Lewis Tappan
and the Evangelical War
Against Slavery

Lewis Tappan

Lewis Tappan
and the Evangelical War
Against Slavery

Bertram Wyatt-Brown

1969
The Press of Case Western Reserve University
Cleveland

To Anne

Preface

*A*t *first glance*, Lewis Tappan may seem to be the
typical American abolitionist. His background was rural New
England, Congregational, and Federalist, all of which qualified
him for a central place in the anti-southern crusade. In his business life he mirrored past and contemporary assumptions about
who the abolitionists were and why they reacted so aggressively
against slavery. During part of his career he was a merchant and
industrialist in Boston. As such, he personally could have served
John C. Calhoun and other southern critics as their image of a
grasping Yankee, blind to the evils of "wage slavery" at home
while bleating about the slaves' clanking chains far away. For
historians with an interest in exposing the economic causes of the
Civil War, who could better exemplify the connection between
the abolitionists' propaganda and the selfish boosterism of northern capitalists than Lewis Tappan, founder of the Dun & Bradstreet Company of New York?

One is almost tempted to say that Tappan welcomed caricature.
He combined the tastes, habits of mind, and sentiments appropriate to the abolitionist with the blackest uniform and gloom-
iest expression that a southern planter could imagine. Like Henry
James's classic antislavery lady, Miss Birdseye, he "belonged to
any and every league that had been founded for almost any purpose whatever," so long as it was benevolent, pious, and teetotal.
In fact, "doing good" seemed to be at times an excuse for not

thinking at all. Crowded convention halls, vestry rooms, lecture galleries, and platforms filled him with the assurance that the world was indeed making progress and that he was a part of the grand march of events. They also provided him with opinions, or at least with those he had not already obtained by an earnest chat with someone with the same inclinations as his own. Like Miss Birdseye, he failed to mature. This was an unfortunate result of events early in his philanthropic work, but the consequence was that he knew less about mankind, "if possible, after years of humanitary zeal," than on the first occasion that he "had gone into the field to testify against the iniquity of most arrangements."[1] It must be sadly admitted that Tappan scored all too well on the familiar checklist of the Yankee do-gooders' grave defects: moral arrogance, obstinacy, cliquish conformity, provincial bigotry, and abrasive manners—with a streak of unpleasant opportunism when circumstances allowed.

It is best to say the worst at the beginning. Yet, Tappan's failings were not the whole man, any more than vindictiveness and the desire for profit exhaust the range of antislavery motivation. He shared with others in the cause a love of those enduring principles that his section and the country at large espoused (but did not fully practice) during the American Revolution and ever afterward. Like William Lloyd Garrison, Wendell Phillips, Theodore Weld, and a host of lesser men and women, he was endowed with courage and even with a remarkable empathy for the Negro, an understanding that, while paternal and rather abstract, far exceeded that of most white Americans from that era to this. Besides, he was a great architect of valuable institutions at a time when the nation was not particularly well served by the few it had. His gifts as a publisher, administrator, and financier of antislavery contributed as much to the greatest nineteenth-century American reform as those of many others whose lives have already received scholarly treatment. And he could be very gentle, particularly with children, whenever he chose to forget some of his evangelical prescriptions.

In somewhat broader terms, too, Lewis Tappan's life of reform can be viewed sympathetically, even if his behavior sometimes fell short of his impossible standards. First, it is important to remember that he and his friends shared the universal characteristics of any reforming class. Sometimes it seems that we expect such men as he to foretell the effects of their actions with the accuracy with which we interpret them in retrospect. Abolitionists did not know that a Civil War lay ahead any more than Lafayette in 1789 foresaw Napoleonic dictatorship. Actually, they rather suspected, at least in the 1830's, that God's vengeance on the South would be a Negro uprising, as in Santo Domingo, and their warnings to the slaveholders monotonously dwelt on that danger and much less frequently on the threat of Union mobilization. In this myopia, if one wishes to call it that, they were not alone. While some southerners solemnly predicted a disintegration of the Union unless agitation ceased, leaders of both sections—Whigs, Democrats, secessionists, Republicans, southern Unionists, and others—as late as 1861 were as unaware of the full import of their actions as politicians today must be about the consequences of the courses upon which they embark. For this reason alone, historians especially should be careful not to confuse their "scientific" skills with an unremarkable hindsight. Moreover, they must realize that these reformers were about as wise and often as obtuse as the other leaders of that period.

Second, a reformer like Tappan was not wholly responsible for the outcome of his agitation. William Lloyd Garrison and Lewis Tappan cannot and need not bear the weight of a later tragedy on their shoulders. It is true that few scholars still curse the abolitionists as heartily as men of a different generation did. But old southern hostilities or half-remembered bits of folklore may still lurk even in the most sophisticated minds. To some it seems fair to blame "extremists" of both sections, North and South, but we simply cannot escape the ultimate moral choice which the antebellum generation had to face—to accept or reject the basic premise of abolitionism: the essential injustice of human bondage. Actually the reaction of their enemies to the abolitionists' generally not outrageous proposals had more to do with the violence of Civil War and Reconstruction than did the activities of the reformers themselves, although it is necessary to add that antisalvery men and women could not fully escape the influence of the violent impulses at work in society at large in the years leading to the war.

Third, the agitator is seldom an intellectual or a politician-intellectual (a breed of academic bureaucrat recently in favor). Lewis Tappan should not be reproached because he did not explore all the sides of an argument, weigh the factors of history and custom, meditate on the power structures and interest blocs against him, and then seek the most efficacious way to compromise divergent opinions or make an expedient withdrawal when opposing forces proved too strong.[2] An agitator is generally one whose compulsive dissatisfaction with prevailing mores is antithetical to the ordinary processes of slow improvement. His benefit to society derives not from his flexibility and institutional loyalty but from a steadfast assertion of principles. As a result, he is prophetic and powerful only if something of his idealism impresses society; otherwise he is ludicrous and pathetic.

It is sometimes observed that the abolitionists were uncommonly guilt-ridden. Their view of reality was supposedly distorted because of their exaggerated sense of personal complicity in evil. Indeed, their words must seem harsh a century or more after the heat of their battles had been dissipated in newer national preoccupations. But Tappan and his co-workers felt themselves oppressed by public indifference. In the face of slavery's undeniable success, they stressed their own feelings of wrongdoing because so many Americans felt few or none. To the abolitionists, slavery was a denial of civilization, while antislavery represented the highest aims of Christian life. To fulfill their mission to "civilize" a barbaric country, they employed the arresting but familiar language of the Bible, the terminology of sin, guilt, depravity, and divine retribution. Rhetorical exuberance was not merely a product of their psychological makeup; it was also a response to their fear of being ignored. The frustration of watching churches, political parties, and ordinary citizens dodging or defending slavery and racial intolerance enraged them. They used religious hyperbole because they felt unable to touch the national conscience in any other way. There was a note of desperation in their appeals to the public because they believed that the nation had lost its sense of integrity, its Christian heritage, and its Revolutionary idealism in an insane rush to make dollars out of the sufferings of the unfortunate. Moreover, it was sound strategy to make their pleas as urgent and forceful as possible in order to shock the respectable northerner and worry the inflexible southerner.

Yet the abolitionists were human beings with the normal afflictions of the species. Obviously more than pure altruism lay behind their efforts. Some kind of personal dissatisfaction, some impulse of the sort that is necessary to tip the human mechanism out of its common state of poise, found expression in antislavery work. Certainly the impulse varied from individual to individual. While there is no substantial evidence in the matter, it is possible that Lewis Tappan's early rivalries with siblings were factors in his choosing abolitionism as a means of self-assertion. (Even so, one must ask why some other means of self-identification or defiance could not have satisfied him as well.) Even when the historical documents are available for this sort of speculation, the results can be absurd and pointless when treated crudely. When abolitionists as a group are classified under some broad psychological heading, there is a danger of oversimplification and sweeping generalization that fail to account for the complexities of human nature.

It has been tentatively suggested that feelings of social inadequacy that set abolitionists apart from their parents' generation and most members of their own may explain their behavior. Glib analyses of the intricate and mysterious impulses of their minds cannot be accepted until the evidence is more convincing and the discipline of psychology mature enough (if possible) to assess in accurate terms the difference between real and imagined anxieties and needs. Furthermore, whatever the reason for abolitionist belligerence, there can be no escaping the fact that, except for the dying empires of Spain and Portugal, the United States was the major deviant from standards of racial justice in the Atlantic community. In other words, in the Western world of the nineteenth century the slaveholders and their northern apologists, not the abolitionists, were men with "abnormal" views. While the rest of the country and the national government were generally isolationist and parochial, the reformers were very much attuned to international currents of opinion.

Finally, the reformer's departure from customary attitudes is always a positive advantage to society. Any nation without a trace of anti-institutionalism must resemble the famous Orwellian specter. Most abolitionists were young men, challenging the preconceptions of their elders and especially of those in power; their language fitted the urgency of their youthful claims for dignity and equality of rights for all citizens, black and white. Most of the abolitionists (many of them trained for the ministry) were not truly anarchistic in the first place, but even those who were can be defended on the ground that their denunciations of the status quo challenged men to review their premises with some sensitivity. A tepid reformism that seeks only to tinker with the social machinery cannot answer this need, at least in a democracy. A society bereft of all radical expression offers little to civilization. It is likely to be stagnant and supremely dull. Abolitionism, far from being a subversive kind of moonshine, struck at the heart of American illusions of self-congratulation. If some institutions were unable to survive the reformers' attacks, they were weak indeed, considering the tiny number of activists and their relatively meager access to the sources of national power. Moreover, the slave system was difficult to dislodge because of southern political-economic power. Slavery was not receding in Tappan's day but expanding with ever-increasing speed across the continent. Why should he or Garrison withhold criticism of Daniel Webster, a timid church father, or of a New York cotton factor whose moral commitment was as flaccid as theirs was strong?

It can be argued that if only abolitionists had been more willing to negotiate with proslavery forces in the first place and if only the nation had been able to create a more satisfactory institutional structure to solve critical problems, their reception in the South would have been warmer and perhaps slavery would have been removed gradually. Fittingly enough, however, the institution was to end the same way it began—by violence. It is hard to see how centuries of Negro peonage could simply have been wiped away by the sweep of a pen on successive bills to lighten the burden of slavery and check its advance. Slaveholders knew that piecemeal measures were no less subversive than "immediate abolition." In our own time legislative gestures, though backed by centralized authority, have proved insufficient and seemingly half-hearted, while they increase anticipations and lead to an understandable disenchantment, even violence. Any relaxation of the slave system would have whetted Negro desires for freedom and perhaps caused the eruption of slave rebellion that the abolitionists often predicted.[3]

My recitation of grounds for admiring Lewis Tappan, his cause, and his labors in it is not meant to answer all the questions about the nature of antislavery, particularly those of a philosophical and controversial kind. For one thing, neither he nor Arthur Tappan was a formulator of antislavery rhetoric and ideas. Though they were men of strong convictions, all their antislavery conceptions were borrowed from their more intellectually gifted friends. Many intriguing questions about the history of antislavery thought, its place in the stream of American ideas, and its later influence upon the character and content of post-Civil War social philosophy are still unanswered. For example, little of value has been written about the role of women in the development of antislavery ideology or, for that matter, about the sexual issues that slavery created in a society trying to become "Victorian." Unfortunately, a study of the Tappans will yield few answers to questions about antislavery thought. For an understanding of the theoretical side, one must turn to such leaders as William Lloyd Garrison, the brilliant Weld-Grimké family, Theodore Parker, Wendell Phillips, and that much-neglected figure, Judge William Jay, whose constitutional views displayed exceptional learning and refreshing practicality. Lewis Tappan did not contribute one memorable or thought-provoking pamphlet or article to the cause, although he wrote many passable ones of the occasional, sentimental, or topical variety. His gifts lay in other directions.

Some controversies will always surround the individual and collective responses of these New Englanders to the tragedy of our race relations. "Motives," Santayana has observed, "are always easy to assign, unless we wish to get at the real one," but one hopes that scholars will continue to search for it. Even if it were possible to penetrate the mysteries of human motivation and to obtain reasonable agreement about the findings, it is unlikely that the clinical approach would lead anyone to love these old reformers any more than the present generation does. Their religious concerns, moral certitudes, and authoritarian ways prevent much reverence for them in a secular and permissive age. And Lewis Tappan's temperament itself provides another dimension to the resistance we may feel to him and his colleagues. Like the goose in the Negro song, which was still too tough to eat after weeks of cooking, he is too much alive and too unyielding to be very palatable. He affronts us with his tenacious beliefs, his countrified sentiments, and his combination of an abstract love for mankind with an appalling disregard for the feelings of others. No amount of biographical adulation can ever quite erase the impression he left of unbending irascibility, impulsiveness, and a curious distance of manner, as though he spoke even to himself from a rostrum. Formalistic men like him do not always lend themselves to the probing of the psychoanalyst. His letters and diaries seldom revealed the inner man—his doubts and his fears—or assessed his own character and motives. His reticence probably came from his early need for privacy in the large and competitive family environment in which he was raised. Moreover, he was a puritan, though not prone to the introspection which is so often attributed to that group. He belonged, as one historian aptly said, "to a race whose typical member is eternally torn between a passion for righteousness and a desire to get on in the world."[4] That impossible duality was very likely to create tensions that would discourage sensitivity, intimacy, and light-heartedness. Yet, we can respect his resilience, his love of life, and his principles.

A word should be added about his brother Arthur. The temptation was very strong to make this a dual biography, but, first of all, there were inadequate sources for the study of Arthur's life. He did not stow away his correspondence, as Lewis did, and he wrote only the curtest of notes to others. Moreover, his career ended abruptly with his retirement in the forties, whereas Lewis was active for another quarter of a century. A gloomy man, he had about him a sad lucidity of soul (to borrow Matthew Arnold's phrase). Money was his passion; to give it away his security. While so obvious a contradiction requires psychological explanation, the materials available are very unhelpful. I did decide, however, that as much about Arthur as was relevant should be included in this book, because not only is the role of Lewis Tappan elucidated thereby but longstanding confusions about the significance, and later insignificance, of Arthur are resolved.

In summary, this book is an attempt to see abolitionism as a generally sensible though by no means unblemished attack on a national problem. Its leaders ought to be remembered not solely for their various imperfections but for their acuteness of moral perception as well. The Tappans and their friends were neither harpies of destruction nor merciful deliverers. They were much too puny, like all of us, for that. But they gave the country a higher conception of what American nationality was supposed to stand for than most of the statesmen of their day.

NOTES

1. Henry James, *The Bostonians* (New York, 1956), 27.
2. See Aileen S. Kraditor, "A Note on Elkins and on Abolitionists," *Civil War History,* XIII (December, 1967), 330–39. I regret that Dr. Kraditor's *Means and*

Ends in American Abolitionism: Garrison and His Critics on Strategy and Tactics, 1834–1850 (New York, 1969) was read in galley too late for my use of the valuable insights offered, but both book and article are surprisingly in accord with the interpretation of Garrisonian abolition presented herein.

3. See the brilliant essay of Richard Hofstadter, "Wendell Phillips: The Patrician as Agitator," in *American Political Tradition and the Men Who Made It* (New York, 1948), 137–63; and on the myopia of prewar politicians see David M. Potter, *Lincoln and His Party in the Secession Crisis* (New Haven, 1962). These remarks are addressed to the points raised by two outstanding scholars: David Donald, "Toward a Reconsideration of Abolitionists" and "An Excess of Democracy: The American Civil War and the Social Process," in *Lincoln Reconsidered: Essays on the Civil War Era* (New York, 1961 ed.), and Stanley Elkins, *Slavery: A Problem in American Institutional and Intellectual Life* (Chicago, 1959). Elkins demonstrates the totality of the slave experience in his first chapters but then contradictorily minimizes its pervasiveness and power in his analysis of the Garrisonians in the final section.

4. Samuel Eliot Morison, *The Maritime History of Massachusetts, 1783–1860* (Boston, 1961 ed.), 22.

Acknowledgments

*I*n *writing this* biography I have enjoyed excellent advice from many quarters. My wife Anne has prodded me to finish it with both a zeal born of gay exasperation and a patient understanding. She has listened to more than one version of nearly all the chapters, offering on every occasion invaluable suggestions. Professors C. Vann Woodward and Wilson Smith marched bravely through the jungle of "Partners in Piety: Lewis and Arthur Tappan," when one form of the early chapters of this book was submitted as my dissertation. Their quick perceptions of its faults were unfortunately not sufficiently acted on at that time, but the example of Dr. Woodward's union of literary excellence and profound historical understanding has been a constant inspiration. Professor Louis Filler not only applied his thorough knowledge of antislavery history to this text, but he also responded to numerous calls for assistance of various kinds with his customary generosity and good humor.

James M. McPherson of Princeton, another scholar with wide-ranging experience in abolitionist sources, offered his comments on the text and also gave much-needed encouragement on more than one occasion, creating for me a debt difficult to express here. Professor Aileen S. Kraditor of Sir George Williams University volunteered to give me particular assistance with the language of this document; she proved to be a true artist in this specialized field.

A number of individuals have aided in the collection of research materials: Mrs. Virginia Roberts of Cotey College; Walter M. Merrill of Witchita State University; Mrs. Willie Lee Rose of the University of Virginia; and Dr. Wesley A. Hotchkiss, General Secretary of the Board of Missions, New York. James B. Stewart of Case Western Reserve University added his fund of information about political abolitionism and also helped me sort out the unspeakable mess which an office fire made of Tappan materials.

It is unfortunate that historians have confined their appreciation of librarians to a few lines in the Acknowledgments; I allow somewhat more space here, but still with the sense of not rendering an adequate accounting. Two ladies deserve grateful mention: Miss Lelia Holloway of the Oberlin College Library and Miss Margaret Lough of the Johns Hopkins University Library. The staffs of other libraries and archives have also been generous with their time: the Alderman Library, University of Virginia; the Boston Public Library (where I mention particularly John Alden); the Chicago Theological Seminary Library; the Fisk University Library; the Houghton and the Widener Libraries of Harvard University; the Howard University Library (where I mention Dorothy Porter); Jay House, Mt. Kisco, N.Y.; the McCormick Theological Seminary Library; the Massachusetts Historical Society; the New-York Historical Society (I mention James J. Heslin); the New York Public Library; the Ohio Historical Society; the Pennsylvania Historical Society; the University of Rochester Library; the William L. Clements Library; the Yale University Library; the archives of the American Bible Society and of the American Sunday School Union; and, above all, the Library of Congress.

I must also thank certain individuals for the facilities they offered: Mrs. Herbert R. Preston and Miss Janet Preston of Baltimore; the residents of Botham's End, Baltimore; and, finally, James Morton Smith and W. W. Abbot, then of the Institute of Early American History and Culture, who provided me with a room and charming company when I was finishing the last chapters in Williamsburg.

A word of appreciation is also extended to the descendants of Lewis Tappan. The late Miss Anna Hulett of Washington, D. C., donor of the Tappan papers to the Library of Congress and granddaughter of Lewis Tappan, located and allowed me to use a small collection of family papers. In addition, I have been generously assisted by Miss Constance Holt of "Roseland," Mr. George C. Holt, whose son is named for Lewis Tappan, Mr. and Mrs. Gardner Richardson of "Plaine Hill," and Mrs. Lucy T. Lythgoe—all of Woodstock, Connecticut.

For financial support I am indebted to the University of Colorado Council on Research and Creative Work for a summer grant that enabled me to finish the research and to the Executive Committee of the Graduate School, Case Western Reserve University, for authorizing payment for the superb typing of the final draft by Mrs. June Howland, Cleveland. The Danforth Foundation made it possible for me to do the major part of the research and writing as a graduate student.

Finally, James P. Baughman, editor of the *Business History Review*, and W. M. Brewer of the *Journal of Negro History*, have granted permission for me to absorb into this book my articles, "God and Dun & Bradstreet, 1841–1851," *BHR*, XL (Winter, 1967), and "The Abolitionists' Postal Campaign of 1835," *JNH*, L (October, 1965).

B. W.-B.

Contents

*Lewis Tappan
and the Evangelical War
Against Slavery*

CHAPTER ONE

The Legacy of Sarah Tappan

Lewis Tappan was already in early middle age when he became an abolitionist. Until the year 1827 his career hardly differed from those of hundreds of New Englanders who left home to make their fortunes. He was more alert than most young men, but he possessed about the average Yankee mixture of ideals and ambition in the pursuit of the dollar. To the casual observer, there was no indication that he would become one of the great reformers of his era. His opinions, tastes, and habits were typical of a merchant trying to make his way up the social ladder of Boston.

There was no family tradition of radical dissent for Lewis to inherit. Neither his father Benjamin nor any other Tappan had ever shown the slightest inclination to challenge society's standards. Abraham Toppan (the name was changed in the late eighteenth century), a tradesman and cooper, arrived in Massachusetts in 1637 from Yarmouth, Yorkshire, and remained a stalwart, orthodox puritan to his dying day. Several Tappans were village ministers, and one taught at Harvard College; but mostly they were farmers and storekeepers, satisfied with their modest positions. Benjamin, a goldsmith of Northampton, rather mystified his son Lewis by his lack of personal ambition. Even after giving up jewelry-making to run a general store, he never earned more than a thousand dollars a year. He did, however, speculate in Ohio land development in the late 1790's, a venture that caused him much anxiety and brought in little extra money. On the whole it was enough for "Benny," as his relatives called him, to provide his family with the necessities of life. A jovial, rather fat man, he enjoyed a neighborly chat at the store more than the selling of muslins and shoe buckles.[1]

Nor was there anything particularly insecure or hostile in the social climate of Northampton which could account in any way for Lewis Tappan's later deviation from the path of a typical New England merchant. His mother and father gave all their children a wholesome home life; they put on no airs, envied no one's superior status, and did not snub those below them. Situated on the banks of the Connecticut River, Northampton was neither rich and sophisticated nor backward and poor. By comparison with the coastal towns, with their bustling piers, grog shops, and well-traveled merchants and sailors, it was sleepy, conservative, and safe. Tappan & Whitney, facing the common, was the only store offering a general assortment of merchandise, and Pomeroy's hostelry was the sole refuge for the thirsty. Once a month the Society for Detecting Thieves and Robbers and Bringing Them to Punishment met before a blazing fire in the tavern's main room. Upstairs the Hampton Musical Society held weekly rehearsals.[2]

Twice a year, however, life quickened somewhat when the judges from Boston visited the county seat of Hampshire on circuit. Lewis, Arthur, and the other Tappan children watched the magistrates parade to the courthouse in powdered hair and cocked hats, led by the high sheriff in his "half-uniform," bearing a sword and staff. In the lower courts Saturdays were given over to punishments, which the city fathers sometimes caused the children to watch from the schoolyard as a timely warning. The effect on the boys of seeing a man administered thirty-nine lashes or his ears cropped was not what their elders expected. The boys used to slip off to inflict an imitation of the morning's torments on some victim of their own.[3] In spite of the excitement of these scenes, the town was unstimulating and provincial.

Like all New England communities, Northampton had its well-defined social classes. Benjamin Tappan was a freeman and pew-holder. When he arrived in 1768 from his Boston apprenticeship, he had to throw away all his checked shirts because only squires were allowed by custom to wear them. The tradition faded in later years, yet he was always conscious that the Strongs, Lymans, Edwards, and Stoddards were gentlemen, entitled to a doffing of the hat and a dignified greeting. The "river gods" of the shire held sway through much of Benjamin's long life, which ended in 1831. As a respectable merchant and upholder of the existing order, he served on General Benjamin Lincoln's staff during the suppression of Shays' Rebellion. Known for his integrity and "Washingtonian" principles, he was consistently re-elected town treasurer, and, perhaps because of his friendship with the shire's favorite son, Governor Caleb Strong, he took a term in the state's General Court in 1811. Benjamin was always eager to see good men elected and "ever prayed," as Lewis said, "that righteous men might be exalted in the nation." Signs of his gradual acceptance into Northampton's social ranks were the marriages of two of his daughters into the Edwards and Stoddard clans.[4] Yet, he never became a deacon of the First Church, a position reserved for the river gods themselves.

One interpretation of abolitionism maintains that the sons of men like Benjamin were likely candidates for the crusade. The reformers' presumed inability to preserve or surpass the social attainments of their fathers, it is argued, prompted in them a fanatical discharge of spleen against southerners and northern conservatives. Even if the theory fitted most other abolitionists (which it probably does not), it clearly does not fit the Tappans. Five of Benjamin's sons easily exceeded their parents' limited personal horizons and modest position in society. Although the social circumstances of their upbringing were almost identical, only two sons became abolitionists. The truth was that all of them were rather condescending about Benjamin's standing in the community, since they enjoyed much more wealth and prominence than he, whether they were antislavery or not.[5] Certainly Benjamin's sons inherited his pride in self-reliance (conformist though he was), his sectional loyalty to Federalism, and his distrust of the slaveholding, deistical aristocrats who supposedly dominated the Jeffersonian party. But too many men with similar backgrounds and attitudes rejected the lonely antislavery conviction for these common tendencies to be counted as causes.

Instead, the origins of Lewis' and Arthur's alienation from established racial prejudices and practices must be located elsewhere. In 1744, some forty-odd years before Lewis' birth, Jonathan Edwards was expelled from the pulpit of the First Church. Like Tappan himself years later, Edwards had disturbed powerful interests and had paid dearly for his temerity. Northampton, although generally a happy place, was still somehow afflicted with the uncompromising and reforming spirit that Edwards had laid upon it in the Great Awakening. From this peculiar source sprang the impulse that drove Lewis Tappan from the complacent life of an ordinary Boston merchant.

To the religious cast of Northampton life, Sarah Tappan adapted herself with brooding satisfaction. In her opinion, the town was a better place than her native Boston, where Congregationalists had become smugly insensitive to the proper demands of Calvinist living. In her day, Jonathan Edwards' pulpit was occupied by the Rev. Solomon Williams, a loyal disciple of his predecessor and an ardent Federalist and defender of the old order. He did not rival Edwards in eloquence or learning, but he helped to preserve the Connecticut River Valley from the spread of Boston's theological liberalism. It was quite fitting that the Tappans lived for a number of years in the old Edwards house on King Street, since both Sarah and Benjamin lived within the structure of his thought as well.[6]

Sarah Tappan, who was always more aggressive about her religion than her easygoing husband, inherited her convictions from her father, William Homes, Benjamin's master in the goldsmith trade. Before the Revolution, William Homes had been a justice of the peace and a tithing man. He rather enjoyed chastising Sunday-morning loiterers, giving them a prod with his staff of office on the way to church.[7] Once, when Sarah was a grown woman, she had stayed out past nine o'clock, and her father had boxed her ears. Sarah assured Lewis that it was customary then for religious parents to treat their children severely and to avoid familiarity.[8] She was not herself as grim as her own mother and father, yet she retained much of their pious reserve. Never had she rebelled against their spiritual authority, finding within its framework the means to encompass all her feelings and thoughts. With her parents, she heard George Whitefield and other great revivalists of the late days of the Awakening, and from these experiences and the influence of her melancholy upbringing she became an extraordinarily intense believer.

Mrs. Tappan was a pietist of the Edwardsean persuasion to her death in 1826. "From my own experience I firmly believe the Calvinistic doctrines to be scriptural," she wrote Arthur in 1807. Of course many other women shared this creed, but Mrs. Tappan brought to it an intellectual depth from an extensive reading of devotional literature and a strength of will distinguishing her from the average country puritan. As Solomon Williams' assistant remarked, "Mrs. Tappan, whether considered as to her intellect or to the energy of her moral character, was no ordinary woman."[9] For this reason, it is important to sketch the nature of her religious thought. She was representative of the devout layman's understanding of the Calvinist faith; it bore directly on the development of her two abolitionist sons.

Puritan theology has too often been caricatured as irremediably authoritarian and conservative. It was not, however, exclusively or necessarily reactionary. Many of the New England clergy had not only supported the Revolutionary cause but had also continued to issue the prophetic call for the regeneration of man and society, not Tory conservatism. Of course, it is true that during Lewis' early years, the Calvinist pastors were allied with the Federalists. Even though these ministers believed that Federalism was their only political safeguard against the French Jacobins' and the Jeffersonians' alleged contempt for priest and property, few of them relished the unfamiliar noise and intrigues of partisan strife. The Calvinist dialectic was attuned to a society of feudal harmonies in the tastes, economy, and customs of its adherents; such a faith could not be wholly embodied in Federalist politics with its stress on Hamiltonian economics and banker enterprise. Moreover, some of the most influential Federalists were tainted with the Unitarian heresy (like the Adams family) or, like Alexander Hamilton himself, with haughty Episcopalianism. While it was recognized that these creeds included many worthy gentlemen, the theological systems were too alien, man-centered, and deistical to please the orthodox.

The Rev. Dr. David Tappan, Lewis' uncle and Hollis Professor of Divinity at Harvard, illustrated in 1799 the discomfiture of some of the New England divines in regard to their political friends when he wrote his younger brother Benjamin at Northampton about the dangers of combining true Christianity with undeviating party loyalty. (Years later, Lewis Tappan was also to encounter similar problems in reconciling antislavery principle with political exigencies.) David Tappan complained: "I have a poor opinion of those federalists & christians however respectable on other accounts, who declaim against French *principles*, & yet resemble them in practice; who speak highly of religion & the clergy in charges to Juries, in Orations, Toasts, or newspaper paragraphs, & yet practically neglect or trample them under foot." The only proper response to the Jacobinism raging through America, warned Dr. Tappan, was an effort by "our rulers & influential citizens," in league with the ministers, to bear "down infidelity, impiety, & vice by the weight of their *examples*." He recommended the writings and activities of William Wilberforce, leader of British evangelicalism, as the proper guide to "ardent piety & patriotism & philanthropy."[10] Indeed, it was Wilberforce whose example and influence later stimulated in the United States the reforming impulse so deeply embedded in the Calvinist creed.

In David Tappan's mind, as in the minds of Sarah and Benjamin, Calvinism was another name for the war against complacency, materialism, and self-pride. According to them, these vices, aggravated by the country's prosperity and heedless expansion, gripped all citizens regardless of their station in society. Perhaps in the first years of the Republic the puritan clergy were too often silent about the failings of their wealthy pewholders, in contrast to the pre-Revolutionary ministers, who did not hesitate to denounce Tory aristocrats in fiery language. Nevertheless, the faith of Jonathan Edwards was not so lifeless that its message of reform was incapable of revival. The church was to survive the death of Federalism, and it was destined to emerge more invigorated than at any time since the first Awakening.

Sarah Tappan was keenly aware of the millennial aims of her creed, that is, the establishment of an American republic in which God, not money, place, or power, would be the sole object of worship. Evangelistic and aggressive though this objective may seem, it was accompanied in Sarah by much of the introspective mood so commonly associated with puritan life. She was also a moral absolutist. The puritans' concept of liberty was certainly never meant to signify freedom to do wrong. Frequently driven by a feeling of her "enslavement" to sin, she was likely to preface her evocations with "Can I hope that thou has set thy love on such a worthless worm as I am!" and told her sons, "Every action of my life has been so wofully polluted with indwelling sin, that without an almighty and infinite atonement, I could never dare to appear before infinite purity; and therefore ought to abhor myself and repent in dust and ashes. . . ."[11] This side of Calvinism is a very familiar one, but it is to be observed that the burden of original sin was offset by the beauty of sainthood.

To the conscientious pietist like Sarah Tappan, the evangelical way offered unsearchable riches. "The Bible," she said, "is full of encouragement to those who diligently seek for true wisdom, and assures us that her ways are ways of pleasantness. . . ."[12] If, as one historian has recently observed, we assume that eighteenth-century Calvinism is exemplified solely by Edwards' *Sinners in the Hands of an Angry God*, the result will be a misinterpretation of the evangelical spirit and consequently of the antislavery movement too. Edwards' gospel message was based on love, not fear alone. Holiness, he thought, was more than mere penance; it included an active desire to carry out God's will on earth. Piety, he said, "consists not only in contemplation, and passive enjoyment, but very much in action." At heart, then, Calvinists like Sarah Tappan carried the seeds of a humanitarian faith.[13] Theological subtleties lay behind the simple framework, as plain as the First Church itself, but Mrs. Tappan's puritanism was a hopeful, though scarcely easy, road to salvation.

Like the more thoughtful evangelicals of her time, she did not live in dread of hell but fashioned her spiritual life around three principal elements: regeneration through the aid of the Holy Spirit and her fellowman; willing submission to the Providence of God as an expression of her love for Him; and the intercession of Christ to sustain her in the struggle against the world and flesh. Having undergone the experience of a "new birth" after hearing a revival sermon at Falmouth in 1769, she was convinced that this method alone was the way to obtain God's grace, a belief which Arthur and Lewis later accepted too. She had no illusions that her children were destined for heaven simply because she forced them to church; instead, they too would have to proclaim their faith before fellow Christians, as she had done.

Out of the interaction of the Holy Spirit, the preacher, and the convicted soul came the spontaneous liberation of the sinner from the shackles of unbelief and the beginning of knowledge. Evangelicals might differ about which party to the event was most responsible for it; Mrs. Tappan and the pietists of her generation gave the Holy Spirit more of the credit than her sons later did. Nevertheless, she too recognized the importance of the inspired preacher, as well as the individual's consultation with scripture and pious friends. Spiritual illumination was a social act, even for her, a shy and reclusive lady. The addition of each convert increased the delight of the congregation and bound the witnesses closer together and to God. Sin, like salvation, was also community business, as any resident of a small town knows. This commonly held opinion fitted well into the theology of a God capable of delivering or chastising a church, town, state, or nation according to its merits. Certainly the ancient tradition of communal responsibility for sin that Sarah helped to pass along was later very much in evidence in the various reform efforts of the Tappan brothers.[14] Thus, the appeal of orthodoxy was not only to men and women with long faces and isolated, crabbed lives, but to ordinary farming people, who accepted its sober cheer with as much routine assurance and sense of rightness as a yeoman's son had in carrying out his daily chores.

Sarah Tappan's idea of the role of the preacher in the conversion "miracle" is also important, since it affected her children's approach as laymen deeply involved in clerical affairs. Being a New Light Congregationalist, she showed no interest in revivals conducted by an uneducated ministry, nor did any of her children. The emotional excesses, the whooping and rolling which critics ridiculed, were not for her. Studying the Bible, praying, and learning God's lessons in daily life, not sudden frenzies, were steps preparatory to a change of heart. On the other hand, too much erudition and too many pulpit flourishes were equally dangerous. Both encouraged self-love and made the approach to God seem unduly easy.[15]

Of equal importance was Sarah's reliance on Christ's redemptive power. Christians, she told Lewis, "believe that this means holiness of heart, evidenced by a constant endeavor to obey all God's commands. . . ."[16] Piety consisted in obedience; happiness was synonymous with holiness. Nevertheless, she was constantly goaded to review her imperfections. Sometimes she felt overwhelmed. Even in midwinter, she spent many nights on her knees and found two or three times during the day to pray for forgiveness. Yet Sarah Tappan, like so many pietists, especially the "saints" of the seventeenth century, relieved her despondency with the truth of Christ's redeeming grace. Total joy then replaced black despair. Such escalations and declensions may seem signs of maladjustment, but Mrs. Tappan had firm command of her mind and a full understanding that, according to the best theologians and most devout laymen of her time, such contradictions were the burden a Christian had to carry. Even her belief in the atonement was cautionary, for victory over man's evil nature required perpetual vigilance. Her faith was always restless, it is true, but it was not neurotic or perverse by the standards of her religion. Sarah's sense of discipline was so vital that its severity sharpened, rather than distorted, her view of reality. To the modern mind, she seems unpleasantly fanatical; yet it must be remembered that her religious environment was closer to that of the puritan fathers than of twentieth-century rationalists. Those puritans, tormented by the same theological issues of good and evil as she, cannot be judged by the tests of a secular society, and no more can Sarah be. And yet, the impressions she implanted in her children were not altogether beneficial, if one considers the highest good to be a happy satisfaction with things as they are. In Lewis and Arthur a sense of personal guilt, derived from Sarah's mixture of joy and defeat, proceeded from their collateral sense of the evil of their community and the nation at large.

The final element that marked Sarah Tappan's understanding of theology was her attitude toward God the Father. In her generation, the incarnation and sacrifice of Christ had already supplanted the earlier Calvinists' concern for the illimitable sovereignty of God. Yet, like all good eighteenth-century supernaturalists, she thought His power was evident in special, rather than ordinary, events. Divine intervention had visited her, she said, in spite of her "barrenness and unfruitfulness." His "invisible hand" had preserved her from drownings, concussions, maimings, and fatal diseases. Her parents had sixteen children; only three survived. When the "throat distemper" carried off two infants, her grandmother begged the Homeses to allow little Sarah to visit her in a healthier neighborhood, but, as Sarah proudly exclaimed, "my parents thought it would be running away from Providence, and refused. . . ."[17] Obviously God intended her for a special calling, and even her own "giddy mirth and vanity" before her conversion did not sway His resolve.

So, too, God in His wisdom took away her adult daughter Eliza, who died unexpectedly in her sleep. Both Mrs. Tappan and Benjamin attended Sunday services as usual, leaving the lifeless body at home. "This was indeed a triumph of faith in God over natural feelings," Lewis later said in admiration.[18] Mrs. Tappan enjoyed some relief from anger and grief in confronting God in His house as both a witness against His judgment on her favorite daughter and a submissive captive of it. Such a conflict of motives would hardly have been unique in the life of a Yankee puritan, but her son Lewis, who later tried to match her self-control, was never able to reach this height of spirituality. Nevertheless, he too believed that all things were mercifully ordered by God, whether the death of a child or the freeing of slaves.

Though fully engaged in these spiritual struggles, Sarah Tappan was a remarkable mother, strong-willed, resourceful, and intelligent. In an age when medicine was more a shadow of hope than a science, she raised ten children to adulthood on her husband's indifferent earnings with just one servant girl to help. Lewis himself was born on May 26, 1788, with the assistance of "Granny" Allen, a midwife who charged a dollar for her services. Instead of calling a doctor when her children were ill, Sarah relied on Buchan's *Domestic Medicine* and pills made from butternut bark, regardless of the complaint. Moreover, she took an interest in her girls' and boys' play and work, allowing them to keep all sorts of pets and seeing to it that there were occasional family festivities and outings. In spite of her sometimes grim outlook, she was a warm, perhaps tenderly affectionate, woman. There was no doubt in any of her children's minds that she loved them without reserve, even if she was not the kind to enjoy a joke or tolerate impertinence.[19]

What preserved quince and healthful farm cooking may have done for the youthful body, the Bible, a remedy to be prized above all things, did for the soul. The children were required to spend the Sabbath getting up their lessons in the *Westminster Catechism* and attending church. Sundays were gloomy, tedious days, by Lewis' own admission. Then, as the last beams of the sun disappeared from across the chest of drawers in the kitchen, Mrs. Tappan used to pull an apple pan cake from the oven, and whichever one of the children knew the lesson best had first choice of the corner pieces. Lewis always cherished the memory that he had never once won the prize. With a shout, the children would rush from the house to play with friends until called home for bed. In later years she admitted to having "drawn the cords too tightly," and Lewis never quite forgave her for "not making it a day of cheerful strictness," as he described the Sabbath he aimed at in his later years.[20]

Following the example set by her father, Sarah was not an indulgent parent. " 'The rod and reproof give wisdom'—'Withhold not correction from the child; for if thou beatest him with the rod, he shall not die'—'Foolishness is bound in the heart of a child, but the rod of correction shall drive it far from him'—'He that spareth the rod hateth his son &c &c,' " were the words Tappan remembered she said as she laid on the strokes when he had not obeyed. Sometimes she took him to the cellar, stripping him and pouring cold water over his head and shoulders. Quoting the Bible during these unpleasant sessions was a mistake, Tappan later observed: "It made me hate the scriptures as much as the rod." When called upon, Benjamin also birched the children, but Lewis found him easy to get along with. If his father had not been bothered by some impudent remark or childish question, he left the children alone. Indeed, he never called Lewis aside for a conversation of any sort, and no close relationship developed between them.[21]

Unlike her husband, Mrs. Tappan tried to exert an influence on her children that would last beyond their childhood days at the homestead. Yet, she deliberately set limits to her own maternal power. In spite of all the puritan advice that she sent after her boys in their careers, she maintained a certain detachment, as if she appreciated their need for independence and recognized that they had to face their destinies alone. Sarah encouraged them to leave Northampton for more promising opportunities; once gone, they did not receive from her any pathetic pleas to return, nor did she urge them to invite her to visit them. Physical absence did not, in Sarah's view, mean any loosening of family ties. It was a curious relationship that she developed with her enterprising sons but one appropriate to a society that honored the family institution yet required easy mobility for sons and daughters.

In one regard, however, Sarah insisted upon absolute obedience. She required the children's loyalty to the family religion, and she pursued them on this topic with a vehemence that betrayed at least a powerful inclination to dominate. It was not enough for them to be respectable, law-abiding, and faithful in church attendance. These were aims sufficient to satisfy most other Yankees of the time but not Sarah Tappan. "Think not a moral character sufficient," she wrote Lewis after his arrival in Boston, "lest with the young man in the gospel, when you are not far from the kingdom of heaven, you should be refused admittance." So eager was she to offer warnings, she neglected in her letters all but the barest family happenings. When Lewis asked for news about his sisters and kinfolk back in Northampton, she replied that "Providence has thus far restrained them from vice, or at least shielded them from infamy; and I enjoy the happiness of thinking they are so, as far as reputation is concerned, but I know, by woful experience, that by nature they are totally depraved. . . ."[22]

At times Sarah's strictures were too much for even the most dutiful of her sons. Lewis once admonished her to pry less, and she thrust back the angry response: "give up your youth to God. . . . You are a probationer for eternity. . . ." Deprived of a happy childhood and adolescence by cold and suspicious parents, frequently called to grieve for dead brothers and sisters, she could not trust the uninhibited spirit of youth and showed an unusual sensitivity to any sign of rebellion. " 'Why cannot my mother write as most people do?' " she imagined Lewis to say to her. " 'Why must she be always preaching . . . ?' My dear child, it is because I wish to see you every thing desirable, and I know the foundations must be laid in true love to God and obedience to his commands."[23]

Lewis and the other pious brothers, John, Charles, and Arthur, learned above all from her not to fear what others said of them but always to follow their own consciences. "What need we care," she wrote Charles, "how little we are in the opinions of our fellow worms, if we may but shine as stars in the kingdom of heaven." As well, she revealed that it was possible to gain authority over others through unremitting religious argument. "Ought I not, by all means in my power," she asked Lewis toward the end of her life, "to enforce the truths I believe on the minds of those most dear to me?"[24] This philosophy of action—to *enforce* rather than to explain—bore a resemblance to the method that Arthur and Lewis carried with them into their evangelical and abolitionist crusades, the spoken word of authoritarian zeal. When they tried to apply it on a universal, rather than her domestic, scale, the results were not as predictable or as lasting as was her grip upon the souls of her sons, even after her death. In the narrow world of the domestic circle, Mrs. Tappan was victorious; confronted with the conversion of an entire nation, the Tappans were bound to suffer disappointments their mother never had to face.

Thus, from the first, the Tappans' parents had backed their religious prescriptions with physical and mental coercion. Lewis never fully developed a spirit of independence about religious matters. He was clever, innovative, and self-assured in business affairs, but he always looked for guidance to those whom he considered touched with God's spirit, and he followed their judgment without directly experiencing the kind of insights they had found.

This failure at the heart of his faith was an ironic result of his mother's very intensity. In part, too, it was a consequence of the fact that he belonged to a new generation that no longer recognized the world of Sarah Tappan or tried to relive the past greatness of the age of Jonathan Edwards.

The other Tappan brothers also showed unmistakable signs of their mother's influence. William, the second eldest, tried to escape the burdens placed upon him by avoiding all responsibilities. He was often in scrapes involving creditors and liquor, the latter a commodity not found in Benjamin's store. Throughout his life, he wandered from job to job, finally dying penniless, a ward of his equally luckless children.[25] On the other hand, Charles and John chose more passive ways, learning to live the religious lives their mother approved, although they too rebelled for a short time in a mild, halfhearted way. Settled and generally prosperous, they did not join unpopular causes. Benjamin, the eldest son, however, rejected his parents' orthodoxy both in religion and politics, though in an aggressive manner that itself was an inheritance from his mother. In 1793, he was graduated from Harvard, coming away with Voltaire as his "theologian" and *The Rights of Man* as his political creed. One of the reasons why the Tappans sent no more of their sons there may have been because they thought that infidelity had become part of the Harvard curriculum. In any case, money was always short; none of the others attended any college. After studying a while with Gilbert Stuart, son Benjamin turned from art to law.[26] In frontier Ohio he was a thoroughgoing Jeffersonian, a deist, and a man of broad intellectual and scientific interests, with only an occasional, bitter letter from Sarah to remind him of what he had left behind.[27] Yet his moral sense was no less strict than that of his pious brothers; after leaving Gilbert Stuart, a heavy drinker, he never touched liquor again.

Arthur, the most modest and retiring of the boys, seldom felt the sting of the rod, but he often heard the voice of warning. For him there were unremitting, torturing headaches. The temptation exists to claim that his physical ailment was a result of his failure to rebel, to however slight a degree, as the other children did. Yet so little record remains about him, especially in the formative years, that such speculations are dangerous.

As the youngest son, Lewis Tappan had to learn quickly how to assert himself in the midst of the clan. He had no intention of letting his brothers—Benjamin, William, John, Charles, and Arthur (his senior by two years)—submerge him in the general family rough and tumble. At school he excelled in the classroom and on the playground. "I had, on the whole," he said, "a happy time at school, being fond of study, ambitious to be one of the best scholars, often a favorite with the masters & a leader among the boys in our plays."[28] But he never thought his education was altogether satisfactory. The selectmen of Northampton had to hire as many as twelve separate instructors in the course of his schooling, most of them indifferently educated themselves, all underpaid, overburdened with work, and harassed with the business of keeping order in the crowded classroom. From the point of view of the hard-working student, these conditions were equally frustrating. The recitation method provided each one with only brief opportunities to participate, while the rest of the time was devoted, Tappan later said, "to catching flies, cutting the desks, or other ingenious modes of killing time."[29]

Limited as it was, Lewis' schooling ended abruptly when he was almost fourteen years old. "It was always a disadvantage to me," he later wrote, "that I became a man too soon."[30] For a year he studied independently, having outstripped his class and his masters. Alert and ambitious, he welcomed the chance to leave home in March, 1804, when he was fifteen. Carrying eight dollars in his pocket and a small Bible, a gift from his father, he boarded the sleigh stage for Boston, as awesome a city as he could possibly imagine.[31] The time he spent there was bound to lead him some distance from the heritage of his town and parents, as it did to so many immigrants escaping the tranquillity of their homes for wider adventures in those early days of the nineteenth century.

NOTES

1. Lewis Tappan, *The Life of Arthur Tappan* (New York, 1870), 15, 411–12; "My Forefathers," 4, 5, 17–21, Lewis Tappan (hereinafter LT) MSS, Library of Congress (hereinafter LC) (all references unless otherwise identified are from the LT MSS, LC); Daniel Langdon Tappan, *Tappan-Toppan Genealogy: Ancestors and Descendants of Abraham Toppan of Newbury, Massachusetts, 1606–1672* (Arlington, Mass., 1915), 3–6.

2. Sylvester Judd, *History of Hadley, Including the Early History of Hatfield, South Hadley, Amherst, and Granby, Massachusetts* (Springfield, Mass., 1905),

380, and Judd's "Early History of Northampton," clipping, scrapbook. The checked shirt had once been a symbol of the "Court party" or rich men's party; see Perry Miller, *Jonathan Edwards* (New York, 1949), 43–44.

3. "My Forefathers," 39; LT, *Arthur Tappan*, 25–26.

4. "My Forefathers," 18, 20, 26, 28; Edwin C. Rozwenc, "Caleb Strong: The Last of the River Gods," *The Northampton Book, Chapters from 300 Years in the Life of a New England Town, 1654–1954* (Northampton, 1954), 63 ff.; "Another Group of Northampton's Famous Children. . . ," April 10, n. d., clipping, scrapbook, and other clippings therein. Benjamin Tappan's life span was 1748–1831.

5. Cf. Donald, *Lincoln Reconsidered*, 19–36. See also Bertram Wyatt-Brown, "Abolitionism: Its Meaning for Contemporary Reform," *Midwest Quarterly*, VIII (Autumn, 1966), 45–48. For a precursor of Donald's provocative thesis, see Frank Tracy Carlton, "Humanitarianism, Past and Present," *International Journal of Ethics*, XVII (October, 1906), 48–55; also Merle Curti, *The Growth of American Thought* (New York, 1964), 366–67. There is something to be said for the view that humanitarians disliked the new order of things, but the reason probably did not stem from fears of personal disadvantage but rather from the sense that their traditional religious and social values were threatened by the changes in society.

6. See Rozwenc, "Caleb Strong," *Northampton Book*, 66; and Virginia Corwin, "Religious Life in Northampton, 1800–1954," *ibid.*, 386–88; "My Forefathers," 27.

7. "My Forefathers," 12; LT, *Memoir of Mrs. Sarah Tappan: Taken in Part from the Home Missionary Magazine, of November, 1828, and Printed for Distribution among Her Descendants* (New York, 1834), 11. Sarah Tappan lived from 1748 to 1826.

8. "My Forefathers," 12; diary, March 28, 1826.

9. Sarah Tappan (hereinafter ST) to Arthur Tappan (hereinafter AT), June [?], 1807, in LT, *Memoir of Sarah Tappan*, 86; LT, ed., "Letters from Sarah Tappan," *The Home Missionary*, I (November, 1828), 123 (see also 122–25).

10. David Tappan to Benjamin Tappan, Sr., July 21, 1799, Simon Gratz autograph MSS, Pennsylvania Historical Society.

11. LT, *Memoir of Sarah Tappan*, 20; ST to LT, April 19, 1819, in *ibid.*, 69; "My Forefathers," 13.

12. ST to LT, June 24, 1807, in LT, *Memoir of Sarah Tappan*, 59.

13. Quoted by Alan Heimert, *Religion and the American Mind from the Great Awakening to the Revolution* (Cambridge, 1966), 110; see also Miller, *Edwards*, 45, 65, 89–91, 128–33; H. Richard Niebuhr, *The Kingdom of God in America* (New York, 1959), 113–19; William G. McLoughlin, "The American Revolution as a Religious Revival: 'The Millennium in One Country'" (review of Heimert's book), *New England Quarterly*, XL (March, 1967), 99–110.

14. Sidney E. Mead, "The Rise of the Evangelical Conception of the Ministry in America (1607–1850)," in H. Richard Niebuhr and Daniel D. Williams, eds., *The Ministry in Historical Perspectives* (New York, 1956), 207–49; Heimert, *Religion and the American Mind*, 102; Curti, *Growth of American Thought*, 372.

15. ST to Charles Tappan, December 24, 1825, in LT, *Memoir of Sarah Tappan*, 116–17.

16. ST to LT, October 1, 1825, *ibid.*, 108.

17. *Ibid.*, 15–16, 19; LT, *Arthur Tappan*, 21.

18. "My Forefathers," 31; LT, *Arthur Tappan*, 17–18.

19. "My Forefathers," 29, 33, *passim*; LT, *Arthur Tappan*, 17–18.

15

20. LT, *Arthur Tappan*, 22–25; "My Forefathers," 24, 50–51; LT to Sophia Sturge, January 29, 1844, letterbook (hereinafter ltrbk.).

21. "My Forefathers," 24–25, 27, 30.

22. ST to LT, April 29, 1806, in LT, *Memoir of Sarah Tappan*, 57; *ibid.*, December 11, 1806, 57.

23. *Ibid.*, July 10, 1807, 60; *ibid.*, December 11, 1806, 58; ST to Charles Tappan, n.d., *ibid.*, 145.

24. *Ibid.*, April 6, 1819, 73–74.

25. "My Forefathers," 30; LT to Benjamin Tappan, Jr. (hereinafter BT), February 2, 1821, ltrbk.; AT to BT, March 15, 1824, BT MSS, LC. The life spans of the sons are: Benjamin, 1773–1857; William, 1779–1855; John, 1781–1871; Charles, 1784–1875; Arthur, 1786–1865; Lewis, 1788–1873.

26. Springfield (Mass.) *Sunday Union*, clipping, scrapbook, May 1, 1904.

27. ST to BT and Nancy Tappan (his wife), April 13, 1819, BT MSS, LC.

28. "My Forefathers," 35.

29. *Ibid.*; LT, *Arthur Tappan*, 19; LT in *New England Palladium and Commercial Advertiser* (Boston), May 10, 1822 (quotation).

30. LT to Mrs. John Bigelow, December 1, 1847, ltrbk.; "My Forefathers," 48.

31. "The Honored Dead," New York *Tribune*, June 25, 1873, clipping, scrapbook; "My Forefathers," 51–52; LT, *Arthur Tappan*, 33; diary, March 13, 1854.

CHAPTER TWO

Boston

*D*uring *his first* few years in Boston, Tappan remained a true son of Northampton. "This town," he wrote his brother Benjamin in 1805, "presents a picture of dissipation and laxness in principles, astonishing to any, who does not consider himself the child of chance, and a votary of vice. Decency and order are thought obsolete by these sons of folly. . . . For myself, I hope to enjoy a sound body & mind, untainted by vice and unsubdued by prejudice."[1] Thus, at a prudish seventeen, the young merchant-apprentice showed his alarm at city life, even though he could barely hide the excitement he felt at being a part of it. If ever his thoughts ran in other directions, his mother's warnings were there to anticipate a fall from grace. Recalling a dream, she wrote him in 1809, "Methought you had, by frequenting the theatre, been drawn into the society of lewd women, and had contracted in consequence of it, a disease, that was preying upon your constitution, and undermining your health; that by recourse to quackery, in hopes, if possible to conceal it you were past recovery."[2]

Tappan was never to lose entirely his fondness for country life, even though he did not return to the hinterlands. Nearly seventy years after he left Northampton, he wrote that his brother Arthur had shown a "peculiar love of the country, and praised its streams, its trees, its flowers, its woods, its roads, its hills, its mountains, with almost youthful delight." Lewis could have been writing about himself.[3]

A number of his relatives also kept an eye on him, making sure that Sarah Tappan's son did not neglect his religious duties. His uncle, David Tappan of Harvard, the only Tappan to enter college teaching, had died in August, 1803. But the pious Mrs. Abigail Waters, an aged great-aunt, and his uncle William Homes, who still operated his father's goldsmith shop, invited him frequently for visits and questioned him closely about his activities. Much more enjoyable for him were the hours spent at sister Lucy's house in nearby Brookline. She had married John Pierce, a Congregational minister, bringing with her Polly Hatch, an orphan raised in the Northampton household, whom he liked for her quick wit and simple charm. John, who was several years older, Charles, a young printer, and Arthur were also working in Boston, so that the four brothers often went on expeditions and to church together.[4]

In spite of the companionship and protection of his relatives, Lewis was often alone. Wiggin, "a disagreeable man," under whom he apprenticed in the dry goods trade, made no effort to include him in his family circle, though Tappan lived on his third floor. Too proud to waste his time hanging around the kitchen talking with the help, he spent most evenings in his chilly room with the blankets wrapped tightly about him, reading history books, manuals on trade, and devotional literature.[5]

As he progressed in his professional attainments, Tappan gradually became more accustomed to urban habits of mind. Mastering the double-entry system of bookkeeping recently introduced from abroad, he showed so much inventiveness and promise that even master Wiggin was impressed enough to lend him capital to start his own business in 1809. Borrowing money also from John Tappan, already a fast-rising dealer in French imports, Lewis tried his luck with a store in Philadelphia. Trade was slow, however, because of the Jeffersonian embargo, so he went to England to establish connections with the exporters of calicoes and await better times at home. On his return, he settled in eastern Canada, but the outbreak of war with England in 1812 interrupted his ventures. Luckily, he was able to bring his goods to the frontier before British confiscation. It took a trip to Washington and a special act of Congress, however, to recover his merchandise from American customs.[6] With prices rising and English goods in high demand, he made a fortune of sixty to seventy-five thousand dollars, a large sum for so young a merchant.[7]

In the meantime Arthur returned to the United States from Montreal, where he had sold blankets for the Indian trade. He had lost heavily in the transfer and had to spend most of the war years trying to collect old debts. Family loyalty was a binding force in the Tappan clan; Lewis was required to share his good luck. When Arthur approached him for a loan, it was soon forthcoming. With the twelve thousand dollars that Lewis lent him without interest, Arthur moved to New York City in 1815 to start an import firm.[8]

With the remainder of his funds, Lewis bought a hardware store in Boston. Young and successful, he was a very eligible bachelor, with every sign of stability and social ease to recommend him. In 1813 he began to court Susan Aspinwall, a pretty, quiet, and pleasant girl of eighteen. She was the daughter of William Aspinwall, a retired physician, who once ran a hospital where smallpox inoculations were given. Although Susan's family was much more distinguished than her suitor's, the Aspinwalls welcomed the match. Her mother shared the Tappan trait of piety, and undoubtedly the young merchant's obviously sound religious training overcame any deficiencies in other respects. In one of few surviving letters, Mrs. Aspinwall advised her daughter, then visiting a friend, "be cautious of speaking about any person. put your trust where it can never be disappointed—don't go out in the Evening—keep near your friend Miss [?]. write me immediately if you have been dancing."[9]

On September 7, 1813, the Rev. John Pierce married Lewis and Susan in the parlor of the large Aspinwall house in Brookline, with only the families of John and Charles to represent the groom's relatives. Susan was dressed in India nankeen and white kid gloves, and Lewis' costume, which he recalled to the last detail some forty years later, was no less stylish. Throughout his career he showed surprising vanity in matters of dress, and on the occasion of his marriage, he must have been especially resplendent in "a blue broadcloth coat, with brass buttons—white jean pantaloons—white marseilles vest—a white cravat—white silk stockings—and shoes." They went to a fashionable watering place for the honeymoon, returning by way of Northampton to visit with the family.[10]

Tappan's marriage helped him in his climb from rural obscurity to metropolitan distinction, but he had already made considerable progress along those lines. Throughout the war period he proved his attachment to Federalist principles, certainly a requirement for the ambitious, by writing pieces for the press attacking "Mr. Madison's War" and urging an immediate settlement. Casting his lot with the younger generation of Federalists—Daniel Webster and Harrison Gray Otis, for example—he did not follow the party extremists, symbolized, though perhaps unfairly, by the crotchety Essex Junto. Instead, he urged the party to adopt some of the techniques of political organization that had made the Jeffersonians popular and to abandon the negative tactics that smacked of snobbery and unpatriotic obstruction.[11] A sign of his growing acceptance in Boston society was his election as secretary of the Washington Benevolent Society, a young men's Federalist club and charity. Yet the domestic responsibilities of raising his children, his business interests, and the decline of the party sapped his once ardent enthusiasm for ward work in Boston in the years following the Peace of Ghent.[12] It was no longer as fashionable as it had been for businessmen to enter the sometimes dirty game of politics.

Rather than seeking new horizons in that field, he chose to busy himself in local charity, a much surer way to win advancement in society. He canvassed for gifts to the Deaf and Dumb Asylum, and to an Asylum for the Insane and a Hospital for the Sick, later known as Massachusetts General, and he subscribed to various causes, including the Asylum for Indigent Boys.[13] With twenty-five of the most prominent Boston citizens, including William Phillips and James Savage, he helped to start the Boston Provident Institution. Although British philanthropists were responsible for the savings bank idea, the Boston experiment was one of the first of its kind in New England. Tappan and other volunteer tellers hoped to encourage the poor to salt away their small holdings to gather modest interest, instead of wasting their money, as Tappan phrased it, by remaining "addicted to useless expenses, decking their persons with finery, and even . . . destroying themselves by the free use of spiritous liquors."[14]

While Tappan's Northampton background may have been partly responsible for his interest in philanthropic work at this time, his attitude was hardly distinguishable from anyone else's in his class. For instance, in 1819 he refused to canvass for the American Bible Society, another effort to save the poor from themselves, because he said it was wrong to ask hard-working people to give when money was so short. Only the very rich should be solicited. Such a stricture hardly fits the pattern of the root and branch reformer. In fact, for Tappan at this stage the aim of doing good was not the renovation of society but rather the exercise of a mild benevolence and the improvement of the existing order of things. Like most of his contemporaries among Boston businessmen, he was a social conservative. What worried him was the alarming spread of "wasteful and vicious habits," as hundreds of rural men and women poured into the city to mingle with Irish immigrants, all looking for work and mostly finding crime, slums, whiskey, and poverty.[15]

The answer to this social problem was education—the traditional American solution to the ills of society—but religious as well as secular education. Bible societies, Sunday schools, and tracts would teach the needy middle-class ideals and methods of hard work and show them the path to "success." Like other merchants and civic leaders, Tappan sought an improved public school system, but he also was enthusiastic about another British import, the Lancastrian experiment, whereby older children were trained by a senior teacher to parrot information and Bible precepts to their younger colleagues in small classes, thus expanding the coverage of instruction at very low cost.[16] Naturally proud of his rise from small beginnings, he thought others should have the opportunity to do likewise. At the same time, Christianity in purer form was thought necessary. "Take away Religion and what prevents the mass of people from violating laws of God and man?" Tappan asked his skeptical brother Benjamin in 1814. Increasingly, members of the possessing classes like Tappan were turning away from the Federalist party as a means to restrain the poor. But the patriarchal habits associated with that party continued. Religious instruction, sugar-coated in the form of moral tales and simple, printed homilies, breathed the spirit of old gentry rule. Tappan gave generously to the American Bible Society (though probably less in depression years), so that the poor would have access to the same source of inspiration he had enjoyed.[17]

It is easy to portray this trend from partisanship to religious activity as a conspiratorial means of controlling the lower classes. Patrician leadership, however, was of such ancient heritage in New England that its influence upon the manner of conducting religious work was hardly a sign of a deeply laid plot. Although increasingly challenged by secular trends, the patricians' style of benevolence was of some value. It encouraged the rich to exercise their social leadership in new ways—the creation and endowment of public institutions, the transmission of foreign ideas and techniques of humanitarian activity to the American public, and the exchange of these concepts and their applications with fellow philanthropists in other parts of the country. The New England elite was not so negative or so narrow that religious action and philanthropy became mere substitutes for the shackles of Federalism.

Certainly Tappan's own motives were not confined to fears of mobocracy alone. While conscious that he had not yet risen to the highest status in Boston society, he considered himself a liberal, generous, and well-informed man who sought only the good of all. His self-satisfaction did not, however, encourage an awareness that something was wrong in the nation that needed instant and wholesale reform; it was a sign of his conformity.

The 1820's were a time for all sorts of organizations designed for self-improvement and the raising up of others. It was as if communal were replacing individual action for the first time, as indeed seemed to many to be the case. The associative principle was approached with a new intensity, a spirit of national and local pride. Soon America was as much oriented toward group action as Great Britain's middle class. "Ours is the age of societies," declared James Stephen, one of their foremost promoters in England. "For the redress of every oppression that is done under the sun, there is a public meeting. . . . For the diffusion of every blessing . . . there is a committee."[18] Tappan was alive to the trend, and it suited his gregarious nature to take full part. He joined lecture groups and a debating society. On one occasion, he extolled the virtues of John C. Calhoun as Presidential timber at a forensic contest in Boylston Hall, but he was mainly interested in how he pitched his voice and presented his case rather than in what he said.[19]

Savings banks, asylums, clubs—including the St. John's Masonic Lodge—and other hobbies and casual interests were all very well, but a man's advancement depended largely on his business successes. Some men were making money from the textile mills springing up along the Massachusetts rivers in the early 1820's. That kind of enterprise was risky, but Tappan decided that the future lay in its direction. Perhaps he also found something of a challenge in brother Benjamin's woolen ventures in Ohio. By the end of 1823, Lewis had bought, for twelve thousand dollars, a quarter partnership in a prosperous mill at Lancaster. His duties in the firm included the purchase of cotton, but he knew so little about it that the other partners, including the wealthy Benjamin Pickman of Salem, forced him to resign after one year of operating at a loss.[20]

Other speculations in cotton and woolen mills, a nail factory, and a bleachery, which was the first calico-printing company in North America, fared quite well for a while. Nevertheless, Tappan had entered the manufacturing business at the wrong time, for a recession struck the country in 1826. Great Britain made matters worse by dumping cheap cottons and iron products on the market, with the result that factories closed down by the score. For the next year, Tappan struggled to restore his fortune. He demanded a new tariff law from Congress to ease the intensity of foreign competition, like most of his business associates abandoning the support of free trade to clamor for government assistance.[21] With some amusement, Benjamin reminded his brother of his inconsistency, and Lewis had to admit, "We are however greatly swayed by interest."[22] Unhappily the Tariff of Abominations of 1828, with its modest protective rates on finished textiles, came too late to help him weather the bad times.[23]

At first he showed an abundance of optimism and resilience; things would get better soon, he thought, and after all, business ventures did add mettle to a man's character. "It requires much fortitude, aye and religious principle to bear up under such disappointments," he had written shortly after his expulsion from cotton-buying. Anyhow, wealth was only a seductive mistress, and these losses "would not greatly harm" him in the long run. Even so, Tappan became increasingly uneasy. Perhaps his financial problems stemmed from something more ominous than just the whims of economic chance. Business failure might be God's timely lesson in humility, when greed absorbed the soul. "My adventuring so largely into the manufacturing business has been a serious injury to me, were I suddenly to escape I sh[oul]d leave everything behind. Thus Providence disciplines us sometimes with prosperity, and then with adversity, and always for our best good," he wrote a relative in 1827.[24]

Since his marriage in 1813, Tappan had lived happily, content with the world as it was, moderate in his political opinions, and satisfied, at least until 1823, with the state of his business. Respected in the community, he had looked forward to a life of security and growing importance in the city life of Boston. In 1823, he moved his family to Brookline in order to be near his wife's family and Dr. and Mrs. Pierce. The house he built next door to the home of Susan's brother Augustus was made of un-hammered blue granite, and it contained the study and library he had always wanted. Here, on his estate of seventeen acres of woods and fields, he could live in the same style and comfort as other merchants of Boston who had left the city for the sub-urbs.[25] With his growing troubles in manufacturing, however, his hopes were soon disastrously shattered.

In view of Tappan's religious training, it is not surprising that financial difficulties should force him to reconsider his spiritual life. Lewis, like John and Charles, had deserted the faith of his fathers and had become a Unitarian under the influence of William Ellery Channing, their pastor in Boston.[26] The great preacher was thought to be a saint in his own time, and all three brothers were attracted by his warmth and eloquence.[27]

Benjamin and Sarah had not objected to their sons' attending Channing's services, for he was a former student of David Tappan at Harvard, although more liberal than his mentor. Arthur too had been a member of the Federal Street Church, but he had left for Montreal before Channing's Unitarian views were fully devel-oped, thus escaping the liberal tendencies that affected the others. By 1815, however, Channing had started to preach a different kind of gospel. In his opinion, the puritan position suffered from three defects: its mistrust of man's moral nature; its belief in an essentially unlovable God; and its faith in the unity of Three Persons within the Godhead, a doctrine neither rational, provable, nor scriptural.[28]

Lewis Tappan could not accept these points uncritically. Be-ginning in 1816, he wrestled with the problem of the Trinity, reading the arguments of orthodox and Unitarian theologians. "Finished Wardlaw's Reply," he wrote in his diary. "Controversial work should be *studied*. . . . Different texts afford learned po-lemicks [*sic*] . . . but it appears to me that most persons, of serious-ness and good sense, who had never before read the scriptures, would, on perusing them, believe in the unity and not the trinity of the Godhead. Am I mistaken?"[29]

Tappan was highly intelligent, but there was a matter-offactness and curious self-consciousness in his mentality that excluded intuitive and mystical experience. Certainly the career he had chosen encouraged him to think along more practical lines. As a result, faith was something he imposed upon himself, as if it were a useful formula, like the little New Year's resolves he made and tried to follow. Mrs. Tappan was aware of his shortcoming, once writing him, "You have drawn up an excellent set of moral duties . . . but the difficulty is no one lives in the habitual practise of them. . . ." She urged him to depend on a "change of heart" instead, as a better way "to do all the whole law. . . ."[30] What he could do, of course, was to read all the pertinent literature and think about all the living examples of sin and goodness around him. These duties he performed faithfully: he kept a record of his reading, and he filled his diary with summations of the character and delivery of the clergymen he heard. The act of writing, and later, under evangelical impulse, the act of doing good works, would somehow make up for his inability to achieve the state of being that he assumed his mother had reached.

Since concepts of theology puzzled him, as elusive and subtle as they are, Tappan was all the more prone to defer to the judgment of those in whom he saw a superior spiritual insight. For a time Channing replaced Sarah Tappan as Lewis' religious instructor, finally convincing him, through goodness of character more than by any other means, that God was One and man was rational. In addition, they suffered a similar bereavement within the same year. In October, 1816, Channing, whom Tappan called "our beloved paster," lost his daughter. The father of two little girls himself, Tappan was especially sympathetic, praying, "May God who 'tempers the wind to the shorn lamb' console the sorrows of Mr. C."[31] Then, following an agonizing illness from consumption, Tappan's eldest child Susan died shortly after Christmas, 1817. In emulation of his mother, Tappan sought to feel a "sweet composure," but he found it hard to become fully resigned. Their grief drew the young couple closer together; it was a long time before they recovered from the loss of so happy and lively a child.

While Channing's example undoubtedly was a factor in Tappan's conversion, there was another and rather practical reason for a young businessman to be his disciple. Unitarianism was a fashionable creed for a merchant with social ambitions. No doubt Tappan was hardly aware that considerations of this sort might affect his attitude, but, because those he admired in society were mostly of that faith, he would have been likely to treat it with deference. Moreover, the Socinian heresy, he discovered, gave a man greater freedom in his habits than the catechism he had learned as a boy. He drank wine, temperately; attended the theater and dances, occasionally; read novels, sparingly; and took spontaneous, childlike delight in parades, debates, ceremonies, and gun salutes—in fact all those things that made life in Boston seem cosmopolitan by any standard with which he was familiar.[32] In contrast, Arthur Tappan had always been more serious about such things. Writing to one of his sisters after a visit to a circus as a young man, Arthur complained, "Fashion! Fashion! How much is society influenced by this little word; how few are able to resist its potency!"[33]

Knowing what his mother's reaction would be, Lewis kept his conversion to Unitarianism secret until finally convinced of the rightness of his course. From 1819, when she first learned of it, until her death in 1826, the only subject of her letters was his immediate return to orthodoxy. She urged him to "shun those fashionable preachers, who prophecy smooth things that will lull you into a false security. . . ."[34] Driven to self-defense, Tappan burst out on at least two occasions, criticizing her for thinking too much about "divine wrath," for constantly referring to her own wickedness in vague but foreboding tones, and for exercising a spiritual tyranny over others in the family. Of course, she was more than his match. After one such retort from her son, Sarah forced him to apologize for bad taste and lack of proper respect.[35]

Tappan's conversion was less absolute than this simple opposition between mother and son seems to indicate. For one thing, his Unitarianism was intermingled with a faithful adherence to much of her philosophy of life, and his later reconversion was therefore somewhat easier. Second, what seemed to stir his enthusiasm more than the belief in the oneness of God was the challenge of spreading the Socinian faith. If it was true for him, it had to be true for all men everywhere. This evangelistic approach to his new creed quite suited his general inclinations.

Unitarians were not very concerned with proselyting, but Tappan could not restrain his interest in institutions, societies, and committees. From the beginning, then, he found many of his colleagues, both pastors and laymen, less involved in philanthropy than he would have liked to see them. In the face of apathy, he tried discreetly but persistently to raise support for a Unitarian missionary in India. He also applauded Channing's efforts in behalf of the American Bible Society and other ecumenical ventures, and he became a counselor of the Society for the Suppression of Intemperance. With Charles as printer and publisher, Tappan for a while edited the *Christian Register,* a Unitarian journal. Yet his most permanent work for his church was the assistance he gave in institutionalizing it. In 1825 he urged the formation of the American Unitarian Association, becoming its first treasurer.[36]

If Tappan expected this movement to galvanize what had been a very uncertain, amorphous body of Congregationalists, he was to be rather disappointed. To some it smacked of harmful sectarianism, which would aggravate an already fierce contest with the aggressive orthodox faction. Others foresaw schisms within their churches and a loss of power and financial support. Tappan, however, believed it was time for the Unitarians to show conviction.

In 1825 a meeting was called at Channing's church to debate the question. The foremost leaders of the faith—Henry Ware, John G. Palfrey, Jared Sparks, and others—attended.[37] Probably not to Tappan's surprise, John Pierce, his Brookline pastor and brother-in-law, opposed the creation of a formal denomination. With impressive dexterity in his pastoral calls and with soporific and uncontroversial lectures from the pulpit, Pierce avoided commitment to either the Unitarian or the orthodox faction within his church.[38] Not surprisingly, therefore, he denounced the "measure of such a party aspect." Tappan replied that Pierce's fears were "groundless" and every so often thereafter criticized him for not being "an ultra Unitarian."[39] For his part, Pierce thought himself neither deficient in spirituality nor unique in his tactics in observing this uneasy religious truce, but he and Tappan remained on friendly terms.

The peace between the two creeds was not to last in Brookline; in fact, it was remarkable that Pierce had delayed a rupture as long as he had, for there was bitter feuding all over New England. At first, the orthodox had suffered demoralizing defeats: Harvard had defected by giving David Tappan's chair in the divinity school to the Unitarian Henry Ware; then the Connecticut empire of Timothy Dwight, president of Yale, had collapsed with the ending of the Congregational Establishment in 1818. Most humiliating of all was the Dedham decision of 1820, in which the Supreme Court of Massachusetts forced the orthodox to surrender church property to the Unitarian minority, whenever Congregationalists seceded and the "parish," which included non-communicants, voted to retain the Unitarian minister. Some grumbled that this was "legalized plunder," and among the Congregationalists it created smoldering resentment and the desire for revenge.[40]

To counteract the liberal trend, the orthodox had to adopt new methods and ideas and to find new leaders. All these elements appeared in the course of time and converged in a general revival of religion, the Second Great Awakening. Armed with these weapons and inspired by a renewal of popular interest in religion, the traditional Calvinists launched an attack on infidelity under the banner of what they called evangelicalism. The term was a broad one, cutting across denominational lines. Basically, it signified the promotion of revivals and voluntary or benevolent associations, and a modified Calvinism, elements that were borrowed or adapted from the democratic trends of the day in order to popularize the faith. From the first, problems arose over the nature of revivals, the character of religious philanthropy, and the degree to which theology had to be altered to meet the needs and sentiments of the public, but in view of the threat of Unitarian growth, old Edwardseans and more flexible Calvinists found themselves forced to unite. While few issues were ever finally resolved, the evangelicals of New England had a general plan of action and lost no time in putting it into effect.

Jedidiah Morse, Timothy Dwight, Joshua Huntington, and Eliphalet Pearson were among the early figures to protest the heresy of Boston, but by the 1820's the mantle of leadership fell to Lyman Beecher, who moved in 1826 from Litchfield, Connecticut, to Boston to take command. Despondent at first over the disestablishment of the Congregationalists in Connecticut in 1818, Beecher had come to see that separation of church and state was really a blessing. "By voluntary efforts," he concluded, "societies, missions and revivals, [ministers] exert a deeper influence than they ever could by queues and shoe buckles and cocked hats and gold headed canes."[41] As one of the founders of the American Board of Commissioners for Foreign Missions in 1810, he was an early advocate of the missionary and Bible movements by which the word of God was to spread across the globe. A raw-boned man, he preached with a rustic accent and a flailing of arms, giving a hint of emotion and excitement, though not so much as to shock the decorum of his Boston listeners.[42] Finally, Beecher collaborated with Nathaniel William Taylor of Yale in publicizing a form of Calvinism based on common sense and directed toward convincing men that salvation through the Redeemer, not God's sovereignty and human depravity, was the essence of Christianity.[43] It was Beecher's dream to unite Congregationalists, Presbyterians, and members of other sects with a Calvinist heritage in a great movement to defeat all rivals and rescue the nation from "the wilderness of popular unbelief."[44]

As the capstone to his campaign in Boston, Beecher in 1828 founded the *Spirit of the Pilgrims,* the co-ordinating journal of the traditionalists. At the same time he stepped up the pamphlet campaign in opposition to the legal victories of the Unitarians, appealing to the higher law of God (appeals to the state judiciary having been exhausted). His bold attacks gave heart to disgruntled Calvinists all over New England.[45] He was a politician more than a theologian, but the identification of religion with things to *do* rather than things to think about was the very key to his success. By this means he was able to exploit the secular predilections of ordinary churchgoers, as well as their fears about a burgeoning, almost chaotic America. Alarmed and forced to the defensive, Unitarians grew increasingly critical of the evangelical movement, withdrew from the benevolent societies, which were dominated by Beecher's Congregational and Presbyterian allies, and accused him of plotting to "seize civil power" by forming a Calvinist political party. Beecher, however, had stolen the initiative; the attacks on him fell short.[46] Stimulated by revivals and a plan of action, the evangelicals were moving with the times.

With growing interest, Tappan watched these controversies develop, read all the pamphlets, and discussed the ecclesiastical war with his friends. It was exciting, particularly when examples of religious feeling dramatically appeared in the everyday life around him. In his factory shed at Ware, Massachusetts, he attended revival services sponsored by his partners for the benefit of the workers and the neighborhood.[47] Six months later, Tappan was attending the Monthly Concerts of Prayer, which he and a close friend named William Ropes introduced to Brookline. (Ropes, a prominent shipper, even carried tracts and Bibles to Russia with him on his business trips.)[48] Pierce was forced to approve, although conservatives in the parish thought the movement disruptive and unbecoming. Tappan enjoyed the emotional overtones of these prayer sessions, which were actually rather mild compared with the shouting, clapping assemblies in the backwoods or in the poorer quarters of the coastal states, where Baptist missionaries labored with powerful effect.[49] Even so, he, liked Beecher, was not opposed to a show of sincere religious exaltation.

Under the stimulus of religious meetings and of gossip about miraculous conversions among the orthodox, Tappan became increasingly aware of Unitarian shortcomings. He began to think that where there was little interest in foreign missions and domestic revivals there must be a lack of Christian spirit. What else could account for the Unitarian opposition to his own modest efforts?[50]

Then one Sunday he returned from church to discover Caleb, the handyman, under deep conviction of sin in his room, crying, as Tappan recalled, " 'Lord Jesus, Lord Jesus, have mercy on me.' " Only the night before Caleb had taken a quiet part in the Monthly Concert session in his employer's parlor. Immediately Tappan rushed in with "medicine suited to the case"—Bunyan's *Pilgrim's Progress* and orthodox sermons hastily selected from the library shelves. With the cook's assistance in reading aloud, Tappan brought relief to the unhappy sinner. Thereafter, Caleb seemed to work with greater efficiency and to bear witness to God, rather in contrast to his previous behavior.[51]

Faced with this and other evidence of God's handiwork, Tappan called on Lyman Beecher, whose distrust of the Unitarians' urbanity Tappan was also beginning to share. He asked Beecher to explain the nature of the Godhead, and in his diary he recorded Beecher's reply: ". . . the scriptures clearly taught the existence of three intelligences . . . and that, somehow or other, these three were One. The *distinction* was revealed, but the *Unity* was a mystery."[52] Tappan promised to think over the explanation and review his Bible.

Meanwhile, his financial situation was becoming graver. Creditors of his manufacturing partnerships were demanding the repayments for which he was liable. His mind crowded with problems both religious and financial, he went to New York City in mid-August, 1827, when Arthur asked for his help during the fall rush.[53] His experience there not only resolved his financial dilemma but also dispelled his confusion about the nature of God and the proper road to take in his search for salvation.

Arthur Tappan's initial progress in commerce was slow; by this time, however, he was the owner of one of the nation's largest silk-importing houses. Although the most reserved member of the family, he had become its most successful businessman. As a boy, Arthur had been too shy to be a leader like his younger brother. Hampered from adolescence by crippling headaches, he could scarcely hide their effects in his relations with others. Weak eyesight may have contributed, but probably suppressed emotional conflicts brought on his attacks. Fears of failure in business, domestic strains, and other anxieties added to his burden, but a belief that he could never rise to Sarah's impossible standard of spirituality may have been the real source of his affliction. Certainly she had managed to imbue him with her own sense of guilt. Painfully shy and humorless, taking little pleasure in social gatherings, Arthur more closely resembled his mother than any of her other children; moreover, he shared her search for joy not in the things of this world but in the faithful pursuit of the path toward the next. Driven by an almost compulsive piety, Arthur Tappan tried to find release in philanthropy, and his profits by the mid-1820's had enabled him to become the most lavish giver in the city.[54] His experiment in Christian living greatly impressed his financially embarrassed brother.[55]

After fastening the great iron shutters in front of the store at 122 Pearl Street, the Tappan brothers commonly made their way together to evening religious meetings. They presented an interesting contrast as they walked along the narrow streets. Both had inherited the Tappan family's hazel eyes, slight build, and delicate features, but Arthur had deeper lines in his face, shaggy brows, and a joyless expression that made him look much older than Lewis—in fact, much older than he really was. Both of them had a glint of quick intelligence in their eyes, but Lewis' expression was always the more animated, purposeful, and open of the two. Mingling with the clergy who treated Arthur with such respect, Lewis Tappan listened to their reports of good works with unflagging pleasure.[56] In company with his brother, Lewis attended various meetings, including those of the American Board of Commissioners for Foreign Missions. Fascinated, he heard one missionary lecture about the grand work being done to convert the "musselmen" of Palestine.[57] Such activity, covering wide and exotic areas of the world, put the Unitarians' lonely outpost in India to shame.

Perhaps Arthur led Lewis to the Bible House on Nassau Street, not far from the silk store. The headquarters of the American Bible Society was the most impressive building in the rising empire of religious associations. Some may have grumbled about the luxury of its furnishings—the red carpet, the canopied throne of the presiding officer, the oil portraits of philanthropists, past and present, along the walls, the row of gilded chairs around the dais for the score of distinguished vice-presidents. As John Pierce had once observed, Lewis had a "love of show," and even as a boy he relished the chance to act on the Northampton community stage. But, after all, such displays were Christian, were they not? Presumably this sort of evangelical ritual and panoply was not frivolous, like Tappan's Masonic lodge or the commercial productions he had once seen in Boston's theaters.[58] How different was this religious enthusiasm in New York from the stodginess of Unitarians at home. Already Massachusetts, which Tappan had once thought the most progressive state in the Union, seemed outdated. "An old state," he wrote Benjamin, "like an old man, is ordinarily fearful."[59]

The purpose of Tappan's visit was not merely to help his brother sell silks or to converse with reverend gentlemen and their patrons. Already heavily in debt to Arthur, Lewis was forced to ask for even more help. Arthur did not disappoint his brother. He offered Lewis a partnership in the New York store; one-quarter of the profits would be Lewis', with the stipulation that one-half of this income, minus family expenses, would be reinvested in the company. The other half would be reserved to pay Lewis' debts to John, who also had lent him large sums, and to Arthur. (In prior months they had met his most pressing engagements.) With thousands to repay, Lewis was grateful for the handsome proposition.[60]

Arthur was a very generous man, not only toward the church but toward his relatives too. Nonetheless, he occasionally used money as a weapon. Once, for example, Benjamin asked him for a loan to start a business of some kind and received this reply: "With my brothers I am willing, in case of *need*, to share my last dollars, but while no such necessity exists I regard myself as the steward of the great Giver of all I possess, and all that He has entrusted to me as sacredly devoted to carrying forward the great work of spreading the Gospel. . . ."[61] He then added how pleased he would be to learn of Benjamin's rejoining the fold of Christianity. The two brothers had always conducted their relations on a very formal basis, but Benjamin was naturally furious over the ill-disguised bribe. Among his irreverent friends in the West, the New York silk-jobber was known as "Saint Arthur."[62] Toward Lewis, however, he proved more magnanimous.

Even so, it may have come as a surprise to Lewis when Arthur insisted on a lone, but pointed, stipulation. During the course of Tappan's stay in New York, Arthur called him to his cubicle in the center of the gloomy warehouse store. Perhaps Arthur ordered a clerk to bring an extra chair. (He had found that the missing convenience speeded the departure of unwanted visitors.) Then he observed, as Tappan recorded in his diary:

. . . that he should be sorry to have me come here to be very active as an Unitarian, in religious matters—building churches, etc. I replied that for sometime I had felt that I might be under some temptation to swerve from my religious opinions from secular or pecuniary considerations; that he must be sensible it was my duty scrupulously to keep my mind unbiased by pecuniary considerations; that I should endeavour to act conscientiously; that I was free to acknowledge that my mind had undergone some change & that I should *not* be active in propagating Unitarian sentiments, with my present views; and that if my mind should alter, on this subject, and I should feel it my duty to make such efforts I should be willing to dissolve any connexion in business, I might form, if he wished it.[63]

After his return to Brookline at the end of the fall trading season, Tappan began a letter to his father, who had lost Sarah the year before, explaining his change of religious feelings. Unable to continue, he went to his library and behind the closed door fell on his knees: "I felt a constraining influence to address God in three persons, and then to pray to Jesus. I was unwilling to rise until the scales had fallen from my eyes, but I did."[64] Just then Susan walked into the room and looked at him "with unusual earnestness. . . ." Refusing to tell her what was on his mind, he finished his letter to his father: " 'I shall therefore withdraw myself from the influence of a denomination with which I have cordially and for a long period acted, and shall put myself under the influences of the orthodox denomination. . . .' "[65] This was a matter for him to write the Tappan clan about, even before he told Susan herself.

Only a short time passed before Tappan was denouncing the outraged John Pierce for not being an enthusiast for orthodoxy. While claiming brotherly affection for his family, he felt obliged to tell his sister Lucy that her husband's "perturbation, indecision, mental distress, bespeak a faith unsettled, a dark path, a dubious way." Shortly afterward, seventy to one hundred parishioners joined Tappan and William Ropes at Dr. Blagden's Congregational church in Brighton. Rather predictably, Pierce, Lucy, and Augustus Aspinwall, Susan's brother, were thoroughly resentful and sarcastic about the "worldly motives" involved.[66]

Susan could hardly have enjoyed the malicious neighborhood gossip that circulated about her husband's change of faith. Being a dutiful wife, however, she tried to follow his course as best she could, supported by his vigorous barrage of arguments. Nonetheless, Tappan had to admit, "Her heart is at war with her mind." Some months later she fully surrendered, perhaps at first for the sake of domestic peace and only later for more elevated reasons.[67]

In order to counteract the rumors, Tappan published a pamphlet setting forth the reasons that he claimed were paramount in his decision. What it demonstrated, however, was not so much his rededication to orthodoxy as the wide gulf separating him from his mother's theocentric faith. His arguments did not treat in any depth the innate sinfulness of man, the concept of regeneration, or even the majesty and mercy of God. The doctrine of election was dismissed as "a merely speculative subject." Man, he asserted, was by nature sinful, but "from a careful attention to the means of grace and from special influences of the Holy Spirit" he could receive the means to redemption. Tappan's explanation of the Trinity consisted of a repetition of Beecher's comment and the remark: "the Orthodox, although they believe the doctrine is true, yet have various ways of explaining their apprehensions of it, all of which, however, include the doctrine." Finally, he summed up his brief discussion of theology with an affirmation of the existence of hell, which, he said, must be true, for "a contrary belief counteracts nearly all the good effects of preaching. . . ."[68] Tappan was no theologian.

The rest of his tract concentrated on the failings of the Unitarians and the contrasting strengths of their opponents. It was not unusual for the evangelicals to define themselves by their differences with "infidels," but Tappan made this argument his chief one. Unitarians prayed too little in their closets, gave too little to religious charity, preached with less fire and conviction, and followed too much the fashions of the world. On the other hand, he asked, "Who are the people, that refrain from doubtful, or positively injurious amusements; who refuse to patronize the theaters; who love social religious meetings; who are in favor of discreet church discipline; who stand up for morality and piety in all places, fearlessly, and at the risk of unpopularity?"[69] It was a queer sort of conversion that could be so easily set on paper as a series of social benefits. It was no less sincere for all that, but it hardly signified a faith identical to his mother's. Almost totally absent was any heartfelt sense of contrition or appreciation of the beauty and mystery of God. For Tappan, as for Beecher and Nathaniel Taylor, the Calvinists' deity had died, to be replaced by One concerned with the happiness of mankind, the growth of the visible church, the extinction of heresy, and the establishment of a moral order which reflected the ethics but not the theology of Calvinism. In brief, Tappan's faith was the dynamic, optimistic faith of middle-class, nineteenth-century America. The basis for a religion with wide appeal had been laid, but "it was the faith of the fathers," as one historian has said, "ruined by the faith of the children."[70]

In spite of its obvious defects, the pamphlet created a sensation in Massachusetts. Within a few days three thousand copies were sold, a large number for a work of this sort. Orthodox zealots were crowing over their new acquisition, who was, after all, one of the principal lay figures in the Unitarian church. From Groton in the western part of the state, where control of the first Congregational church was then being hotly contested, a young schoolmaster named Elizur Wright wrote his fiancée in Boston, "It is to be hoped that great good will result. . . . Mr. Wilder told us the other day that some months since he called on the pious mother of these Tappans who told him that She had not for ten years omitted for a single day to pray for this Son Lewis in Boston, and she had strong confidence that he would at last be converted."[71] Indeed, Sarah knew her son's disposition better than Tappan did himself.

When Tappan reverted to Trinitarianism, he adopted a tradition popular among the American and British evangelicals of his day by claiming that his return to Calvinism, along with that of fourteen of his mother's descendants, including John and Charles, was solely due to her influence. To memorialize Sarah's triumph, he later compiled a book of her letters. In the preface, he fully apologized for having "deprived himself, during her life, of sweet communion with her in religious fellowship," but, he continued, he looked "forward with hope that maketh not ashamed, to the period when he may be permitted to bow before the throne of the Lamb and exclaim with her, 'My Lord and my God.' "[72]

In the meantime, he was busy concluding his affairs in Boston, saying good-bye to William Ropes and the group of triumphant Israelites from Pierce's church and explaining his actions to still doubtful in-laws. John and Charles, who had also recently returned to the fold, defended him, but to unfriendly critics Tappan had to turn what he called, as one would expect, "the other cheek." "My motives are impeached," he said, "and much obloquy will be thrown upon me. I pray God I may be humble, patient & firm, esteeming it an honour to be slandered—falsely—for the cause of my Saviour."[73] On January 28 at two in the morning he left on the stage for New York, after kissing his wife and five children good-bye. He and Susan had decided that, for financial reasons, as well as for the health of their family, it would be better for her and the children to remain in Brookline until the property was sold. "It was painful to leave my family, and a place so dear to me, and I could not do it without much emotion," he confessed.[74] It was the end of a way of life. It was also the end of his happiest years of marriage to Susan, for she never quite reconciled herself to losing her pleasant associations with friends and kindred in Brookline. Within a few days, Lewis was wholly occupied in that orthodox and benevolent world of Arthur Tappan.

NOTES

1. LT to BT, June 28, 1805, BT MSS, LC.
2. ST to LT, June [?], 1809; LT, *Memoir of Sarah Tappan*, 64–65.
3. LT, *Arthur Tappan*, 31–32; see also "My Forefathers," 51.
4. Joshua Huntington, *Memoir of the Life of Mrs. Abigail Waters* . . . (Boston, 1817); LT, *Arthur Tappan*, 33–34, 40; Harriet F. Woods, *Historical Sketches of*

Brookline, Mass. (Boston, 1874), 178 ff., 251–52; Arthur W. Brown, *Always Young for Liberty: A Biography of William Ellery Channing* (Syracuse, 1956), 68.

5. "The Honored Dead," New York *Tribune,* June 25, 1873.

6. "Chronological Resume," 1807–1812; see also "Scrapbook and Summary Book," September 1, 1855, 54, and September 1, 1859, 285; Benjamin Tappan, Sr., to BT, July 4, 1812, BT MSS, LC; LT to Thomas Aspinwall, February 25, 1813, ltrbk.; Boston *Daily Advertiser,* March 2, 1813.

7. LT to Mrs. John Bigelow, December 1, 1847, ltrbk.; LT to BT, December 27, 1813, ltrbk.

8. LT, *Arthur Tappan,* 53–60; "Chronological Resume," 1815, 1817; see also LT's copies of a petition to Hon. William Reed, Benjamin Tallmadge, Samuel Taggart, *et al.,* in regard to Arthur's situation, June 16, 1812, ltrbk.

9. Mrs. William Aspinwall to Susan Aspinwall, n.d., transcript by author from a private collection; Algernon Aikin Aspinwall, *The Aspinwall Genealogy* (Rutland, Vt., 1901), 82.

10. *Lewis Tappan's Wedding Journey, September 7, 1813* (n.l., n.d.), 15, in author's possession. The original reminiscences were lost.

11. LT (signed "Washington"), in Boston *Repertory and General Advertiser* June 5, 1812; LT (signed "Peace"), in *ibid.,* August 4, 1812; LT (signed "Spectator"), in Boston *Daily Advertiser,* March 5, 1813; LT (signed "Spirit of the Times"), in *ibid.,* March 16, 1813; LT, "Public Festivals," in *ibid.,* March 17, 1813; LT to Isaac Hastings, February 25, 1813, ltrbk.; LT to Thomas Aspinwall, February 25, 1813, ltrbk.; LT to BT, December 27, 1813, ltrbk.

12. *A Directory Containing the Names, Places of Business, and Residences of the Members of the Washington Benevolent Society of Massachusetts from its Commencement* (Boston, 1813), 65; and diary, September, 1814, October-November, 1816, December 7, 1816, February 23, 1817; LT to BT, May 17, 1821, BT MSS, LC; see also *ibid.,* October 19, 1820, and July 24, 1824.

13. Diary, November 2 and December 26, 1816, and May 26, 1814; LT in *New England Palladium* (Boston), March 12, 1822; N.I. Bowditch, *A History of the Massachusetts General Hospital* (Boston, 1851), 23, 417.

14. LT, *New England Palladium,* November 29, 1816; see also *ibid.,* November 22 and December 6, 1816; diary, November 16 and 23, 1816; *The Constitution, Plans, and By-Laws of the Provident Institution for Savings in the Town of Boston . . .* (Boston, 1818); and *One Hundred Years of Savings Bank Service* (Boston, 1916), 11 ff.

15. LT, *New England Palladium,* November 29, 1816.

16. LT, *ibid.,* May 3, 1822; see also LT, *ibid.,* April 26, May 10 and 14, 1822. Lancastrian experimentation generally appealed to young Federalists: see David Hackett Fischer, *The Revolution of American Conservatism* (New York, 1965), 49.

17. Diary, October, November, December 7, 1816; LT to BT, May 21, 1814, which is also quoted by Fischer, *Revolution of Conservatism,* 48.

18. Sir James Stephens, *Essays in Ecclesiastical Biography* (London, 1849), I, 382.

19. Diary, May 5, 1824; see also LT to BT, February 21, 1825, BT MSS, LC.

20. Andrew E. Ford, *History of the Origin of the Town of Clinton, Massachusetts, 1653–1865* (Clinton, Mass., 1896), 155; see also LT to BT, February 21, 1825, BT MSS, LC. Susan Tappan's sister-in-law was the daughter of the senior

partner of the firm, David Poignard; see Susan Tappan to Louisa Elizabeth Poignard Aspinwall, November 2, 1823, transcript by the author from a private collection. Benjamin Pickman, a noted shipper and investor of Salem, was instrumental in having Tappan removed.

21. LT to BT, January 11, 1827, BT MSS, LC; "The Honored Dead," New York *Tribune*, June 25, 1873; diary, June 2, 1827.

22. LT to BT, October 31, 1823; see also LT to BT, August 30 and October 19, 1820, July 24, 1824, BT MSS, LC.

23. LT to William P. Green, Norwich, Connecticut, December 28, 1849, ltrbk., in which he claimed a loss of eighty thousand dollars in the Ware Manufacturing Company alone; LT to John Tappan, December 5, 1847, ltrbk. For nationalistic reasons, Tappan also favored a high tariff on imported raw wool to protect American sheep-raisers; see LT to Samuel Lathrop (a Massachusetts congressman), November 30, 1826, Simon Gratz autograph MSS, Pennsylvania Historical Society.

24. LT to Henry Edwards, October 19, 1827; diary, November 8, 1824.

25. LT to BT, February 21 and May 14, 1825, BT MSS, LC; diary, December 25, 1826; *Land Ownership in Brookline from the First Settlement with Ten Maps* (Brookline Historical Society, 1923), publ. no. 5, Map VI; Woods, *Historical Sketches of Brookline*, 171; John Gould Curtis, *History of the Town of Brookline, Massachusetts* (Boston, 1933), 186–87.

26. LT to Sophia Sturge, January 29, 1844, ltrbk.; LT, *Arthur Tappan*, 36.

27. LT, in New York *Evangelist*, clipping, scrapbook; diary, May 15, 1825.

28. LT to Sophia Sturge, January 29, 1844, ltrbk.; Brown, *Always Young for Liberty*, 31, 71–75; LT, *Arthur Tappan*, 36, 62, 63.

29. Diary, January 26, 1816; see also *ibid.*, August 31, 1817.

30. ST to LT, April 8, 1819, *Memoir of Sarah Tappan*, 72; see diary, January 1, 1826.

31. Diary, October 27, 1816.

32. *Ibid.*, 1814, 1816, November 13, 1824, April 2, 1825; on his later hostility to theaters, see clipping from *Independent*, July 9, 1857, scrapbook, 226.

33. AT to a sister, May 14, 1808, LT, *Arthur Tappan*, 50.

34. LT, *Memoir of Sarah Tappan*, 115.

35. ST to LT, May [?], 1820, *ibid.*, 79; October 1, 1825, *ibid.*, 106.

36. "Chronological Resume," 1818, 1819, 1821, 1826; LT and George Bond, "Circular Letter on the Rev. Mr. Adams's Calcutta Mission," June 5, 1824, Jared Sparks MSS, Houghton Library, Harvard; LT to Moses Grant, June 13, 1824, Grant Autographs, Boston Public Library; diary, May 25, 1825, December 26 and 31, 1826.

37. The Rev. John Pierce, journal, January 27, 1825, Massachusetts Historical Society.

38. William Buell Sprague, *Annals of the American Pulpit. . .* (New York, 1857–69), VIII, 333–34, 340.

39. Diary, November 1, 1827, Tappan's report of a conversation with Pierce; see also Pierce journal, January 27, 1825, Massachusetts Historical Society.

40. Joseph S. Clark, *A Historical Sketch of the Congregational Churches in Massachusetts, from 1620 to 1858* (Boston, 1858), 250, 262–63; Sidney Earle Mead, "Nathaniel William Taylor (1786–1858) and the New Haven Theology: A Study in Background and Development," Ph.D. dissertation, University of Chicago, 1940, 69–70 (published as *Nathaniel William Taylor, 1786–1858 . . .* [Chicago, 1942]).

41. Barbara M. Cross, ed., *The Autobiography of Lyman Beecher* (Cambridge, 1961), I, 344; Sidney E. Mead, "Lyman Beecher and Connecticut Orthodoxy's Campaign against the Unitarians, 1819–1826," *Church History*, IX (September, 1940), 229; George L. Walker, *Some Aspects of the Religious Life of New England*. . . (New York, 1897), 160–61, 163; George M. Stephenson, *The Puritan Heritage* (New York, 1954), 114–15.

42. Lyman Beecher Stowe, *Saints, Sinners and Beechers* (Indianapolis, 1934), 49–51; Cross, *Beecher Autobiography*, I, xxix; and Charles C. Cole, *The Social Ideas of the Northern Evangelists, 1826–1860* (New York, 1954), 28–29.

43. Mead, "Taylor and New Haven Theology," 54–73, 87, 90, 94; Walker, *Some Aspects of Religious Life*, 151–52.

44. George Burgess, *Pages from the Ecclesiastical History of New England During the Century Between 1740 and 1840* (Boston, 1847), 126; see Beecher's declaration of war, *Christian Spectator*, I (1819), 3–4; Mead, "Taylor and New Haven Theology," 114.

45. Clark, *Historical Sketch of Congregational Churches*, 236, 262–63; Edward R. Tyler to Elizur Wright, April 13, 1827, E. Wright to his parents, December 25, 1827, E. Wright to Susan Clark, February 13, 1828, Elizur Wright MSS, LC.

46. *Christian Examiner* (Boston), V (July and August, 1828), 298, reviewing Beecher's *Vindication of the Rights of the Churches of Christ;* see also *ibid.,* IV (March and April, 1827), 136; cf. Burgess, *Pages from Ecclesiastical History of New England*, 101–3.

47. Diary, November 19, 1826; LT's partner in the woolen mill was S. V. S. Wilder, a noted philanthropist.

48. *Ibid.,* August 16, 1827; Harriet Ropes Cabot, "The Early Years of William Ropes & Company in St. Petersburg," *American Neptune*, XXIII (April, 1963), 134–35.

49. LT to Sophia Sturge, January 29, 1844, ltrbk.; C. C. Goen, *Revivalism and Separatism in New England, 1740–1800: Strict Congregationalists and Separate Baptists in the Great Awakening* (New Haven, 1962), 282–85.

50. Diary, May 25, 1825, January 23, 1828.

51. LT to Sophia Sturge, January 29, 1844, ltrbk.

52. Diary, August 17, 1827.

53. Diary, December 25 and 31, 1826, May 4 and September 29, 1827; LT to Henry Edwards, October 19, 1827, *ibid.;* and LT to BT, July 26, 1827, BT MSS, LC.

54. LT, *Arthur Tappan*, 86.

55. *Ibid.,* 74; LT to BT, September 26 and October 5, 1829, BT MSS, LC.

56. Diary, September 20, 1827; LT, *Arthur Tappan,* frontispiece.

57. Diary, October 11, 1827.

58. *Ibid.,* October 19 and November 1, 1827; "My Forefathers," 36–37; New York *Evangelist*, April 20, 1833; diary, February 5, 1829.

59. LT to BT, January 5, 1828, BT MSS, LC.

60. Diary, October 8, 1827.

61. AT to BT, March 5, 1829, BT MSS, LC.

62. J. Neef to BT, January 8, 1834, *ibid.;* AT to BT, May 8, 1829, *ibid.*

63. Diary, October 8, 1827; LT, *Arthur Tappan,* 85.

64. Diary, October 30, 1827.

65. *Ibid.*

66. *Ibid.*, December 8 and 18 (1st quotation), 1827, January 20, 1828 (2nd quotation), and *passim;* Edward R. Tyler to Elizur Wright, April 13, 1827, Elizur Wright MSS, LC.

67. *Ibid.*, January 5 and 6, February 16, March 5, April 26, 1828.

68. LT, *Letter from a Gentleman in Boston to a Unitarian Clergyman of that City* (Boston, 1828), 14, 17.

69. *Ibid.*, 11; Martin E. Marty, *The Infidel, Free Thought and American Religion* (Cleveland, 1961), 105.

70. Joseph Haroutunian, *Piety v. Moralism: The Passing of the New England Theology* (New York, 1932), 281; see also Henry Ware, Jr., *Reply of a Unitarian Clergyman to the 'Letter of a Gentleman of Boston'* (Boston, 1828); *Christian Examiner* (Boston), V (January and February, 1828), 89–90; Boston *Recorder,* March 7, 1828.

71. E. Wright to Susan Clark, February 13, 1828, E. Wright MSS, LC; Wright to his parents, February 16, 1828, Weston MSS, Boston Public Library; Wright to Reuben Hitchcock, February 26, 1828, Hitchcock Family MSS, Western Reserve Historical Society.

72. LT, *Memoir of Sarah Tappan,* 5.

73. Diary, February 16, March 5, 1828.

74. Diary, January 28, 1828. Tappan's children were Juliana, 11 yrs.; Susan, 9; William, 8; Lewis Henry, 6; Eliza, 4; Lucy, 2. See diary, January 1, 1828.

CHAPTER THREE

The World of Arthur Tappan: "Silks, Feathers and Piety"

*W*hen *Lewis Tappan* arrived in New York, he joined some friends at a family boardinghouse, where he soon arranged with the landlady a daily schedule of religious exercises. A bell was rung at ten o'clock each night, summoning the residents to evening prayer. A Mr. Sturgis objected and apparently left in high dudgeon, but Tappan and his friends promised to pay for the vacancy until a more amenable lodger could be found.[1] Religious houses and hotels of this sort grew very popular with the evangelicals during the era.

Prayers at his quarters and unsparing work at the store did not entirely cure him of lonely thoughts of "sinful indulgence." Separated from his wife and family, he was often depressed and restless. Shortly before their arrival from Brookline in October, 1828, he had a particularly serious struggle against his baser impulses. "I have been, this week," he wrote in his diary, "sorely assailed by a grievous temptation. . . . When I entertained such thoughts God's restraining grace seemed to be withdrawn. . . . But at length on the eve of committing sin a heavenly influence seemed to come over me . . . entreating me not to forfeit my hopes of heaven for the sins of this world." He did not commit the sin.[2]

With the zeal of a new convert, Tappan tried to live up to all the regulations of the evangelical creed, but at times he had moments of temptation of a less formidable character. On the Fourth of July, citizens of New York watched a "magnificent set of fireworks" at Castle Gardens near the Battery. Tappan longed to be there, but others in the boardinghouse persuaded him that it was frivolous display. Instead, he reluctantly took his place in the parlor, and the ladies sang several numbers from the Rev. Asahel Nettleton's revivalist hymnbook, *Village Hymns*.[3] Later, he and Horace Bushnell, a young friend of the Tappan brothers and later a prominent Congregational theologian, visited Niblo's Gardens. Lanterns swung in the breeze, and a band played gaily. "I do not know as such amusements are injurious in a city like this," he mused, rather uncomfortably. "There was nothing indelicate or profane."[4]

But he had not come to New York to enjoy light entertainments, and from morning to night he was "chained to the oar," as he told brother Benjamin, at Arthur Tappan's silk company. On some days during the fall or spring rush, the clerks wrote as many as thirty pages in the ledgers. The store itself was a granite, three-story building on the Pearl Street side of Hanover Square, as fashionable a site as the city then could offer. Meandering up from the Battery as if "laid out by some patriotic cows," Pearl Street was the center of New York trade.

Lewis' job was to manage the daily operations. He supervised the twenty or more clerks and bookkeepers, saw that shipping consignments arrived or left on time, stocked the sample bins of straw hats, umbrellas, and ladies' stockings, and interviewed prospective employees. The rips, creaks, bangs of crates being opened or hauled by pulley upstairs, the shouts of workmen, the rumble of carts outside, the curses of draymen and constant tramp of people on the wooden sidewalks made a frightful din. Tappan had no trouble adjusting to the organized frenzy of Manhattan, and he even came to love it. "It is delightful to me to have occupation, that is my hobby," he told Benjamin.[5] Arthur, on the other hand, never grew accustomed to the pace of urban life.

There in the midst of this strenuous activity sat Arthur Tappan, bent over heaps of invoices, memoranda, and bankbooks. Over the low partitions of his office he kept an eye on customers and clerks, but most of his time was devoted to receiving orders for goods from all over the country, especially the South, and to placing orders with his suppliers in England and Italy. It required skill to anticipate what fashions would be popular and to gauge the state of the market. Sometimes he left the office, burdened with business anxieties, to lie on his couch at home, a handkerchief over his face, while his wife ordered his daughters to leave him undisturbed. "He has a waspish temper," Lewis had to admit after one small dispute, but he understood his brother's headaches and genially made allowances for them.[6] Actually, it was for reasons of health that Arthur had been so pleased to have Lewis join his firm, in order to "relieve" him "of some care."[7]

Within a month after Lewis arrived, Arthur bought a house in New Haven and moved his family there for all except the winter months. Leaving on Friday or Saturday and returning to town on the overnight steamer that docked Monday morning, he at last had found a way to escape the noise, grit, and vexations of the city. Although his wife Frances had grown up in the New York home of Alexander Hamilton after her parents' death, she too was glad of a chance to enjoy a peaceful, healthful atmosphere. (Her father had been one of Hamilton's closest friends during the Revolution, and he had brought her up from the age of two.[8] This commutation—for that is the word for it—from Connecticut to Manhattan allowed Arthur to maintain a spiritual retreat in his native New England, where the values of country Calvinism still prevailed.

Nearby was Yale; Arthur's next-door neighbor and close friend was Nathaniel William Taylor, who was the leading theologian of the college's seminary and Lyman Beecher's partner in the orthodox crusade. The house that Tappan had bought from Samuel F. B. Morse, the famous inventor, had originally been the home of Jedidiah Morse, one of the earliest and most politically conservative leaders of revived Calvinism. Refreshed by his associations in the quiet college town, Arthur could return to fulfill his pledge to transform "Babylon," as he often considered New York, into Zion. Business lay before him on his desk after the weekends, and he did not neglect his duties. Yet "the prominent thoughts in his mind," as Lewis remarked, "were the sayings of his Master: 'The field is the world'—'Occupy till I come.' "[9]

Religion and capitalism combined in Arthur in an unusual manner. He ran his business as if he were a parsing Latin schoolmaster. The clerks were required to live in boardinghouses similar to Lewis' residence. They were urged to be at home by ten o'clock.

The young men also were expected to attend church at least once a week. A small room on the third floor might frequently be set aside for the reading of morning prayers and the performance of devotionals. The "Bethel," as that chamber was called, was often in use during revival seasons. Naturally, the clerks were not to visit theaters or consort with actresses, for such habits might lead to a loss of interest in religion or even to unspeakable degradations. The monastic rule was harsh, but Arthur felt a responsibility to the New England parents who had sent their sons to study in the successful firm. Although the young men learned a great deal, they were ill paid. A clerk of twenty-one, with previous experience in a country store, received three hundred dollars a year, with an annual raise of fifty dollars for the five-year term of the contract. The rigorous course was worth the trouble, however; for Arthur Tappan, while forbidding and taciturn, was generous in helping the promising graduates start their own independent careers.[10]

In the management of business itself, Arthur Tappan followed traditional Christian teaching. Contrary to then current practices, he sold for cash or quickly redeemed promissory notes, at fixed prices, avoiding long-term loans and the usurious rates associated with them. He made his profits from, in the phrase, low markup and high volume. Such innovations evoked wonder, since even stores on London's Regent Street allowed Arabian haggling over prices. To the country traders, unused to city ways and suspicious of being cheated, Arthur's method was most attractive. They could depend on his honesty and fair-dealing. Even A. T. Stewart, pioneer of the American department store, was said to have been forced once to reserve the goods he had purchased until he could return with cash in hand.[11]

Yet Arthur's ethics looked back as far as Cotton Mather, not forward to J. C. Penney. Dependence upon the credit system, Lewis Tappan wrote in a pamphlet years later, tempted men to speculation and greed, to the neglect of their families, and eventually to ruin. Exchange for hard cash, he maintained, was the Christian way to trade. Many other businessmen of the day paid lip-service to thrift and the doctrine of pay-as-you-go; Lewis, however, speaking from his own experience of 1827, meant every word, though even he sometimes failed to live up to the principle.[12] For a time, at least, these rocklike ethics grossed Arthur Tappan and Company over a million dollars annually. If his profits are figured at a conservative six per cent and the shares of his minor partners are deducted, Arthur's personal income may have been somewhere between twenty-five and thirty thousand dollars, perhaps more.[13]

"A cracker and a tumbler of cold water sufficed for Arthur's luncheon," Lewis later recalled. Arthur's family's expenses were equally modest, because money, he believed, was entrusted by God to his care. "At the GREAT ASSIZE" he would have to submit his accounts, and "luxurious living" or "vain show" would appear on the debit side. Therefore, the residue he spent to fulfill his evangelical dream, "the conversion of the world."[14] His vision of a perfect Christian society was somewhat similar to that of his puritan ancestor Abraham Toppan and Abraham's contemporaries in Massachusetts, but the methods necessary to achieve it were strictly "modern" by Arthur's standards. The country was no longer empty wilderness; it was full of enemies of his faith who had to be conquered and converted. The task could be done only with the means at hand, the profits from "silks, feathers" and the inspiration of his New England "piety."[15]

Like any other party, the evangelicals had their partisan machinery, "those godlike institutions" of the tract, Bible, Sabbath school, and temperance and missionary societies. Each May, the party members—Methodists, Baptists, Dutch Reformed, but especially Presbyterians and Congregationalists—gathered in New York to plan new campaigns, which were to grow in strength "till the millennial day shall be ushered in with the songs of a regenerate world."[16]

Although Calvinists were particularly attracted to this disciplined brand of Christianity, a smattering of well-born Episcopalians, in imitation of the broad churchmen of the English church, joined the movement, adding a certain luster to the subscription lists: William Jay, son of John Jay; John Pintard, a New York financier; Richard Varick, an aged Federalist and wealthy patroon; and the Rev. James Milnor, a former Federalist politician, were among this group. Of course, the Calvinists could also claim some distinguished men: Elias Boudinot, an early supporter of the Bible Society; Stephen Van Rensselaer, the richest landowner of New York; and Theodore Frelinghuysen, senator from New Jersey, whose devotion to Sunday schools was exceeded only by that to Henry Clay.[17]

These luminaries considered the religious education of the

masses essential to the nation if anarchy were not to seize the country, an opinion common among the higher classes of society but one that evangelicals took as a principle of action. Typical was the attitude of John Pintard, who supported a Society for the Prevention of Pauperism but could note in disgust that "the scabby sheep" of "that sink of pollution," Five Points in the Irish quarter, would have nothing to do with it.[18] In England, social conservatism played an important role in formulating the program of William Wilberforce and the Quaker and Anglican evangelicals, whose societies set the pattern for American churchmen.[19] Conservatism was also bound to be a part of the movement here, but American evangelicalism did not derive its strength from the wealthy alone. The Tappan brothers felt a little uncomfortable in the society of these ponderous gentlemen in smallclothes, even though sharing their social views. Lewis Tappan, for instance, acknowledged that "Christianity is the conservator of all that is dear in civil liberty & human happiness; and that infidelity sets loose all the base passions of our nature."[20] Yet he did not view religion as simply a means to preserve social inequalities and to protect the rule of the "wise and good." In fact, evangelicalism, for all its elitist shadings, was not, in his mind, incompatible with democracy. The aim was chiefly to make everyone equally good, the standard being the ethics of his New England upbringing.[21]

The Tappans had known, and were to know, near poverty themselves too often to despise the poor as such, but they were not free of the snobbery of the times. In 1830, Lewis wrote Mathew Carey, a Philadelphia philanthropist, that the improvement of the condition of the poor was a matter of charitable paternalism. "The rich ought to furnish coarse work for poor females & pay them liberally," he said, "even if such is created on purpose." If the wealthy man doubled "his family washing," he would be doing society a great favor. "But," he concluded, "in this mercenary, close-fisted world, how slow mankind are to obey the dictates of enlightened humanity!" Rather naturally, Lewis did not believe that the humble were entitled to a breezy familiarity with their betters. In 1844, he advised his future son-in-law, Henry C. Bowen, to "dare to be singular" by not inviting his store clerks to the wedding, because to do so would hardly be "proper."[22]

Autocrats in the management of the silk firm, the Tappans were unlikely to approve trade unionism, which was beginning to develop in the late 1820's. But they objected to Frances Wright, the Owens, George Henry Evans, and other labor reformers not so much on the grounds of their economic opinions as of their freethinking. One entry in Tappan's diary disclosed that he had read a pamphlet entitled " 'Infidelity Displayed' by a mechanic, in answer to Miss Wright—a pretty smart performance."[23] Later on, however, he became more sympathetic to labor reform. In 1847, for instance, he wrote George Henry Evans, who was seeking support for a long list of reforms, that he favored the imposition of legal limitations on landholdings and the institution of the ten-hour day for public employees and those who worked in companies with charters granted by state governments. It would seem that Lewis' association with the cause of the slave tended to liberalize his approach to other problems, for in supporting Evans' program of 1847 he had to overlook Evans' long-standing hostility to evangelical Christianity.[24]

Equally dangerous and antirepublican in the evangelical mind as atheistic labor advocates were Catholics and Masons. The mysterious disappearance in 1826 of William Morgan, an ex-Mason who was about to expose his knowledge of the rituals, excited religious people, especially in New York and New England, and they rallied to the Anti-Mason party. After a twenty-year membership in the St. John's lodge, Tappan had resigned from the order sometime before leaving Boston. In New York he attended several Anti-Mason meetings, and he subscribed to the *Ohio Star* of Ravenna, the party's leading journal across the Alleghenies. He wrote the editor that the fraternity's rituals were "PROFANE AND BLASPHEMOUS," its duties a waste of "much valuable time," its values a hindrance to "the course of justice," and its power a threat "to the freedom of our political institutions." By limiting membership to gentlemen of political and social standing in their neighborhoods, the Masons were indeed resented by those who found themselves ineligible for admission. Much of the Anti-Mason rhetoric was rather vicious and bombastic, but it was also indicative of a concern about elitism in a society that only recently had emerged from the restrictiveness of New England squire-archy. Tappan's sympathy for Anti-Masonry obviously had more than a casual relation to his loss of status and wealth in Boston, yet there was more motivation than that. To the evangelical mind, Masonry was a heathenish substitute for the church and Bible, a dangerous rival for the allegiance of uncommitted Americans. For this reason Charles Tappan (whose social position was well assured) became involved in Anti-Masonry and even served as a Boston delegate to a Massachusetts Anti-Mason convention.[25]

Arthur Tappan, on the other hand, apparently ignored this issue, though he did show interest in anti-Catholicism. George Bourne, who ran a fanatical paper in New York to expose Jesuitical conspiracies, had Arthur's full support for a while. Bigotry cannot be defended, whatever its objective; yet it may accurately enough be observed that, however ugly or virulent their hostility became in the antebellum years, neither the Anti-Masons nor the anti-Catholics ever matched the degree of violence and power of the racial bigots, whose fury the Tappans were soon to experience themselves.[26]

In spite of their disapproval of Masonic snobbery, the evangelicals were not very egalitarian in their own circles. Prominent Episcopalians and Calvinists usually monopolized the center of the evangelical stage, radiating an aura of respectability. The real dependence of the movement, though, was upon the middle-class farmers and townsmen near the Erie Canal and along the rivers of New England. These were men and women whom the Tappans admired. As one Ohio storekeeper said, religious people like himself loved "the habits that are most like the middle class of society," and the Tappans were a corroboration of this observation.[27] Self-confident, assertive, and eager to make others conform to their standards, evangelicals were united on a common project. Even their language breathed their involvement with things both material and spiritual; in the words of a writer in the New York *Evangelist,* they all pressed for the construction of a "great moral railroad upon which the chariot wheels of mercy" would roll through the land.[28]

It was not easy, however, to consolidate the movement, since the crusaders came from different denominations divided by long-standing disputes. In upper New York state, Congregationalists of puritan descent had mingled with Presbyterians whose fathers had arrived in New York City in the eighteenth century from Scotland and Ireland. Their common Calvinist theology had led them to pool their resources for westward missionary advancement in a venture known officially as the "Plan of Union" of 1801. But the upstate "Presbygationalists" of the Plan of Union churches, organized on the hierarchical lines of the Presbyterian church but often ministered to by Congregationalists, had adopted too liberal and optimistic a theology to please the Scots Presbyterians and Dutch Reformed in New York City. The downstate Calvinists mistrusted any tampering with doctrines merely to please prospective converts.[29] The Tappans were to play a role in this division, but these rivalries were less important to them than the task of creating a benevolent system to "enlarge the kingdom of our Lord and Savior Jesus Christ."[30]

In all his philanthropic career, Arthur Tappan never gave a public address of any length. Even his correspondence was usually brief. Since he left literary production and oratory to others better equipped by education and talent than himself, his only means of expression resided in the metallic eloquence of his money. In 1829, the evangelicals laid plans for a large-scale assault on the unchurched and the heretical, particularly those of the West. The churchmen feared that if that section were lost to Catholic, Universalist, anti-mission Baptist, and other hostile forces, afflictions would fall upon all the political and religious institutions throughout the whole of the country. Arthur Tappan took interest in the reports of woeful conditions out West that Calvinist missionaries brought to his attention. He not only gave them personal funds to carry on their work but decided upon a concentrated effort to aid the western strategy. It is likely that he took to heart the frantic words of Theodore Frelinghuysen, who predicted that, without such a program, "floods of wickedness will by and by come over us, that will sweep away the last vestiges of hope and freedom" in the East. The area of most immediate concern to Arthur Tappan was the Northwest, which the evangelicals referred to as the "Mississippi Valley." While the southern reaches of the river were nominally included in the "Valley" project, as the crusade was called, Arthur determined to make the Trans-Allegheny West especially safe for the expansion of New England culture and religion.[31]

Each of the major benevolent societies was a recipient of Arthur's determined generosity. In May, 1830, an announcement was made of an anonymous gift of $5,000 to the debt-ridden American Bible Society, then threatened by the withdrawal of disgruntled Methodists. The money (all of it Arthur's) would heal the split and unite the organization behind Tappan's aim "to supply every family in the United States with a Bible." There had been considerable difficulty in getting the rather stodgy Bible group to act, but, using his promise of a large financial reward for all it was worth, Arthur finally succeeded. Inspired by his gift, Bible Society agents and volunteers dunned other city merchants and country people, with each successful effort quickening the response to the next appeal. The campaign produced a total of $50,000.[32] As Lewis Tappan later declared, Arthur could with ample reason say, " 'Lord, thy pound hath gained ten pounds.' "[33]

Turning his attention to the recently formed American Sunday School Union, Arthur offered $4,000, conditional upon the raising of $100,000 from other sources, for the purpose of filling the religious needs of the Mississippi Valley settlers. He wrote the Union officials: "Will not your Board resolve *to have a Sabbath School formed within two years in every town* in that interesting portion of the country?" Two weeks later, Christians of Philadelphia, where the society had its headquarters, raised $22,000 at a single rally. That achievement was the work of Robert Baird, a young, enterprising agent of the Sunday School group. It was Tappan, however, whose benevolence provided the initial impetus. Baird then organized a similar meeting in New York. Jonas Platt, a judge from Utica, told the large audience that an anonymous donor had helped to revive what had seemed only a few weeks earlier a "languishing" enterprise. "There is something in grand resolutions," he eulogized, "which takes hold of the feelings and stimulates the mind to action."[34] Another $11,000 in New York bank notes swelled the treasury of the Sunday School cause in response to Platt's appeal, Baird's efficient management, and Tappan's example. Indeed, so emphatic was the response that Tappan canceled the original condition of his donation; the fund was oversubscribed.[35]

Any co-ordinated evangelical crusade had to include the powerful American Tract Society, which Arthur himself had helped to found in 1825. At a meeting held in the City Hotel, he had given $5,000 for the purchase of up-to-date steam presses for the churning out of moral messages.[36] In an executive meeting in 1829 at the newly occupied Tract House on Nassau Street, he was reported to have said, " 'I want to give two tracts to every family in the valley of the Mississippi, so none shall be passed by. I will give $1,000 to this object.' "[37] Nor could he overlook the claims of the American Home Missionary Society. This body, an amalgamation of Congregational and Presbyterian missionary societies, concentrated its energies upon the New York and Ohio frontier regions where so many New Englanders were in need of aid in recreating the institutions they had left behind. Since Tappan took special delight in the rising temperance cause, he set up a fund of $2,000 for those congregations in the Home Missionary "diocese" that expelled drinkers from their churches.[38]

Arthur Tappan had already started to devote his fortune to the increase of missionaries by vigorous support of Calvinist seminaries, even before the Valley campaign was launched. In the mid-1820's he had tried to strengthen religious colleges by making donations and endowing professorships, so that they could send out ministers to bring the gospel tidings to isolated communities. Auburn, a western New York school for Congregationalists and Presbyterians; Andover, a Congregational center, founded in compensation for the loss of Harvard to Unitarianism; and Kenyon, a new Ohio college founded by Episcopal Bishop Philander Chase, all received thousands of dollars from the zealous merchant.[39]

After the Valley plan was anounced, however, Arthur seemed to prefer to give his money through the national benevolent societies rather than directly to local institutions. Honored by being selected as president of the reorganized American Education Society in 1826, Tappan took special interest in this primarily Congregational venture. Most of the conservative Presbyterians refused to co-operate with it, because of the supposed Arminian tendencies of its most active members. To avoid the appearance of sectarianism, Elias Cornelius, the American Education Society's able secretary, established a rule that only pre-ministerial undergraduates would receive aid; they could then choose their denominational calling without embarrassing the sectarian feelings of those involved in the charity. Over several years' time, Tappan, through the Society's agency, paid the tuition of about one hundred students, mostly Yale undergraduates, and provided others with small stipends.[40]

By 1832 Arthur Tappan was guiding the entire complex of voluntary associations along the road toward an ever more belligerent puritanism. "Our great benevolent system," wrote one admirer, "owes its expansion and power . . . to his influence. His example inspired the merchants of New York. . . , leading them to give hundreds and thousands where before they gave tens or fifteens."[41] Arthur's stature in evangelical circles matched his generosity, concealed though he may have intended it to be. Among his many official and honorary titles were the following: president of the American Education Society; finance chairman of the Tract

Society; manager of the Bible Society; auditor of the Home Missionary Society; life director of the American Seaman's Friend Society and of the Society for Meliorating the Condition of the Jews (for Christianized Jews only); treasurer of the Society for Promoting Common School Education in Greece (in response to an appeal by a Congregational missionary); trustee of the Mercantile Library Association (for the benefit of the merchant-apprentices, to counteract the temptations of the city). Overcome by Tappan's extraordinary gifts, John Pintard declared, "He is truly a wonderful benefactor & if his life sh[oul]d be spared & prosperity, his benefactions may am[oun]t in a few years to half a million. . . . I wish we had more Arthur Tappans."[42] Such praise was to be rare once Arthur joined the abolition movement; for the time being, however, he was acclaimed by clergy and laity. Idolizing his brother and his principle of Christian stewardship, Lewis rhapsodized, "This is *enjoying* riches in a high degree, and is making one live after his death in the good he achieves while living."[43]

There is no way of knowing how much Arthur Tappan contributed, since he probably did succeed in keeping many gifts secret. Regardless of his intent, however, the left hand inevitably came to know something of what the right hand was doing. One may speculate about the satisfaction he derived from the paradox of being honored publicly for "anonymous" giving. In any case, Tappan was undoubtedly one of the largest contributors to religious causes in his day, and his principle of extravagant giving during his lifetime was not buried with him; most of the institutions he founded and supported have continued to the present day. Moreover, his concept of acting upon a comprehensive scale paralleled in philanthropy the trends toward cultural, economic, and political unity in antebellum America.[44]

Although he could not match his brother's level of "doing good," Lewis Tappan, in company with hundreds of others, performed the muscular work by which these national enterprises were sustained. At the store he sold Arthur's cheap silks, "pins, bobbins, fans &c" all day. "Don't turn up your nose, your Honour," he wrote Judge Benjamin Tappan, for the sales were "on a large scale to be sure."[45] In his spare time, Lewis went about his Father's—and his brother's—business.

In company with the Rev. Joshua Leavitt, a young minister from

Yale Seminary whom Arthur had befriended, Lewis passed out the Bible and "its delightful companion, the tract."[46] They roamed the wharves of the East River; they entered the dingy stores and taverns of Five Points; they stopped in the countinghouses of Wall and State Streets. To each person they met they gave a tract, or, if rebuffed, perhaps a word of warning. By May, 1831, Lewis Tappan and the other distributors in the wards of the city had dispensed six million pages.[47]

Delivering tracts became a lifelong hobby, and Lewis usually included a short religious verse or printed homily in letters he sent to friends. During the height of the religious campaign for the West, he chaired one of the local rallies, perhaps too exuberantly to suit all those present. Gardiner Spring, pastor of the Brick Presbyterian Church, complained that too much levity would cause "the ark" to "tremble."[48] Tappan's zest was to create more serious difficulties for another cause he and Arthur supported. Taking issue with the Jacksonians who favored the least possible connection between church and state, evangelicals campaigned for Sunday closing laws. Especially disgraceful in their eyes was a Congressional act requiring postal clerks to work on Sunday. To lobby for a change "in all the arrangements of business at the seat of government," they formed the General Union for Promoting the Observance of the Christian Sabbath. Not only these government employees were to regain their day of rest but also those working in bakeries, foundries, abattoirs, stores, and taverns, and even on whaling ships. Christians were exhorted to leave "all worldly conversation and amusement" for other days of the week, and Sunday travel was to be confined to a walk to church.[49]

Ignoring Lyman Beecher's plea to be "juditious [sic]," Lewis Tappan did his part to make perfect Sabbath-keeping ridiculous to critics and tedious to his friends. As secretary of the Sabbath Union, he gave the organization's backing to Josiah Bissell, a Presbyterian land promoter of Utica who started a six-day stage line called the Pioneer. Good Christians were expected to travel by this means rather than on those stages that moved on Sunday. Not only was Bissell's effort a financial disaster but it also made Sabbatarianism seem a lunatic cause to the unsympathetic. So great was the reaction, particularly from the Universalists, that Beecher wrote Tappan, "I am a little afraid that our good brother Bissell may need some caution on the subject. Having been obliged to raise the steam so high to get under way—it may not occur to him that the Pressure may be too great for necessity or prudence in the remainder of the voyage."[50] Tappan, however, continued his support of six-day stages, and he argued for some of the still more questionable attempts to return to the customs of an age that had not known steam transportation, factories, and humming cities. "If it be necessary to violate the holy Sabbath habitually in order to manufacture any article of luxury or convenience, Christians ought to dispense with the use of such articles," he wrote in the New York *Evangelist*. On this basis, he questioned the necessity of churches' lighting their services with gas supplied by companies operating on the Sabbath.[51] In view of the Sabbath Union's notoriety, it was hardly surprising that it soon languished from confusion and lack of support, to Tappan's mortification. William Jay, a prominent leader in the Sabbatarian cause, complained that Christians had only themselves to blame, since so many of them had united with "avowed infidels in slandering those who are striving to rescue the Sabbath from legalized profanation." In spite of a well-organized petitions campaign, which set the precedent for a later antislavery petitions effort, Congress refused to repeal the offending postal statutes. Sabbatarianism did, however, have enough strength to induce the sympathetic Charles Wickliffe, Postmaster General in John Tyler's cabinet, to close down eighty thousand miles of postal routes on the Lord's day in 1843. By the time of this rather savage revenge for all the past Sundays lost for God, Lewis Tappan was too much engaged in other, more important matters to enjoy the belated victory.[52]

Lewis fared somewhat better with another venture in uniting religion with ordinary life. In 1827 Arthur had founded the New York *Journal of Commerce* as a rival to the theater and liquor-advertising gazettes of the city. Distributed free of charge at first, the paper devoured thirty thousand dollars of his money in short order. Moreover, Arthur had been unwise in his choice of the editor. The Rev. William Maxwell, who headed the Virginia Presbyterians' Union Seminary, was placed in charge, though his duties were not so defined as to require him to leave his isolated location near Farmville, Virginia. Maxwell was unable to prove that religious and commercial news could profitably flourish in the same journal. Given full control of the paper by his brother, Lewis ran it for several months and then negotiated its sale to a hatchet-faced Connecticut puritan named David Hale, under whom it quickly grew into a leading financial and political sheet.[53]

In these efforts there ran a dual theme of preparing the way for God's kingdom on earth and of returning the nation to its more religious, more orderly past. Some historians have found that the rhetoric and belief of the Jacksonians were more attuned to romantic visions of what rural life and yeoman traditions once were than to a liberal future. Many other Americans sought the promise of stability and respect for decency in a similarly romantic retreat in eighteenth-century puritanism. There was also grave fear that unless orderliness and devotion to God, enforced by law and pious example, replaced the turbulence of the youthful society, the Christian republic would die, not from external injury but from self-administered poisons. Brother Benjamin, with his rationalistic and Jeffersonian faith, did not approve of so gloomy a view and he warned Lewis not to place faith in efforts to repress a dynamic people in the name of order. "History & experience" proved that every attempt to do so, from their childhood in Federalist New England to the present, had failed, and, the Jacksonian political leader added, "I trust it will ever be so. . . ." But Benjamin did not expect to persuade Lewis, who had stared too long "at the dark side of the shield" to see the brightness on the other side.[54] And indeed, Lewis was unmoved. Later, he, like other abolitionists, would identify as the source of the selfishness, malice, and violence that threatened the country its most obvious and most institutionalized form—Negro slavery. But before the New York Tappans entered the antislavery cause, they encountered a resistance which indicated that the disease of intolerance was not confined to the southern states alone. Unafraid, they set about to create a restrictive Christian society that many northerners, including their Ohio brother, did not want. This effort failed in most respects, but it left its imprint upon American culture.

NOTES

1. Diary, February 1, 3, 4, and 23, 1828.
2. *Ibid.*, October 4, 1828; see also March 16 and September 18, 1828.
3. *Ibid.*, July 5, 1828; see Cole, *Social Ideas of Northern Evangelists*, 21.
4. Diary, September 19, 1828; also October 16, 1829; [Edward Ruggles], *A Picture of New York in 1846* (New York, 1846) 67.
5. LT to BT, July 8, 1829, BT MSS, LC; Thomas Picton, *Rose Street: Its Past, Present and Future* (New York, 1873), 3 (quotation); Thomas V. Eaton, "An

Old Street in New York," *American Historical Magazine,* II (1907), 546–57; John Fowler, *A Journal of a Tour . . . of New York . . .* (London, 1831), 221–22; William E. Dodge, *Old New York: A Lecture* (New York, 1880), 10; Edward Waylen, *Ecclesiastical Reminiscences of the United States* (New York, 1846), 4; AT's advertisements in New York *Journal of Commerce,* August 30, 1828, March 24, 1829; Joseph A. Scoville [Walter Barrett, pseud.], *The Old Merchants of New York City* (New York, 1863–72), I, 229 (Scoville is notoriously inaccurate but sometimes interesting); LT, *Arthur Tappan,* 389.

6. Diary, July 18, 1828 (partially erased); LT, *Arthur Tappan,* 85, 391.

7. AT to BT, March 21, 1828, BT MSS, LC.

8. LT, *Arthur Tappan,* 69, 257, 262, 352; New York *Independent,* August 27, 1863; Benjamin Tappan, Sr., to BT, March 26, 1828, and LT to BT, November 17, 1831, BT MSS, LC.

9. LT, *Arthur Tappan,* 85.

10. *Ibid.,* 287, 389; Thomas Bellows Peck, *The Bellows Genealogy . . .* (Keene, N.H., 1898), 362–63; Scoville, *Old Merchants,* I, 230–31, 234–35; LT to Mrs. John Bigelow, December 1, 1847, ltrbk.

11. Nathaniel T. Hubbard, *Autobiography . . .* (New York, 1875), 9–10; LT, *Arthur Tappan,* 61–62; Roy A. Foulke, *The Sinews of American Commerce . . .* (New York, 1941), 282–83.

12. LT, *Is It Right to Be Rich?* (New York, 1865); Robert A. Feer, "Imprisonment for Debt in Massachusetts before 1800," *Mississippi Valley Historical Review* (hereinafter *MVHR*), XLVIII (September, 1961), 264; see also Donald, *Lincoln Reconsidered,* 33–34.

13. LT, *Arthur Tappan,* 61–62.

14. New York *Evangelist,* May 22, 1830, and LT, *Arthur Tappan,* 86, 388.

15. *Evangelical Magazine and Gospel Advocate* (Utica), June 26, 1830.

16. New York *Evangelist,* May 22 and 29, 1830.

17. Charles I. Foster, *An Errand of Mercy: The Evangelical United Front, 1790–1837* (Chapel Hill, 1960), 252; Bayard Tuckerman, *William Jay, and the Constitutional Movement for the Abolition of Slavery* (New York, 1894), 12; Robert W. July, *The Essential New Yorker, Gulian Crommelin Verplanck* (Durham, 1951), 18.

18. John Pintard to Eliza Pintard Davidson, December 16, 1828, in Dorothy C. Barck, ed., *Letters from John Pintard to His Daughter Eliza Noel Pintard Davidson, 1816 to 1833* (New York, 1940–41), III, 52, and March 27, April 4, 1832, IV, 32; Clifford S. Griffin, *Their Brothers' Keepers: Moral Stewardship in the United States, 1800–1865* (New Brunswick, 1960), 308.

19. Foster, *Errand of Mercy,* 7–10, and Chapter II, 11–27. See Ford K. Brown, *Fathers of the Victorians: The Age of Wilberforce* (Cambridge, England, 1961), 5; Griffin, *Brothers' Keepers,* 10–12; cf. William B. Hesseltine, "Four American Traditions," *Journal of Southern History,* (hereinafter *JSH*) XXVII (February, 1961), 6–7.

20. LT to BT, December 12, 1829, BT MSS, LC.

21. Cf. Griffin, *Brothers' Keepers.*

22. LT to Henry C. Bowen, May 25, 1844, ltrbk; LT to Mathew Carey, May 1, 1830, Simon Gratz autograph MSS, Pennsylvania Historical Society.

23. Diary, March 3, 1829. Alice J. G. Perkins and Teresa Wolfson, *Frances Wright, Free Enquirer* (New York, 1939), 233, blame the Tappans for launching

a witch-hunt against Fanny Wright in the *Journal of Commerce*. Probably it was the later owner, David Hale. On Fanny Wright's opposition to the Tappans' causes, see her paper the *Free Enquirer* (New York), February 18, March 4 and 18, 1829.

24. LT to George Henry Evans, Secretary of the Central Committee of the National Reformation Association, October 11, 1847, ltrbk.

25. LT to R. W. John Dixwell, M.D., September 26, 1814, ltrbk.; diary, October 15, 1829; *Anti-Masonic Review and Magazine* (New York), I (No. 3, 1828), 100; *An Abstract of the Proceedings of the Anti-Masonic State Convention. . .* (Boston, 1830), 3; quotation (supplied by Robert Gould) is from *Ohio Star* (Ravenna), March 10, 1830; cf. the more hostile views of Richard Hofstadter, *The Paranoid Style in American Politics, and Other Essays* (New York, 1965), 14–23, and David Brion Davis, "Some Themes of Counter-Subversion: An Analysis of Anti-Masonic, Anti-Catholic, and Anti-Mormon Literature," *MVHR*, XLVII (September, 1960), 205–44. While the evangelicals' biases were not very wholesome, the hysterical reactions of otherwise urbane conservatives to the antislavery agitation were far more indicative of a deep-seated malaise than the antics of the Anti-Masons, etc. Yet, so far there is no published psychological analysis of anti-abolitionist "paranoia."

26. Gilbert Hobbes Barnes, *The Antislavery Impulse, 1830–1844* (New York, 1933), 33, 212n; Ray A. Billington, *The Protestant Crusade, 1800–1860: A Study of the Origins of American Nativism* (New York, 1952), 101, wherein a Rev. Mr. Arthur Tappan is named as a leader of the movement, either a coincidence or an error.

27. Luther Dodge, Cleveland, Ohio, to Henry Cowles, Ohio, December [?], 1839, Treasurer's Office Files, Oberlin College, Oberlin, Ohio.

28. New York *Evangelist*, May 29, 1830; Foster, *Errand of Mercy*, 178.

29. Whitney R. Cross, *The Burned-Over District: The Social and Intellectual History of Enthusiastic Religion in Western New York, 1800–1850* (Ithaca, 1950), 18–19; William G. McLoughlin, *Modern Revivalism: Charles Grandison Finney to Billy Graham* (New York, 1959), 15, 18; Samuel J. Baird, *A History of the New School, and of the Questions Involved in the Disruption of the Presbyterian Church in 1838* (Philadelphia, 1868), 212, 256–57, 271, 283–92; George Punchard, *History of Congregationalism from About A.D. 250 to the Present Time* (Boston, 1881), V, 51–59.

30. New York *Evangelist*, April 24, 1830; Foster, *Errand of Mercy*, 187.

31. New York *Evangelist*, May 8, 29, 1830; Foster, *Errand of Mercy*, 179–207 (which contains the most extensive scholarly account of the western campaign); LT, *Arthur Tappan*, 74–75.

32. AT, Theodore Dwight, John Bingham, John Keese, and Elijah Pierson to Richard Varick, president, May 21, 1829; AT to [Nitchie], August 26, 1829, American Bible Society MSS, Bible House; see also AT's remarks in *American Sunday School Teachers' Magazine*, VIII (September, 1830), 283.

33. LT, *Arthur Tappan*, 397.

34. New York *Evangelist*, June 26, 1830; AT to Frederick W. Porter, secretary, May 19, 1830, American Sunday School Union (hereinafter ASSU) MSS, ASSU headquarters, Philadelphia.

35. New York *Evangelist*, May 29, June 26, 1830; Ellen Harriet Thomsen, "Protestant Westward Migration, Sunday Schools for the Mississippi Valley," *Journal of*

the Presbyterian Historical Society, XXVI (March, 1948), 44; *Proceedings of the Sixth Annual Meeting.* . . (Philadelphia, 1832), 72 (AT gave $4,100.00 of a total fund of $118,181.10 [p. 75]); Robert Baird to Porter, June 22, 1830, and AT to Porter, May 24, 1830, ASSU MSS, ASSU, Philadelphia.

36. *The Address of the Executive Committee of the American Tract Society to the Christian Public* (New York, 1825), 20; American Tract Society, *Arthur Tappan, Tract No. 677* (New York, n.d.), 1; LT, *Arthur Tappan,* 66–67, 74; Barcke, ed., *Letters from Pintard,* III, November 17, 1830, 192.

37. *Tappan, Tract No. 677,* 2.

38. AT to treasurer, American Home Missionary Society, January 2, 1832, with notation on February 13, 1832, by W. Knowles Taylor that the proposal was accepted, American Home Missionary Society MSS, Chicago Theological Seminary Library; New York *Evangelist,* April 10, 1830; Colin B. Goodykoontz, *Home Missions on the American Frontier.* . . (Caldwell, Idaho, 1939), 35–36, 39, 43n.

39. LT, *Arthur Tappan,* 65–66; John Quincy Adams, *A History of Auburn Theological Seminary, 1818–1918* (Auburn, N.Y., 1918), 58; "Book Table," New York *Independent,* October 6, 1870.

40. LT, *Arthur Tappan,* 88; *Liberator* (Boston), March 26, 1831; for criticism of the American Education Society's policies, see Old School Presbyterian Baird's *A History of the New School,* 283–92.

41. *Tappan, No. 677,* 3; see also William A. Hallock, *"Light and Love": A Sketch of the Life and Labors of the Rev. Justin Edwards, D.D., The Evangelical Pastor* . . . (New York, 1855?), 327.

42. Barcke, ed., *Letters from John Pintard,* III, November 17, 1830, 192; LT, *Arthur Tappan,* 74, 88; *American Seaman's Friend Society, Fourth Annual Report* (New York, 1832), 22; *Israel's Advocate,* May 5, 1827; *Rights of All* (New York), May 29, 1829.

43. LT to BT, September 26, 1829, with addition dated October 5, 1829, BT MSS, LC.

44. The following are among the surviving institutions which he helped to found: New York *Journal of Commerce,* American Tract Society, American Seaman's Friend Society, American Missionary Association, Magdalen Asylum (now Inwood House, Bronx, N.Y.), Mercantile Credit Rating Agency (now Dun & Bradstreet), Oberlin College, Lane Seminary (now Virginia Theological Seminary, Chicago), and Mercantile Library Association (New York City).

45. LT to BT, March 14, 1828, BT MSS, LC.

46. New York *Evangelist,* May 29, 1830.

47. Diary, 1828–29, *passim.,* especially October 17, 1829; Boston *Recorder,* February 17, 1830; New York *Evangelist,* April 23, 1831.

48. Boston *Recorder,* February 17, 1830; New York *Evangelist,* April 23, 1831.

49. LT, *Arthur Tappan,* 96–102; *The Address of the General Union for Promoting the Observance of the Christian Sabbath* . . . (Auburn, N.Y., 1828), 22.

50. Lyman Beecher to LT, May 21, 1828, Beecher Family MSS, Yale University Library.

51. LT, "Gaslight to Churches," New York *Evangelist,* August 20, 1831.

52. New York *Evangelist,* May 12, 1832; Griffin, *Brothers' Keepers,* 119–22, 238; *Western Recorder* (Utica), May 25, 1830; Cross, *Burned-Over District,* 134; Jay, quoted in LT, *Letter to Eleazar Lord, Esq. in Defense of Measures for Promoting*

the Observance of the Christian Sabbath (New York, 1831), 4; *Emancipator* (Boston), October 5, 1843.

53. LT, *Arthur Tappan,* 91–96, 415–18; diary, August-December, 1828; Joseph P. Thompson, *Memoir of David Hale* (New York, 1850), 47–54; Scoville, *Old Merchants,* I, 233; cf. Barnes, *Antislavery Impulse,* 208–9, fn. 7, an exaggeration of the sums involved. See also W. H. T. Squires, "William Maxwell," *Union Seminary Review,* XXX (January, 1919), 45.

54. BT to LT, August 19, 1837, BT MSS, Ohio Historical Society.

CHAPTER FOUR

Yankees versus *Yorkers*

In spite of the outward simplicity of the evangelical movement, it was a crusade of peculiar contradictions. Its advocates claimed to be "profoundly serious," not "solemn triflers," and yet they appealed to an anti-intellectual emotionalism. They aimed at the conversion of souls, but they chiefly stressed social issues— the use of alcohol, the violation of the Sabbath, and indulgence in gambling among them. Believers in the self-reliant, independent spirit, they created societies to promote conformity. Though they spoke of the need to reach all sections of the land, they confined themselves to spreading the sectional culture of New England. In spite of their general appeal to the great mass of common people everywhere, a strong and none too pleasant smell of elitism of the old Federalist variety clung to their efforts. While loudly approving the constitutional injunction against a national religious establishment, they tried to impose their ideas and their regulations upon common schools, post offices, and other public agencies. Though they professed to be disinclined to doctrinal difference themselves, they found it hard to tolerate in others. Firm in their loyalty to Calvinist orthodoxy, they nevertheless believed that men were basically good and redeemable. As a friend of William Ellery Channing observed, "they have gradually and almost imperceptibly quitted Calvinism for Arminianism; therefore they feel less confident of being amongst the elect, and take more pains to work out their own salvation, not only by religious observances, but by deeds of beneficence and mercy."[1] Such paradoxes as these were not uncommon, as Alexis de Tocqueville pointed out, in a democratic society.

These contradictions were present in the efforts of the Tappans but of many others as well. Pleased with the results of Lewis' success in handling the finances of the *Journal of Commerce,* Arthur had "his efficient auxiliary" elected to the select club he had founded, called the Association of Gentlemen. Although the group was too amorphous in membership properly to be called a club, its members did collaborate on a number of religious projects. Among Arthur's Association friends were Anson G. Phelps, David Low Dodge, Eleazar Lord, Knowles Taylor, Zachariah Lewis, Silas Holmes, Peletiah Perit, Jonas Platt, his son Zephaniah, and Moses Allen.[2] Humorless, shrewd, and wealthy, these were mostly men from rural Connecticut in the mercantile and banking trades. In God's realm they may have been among John Calvin's elect, but in this world they were pious *nouveaux riches.* Their common Congregational upbringing made them likely rebels against the local, aristocratic Presbyterian hierarchy. Respectable and sensible, they did not join the antislavery crusade, but for a while they co-operated with Arthur Tappan's other schemes.

Being used to the self-sufficiency of Congregational worship and fired with the possibilities of liberal orthodoxy, the Yankee churchmen yearned for a greater voice in church matters than Presbyterian pre-eminence allowed. The ecclesiastical government of presbytery, synod, and general assembly was too rigid and stifling to suit these "Sons of the Pilgrims," as Lewis Tappan called them. In a letter to Lyman Beecher in Boston, he complained that the entrenched Presbyterian clergy "keep in obscurity many persons who might be highly useful."[3]

The increased tempo of migration from New England into New York City threatened the older churches. If ever Arthur and his friends created a rival Congregational system, the incoming Yankee clerks and mechanics, some of whom were to become the future elders and wealthy laymen, would join them. "I have all the feelings of an eastern man, and but little of the Presbyterian except the name," wrote Arthur Tappan to his friend Elias Cornelius of the American Education Society. Thus, the conflict was not merely the laymen's jealousy of clerical authority; Yankee was pitted against Knickerbocker, yeoman against urban sophisticate, rural pietist against timid keepers of the Ark.[4]

Spurred by his success in leading a group from Pierce's church in Brookline, Lewis Tappan within a month of his arrival began to plot the same kind of effort in New York. With Lyman Beecher to advise him and Arthur to lend financial support, Lewis proposed a chain of Congregational churches, which he planned to create by a method as old as New England puritanism itself. Selected laymen of the parent church were to nurture a struggling mission to maturity, at which time a "colony" would break off and grow. Almost at once, Dr. Gardiner Spring, the city's foremost Presbyterian conservative, vetoed the "Pilgrim" movement. Bitterly Tappan complained, "The Dutch & other interests here have paralyzed even N[ew] England men, and they feel the benumbing influence of timidity, & a compromising spirit, and a fear of man." Preoccupied with his own struggles against Boston's multiplying sins, Beecher advised a hasty compromise with Spring, who then quietly but forcefully sapped the movement of its strength. As a result, only one new church was founded to compete with the old.[5] Obviously, sterner measures would be necessary. It was all too clear to the Association of Gentlemen that the temple crowd not only niggled in the matter of church expansion but also opposed some of its benevolent campaigns.

The times favored insurgents—in religion, politics, economics, and every other area. Why was the blandness of the administration of James Monroe replaced so suddenly by the acrimony of the late twenties? A full accounting of the reasons cannot be given here. It should be noted, however, that no period was more concerned with ideological issues than the age of Jackson. Too often we are tempted to think of this time as one of boastful optimism and sureness of purpose. Yet prosperity and broadening opportunities breed their own varieties of disquiet. The "age of the common man" was no exception. Drastic social changes that dismantled old customs, orthodoxies, and privileges were under way as Americans pushed into close Eastern cities and the open West. As a means of identifying themselves in a time of constant flux, many Americans rallied to such easily identified national ideas as democracy, liberty, piety. Exclusiveness is a necessary element in that kind of identification, and to one faction it was as if the others stood for something diametrically opposed, something dangerous and anti-American.

As a result, Anti-Masons, anti-Catholics, anti-Sabbatarian Universalists, and anti-Universalist Sabbatarians were all convinced that the schemes of "tyrants" and "traitors" threatened national integrity. Certainly the contest of the Jacksonians against the Monster Bank of the United States was another example of the demonic theory of politics at work. All these groups were searching for the road back to the pristine virtues of an earlier, stable period. The evangelicals sought the simplicities of the puritan era, when Catholics, "infidels," and worshipers of Mammon belonged in the stocks, or at least were excluded from polite society. Their opponents, equally appealing to the nation's heritage, feared that a church militant would destroy the republican traditions of the Founding Fathers. Americans were trying to describe themselves, not an easy job for a nation that represented so many noble aspirations and yet fell so far short of squaring them with reality. Under the same impulse abolitionists would later hope that their definition of what it meant to be an American would prevail. But it would have been remarkable if they had not formed their views in the terms of the day. As a result, chauvinism, nostalgia, and, many years later, an exploitative use of violence and even murder—these and other varieties of distortion—led them to "discover" the machinations of a "great slave power" conspiracy ready to surrender white freedom to the perpetuation of black enslavement. Militancy, hatred, and insecurity were woven into the fabric of the "happy republic" of Jackson's period. As Fanny Wright pointed out, "It is . . . the spirit of the age to be a little fanatical."[6]

Religious interest in the state of New York was reaching a pinnacle of "holy excitement," as in politics Jackson's passionate campaign for the Presidency had recently shown the same spirit of restlessness. Preachers, laymen, and religious journalists talked grandly of "ushering in the millennium," "girding up the loins," "the returning of the apostolic age," "the march of empire westward." Even some pietists were starting to weary of this rhetorical exuberance, but the words expressed the hope of a resurgent Protestantism that was expanding with the nation.[7]

Both a leader and a follower of this religious upsurge was Charles Grandison Finney. He was a Connecticut-born immigrant to western New York, where he practiced law before his conversion. Using his courtroom techniques to powerful effect from the pulpit, Finney stirred thousands of settlers to a new awareness of religious truth. Many of those whom he converted were already

63

Christians, but he contended that the cause required the rededication of old church members as well as the addition of new. "Without revivals," the New York *Evangelist* warned, "our benevolent societies will plant and water in vain."[8] To push their campaign forward, the Association of Gentlemen chose two tools: a journal to publicize revivals and benevolent enterprises, and a revival in the city churches conducted by Finney himself.

The first was an immediate success, unlike the *Journal of Commerce*. Under the Rev. Joshua Leavitt, a hot-tempered but efficient editor, the New York *Evangelist* quickly circulated among religious people throughout the state.[9] Importing Finney to New York in order to bring " 'seasons of refreshing in the presence of the Lord' " was altogether a more difficult task. His Gospel message and his measures—the four-day protracted meetings, his consultation with the sinner in the "anxious seat," the outbursts of groans and sighs in the congregation—smacked too much of backwoods Methodism to suit the traditional Calvinists. Even Lyman Beecher, Asahel Nettleton, and others who believed in revival measures were skeptical and, in 1827, tried to elicit from Finney a promise to be more moderate. The New Lebanon Conference, which Beecher and Nettleton organized, was a failure. Finney and his revivalist disciples refused to alter their course. It did not worry Arthur Tappan that Finney rejected human depravity, election, and predestination in order to bring the hope of salvation to the distressed and sinful, for he looked solely to results. (Lewis, still under Beecher's influence, was somewhat slower to accept the Finneyite measures.) Actually, Finney had gone only a little further than Beecher and Nathaniel William Taylor in embracing the doctrine of human free will and perfectibility. His oratory could be likened to the "Refiner's fire," bringing forth "blazing evidence" of God's mercy, and such zeal and success obliterated from Arthur's mind any doubts about his theology. Nonetheless, opposition, based on propriety and dogma, but mostly jealousy, was bound to arise.[10]

Finney himself was reluctant to beard the conservatives in their own strongholds. A cold or skeptical audience had no attraction for him, since responsive congregations in Rochester, Utica, and other towns clamored to hear him. After many earnest pleas from Dodge, Phelps, Platt, and Arthur Tappan, Finney consented to stage a short revival in the summer of 1828 at Dr. Spring's Brick Presbyterian Church. Lewis went to hear him but came away somewhat disappointed because Finney "did not so affect the audience or have so great an impression of abilities as I had expected." As he spoke in the big city church, the preacher had undoubtedly sensed Spring's icy disapproval.[11]

Finney at first refused to accept a permanent parish in the city, and the Association soon located other revivalists from the western part of the state. In hiring them, the Tappans and their friends looked for preaching power, not intellect. "There is too much '*theology*' in the church now, and too little of the Gospel," Lewis observed.[12] The Association of Gentlemen recruited one of Finney's ablest associates, Joel Parker, who began the first "free church," and other revivalists soon followed. To attract the young apprentices and businessmen from New England, the Tappans subsidized "free churches," in which the current practice of auctioning off the pews was abolished and the poor could sit where they wanted. Organized into the "Third Presbytery," the free missions boasted a total membership of 3,863 by May, 1832. While Arthur's money helped to start these ventures, it was Lewis who hired the upper rooms of grocery stores, publicized the enterprise, and moved from mission to mission as the system expanded.[13] Once drawn into the work of aiding revivals, Lewis gradually relinquished his critical view of Finney's controversial revival techniques. Although the Third Presbytery was to have a short history, it was the center of strength for the Tappans' local reform efforts, including abolitionism.

At the same time that Arthur Tappan had launched a campaign for the conversion of the West, he turned his attention to the depraved at home. One of the most formidable obstacles to municipal regeneration, he thought, was the evil of prostitution. He appointed the Rev. John R. McDowall as his curate to "the daughters of guilt and sorrow," as the evangelical phrase went.[14] McDowall, a young licentiate of Princeton Seminary, plunged into his work with a zeal that displayed a certain morbid fascination with sexual vice. Arthur Tappan himself was also bold enough "to explore the recesses of Satan" and to "snatch" the prisoners "from the roaring lions who seek to devour." The criticisms of the "ungodly and self-righteous," Lewis maintained, deterred the senior merchant not a moment. "On the contrary," he wrote in his biography, Arthur Tappan "gloried in all the soiling that attaches to one in such efforts."[15]

Years before, Arthur Tappan had inspected the Magdalen Asylum in London, where, the trustees assured him, the inmates responded in a heartening way. Adopting the British procedure, he and the Association rented a boardinghouse for prostitutes in Five Points, with McDowall as superintendent. Daily Bible readings, regular meals, and the promise of respectable employment seemed to work well for a while.[16]

Tappan and McDowall had no conception of the reasons for prostitution. Social sins were to them as easy to understand as they were to John Bunyan's pilgrim when he visited Vanity Fair. Christian example, preaching, and personal consultations with these "females who have deviated from the path of virtue" would turn them from evil to good, they asserted.[17] Simple country men, they had a simple country view of city vice. If their more sophisticated British pace-setters had no better solution, how much less prepared were these well-meaning rural churchmen to deal with a complex social and moral phenomenon. Large doses of Mosaic law had sufficed for their own resistance to temptation. Why could that prescription not be applied universally?

Moreover, their solution to the nation's drinking problem—a formidable one, owing partly to the low price of rum and whiskey—followed the same lines. If palatable enough, a substitute beverage could entice the intemperate away from vice. Arthur Tappan advertised a "non-alcoholic" burgundy from France. This "pure juice of the grape" was intended as well to replace communion wine, so that total abstinence would not end at the altar rail. Arthur also expected that the profits from the burgundy sales would be high when he placed the product on his list of goods at the Pearl Street store.[18]

If inducements of a milder kind were not sufficient, Lewis Tappan and his friends stood ready with coercive measures. They organized Christian spy cells to watch tavern-keepers and other dispensers of pleasure and report the infractions of long-ignored city ordinances to the proper authorities. "When city functionaries . . . perform their duty," he said, "a moral purification will take place."[19] "Edified and pleased" with the police work, the crusaders plastered Manhattan walls with notices like "QUIT DRAM DRINKING IF YOU WOULD NOT HAVE THE CHOLERA." This particular warning appeared during the great epidemic of 1832. Times of suffering and death, Lewis wrote in the *Evangelist*, were especially advantageous for bringing sinners to their knees. Indeed, he correctly boasted that there was nothing "half-way" about the Tappan brothers' measures.[20]

All these activities were bound to arouse opposition. Benjamin Tappan was only one of the many critics who found his brothers' efforts "sickening." Lewis, of course, had a ready reply: "Surely, my brother, as men of sense you infidels should keep up with the age. This is a century of inventions."[21] But antievangelicals had just as easy access to city walls, the press, and mass rallies as did Christians. Tappan once outraged a tailor who refused to sign his petition to stop the Sunday mails by warning him, "I shall report you to my brother and his connexions, and you shall have no more of our custom!"[22] The storekeeper made sure that the incident got full publicity in the local press.

Opposition grew as the evangelicals became more aggressive. Jumbled together in dismal quarters, "but a step into Hades," the poor and their politicians came especially to despise Arthur Tappan, whose name was "a running title to volumes of recorded sneers and sarcasms." The merchant heard his benevolent associates called "a pack of sanctified plunderers," bent upon "sectarian aggrandizement."[23] Even less zealous Christians were upset. One remarked, " 'I should be willing to contribute say fifty dollars or so; but I look along, and see Arthur Tappan's name for five hundred, and [so] I won't give a cent.' " And a sly churchman with a grudge declared in the *Evangelist* that silk goods were immoral, being items of luxury which required the supervision of silk worm culture by some peasant deprived of the benefits of the Sabbath. (Lewis was not amused, for he wrote a stout rejoinder.)[24]

While the Tract Society printed up its penny sheets, the opposition hawked satirical poems on the streets. One of them described Arthur Tappan as "St. Arthur de Fanaticus," and in another verse as Don Quixotte [sic]." Another poem poked fun at the Sabbatarian Union and "A. T. Burgundy":

> Arthur Tappan, Arthur Tappan,
> Suppose it should happen—
> Mind, I'm only *supposing* it should—
> That some folks in the Union,
> Should take your *Communion*
> Too often by far for their good![25]

The effort to close the post offices on Sunday had led to the staging of numerous antievangelical rallies all over the North in 1829 and 1830, and the public reaction to the Magdalen affair in New York City was no less serious. In the middle of the summer of 1831, the trustees of the Magdalen Society published a general account of Manhattan prostitution. Far from objective or scientific, the Magdalen report estimated that ten thousand women were engaged in the trade. Unless something were done about it, the pamphlet warned, "multitudes will probably be immolated on the altar of the destroying demon of debauchery."[26] Conservatives thought it was deliberate pornography, city boosters protested that it was slanderous to New York's good name, and politicians of Tammany Hall condemned it as a conspiracy of clerical do-gooders.

With the exception of David Hale's evangelical *Journal of Commerce*, the city dailies denounced Arthur Tappan and the other Magdalen trustees. Businessmen and politicians organized protest rallies to finance a libel suit against the society. Applauding one of these meetings, the *Working Man's Advocate* declared, "The people have marked them. They may quaff their A. T. Burgundy, but they will gain no credit with workingmen. . . ." There was even talk of mobbing Arthur Tappan's city residence on Gold Street.[27]

Astonishingly, responsible men were almost as aroused as city editors and ward heelers. General Robert Bogardus, a crusty mossback and Manhattan's wealthiest real estate speculator, officiated as chairman in an anti-Magdalen meeting, a post he later occupied during an antiabolitionist riot as well. Other Knickerbockers present were Elisha Tibbitts, an insurance-company executive; John Delafield, later a founder of New York University; Philip Hone, a rich auctioneer and former mayor. Hone may have been repaying the Tappans for their public hostility to the monopolistic auctioneering system, but what unified all these civic leaders was a common resentment of the rising "social influence of New Englanders in the City."[28]

The strongest reaction came from several Tammany leaders, including Preserved Fish, a lusty ex-Federalist ship-owner, and James Watson Webb, editor of the Tammany organ, the *Morning Courier* (later the *Courier and Enquirer*). Back in 1827, Arthur Tappan's *Journal of Commerce* had consistently scooped rival papers by operating a boat to meet incoming ships with the latest news from overseas. Webb never forgave him for accelerating the already quick pace of competition among the city's fifty journals. Even after the paper was sold, Webb continued his harassment.[29]

Although Preserved Fish (the evangelicals nicknamed him "Pickled Herring") and Webb were to collaborate with the Whigs, it is safe to say that most of the opposition to the evangelicals came from the Democratic party. Drawing support from Catholic and immigrant sources as well as from the free-wheeling elements of the South and West, Jacksonians had already sounded the alarm against a "church and state" party of Sunday-school-trained theocrats. They pointed to the Anti-Mason party as an example.[30] But their chief target was a short, tactless pamphlet by the Rev. Dr. Ezra Stiles Ely of Philadelphia. Brought up in the Connecticut tradition of intimate ties between the established Congregational church and the Federalist party, Ely called upon his half-million fellow Presbyterians to unite in electing God-fearing men to office, and the Jacksonians leaped on the document as a sign of a "Christian" conspiracy. Arthur Tappan, dubbed the "leader of Presbyterian Christianity," was unfairly linked with Ely's program, even though he was really opposed to a close and impure connection between partisan politics and religion. Certainly he did not believe that General Jackson, the eccentric Dr. Ely's choice for President in 1828, represented the best that America could produce in the way of religious and political orthodoxy.[31]

The Tammany machine welcomed the outcry against the Magdalen Society as a way to resolve its own tensions. Only recently, the Wigwam oligarchy had faced a reform-minded set of challengers. Calling themselves the Workingmen's party, they had done well in a municipal election in 1829. Preserved Fish, G. D. Strong, and other Tammany men may have hoped to tempt their hot-eyed, idealistic rivals with lucrative positions, and, indeed, some party leaders did break ranks. Hence the "prodigious" and unmerited "excitement" over the Magdalen report: these ex-reformers and their Tammany bosses had in common an antipathy to clericalism, and a more useful rivet for the disjointed machine could hardly have been found.[32]

The hostility of Tammany Hall lasted for some time. It was fed by the caustic but talented invective of Theophilus Fisk, a Universalist minister and Democratic party pamphleteer, Frances Wright, the labor leader and free-thinker, and Mordecai M. Noah, a newspaperman, playwright, and, by Jackson's appointment, Surveyor of the Port.[33] Fisk and Noah would emerge again as opponents of the abolitionist menace. As late as 1835, Churchill C. Cambreleng, Democratic Congressman from the city, assured the South that the Tappanite abolitionists were the same tiny band of "Church and State" fanatics who had been "annually petitioning Congress about the Sunday mails."[34] To him, as to the Democratic party as a whole, both abolitionism and evangelical reform were troublesome, crankish, and subversive.

Arthur Tappan was used to the lampooning of versifiers and editors, but he was taken aback by the volume of the criticism and the respectability of some of his opponents. After a few months he withdrew from the Magdalen Asylum, despite McDowall's pathetic cry of a cowardly betrayal. Tappan replied stiffly, "The assertion that the efforts of the Society were discontinued because of the opposition of the unprincipled . . . is without foundation. The true cause was the discouraging fact that we saw *no* fruits of our labors. . . ."[35] It was the first evidence he had found that perhaps the millennium was harder to reach than he had originally anticipated. The lesson was not really learned, however, for the Association of Gentlemen turned to preventive measures instead. A society was formed to publish moral tracts against social vices, for distribution to Sunday school children. Tappan's retreat showed a certain conservative inclination that was later to qualify his abolitionism. Without friends or money, McDowall continued his labors until his death at a relatively early age from exhaustion and tuberculosis.[36]

While Arthur Tappan withdrew in some confusion from Christian efforts, Lewis pressed on with a zeal matching that of his opponents. "Their enmity and clamor," he said, "are evidence of the righteousness of the cause. He that sitteth in heaven will laugh."[37] Obviously, the city was fast heading for ruin; the only way to stop it was to try once more to bring brother Finney from the hinterlands. To prepare the way, Lewis begged churchmen to "wrestle in prayer," "to fight manfully the good fight of faith," and to "run and be not weary; walk and not faint." "Less foolish tattling and jest" in business hours and more "weeping over dying sinners" was his message. To judge from the muscularity of his sermon, he was directing his attention to the young men and women of his free missions; but Finney, he reasoned, could do a far more effective job.[38]

Early in 1832, Tappan began to negotiate with a reluctant

circus-owner for the lease of a theater near Five Points on Chatham Street. "The *sensation* that will be produced by converting the place with slight alterations into a church will be very great; and curiosity will be excited," Tappan reported to Finney. As an extra inducement, he slyly added, "Would it be murdering souls to draw away half of Dr. Spring's congregation?" Moreover, he found a suitable residence nearby for the preacher's family, giving a little domestic advice in the bargain. Mrs. Finney should not be allowed to furnish it with unnecessary luxury, he counseled, though he confessed his own failures along these lines: "I should have a civil war in my house if I were to go through & clear it of superfluous furniture & my wife is a tolerably reasonable woman."[39]

Finney was taken somewhat aback by all this strenuous activity, when he really wanted to remain in the West. Theodore Weld, one of his young disciples, warned him that New Yorkers were "whirling in all the hustle and bustle and chaffering and purchasing, confused and perplexed with the details and statistics of filthy lucre," and Finney was inclined to agree. Although he had managed to turn down the blandishments of Arthur's Association for Gentlemen for years, he could not withstand the pressure from Lewis Tappan for long. He and his family arrived in time to be present at the anniversary celebrations of the national benevolent societies, held in Tappan's new auditorium in May, 1832.[40]

While big enough to "accommodate ever so many anxious," as Tappan boasted, the Chatham Street Chapel was a drab barn of a place, without carpeting to soften the noise of spectators' tramping in and out during the services. In addition, it squatted in the midst of the slums, discouraging "decent" people from attendance. Finney had good reason to fear that the whole building might collapse under the weight of a packed house.[41] In spite of these drawbacks, Tappan saw his project as an American version of Exeter Hall, gathering place in London for British evangelicals which had been completed the year before. Just as this dusty "Devil's Temple" was a poor reflection of its British counterpart, so too was the American evangelical movement a crude imitation of the foreign cause. In Britain wealthy merchants and dissenting clergymen, Quakers and Anglicans, supported an amazing array of charities, which, along with their antislavery, Bible, and other large efforts, included such bizarre causes as the Ladies Association for the Benefit of Gentlewomen of Good Family, Reduced in

71

Fortune below the State of Comfort to Which They Have Been Accustomed; the Society for Returning Young Women to Their Friends in the Country; and the National Truss Society for the Relief of the Ruptured Poor.[42] But if the Americans lacked the money to support so varied an array of projects, they made up for it in the zeal with which they promoted the ones they had.

Certainly Lewis Tappan drove ahead, even faster than Finney liked. For the most part, the old Association of Gentlemen slipped away, tired of Lewis' "harshness, censoriousness & driving matters," as Tappan himself admitted. Once in a while, he was forced to confess, "Bro. Finney, I know that I have not that communion with Christ that I should have. . . . Pray for me, that I may be broken hearted, & saved from the [snares?] of the devil." The great revivalist had little impact on him, however, for Tappan took a much sterner view of sinners and sin than Finney himself. For instance, he believed that a Christian could not marry outside his faith without losing all hope of salvation. He published a tract which explained that though such couples (mainly Catholic-Protestant) might "expect happiness," God "bids sorrow encircle them, distress and affliction in various forms, and poverty beset them. . . . 'OH, DO NOT THIS ABOMINABLE THING THAT I HATE.' "[43] It was more than Finney could take, and he later burst out that Tappan was a "pious fraud" in trying to impose his ideas about "forbidden unions" upon the Chatham Street congregation.[44]

Tappan did, however, believe in Finney's Arminian doctrine that all men were capable of salvation, given the grace of the Holy Spirit, a heartfelt willingness, and the inspiration of a revivalist, but he was somewhat ruthless in forcing the process along. "Is it not right policy to go ahead without stopping for the snares of enemies or the stumbling of friends [?]" he asked. "If a measure is decried, come out with a bolder."[45] Finney himself often preached in that vein, but his personal code was different. Being a pietist, he was concerned with the inner workings of man, and he enjoyed his power to persuade. Tappan, on the other hand, lacked that ability; he relied instead on force. This was the difference that prevented Finney from putting his name on the rolls of benevolent societies, even though he preached against the sins they sought to suppress. It was the reason why Finney never became a root and branch abolitionist, while Lewis Tappan adopted that course with the same spirit with which he sought to expel religiously mixed couples from the church.

He was not the first of the two brothers to take up abolitionism, an honor that fell to Arthur. "What a faithful steward of the Lord! His heart is a perpetual fountain of benevolence, which waters the whole land—always flowing, and never diminishing," wrote a young New Englander about him.[46] Although Arthur Tappan never welcomed this sort of praise, William Lloyd Garrison was beside himself with gratitude to the merchant. The two reformers had met in the summer of 1830, the year in which the evangelical campaign for the West had begun. Antislavery was beckoning Arthur Tappan "to be up and doing."

NOTES

1. Lucy Aiken to William Ellery Channing, December 26, 1828, in Anna Letitia Le Breton, ed., *Correspondence of William E. Channing, D.D. and Lucy Aiken, from 1826 to 1842* (Boston, 1874), 29; for examples of these conflicting sentiments, see B. B. Edwards, *Memoir of the Rev. Elias Cornelius* (Boston, 1834), 244–45, 281, 287–88.

2. AT to BT, March 21, 1828, BT MSS, LC (quotation); diary, February 23, 1829. "Association of Gentlemen" appeared on the masthead of the *Evangelist* but otherwise was seldom used officially. Barnes, *Antislavery Impulse*, 35, uses the term loosely to describe the later group of antislavery merchants as well as these earlier philanthropists, without properly distinguishing between them. LT compiled a list of *Journal of Commerce* supporters; see diary, January 14, 1829. AT's collaborators also appear in Finney Correspondence, Oberlin College Library. Peletiah Perit, AT's best friend, was a merchant's son from Norwich, Conn. (*National Cyclopedia of American Biography* . . . [New York, 1921], I, 499–500); Silas Holmes, shipper, Stonington, Conn. (Robert G. Albion, *The Rise of New York Port [1815–1860]* [New York, 1939], 109); John Rankin, lineage unknown; Zephaniah Platt and Jonas Platt, close friends of Finney (McLoughlin, *Modern Revivalism,* 50); Knowles Taylor, from Connecticut, silk merchant (Scoville, *Old Merchants,* II, 24). For Dodge's and Phelps's Connecticut origins, see Richard Lowitt, *A Merchant Prince of the 19th Century, William E. Dodge* (New York, 1954), 8–9, 14. Moses Allen, probably from Connecticut, was a New York banker (Griffin, *Brothers' Keepers,* 179).

3. LT to Lyman Beecher, February 16, 1828 (copy), diary; Walker, *Congregationalists,* V, 150–51; Dixon Ryan Fox, *Yankees and Yorkers* (Port Washington, N.Y., 1940), 209; L. Nelson Nichols, *The History of the Broadway Tabernacle of New York City* (New Haven, 1940), 83–84; Albion, *Rise of New York Port,* 245–46.

4. Timothy Dwight, *Travels: In New-England and New-York* (New Haven, 1822), III, 468; Albion, *Rise of New York Port,* 250–251; AT to Elias Cornelius, April 19, 1830, in LT, *Arthur Tappan,* 83; see also David Low Dodge to Charles Grandison Finney, March 18, 1827, Finney MSS, Oberlin College Library, for

typical attitude of the group toward theological speculation. See also Lowitt, *Merchant Prince,* 194–95.

5. Diary, February 16, March 7 (quotation), 19, and 22, April 6, 10, 16, 17, and 19, May 13, July 9, 16, and 22, 1828.

6. *Free Inquirer* (New York), February 18, 1828; David Brion Davis, "Some Ideological Functions of Prejudice in Ante-Bellum America," *New England Quarterly,* XV (Summer, 1963), 115–25.

7. New York *Evangelist,* April 24, May 22, 1830.

8. New York *Evangelist,* May 22, 1830.

9. Barnes, *Antislavery Impulse,* 20–21; Cross, *Burned-Over District,* 107–8.

10. New York *Evangelist,* March 8, April 24, 1830; William G. McLoughlin, ed., *Lectures on Revivals by Charles Grandison Finney* (Cambridge, 1960), viii, and McLoughlin, *Modern Revivalism,* 17, 46, 50, 52; Gardiner Spring, *Life and Times of Gardiner Spring* (New York, 1866), II, 222–26; Lowitt, *Merchant Prince,* 194–95; *Christian Examiner,* IV (July and August, 1827), 357–70; *Letters of the Rev. Dr. Beecher and Rev. Mr. Nettleton, on the 'New Measures' in Conducting Revivals* . . . (New York, 1828); Beecher to Nettleton, June 10, 1828, Beecher Family MSS, Yale University Library; Shepherd Knapp, *A History of the Brick Presbyterian Church in the City of New York* (New York, 1909), 157.

11. Diary, June 20, 1828.

12. LT to Theodore Weld, October 25, 1831, in Gilbert H. Barnes and Dwight L. Dumond, eds., *Letters of Theodore Dwight Weld, Angelina Grimké Weld, and Sarah Grimké, 1822–1844* (New York, 1934), I, 52; McLoughlin, *Modern Revivalism,* 52, 58–59; LT to Finney, March 17, 1831, and August 17, 1832, Joshua Leavitt to Finney, February 28, 1831, Finney MSS, Oberlin College Library.

13. New York *Evangelist,* May 26, 1832; LT, "Plan of Benevolence," *ibid.,* April 7, 1832; LT, "Free Church System," *ibid.,* March 31, 1832; Charles C. Cole, "The Free Church Movement in New York City," *New York History,* XXXIV (July, 1953), 284–97.

14. New York *Evangelist,* July 2, 1831; *Orthodox Bubbles, or A Review of the "First Annual Report of the Executive Committee of the New York Magdalen Society"* (Boston, 1831), 8, probably written by Theophilus Fisk.

15. LT, *Arthur Tappan,* 110–12, 124–25.

16. *McDowall's Journal* (New York), June, 1833; *Working Man's Advocate,* July 28, 1831; *Orthodox Bubbles,* 8–9. See also LT, *Arthur Tappan,* 114. AT was also accused of allowing debtors to starve only a short distance from his home; see *Gospel Herald and Universalist Review* (New York), December 4, 1830, 403.

17. New York *Evangelist,* October 8, 1831; LT, *Arthur Tappan,* 111.

18. *Priestcraft Unmasked,* September 17, 1831.

19. LT, *Arthur Tappan,* 123; diary, July 23, 1828; *Working Man's Advocate,* June 29, 1832.

20. Diary, July 23, 1828; New York *Genius of Temperance,* May 9, 1832; LT in New York *Evangelist,* July 21, 1832.

21. *Evangelical Magazine and Gospel Advocate,* June 26, 1830; LT to BT, August 21 and September 18, 1830, and July 9, 1831, BT MSS, LC.

22. *Working Man's Advocate,* January 30, 1830.

23. Barnes, *Antislavery Impulse,* 50; *Working Man's Advocate,* July 28, 1831; *Evangelical Magazine and Gospel Advocate,* June 26, 1830.

24. *Emancipator* (New York), August 24, 1833, from *Baptist Repertory*, August 16, 1833; New York *Evangelist*, September 3, 1831.

25. *Priestcraft Unmasked*, July 15, 1830, 116; *Fanaticism Unveiled: A Satirical Poem* (New York, 1834), a dull work in the style of "Hudibras," probably by James Watson Webb.

26. New York *Evangelist*, October 8, 1831.

27. *Working Man's Advocate*, July 19, 1831. Walter E. Hugins, *Jacksonian Democracy and the Working Class* (Stanford, 1960), 135, asserts that anticlericalism played a declining role in city politics, but later, when abolitionism was associated with anticlericalism, it recovered strength. The *Working Man's Advocate* was less vociferous in opposition to abolitionism than Webb's *Courier and Enquirer,* but it was still quite irresponsible in its attacks. LT, *Arthur Tappan*, 116.

28. Stewart H. Holbrook, *The Yankee Exodus: An Account of Migration from New England* (New York, 1950), 273; Albion, *Rise of New York Port*, 250–51; Barnabas Bates, *An Address Delivered at a General Meeting of the Citizens of the City of New-York . . .* (New York, 1830). On Bogardus, see Maria S. (Bogardus) Gray, *A Genealogical History of the Ancestors and Descendants of General Robert Bogardus* (Boston, 1927), 95–104. He paid the largest taxes in the city: *Working Man's Advocate,* January 2, 1830; *Morning Courier and New York Enquirer,* December 29, 1829. On Tibbitts, see Dixon Ryan Fox, *The Decline of Aristocracy in the Politics of New York* (New York, 1918), 21, 157; *Journal of Commerce,* December 22, 1829; and *Working Man's Advocate,* December 29, 1829. On Delafield, see Bayard Tuckerman, ed., *The Diary of Philip Hone, 1828–1851* (New York, 1889), I, 27, and *Working Man's Advocate,* August 27, 1831. On Hone, see Allan Nevins, ed., *The Diary of Philip Hone, 1828–1851* (New York, 1927), I, 43, 45. Antievangelicals thus counted aristocrats in their ranks—perhaps even more of them than the evangelicals could muster.

29. On Preserved Fish, see Albion, *Rise of New York Port*, 243, 247, and Nevins, *Hone Diary,* I, 48, 114, 284; *Journal of Commerce,* December 22, 1829; *Working Man's Advocate,* September 15, 1832. On Webb, see Thompson, *Memoir of David Hale,* 54–55; Frank L. Mott, *American Journalism: A History, 1690–1960* (3rd ed.; New York, 1962), 260–61. On liquor dealers, see William Hogan (at meeting) in *Working Man's Advocate,* August 27 1831, and Scoville, *Old Merchants,* II, 115–20. For ward leaders, see G. D. Strong in *Working Man's Advocate,* August 27, 1831. On Alderman (Ebenezer?) Whiting, see Hugins, *Jacksonian Democracy and the Working Class,* 120. Newspapermen attending the meeting were John Lang of the New York *Gazette* and John I. Mumford of the New York *Standard;* Scoville, *Old Merchants,* III, 193–95.

30. Leader of this Jacksonian element was Richard Mentor Johnson, Kentucky senator and representative and writer of two Sunday Mail Reports. See editorial from New York *Sentinel,* November 1, 1830, from *Priestcraft Unmasked:* "Tappan and Bissel care as little about the principle of Anti-Masonry as the Khan of Tartary does. But they care a great deal about the anti-masonic excitement! It is an excellent tool" for religious tyranny. On Preserved Fish, see E. S. Ely's *Philadelphian* (Philadelphia), April 2, 1830, 54.

31. *Gospel Herald and Universalist Review,* February 27, August 14, September 11, October 9, and December 4, 1830; Theodore Clark to Theodore Weld, November 30, 1829, Weld MSS, William L. Clements Library; Lee Benson, *The Concept of Jacksonian Democracy: New York as a Test Case* (Princeton, 1961), 194;

Journal of Commerce, December 22, 1829; *Orthodox Bubbles,* 23; Ezra Stiles Ely, *The Duty of Christian Freemen to Elect Christian Rulers* (Philadelphia, 1827), 12; see also John R. Bodo, *The Protestant Clergy and Public Issues, 1812–1848* (Princeton, 1954), 46–48; "Notes," *Journal of the Presbyterian Historical Society,* II (September, 1904), 321–22; Arthur Schlesinger, Jr., *The Age of Jackson* (Boston, 1945), 137–43.

32. See Hugins, *Jacksonian Democracy and the Working Class,* 24–28, which notes the movement toward union with Tammany, but, unlike Benson, *Concept of Jacksonian Democracy,* 35, 35n, and 195–96, mostly ignores the importance of the clerical issue in assisting this connection. New York *Evangelist,* August 6, 1831. Workingmen's party leaders at the anticlerical rallies were John Morrison, Thomas Hertell, Edward J. Webb, and Barnabas Bates. Equally anticlerical were Frances Wright, George Henry Evans, Nathan Darling, George V. McPherson, and Gilbert Vale. On Beecher's view of anticlericalism in the Workingmen's movement, see Lyman Beecher, *Works (Lectures on Political Atheism and Kindred Subjects)* (Boston, 1852), I, 92–93.

33. LT to Governor William H. Seward, November 2, 1842, William H. Seward MSS, Rush Rhees Library, University of Rochester; Isaac Goldberg, *Major Noah: American-Jewish Pioneer* (Philadelphia, 1944), 230; Theophilus Fisk, *The Nation's Bulwark . . .* (New Haven, 1832); and Schlesinger, *Age of Jackson,* 138, 169–70.

34. Churchill C. Cambreleng to Richard N. Baptist, of Mechlenburg, Virginia, September 16, 1835, in Washington *Globe,* February 13, 1836. See also *Ohio Watchman* (Ravenna), September 26, 1835: abolitionism "is considered here another scheme of the Clergy, to raise a party in our country with themselves at its head, thus to increase their importance and power. . . ."

35. LT, *Arthur Tappan,* 118.

36. *Ibid.,* 119; New York *Evangelist,* October 8, 1831.

37. LT in New York *Evangelist,* September 24, 1831; *ibid.,* August 6, 1831.

38. "Revival Hints," New York *Evangelist,* February 2, 1832; LT in *ibid.,* May 26, 1833; Nichols, *Broadway Tabernacle,* 49–50. LT to Finney, February 2, 1831; A. Brown to Finney, September 13, 1830, and February 2, 1831; Baxter Sayre to Finney, February 9, 1831; O. Smith to Finney, February 17, 1831—all in Finney MSS, Oberlin College Library. Finney to George Washington Gale, February 16, 1831, Weld MSS, Clements Library.

39. Quotations above from LT to Finney, March 16 and 22, April 11, June 28, 1832, Finney MSS, Oberlin College Library. See also LT to Andrew Reed, February 1, 1835, in New York *Evangelist,* February 21, 1835, on the free church movement.

40. Weld to Finney, February 28, 1832, in Barnes and Dumond, *Weld Letters,* I, 66–67; LT to Finney, March 16, 1832, Finney MSS, Oberlin College Library; New York *Evangelist,* April 14, May 5 and 12, 1832. Barnes, *Antislavery Impulse,* 22, attributes the Chatham Chapel enterprise to AT, not LT. AT merely donated one thousand dollars to the cause. Bernard A. Weisberger, *They Gathered at the River: The Story of the Great Revivalists and Their Impact upon Religion in America* (Boston, 1958), 125, while generally accurate and certainly perceptive, claims LT "offered to buy" the theater; he only leased it and contributed a small sum to help pay the lease.

41. LT to Finney, March 22, April 11, 1833, Finney MSS, Oberlin College

Library. The chapel was close to the later site of the Brooklyn Bridge exit. *Liberator,* May 24, 1839.

42. Quotation, Joel Parker to Finney, March 14, 1832, Finney MSS, Oberlin College Library; Brown, *Fathers of the Victorians,* 330–35, 340.

43. LT to Finney, April 7 and 19, 1832, September 6, 1833, Finney MSS, Oberlin College Library. This was probably an English tract that LT edited for reprinting in New York *Evangelist,* January 26, 1833.

44. *Ibid.;* diary, February 25, March 19, 1836.

45. LT to Finney, September 6, 1833, Finney MSS, Oberlin College Library; quotation, August 17, 1832, *ibid.;* James E. Johnson, "The Life of Charles Grandison Finney," Ph.D. dissertation, Syracuse University, 1959, 47, 68.

46. William Lloyd Garrison to Simeon S. Jocelyn, May 30, 1831, "Miscellaneous Manuscripts," Yale University Library.

CHAPTER FIVE

A Pilgrim's Progress

*O*ne *midsummer day* in 1830, Lewis Tappan, busy with a shipment of Italian parasols or silk handkerchiefs, looked up to see a stranger enter. The young man introduced himself as William Lloyd Garrison. He had a face, Tappan later recalled, that beamed with "conscious rectitude," but his expression did not tally with the cut of his clothes: in those days, he dressed like a dandy. Perhaps on first sight Lewis mistook him for one of the drummers who constantly crowded the aisles of the store. Instead, Garrison belonged to that group of religious young men who invariably asked for a word with the senior partner. Like them, he was solely interested in the proceeds from the till, not the goods offered on the counters. His commodity was reform and his business reference, a recent martyrdom. The two men walked back to the cluttered office of Arthur Tappan.[1]

A short time before, Arthur Tappan had learned of Garrison's arrest and imprisonment in Baltimore on a charge of libel. Garrison had accused a shipmaster of his native Newburyport, Massachusetts, of "domestic piracy" for transporting slaves to the lower South and proclaimed that the crime fitted the man for eternal punishment in the "lowest depths of perdition."[2] Garrison's words appeared in the *Genius of Universal Emancipation,* a small reform journal that he and a remarkable Quaker named Benjamin Lundy had been printing in Baltimore. Arthur had met Lundy in March, 1828, when he had come in search of funds to run his struggling paper. Approached by so many other earnest mendicants, Tappan had politely refused him, but in Garrison's plight he saw a symbolic sacrifice of Yankee freedom. "I have read the sketch of the trial of Mr. Garrison with that deep feeling of abhorrence of slavery and its abettors which every one must feel who is capable of appreciating the blessings of liberty," he wrote Lundy. Enclosed was a check to release Garrison on bail.[3]

In later years, Lewis Tappan remarked that Arthur felt about vice as he would about a toad in his pocket. The description fitted the sentiments of Garrison, too. He had grown up under the strict tutelage of a Calvinist Baptist mother whose husband had deserted her for the evils of drink. The "galling bondage" of tight corset lacings, the enslavement of gamblers to the lottery ticket, the craving of smokers for tobacco, and the addiction of drunkards to the "tippler's stand" were just as repugnant to Garrison as to his benefactor. On these grounds, he amply qualified for Tappan's "orthodox money."[4] Besides, Garrison had personal charm, though it was devoid of humor, and Arthur Tappan was highly impressed. He was somewhat disturbed to learn after due investigation that Garrison's business qualities were doubtful, but his informants assured him that the young editor had a "talent at writing and . . . zeal in the cause. . . ." Garrison received what he had come to get—one hundred dollars to carry on his work. The sum was hardly sufficient for his long-range projects, but it welcomed him to Arthur Tappan's coterie of subsidized reformers. With money from other philanthropists, Garrison issued the first number of the *Liberator* in Boston on January 1, 1831.[5]

The Tappan brothers had long taken a mild interest in the slavery issue. As young men, they had read of William Wilberforce's dramatic struggle in England to outlaw the foreign slave trade. Having signed agreements with the United States and other powers, the English government operated a flotilla of patrol ships to retrieve African slavers bound for the Americas; the Negroes on board were returned to the colony of Sierra Leone. Under the leadership of the aged Wilberforce and of Thomas Clarkson, British Evangelicals of the 1820's were pressing their agitation for Parliamentary abolition of West Indian slavery. The pace quickened in 1824, when British reformers accepted the arguments of Elizabeth Coltman Heyrick, who wrote a pamphlet called *Immediate, Not Gradual Abolition,* and each year the day of delivery seemed closer. The Tappans were aware of these events in England, and they wondered how British ideals might be applied in America, where the Negro issue was so much more difficult to solve.[6]

For many years the American conscience had been restive about slavery. Doctrines of the Enlightenment, Revolutionary sentiment, abandonment of white bonded servitude, the breakdown of squirearchies, and the rise of middle-class prosperity contributed to the gradual extinction of Negro slavery north of the Delaware. Yet this easy regional emancipation did not immediately stir Yankees to export their convictions to the South. Apathy and ignorance on the question generally prevailed in the free states, and even the debates over Missouri's admission (1819–21) aroused little interest outside Congress. Aside from an occasional church or legislative resolution in the North, antislavery activity during the Jeffersonian years took place primarily in the South, particularly in the mountain areas of Kentucky and Tennessee and in Virginia and Maryland. Jeffersonian principles of freedom and the declining need for slaves in parts of the upper South led scores of masters to free their bondsmen in imitation of George Washington, Patrick Henry, and other Revolutionary fathers. Moreover, some churchmen and missionaries of the Baptist, Methodist, and Quaker faiths encouraged discussion of the evils of the institution, though their influence declined as contrary economic and social pressures were felt. In the early years of the republic, outsiders were not compelled to broadcast their messages from northern sanctuaries. Men like Benjamin Lundy and his Quaker colleague Elihu Embree met constant harassment, but they were at least able to survive in the South. For instance, Lundy traveled to Missouri to help organize a futile campaign against a proslavery constitutional convention, an undertaking few would have dared at a later date.

Hampered by prevailing racist sentiments, forced to the defensive on such irrelevant issues as "intermarriage" and the horrors of Negro rape, and crippled by an association with the panacea of Negro deportation, the southern antislavery movement was too conservative to be vigorous or promising. Slavery was a profitable business, especially in the Southwest, where crop income generally kept pace with expanded cultivation, and in the older South, which provided the labor force for the new lands at increasingly higher prices. Even Jefferson was not above observing that "a child raised every 2. years is of more profit than the crop of the best laboring man." By the time of his death in 1826, however, many planters had grown intolerant of the liberal view that slavery was a deplorable but necessary evil, a position which encouraged hypocrisy, confusion, and doubt among the whites and restiveness among the blacks. Conscious of British agitation, uneasy about Negro loyalty after the Vesey Plot, and alarmed by growing signs of northern power and hostility, southern masters were anxious to close the doors to further talk of emancipation, gradual or otherwise.[7] Yet pockets of liberalism remained, constantly creating in Yankee reformers like the Tappans false hopes and then bitter disillusionment and frustration.

Garrison's trip from the Baltimore jail cell to Arthur Tappan's store thus signaled more than a new beginning for the young reformer. It represented the end of one era in antislavery history and the opening of another. No longer could antislavery men reside in relative peace below the Mason and Dixon line. At one time Monticello may correctly have been called the antislavery capital of the nation, but by 1831 that center had shifted to a Boston attic, a more congenial site for plotting what turned out to be a revolution.

The movement for "immediate abolition" began as a direct extension of evangelical Christianity. In the columns of the *Liberator*, Garrison stated his goal as he developed it: the universal, immediate, and unqualified emancipation of all American slaves. Basic to his creed, just as to revivalism, was the conviction that sin was conscious, active disobedience to God. Being willful, it could be remedied only by conversion and penitence. "I take for granted," Garrison wrote in the tone of the zealous preacher, "that slavery *is* a crime—a damning crime: therefore my efforts shall be directed to the exposure of those who practise it."[8]

In his terms, complicity with evil was evil itself. Consequently, slaveholders were not the only sinners; so were all those who supported or refused to denounce them. On this ground Garrison rejected as utterly immoral the British plan of compensating owners. Nor would he accept an apprenticeship system to ease the transition, as Wilberforce recommended, for if man was by nature a rational being, as current theory had it, the slaves would not require a period of discipline and instruction.

Some historians maintain that immediate abolition was a political program, fraught with inconsistencies and ambivalences. But in Garrison's mind the formula was merely an extension of the revivalistic experience of instantaneous conversion—a religious, not a secular, act. Elizur Wright, one of Garrison's earliest disciples, made this distinction between what he called a plan of action and a doctrine in a pamphlet which he wrote in 1833. (Unfortunately, neither Lewis nor Arthur made identifiable contributions to antislavery theory, so that what they believed when they joined the movement must be understood through the record others have left.) Immediate abolition belonged to the category of doctrine and resembled such other doctrines as the Ten Commandments and the natural right of man to free speech. The "plan" which abolitionists proposed was merely "to promulgate the doctrine" of immediate abolition, leaving its actual accomplishment in the hands of those whose consciences they touched.

For thousands of years, Wright observed, Christians had urged "immediate, *entire* repentance; of course they expect, 'what fools!' to convert the whole world at a blow!" Antislavery men were taking the same point of view. They were not more unreasonable in preaching immediacy than a preacher who refused to advocate *"the gradual abolition of sin."* Immediate emancipation was not radical or silly, Wright believed, since any other proposal encouraged the universal inclination of men to procrastinate. Wright implied that abolitionists might secretly rejoice in the success of any gradual scheme of emancipation (which did not include expatriation), even though they would continue to denounce piecemeal reform for strategic reasons.[9]

Immediate abolition was not intended as a plan of political action; advocates of the religious doctrine of immediatism wished to set forth the ideal to which all good Christians must eventually bear allegiance. The doctrine was conservative in that it sought conversion only through pietistic, not coercive, means. Even Congress was supposed to have little power over slavery where it already existed. But the doctrine of immediate emancipation was undeniably radical in tendency. It stressed hatred of a sin, and that hatred soon shifted to hatred of the sinner. Nor did abolitionists themselves always bear Wright's careful definitions in mind, and the movement underwent considerable alterations as time and circumstances changed. Above all, immediate abolition was extreme in nature, because, doctrine though it was, it had profound political consequences: erasure of hundreds of millions of dollars worth of chattels and the transformation of that property into millions of new, uneducated, and untested citizens, with sweeping effects upon existing institutions, customs, and social relations. Two centuries of racist habits had been instilled into the American people, and yet the abolitionists were demanding that the nation begin afresh! It is hardly a wonder that planters shuddered when they pondered the implications for them, their economy, and their culture.

Abolitionists, however, saw no suggestion of danger in their plan. Reared for the most part in rural and conservative sections of the North, they were more amused than angered to find themselves regarded as fanatics. What could be more "conservative" than restoring to slaves their inherent rights and then placing them within the protection of the law? Was it anarchy to urge the removal of the very motive for slave revolt? As for "amalgamation" and, as Elizur Wright once put it, "all that sort of stuff," was there not more of this "whitening" process under slavery than there would be under conditions of free choice? Abolitionist logic could be telling.

At the same time, these reformers so grossly overestimated southern goodwill and underrated northern racial prejudice that one must question their political wisdom while admiring their moral fortitude. According to Wright, his associates expected abolition to come about gradually; first, one or two "benevolent" masters, then a trickle, and finally "dense masses" would awaken and rush to the abolition banner. Meanwhile, he admitted, other slaveholders would threaten "loudly to secede from the Union! madly prating about the invasion of sacred rights . . . and riveting tighter the fetters of helpless victims." These threats of separation and cries of anguish were, in his view, mere bluffs. Somehow— here the reformers' logic became conspicuously unclear—the process toward freedom would continue until all could "hear the trumpet of the world's jubilee announcing that the last *fetter* has been knocked off from the heel of the last *slave*."[10] The plot *had* to come out happily; God would see to it.

Abolitionists were on the whole not a thoughtful set, in spite of their instinct for transforming political defeats into moral victories. One does not turn to the Tappans, to Garrison, or to Elizur Wright for a profound theological or philosophical disquisition on freedom and servitude in the style of John Stuart Mill. And as it happened, slavery was not to be smothered by a blanket of weighty words in any case, but by grimmer and costlier means. Of course the abolitionists did very little to initiate plans for peaceable, piecemeal, institutional reforms; instead they concentrated most of their attention upon the publicizing of doctrine. But the issue they faced was essentially a matter of power, not of technique. Garrison fashioned his tools according to the principles of power, drawing heavily from his religious upbringing for his materials. As Thomas Wentworth Higginson later noted, Garrison's "vocabulary" was not a product of mindless fanaticism but was "the logical result of that stern school of old-fashioned Calvinism in which he had been trained."[11] Such an education did not give him a balanced view of immorality; to his mind nothing was more immoral than the right of one man to own, sell, and forcibly control another. Aware of the enormous strength of the opposition in both sections of the country, he made his language fit the situation. It was harsh, concrete, and specific. He set the standard by which all other abolitionist polemics had to be judged. Rejecting a tone of querulous intellectualism, Garrison followed the advice of Lyman Beecher, whom he had often heard in Boston in the late twenties: "Controversy has always been the great instrument of recovering individuals and communities from the dominion of error. Abuses never reform themselves. Depravity never purifies itself." Garrison took Beecher at his word: "I am in earnest—I will not equivocate—I will not excuse—I will not retreat a single inch—AND I WILL BE HEARD."[12]

Some years passed, however, before Arthur Tappan would hear, and in the meantime he remained a member of the American Colonization Society, a repository for the last impulse of southern liberalism.

In spite of its inadequate philosophy of action, the American Colonization Society was the only truly national organization that even pretended to deal with the slavery issue. Indeed, there were several manumission societies in existence, led by New York and Philadelphia Quakers and aristocrats. These societies did function every year or so as a united national body by inviting a few "Friends of Humanity" from the South to join them in convention. At one time the manumission groups had included such men as Benjamin Franklin, Alexander Hamilton, and John Jay. But once they had won victories over their state slave systems, these groups deteriorated into local charities with parochial aims. The Tappans never showed much interest in them as a result. The point is rather important because it helps to show that Garrison was the real pioneer of antislavery and did not simply capitalize on a sentiment already aroused and institutionalized. Moreover in the manumission groups the cleavage between the newly arrived immigrants from New England and the older New York society is once again revealed and the lack of co-operation between the manumissionists and the evangelical abolitionists made somewhat clearer. They had very little in common.[13]

Only in the American Colonization Society was there a union of the conservative antislavery elements and the evangelical reformers, short lived though it was. The Society's approach was gradual, if not opportunistic, the chief premise being that Negroes could not survive in freedom in a white man's country. Most of the Tappan brothers' associates thought colonization was a satisfactory solution to a sticky moral issue. Lyman Beecher, for instance, inveighed against the gradualists in the temperance movement, but he supported the colonization scheme, an anomaly that Garrison soon called to his attention.[14] But Negro expatriation attracted some support in the upper tier of southern states, where planters found slavery less profitable than in the sugar and cotton belts. Such participation created the possibility that the movement would become a co-operative non-sectional venture.

It was only natural that Arthur Tappan should be drawn into the colonization movement, although his interest was not aroused until he became aware of its business possibilities. A United States Navy surgeon recognized an elderly slave in Natchez, Mississippi, to be Abdual Rahahman, a prince of a royal African house and a grandson of the King of Timbucktu. Charles Tappan, who had already joined the Colonization Society, arranged for the slave's purchase from his master, and the Rev. Thomas Gallaudet, a Hartford clergyman, brought him to New York City to raise funds for his return to Africa. Arthur Tappan met Abdual and was delighted with his "princely bearing, and intelligence."[15] He reasoned that the Negro could open the hinterland to trade through his family connections, and a lively commerce might develop with the United States.

Dreams of imperial and economic glory had played a part in the founding of the Society's colony of Liberia from the very beginning. Sierra Leone, the British prototype for the American experiment, was supposed to be doing well under the banner of evangelical Christianity and the Union Jack. Friends of Liberia hoped for similar success. "It has at times crossed by mind," wrote Arthur Tappan to Ralph Gurley, secretary of the American Colonization Society, "that it would be a good thing to have . . . vessels . . . to sail regularly from this city for Liberia for the double purpose of transporting coloured people and carrying on a trade with the Colony."[16] Since such a scheme would eliminate many of the financial and shipping problems of their colony, Gurley and Charles Tappan were delighted.[17]

Following Arthur's example, Lewis attended meetings to form local chapters and gave his advice freely.[18] Meanwhile, Arthur pledged one hundred dollars to a campaign for matching funds initiated by Gerrit Smith, a wealthy philanthropist of the Genesee Valley, New York. In addition, he accepted a vice-presidency of the African Education Society, a subsidiary of the American Colonization Society.[19] But his chief interest in Liberia centered about his packet venture. He consulted shippers about the market for palm oil, camwood, ivory, and other native products and took special pains to have the advice of Dr. Richard Randall, a newly appointed director of the colony and an expert on African commerce. Randall did not disguise the fact that New England rum was Liberia's major import, but Arthur overlooked the moral question, for the moment at least. When Randall and the prince left for Liberia at the end of 1828, they carried Arthur's wishes for successful negotiations with the natives.[20]

Word from Africa was slow to reach Tappan's desk. In the meantime, he wrote Gurley, "My interest in this subject is in no degree abated, and as soon as we learn the reception that Prince's letter, by Dr. Randall has met with from his kinsmen I shall be better able to decide on the course I will take." Claiming that his sole motive was "the spiritual good of the Africans," Arthur Tappan predicted that "a friendly intercourse with the interiour" would soon "prepare the way for the introduction of the blessings of civilization and Religion."[21]

Unfortunately, Randall and Rahahman both died of tropical fever on their arrival. Arthur Tappan's concern did not survive the news. Bluntly he wrote Gurley, "I feel obliged to relinquish all thoughts of [the commercial enterprise] for the present." As if the unappealing aspects of Liberian trade had previously escaped his notice, he demanded that the Colonization Society "discountenance & if possible prohibit the introduction of distilled spirits into its settlements," or he would never feel it his "duty to aid it."[22] He then had his name removed from Gerrit Smith's list of pledged supporters, "the conditions not having been realized." As a consolation, he offered the society one hundred dollars for its school in Monrovia, the capital.[23]

This sudden reversal was greeted with consternation at the Washington headquarters of the Colonization Society. Unless the directors could "act decidedly," Gallaudet warned, evangelicals with temperance scruples would repudiate the scheme forthwith. The rum trade, however, was the backbone of the colony's economy. Much to the relief of the officers, Tappan did not immediately advertise his defection, and the colonists were allowed to continue their rum-drinking without interruption.[24]

Disheartened by his venture into African matters, Arthur Tappan turned to another cause that he thought more promising. In June, 1831, the merchant went with Garrison and Simeon S. Jocelyn, a young Congregational minister, to the First Annual Convention of People of Color in Philadelphia. Jocelyn, who served a Negro church in New Haven, had drawn up a plan for a Negro training school to be located near Yale College, and Connecticut state legislators, whom he had addressed on the subject, had led him to hope for state support. Arthur Tappan was easily won over to the scheme. The three reformers laid the project before the Negro delegates, and the merchant promised to give substantial aid if sufficient funds were forthcoming from other white and Negro sources.[25] The convention applauded Jocelyn's proposal. Here at last were some white philanthropists who offered the black race a means of advancement in America rather than simply free passage to a savage and pestilential African outpost.[26] Arthur Tappan was enthusiastic about the college idea because of his own convictions of the value of moral and utilitarian instruction. Despite his support, years of agitation and even civil war had to pass before his dream of bona fide college education for Negroes was fulfilled. At least Jocelyn's plan was a start.[27]

Arthur Tappan's visit also opened his heart to the conditions of the free black people of the North. Interviews with James Forten, a wealthy sail-maker of Philadelphia, and "other intelligent and influential men of color" had a profound influence on him. Except for the color of their skins, they seemed to him no different from other upstanding Americans. They told him about the deplorable state of the members of their race, both freemen and slaves. A riot in 1829, for instance, had driven thousands of free Negroes of Cincinnati into Canadian exile. There cold and disease carried off many of them. The riot served grim notice that men of the North could be as brutal as many slaveholders were. Moreover, Arthur was told that most Negroes feared and despised the colonization idea, and Tappan's growing convictions about the immorality of the Liberian venture were thereby reinforced.[28]

Expecting Christians to support the New Haven college, Tappan endorsed it publicly: "We owe it to the cause of humanity, to our country, and to God to raise [the Negroes] from the depths of their degradation and misery. . . ." Only a handful, including Ezra Stiles Ely and two Episcopal bishops, William White and Henry Onderdonk, followed Arthur's lead. Meanwhile, Samuel Cornish, a Negro Presbyterian cleric of New York, began soliciting funds among the northern black communities. His energy and devotion, however, could not make up for the disappointing lack of interest among white Christians.[29]

The Philadelphia conference also produced the impulse for the founding of a national antislavery society. Arthur Tappan participated in discussions with Garrison, Benjamin Lundy, Cornish, and two Quakers of Philadelphia about the need for such an organization. In the July issue of the *Genius of Universal Emancipation*, Lundy announced that an association to overthrow slavery would shortly appear "upon an enlarged and extensive plan." The *Genius* statement was the first public notice that Garrison's long-standing proposal had gained a favorable response, and as a result of his own efforts. Events shortly followed, however, that forced Tappan to reconsider the advisability of the proposal.[30]

Meanwhile, the plans for the New Haven school were developed. Having bought some choice acres not far from Yale, Tappan expected the professors to offer their services at nominal cost. Admittedly, the courses were to be mostly practical, mechanical instruction, but, it was thought, modest attempts would fit modest Negro needs and capabilities and would help assuage white hostility. This was a rather condescending approach, but well-intentioned and even radical for the times. Gradually, Arthur Tappan fell under Garrison's influence, an alteration that caused his brother Charles to observe testily to Gurley, "I wish Arthur Tappan had let him lay in Baltimore jail. And now, what shall I say more."[31]

The plan turned out to be as ill-fated as Tappan's Magdalen enterprise. In late August, 1831, Nat Turner inspired a slave uprising in Southampton County, Virginia, in which about fifty-five whites lost their lives. Although quickly suppressed, the massacre united southerners and northerners in hysterical condemnation. Applauding the brutal punishment of many innocent Negroes as well as the guilty, citizens blamed Garrison and his *Liberator* for stirring slave rebellion.[32] Arthur Tappan immediately responded to this absurd slander by sending Garrison another draft "to be applied to the distribution of your paper to the leading men of the country." In addition, he offered him one thousand dollars for legal defense if that proved necessary.[33]

The Turner Insurrection and Garrison's presumed complicity wrecked all hopes for the Negro school. At a rally in New Haven seven hundred residents protested that the school was "incompatible with the prosperity if not the existence of the present institution of learning. . . ."[34] No professors from Yale joined Jocelyn and Roger Sherman Baldwin, a New Haven lawyer, in defending the Negro academy against the angry crowd. Besides, Yale professors felt no obligation to offer their services at whatever price, a position in such matters taken by most academicians elsewhere. Not long after the protest meeting, Arthur Tappan's wife and children awoke to hear shouts of "Magdalen" and "Immediate Emancipation" mingled with the "most obscene and blasphemous" curses and the noise of shattering window glass. The rioters were probably Yale undergraduates out on a spree, but their action was a fair reflection of the community's hostility.[35]

The protest rally, the college rowdies, the indifference of Yale's scholars, and the controversy over his Magdalen Asylum forced Arthur Tappan to reconsider. If New Haven refused to welcome the effort, he reasoned, what community in the North would? As riots and subtler signs of fear and scorn swirled about them, abolitionists, it seemed, were correct in attacking the slave system and racial prejudice as national, not sectional, tragedies.

Despite his disappointments, Arthur welcomed the news that in early December Garrison had formed the New England Anti-Slavery Society with a few friends (all of whom were as rigidly orthodox as Garrison and the Tappans). Garrison in turn felt sustained in his course of action by Tappan's steadfastness in the face of riots and discouragements. "It may be safely affirmed that no man in the nation," he wrote in the *Liberator*, "is doing so much for the temporal and eternal happiness of his fellow men as Arthur Tappan," despite the assaults of "miscreants and libellers. What a posthumous reputation he is building—broader than our continent, higher than the pyramids, and brighter than the sun!" Garrison, more than ever, needed Arthur Tappan's help—his name on the roster of a national abolition society.[36]

As Lewis Tappan observed, Arthur did not care for flattery, being "always more severe with himself than with his fellow men." The time was not ripe for such a plan, Arthur thought. In addition, he was himself still unprepared. One of his daughters had died during the Magdalen crisis, and he had incurred enough criticism for himself and his family to bear for a while. "The Southampton affair has paralysed our Philadelphia friends," wrote Tappan to Garrison, as an excuse for delay, "and nothing has been, or can be done there now, towards organizing a National Society. Nor can money be raised there now, for the proposed College which I fear cannot be secured this year."[37]

Nor was Tappan pleased with the way Garrison was conducting himself. No more *Liberators* should be sent to South Carolina, Arthur said, with his name on the copies as the donor. "While I would not wish to shrink from duty, I do not wish unnecessarily [to] excite the wrath of my fellow men. I should do no good by being known to disseminate your paper, and should probably have my ability to do good considerably diminished by the loss of my Southern customers."[38] It was a realistic assessment, though in making it Arthur obviously fell short of Garrison's boldness. Anonymity was not compatible with reform, but Arthur Tappan was too cautious to recognize the fact. For a short time, he continued to move only in the shadows, particularly in his handling of the Crandall affair.

Prudence Crandall was a schoolmistress of Canterbury, Connecticut. A nearby Negro farmer asked her to enroll his daughter, and she complied, only to meet furious resistance from her neighborhood. She then advertised in the *Liberator* her intention to "teach colored little misses." The villagers organized themselves to restrain her through economic pressure and threats of violence. To force her to close, the state legislature passed in May, 1833, a law against schools for non-resident Negroes. At once, Andrew Judson, a colonizationist and lawyer of Canterbury, began her prosecution. The familiar arguments that education itself would

suffer and that the town would fast become a haven for disgruntled blacks elsewhere were heard on every hand, just as these
themes had played their part in the New Haven outcry shortly
before.[39]

Miss Crandall had few local friends, but among them was the
Rev. Samuel J. May of Brooklyn, Connecticut, an outspoken
but gentle Garrisonian and the only Unitarian minister in the
state. Years later, May told a large abolitionist gathering how
important Arthur Tappan's quiet role had been. When all seemed
lost, he said, the merchant wrote him, "Consider me your banker.
Spare no necessary expense. Command the services of the ablest
lawyers." Arthur Tappan recognized the significance of the case,
for it set a ruinous precedent of racial prejudice enforced by New
England law. In total expenditure, he gave some six hundred
dollars for legal and journalistic costs.[40]

The money was spent in vain. Miss Crandall won her case upon
appeal to the Connecticut Supreme Court on a technicality, but
public antipathy forced her to shut down her school. In addition,
the court evaded a clear-cut decision about the constitutionality
of the so-called "Black Law," which therefore remained in force
for a number of years.[41]

Once again Arthur Tappan had tested the depth of northern
hostility toward the black man, but the time was drawing near
when silent charity would be inadequate. Arthur Tappan was not
a moral coward, hesitant though he was at times. No conservative
institution could force him to surrender his principles; even the
pressure of economic retaliation was never to change his course.
As early as January, 1832, he had written Garrison, "I fear with
you that we are to see the free colored people subject to a cruel
persecution to make them disposed to emigrate. We have reason
to fear as a people the vengeance of Heaven for the sins [we are]
guilty of . . . to the [people] of Africa."[42]

This feeling of guilt was not alien to Garrison himself. At the
Negro convention in Philadelphia, he had peered through his
steel-rimmed glasses and remarked to the delegates that he never
rose to address a black audience "without feeling ashamed of
being identified with a race of men who have done you so much
injustice, and who yet retain so large a portion of your brethren
in servile chains."[43] Far from being a sign of emotional instability
or destructiveness, the abolitionists' sense of guilt was a creative
force. Under its influence, thousands of New Englanders and other

Americans were gradually prepared by antislavery polemics to recognize a feeling of national responsibility for Negro bondage. At times, to be sure, abolitionists were overly susceptible to feelings of shame, magnified perhaps by the romantic notions of their time, but their acute awareness of past and contemporary insensitivity to racial cruelty spawned a modern reform, even if the source of that perception lay deep in the heritage of eighteenth-century religious and political thought.

Arthur Tappan was never able to escape the conviction of his own depravity, instilled in him in childhood. Perhaps good works were his means of expiation and, paradoxically, an affirmation that sin had passed him by. Yet it can be argued that his mind, though strained by a heavy weight of scruples, must have been highly resilient to sustain them so well. His constructive achievements attested to his abilities and mental stamina. If the measure of "normal" behavior is the degree of conformity to society, Tappan must be called a peculiar, maladjusted man. But if the test is the capacity to overcome personal distress and follow a creative though unorthodox path, he was no crank. It was from his inner fears that the compulsion to reform sprang. In later years, he joined Lewis Tappan in accepting a form of Christian perfectionism, another way of escaping the bloodmark of total depravity. A restless conscience, goaded by the twin prods of a conviction of human sinfulness and a sense of election, drove him from one reform to the next, until slavery came to symbolize for him all the evil and corruption in the land. From his endowment of the Tract House to his association with Garrison, Tappan had progressed along a road toward spiritual satisfaction, a road that turned out to have no end.

From the grave of Sarah Tappan came the words, "I feel that I am depraved in the whole man; that in me naturally there is no good. . . ," and immediately following, the opposite and hopeful conclusion, "and it is my happiness that I may go to him as a guilty, weak and helpless creature. . . . He has promised never to leave nor forsake me, and I can trust his word. It is this comfort, my dear child, that I wish you to enjoy." Like her son, Sarah had feared that America was turning against God. She had expressed this conviction in pietistic terms, urging each individual to examine "how far he is instrumental in bringing down this judgment of God upon a guilty land."[44] In the characters of Arthur and Lewis, her sense of doom was translated into humanitarian goals; guilt about man's relation to God became guilt about man's relation to man, a healthy and constructive impulse. Such an impulse is more inspirational than the kind of bland do-goodism that is too easily forgotten when the going gets tough.

It is not strange that so powerful a force for action should create constant tensions. Beneath Arthur's quiet demeanor was a turbulence of emotion that he generally held rigidly in check. Occasionally, he burst forth with deep affection. "It was remarked," said Lewis, "that if he hurt the feelings of any one, by undue severity, he was quick to express regret. This he would do even to children, and sometimes with tears in his eyes." There was genuine love in the man, and when it appeared, as in the Crandall case or in his hopes for the New Haven school, his habit of mind loses something of its quixoticism. The balance, however, was hard to sustain. Quick to sympathy, quick to querulous, inhibited irritations, he sought an elusive stability in Christian reformation, in which dreams of recreating a bygone puritan haven and a vision of the American democratic promise intermingled. Denied the usual means of expression of love and anger by his infirmities, he had to use "deeds, not words" to save himself from crippling introspection, indecision, and despondency. " 'I ought never to have been married,' " he often said, " 'for my headaches make me so unsocial and unable to add to the happiness of my family.' "[45]

It is peculiarly difficult to judge a religious man's motives and accomplishments in terms either of his own professions or of accepted standards of conduct. "The novelist or dramatist can easily unmask a Tartuffe or Trusty Tompkins or the Rev. Mr. Stiggins, but Torquemada and Oliver Cromwell and Henry Edward Manning and Mr. Gladstone are far more difficult problems," wrote David Knowles.[46] If by some forgivable hyperbole, Arthur Tappan is admitted to this illustrious company, he poses the same dilemma. Sometimes heroic, sometimes shifty, he was ever fallible, always human. If one were to search the abolitionist host for a representative saint, neither he nor Lewis would pass the scrutiny of an honest devil's advocate. Indeed, if there was such a reformer, he is not to be found in these pages. Yet some abolitionists had their moments of greatness and self-sacrifice. Likewise, the Tappans cannot serve as examples of members of a misplaced class unable to cope with the realities of the world or as models of the destructive, neurotic American agitator. The

Tappans often seem alien to their own time and to ours. But they had inherited a rich cultural heritage, restricted in some ways though it appears in retrospect. It provided them with all the spiritual and mental equipment necessary for material success— yet they tried in some measure to identify themselves with people least endowed with their resources. That effort of sympathy, halting and imperfect perhaps, cannot be overlooked, scorned, or labeled unreal and twisted. Most clergymen and politicians did not even try to imagine what it was like to be another man's slave. The abolitionists at least made the attempt.

During the period when revelations of national iniquity weighed heavily upon the senior merchant's soul, his junior partner showed little anxiety for the fate of the black race in America. Lewis Tappan was not present at the Philadelphia convention in 1831; his children did not share the fears of their cousins in the New Haven riot. He did nothing in the defense of Prudence Crandall, and his interest in Garrison extended no further than reading the *Liberator* on a subscription that Arthur paid for.[47] Yet Lewis, too, was equipping himself for the plunge into antislavery, the most despised and most imaginative of American nineteenth-century reforms. When Arthur Tappan departed from the shades of Doubting Castle, to use Bunyan's allegory, and when he entered upon the open land of Beulah, brother Lewis was not far behind.

NOTES

1. LT, *Arthur Tappan*, 163; Wendell Phillips Garrison and Francis Jackson Garrison, *William Lloyd Garrison, 1805–1879* . . . (Boston, 1885–89), I, 55, picture opposite 56, 192, 220–21 (n. 4); and LT to William Lloyd Garrison (herinafter WLG), January 29, 1870, in *ibid.*, IV, 255.

2. *A Brief Sketch of the Trial of William Lloyd Garrison, for an Alleged Libel on Francis Todd of Newburyport, Massachusetts* (Boston, 1834 ed.), 7.

3. AT to Benjamin Lundy, May 29, 1830 (typewritten transcript), WLG MSS, Boston Public Library (hereinafter BPL). Austin Willey, *The History of the Antislavery Cause in State and Nation* (Portland, 1886), 29, 53, claims Eben Dole, an evangelical of Maine, gave half the sum for Garrison's release. Merton L. Dillon, *Benjamin Lundy and the Struggle for Negro Freedom* (Urbana, 1966), 128.

4. LT, *Arthur Tappan*, 42–43; New York *Evangelist*, April 10, May 15 and 22, 1830; *Priestcraft Unmasked*, July 15, 1830, final quotation; Garrison and Garrison,

Garrison, I, 266–67; John L. Thomas, *The Liberator, William Lloyd Garrison: A Biography* (Boston, 1963), 10–20.

5. AT to WLG, August 9, 1830, WLG MSS, BPL. On Garrison's congeniality, see Martin B. Duberman, "The Abolitionists and Psychology," *Journal of Negro History* (hereinafter *JNH*), XLVII (July, 1962), 183–91.

6. See David Brion Davis, "The Emergence of Immediatism in British and American Antislavery Thought," *MVHR*, XLIX (September, 1962), 209–30. See LT to Dr. Worcester, February 14, 1825, ltrbk. Cf. Barnes, *Antislavery Impulse*, 33–35; Thomas F. Harwood, "British Evangelical Abolitionism and American Churches in the 1830's," *JSH*, XXVIII (August, 1962), 287–306.

7. *Liberator*, July 30, 1831. See William W. Freehling, *Prelude to Civil War: The Nullification Controversy in South Carolina, 1816–1836* (New York, 1966), 49–86, a very convincing chapter; Dillon, *Lundy*, 12, for quotation from Jefferson, and 10–33; Donald G. Mathews, *Slavery and Methodism: A Chapter in American Morality, 1780–1845* (Princeton, 1965), 3–87, which explains the early fervor and rapid decline of Methodist antislavery; Arthur Zilversmit, *The First Emancipation: The Abolition of Slavery in the North* (Chicago, 1967), 226–29.

8. Garrison and Garrison, *Garrison*, I, 227, from *Liberator*.

9. Elizur Wright, *The Sin of Slavery and Its Remedy* . . . (New York, 1833), 20–21, 40, 42, 47. Cf. Barnes, *Antislavery Impulse*, 31–34, 42–44, 48–49, 101–3; see also Anne C. Loveland, "Evangelicalism and 'Immediate Emancipation' in American Antislavery Thought," *JSH*, XXXII (May, 1966), 172–88; John L. Thomas, "Antislavery and Utopia," in Martin B. Duberman, ed., *The Antislavery Vanguard: New Essays on the Abolitionists* (Princeton, 1965), 246–47; Donald G. Mathews, "The Abolitionists on Slavery: The Critique behind the Social Movement," *JSH*, XXXIII (May, 1967), 163–82.

10. Elizur Wright in *Liberator*, December 1, 1832; Wright, *Sin of Slavery*, 47. See also Mathews, "Abolitionists on Slavery," 166–67.

11. Thomas Wentworth Higginson, *Contemporaries* (Boston, 1899), 251; cf. Dwight L. Dumond, *Antislavery: The Crusade for Freedom in America* (Ann Arbor, 1961), 174; Barnes, *Antislavery Impulse*, 174–75.

12. *Spirit of the Pilgrims*, I (January, 1828), 14; *Liberator*, January 1, 1831.

13. Careful checking of the New York Manumission Society Minute Books at the New-York Historical Society did not reveal a single reference to AT. Charles C. Andrews, *The History of the New-York African Free-Schools* . . . (New York, 1830) suggests that local Negro abolitionists worked with this Society, but no white evangelicals were involved. AT was accused of disapproving of the Manumission Society's work, but that charge was denied in *Emancipator* (New York), September 21, 1833. Barnes, *Antislavery Impulse*, 213, n. 9, attempts to show that LT was a member of the Manumission Society but offers no explicit evidence. The brothers were, however, involved in the Phoenix Society, which had racially mixed membership and performed various educational services for the Negro community: LT, *Arthur Tappan*, 157–62.

14. *Liberator*, July 9, 1831.

15. Thomas H. Gallaudet, *A Statement with Regard to the Moorish Prince* . . . (New York, 1826); LT, *Arthur Tappan*, 141–42; P. J. Staudenraus, *The African Colonization Movement, 1816–1865* (New York, 1961), 162; *African Repository and Colonial Journal*, IV (October, 1828), 243–50.

16. Staudenraus, *African Colonization Movement*, 150–66. See also Thomas P.

Martin, "Some International Aspects of the Anti-Slavery Movement, 1818–1823," *Journal of Economic and Business History,* I (November, 1928), 137–48. Quotation, AT to Ralph Gurley, September 13, 1827, American Colonization Society (hereinafter ACS) MSS, LC; see also Isaac Orr to Gurley, February 20, 1829, ACS MSS, LC.

17. T. H. Gallaudet to Gurley, November 8, 1828, and John Tappan to Gurley, July 24, 1827, ACS MSS, LC; Staudenraus, *African Colonization Movement,* 159–61.

18. Staudenraus, *African Colonization Movement,* 76; LT to Knowles Taylor, May 22, 1828, ACS MSS, LC; diary, May 12 and 21, 1828; *African Colonization: Proceedings of the New York State Colonization Society* . . . (Albany, 1829); cf. Barnes, *Antislavery Impulse,* 210–11, n. 24.

19. "The Great Object Advanced," *African Repository,* IV (February, 1829), 379; *Report of the Proceedings at the Formation of the African Education Society* . . . (Washington, 1830), 5; Staudenraus, *African Colonization Movement,* 128; cf. Ralph V. Harlow, *Gerrit Smith, Philanthropist and Reformer* (New York, 1939), 60–65.

20. AT to Gurley, March 27, 1829, ACS MSS, LC, and AT in *Liberator,* July 6, 1833. Both references indicate that AT was well aware of the rum trade at this time.

21. AT to Gurley, March 27, 1829, ACS MSS, LC.

22. *Ibid.,* November 15, 1829.

23. *Ibid.,* September 27, 1830.

24. Gallaudet to Gurley, *ibid.,* June 8, 1830. See also June 21, 1830.

25. LT, *Arthur Tappan,* 146–47; *Rights of All* (New York), September 18, 1829; Robert A. Warner, *New Haven Negroes: A Social History* (New Haven, 1940), 54; Leon F. Litwack, *North of Slavery: The Negro in the Free States, 1790–1860* (Chicago, 1961), 123; WLG to S. S. Jocelyn, May 30, 1831, miscellaneous MSS, Yale University Library.

26. LT, *Arthur Tappan,* 137; William Lloyd Garrison, *An Address Delivered before the Free People of Color, in Philadelphia, New-York, and Other Cities, During the Month of June, 1831* (Boston, 1831), 27.

27. See General O. O. Howard (a founder of Howard University) to John Tappan, December 8, 1870, O. O. Howard MSS, Bowdoin College, in which Howard described the influence that Arthur's New Haven idea had upon his educational thinking.

28. LT, *Arthur Tappan,* 135–37; Henry Wilson, *History of the Rise and Fall of the Slave Power in America* (Boston, 1875), I, 365; *Minutes and Proceedings of the First Annual Convention of the People of Colour* . . . (Philadelphia, 1831), 15–16.

29. AT, quoted in Barnes, *Antislavery Impulse,* 28; *ibid.,* 26; Oliver Johnson, *William Lloyd Garrison and His Times* (Boston, 1880), 121; see also New York *Evangelist,* July 30, 1831; *Minutes . . . of the First Annual Convention,* 7; *Liberator,* September 21, 1831.

30. *Genius of Universal Emancipation* (Washington), July, 1831, 35; New York *Evangelist,* September 10, 1831. There is much reason to doubt Barnes's assertion in *Antislavery Impulse,* 33, 35, that LT and Theodore Weld were involved in antislavery meetings prior to the Philadelphia meeting of WLG and AT with Lundy and the Negro abolitionists. Supporting this criticism of Barnes is Roman

J. Zorn's "Garrisonian Abolitionism, 1828–1839," Ph.D. dissertation, University of Wisconsin, 1953, 134–35.

31. WLG to Ebenezer Dole, July 11, 1831, and Jocelyn to WLG, July 26, 1831, WLG MSS, BPL; Garrison and Garrison, *Garrison,* I, 259–60; Charles Tappan to Gurley, August 18, 1831, ACS MSS, LC (quotation); *The Abolitionist,* I (May, 1833), 77.

32. Garrison and Garrison, *Garrison,* I, 237–41 and notes, 260.

33. AT to WLG, September 12, 1831, WLG MSS, BPL; *ibid.,* October 18, 1831.

34. *Niles' Weekly Register* (Baltimore), October 1, 1831.

35. AT to WLG, October 18, 1831, WLG MSS, BPL.

36. *Ibid.,* October 18, 1831; *Liberator,* October 22, 1831; Garrison and Garrison, *Garrison,* I, 277–80; AT to WLG, January 21, 1832, WLG MSS, BPL.

37. *Columbian Centinel* (Boston), August 6, 1831; AT to WLG, January 21, 1832, WLG MSS, BPL.

38. AT to WLG, October 12, 1831, WLG MSS, BPL.

39. James Truslow Adams, "Prudence Crandall," *Dictionary of American Biography;* Samuel J. May, *Some Recollections of Our Antislavery Conflict* (Boston, 1869), 39–53; Russel B. Nye, *Fettered Freedom, Civil Liberties and the Slavery Controversy, 1830–1860* East Lansing, 1949), 83; John Codman Hurd, *The Law of Freedom and Bondage in the United States* (Boston, 1862), II, 45–46; Helen H. Catterall, *Judicial Cases Concerning American Slavery and the Negro* (Washington, 1926–37), IV, 430–33; *Liberator,* March 2 and April 6, 1833.

40. May, *Recollections,* 57–62; see also May in LT, *Arthur Tappan,* 158; Litwack, *North of Slavery,* 130.

41. Hurd, *Law of Freedom,* II, 46; Anna T. McCarron, "The Trial of Prudence Crandall for Crime of Educating Negroes in Connecticut," *Connecticut Magazine,* XII (Summer, 1908), 225–32.

42. AT to WLG, January 21, 1832, WLG MSS, BPL.

43. Garrison's remarks in *Address . . . before the Free People of Color,* 3.

44. ST to LT, August 8, 1807, in LT, *Memoir of Sarah Tappan,* 61; ST to AT, June [?], 1807, in LT, *Arthur Tappan,* 47. It is time for historians to recognize that Freudian psychologists and those behavioral scientists who adhere to the stimulus-response interpretation of social arrangements have not offered the only explanations of human behavior. See Duberman, "Abolitionists and Psychology," which applies the humanistic "growth psychology" of Gordon Allport and others to a historical setting; see also, Gerald W. McFarland, "Historians of American Reform: Working toward a Doorless Corner?," paper presented to the Society for Religion in Higher Education, Oberlin College, August, 1966. Cf. Elkins, *Slavery,* 147–92; Donald, *Lincoln Reconsidered,* 19–36; and George M. Frederickson, *The Inner Civil War: Northern Intellectuals and the Crisis of the Union* (New York, 1965).

45. LT, *Arthur Tappan,* 380, 392.

46. David Knowles, *The Historian and Character* (Cambridge, England, 1955), 9.

47. AT to WLG, September 12, 1831, WLG MSS, PBL.

CHAPTER SIX

National Antislavery Begins

O*n a visit* to New York in 1831, Charles Grandison Finney suggested that Lewis Tappan, then looking for a school for his two sons, send them to a manual labor school in western New York that was exciting much attention in evangelical circles. Out of this chance decision, Tappan was to be drawn directly into the abolitionist cause. Finney had pointed out that tuition was cheap, only $5.50 a quarter, and Tappan, still serving what he called his "penitentiary years," was most receptive. The Calvinism of George Washington Gale, the headmaster, and the country air created a finer academic atmosphere, he thought, than anything a school in New York could offer.[1]

Oneida Academy was just beginning its period of greatest influence as a training center for reformers. "Such a motley company!" one graduate reminisced. Among the students were Theodore Weld, Henry B. Stanton, and a number of lesser abolitionists, the western missionary Josiah Grinnell, an Indian with the "inelegant" name of Kunkapot, "young casuists, others the wards of rich reformers. . . , mulattoes removed from their sable mother . . . , enthusiasts, plow-boys and printers. . . ."[2] Gale, who had been Finney's theological tutor, believed in a strict physical and moral regimen. The day began with a call to prayers at four in the morning; recitation lasted till breakfast at six, and the rest of the day was spent in alternating sessions of work on the farm and classroom study. Meals were spartan: codfish and potatoes twice a week, a strip of meat for the four or five non-vegetarians, bread and milk at all the meals, and an occasional serving of pudding. Instead of idly stuffing their bodies, students crammed their souls with such fare as, "Which is the greater obstacle in the way of Christianity in the United States. . . , Roman Catholicism or Infidelity?"[3] Such was the atmosphere of Oneida.

Delighted with his sons' letters about the amazing doings at Oneida, Lewis Tappan went to the commencement exercises in August, 1831. William, he found, was in charge of fourteen pigs, getting up at dawn to carry their swill in pails on a yoke. The boys were only eleven and twelve, but seven hours of sleep a night and hard daily toil were supposed to be good for them. William survived the ordeal with no visible effects, but Lewis Henry was less fortunate. He died in 1838 of rheumatic fever at the age of seventeen. Happy and excited at first, however, the boys fell under the sway of Theodore Weld, their "Monitor-General," and introduced him to their father. Through Weld's influence, they underwent a short conversion, in January, 1832, though they rebelled against it during later adolescence. With parental pride, Tappan wrote out William's comments for brother Benjamin's edification: " 'Dear Father, How I long to tell you my feelings. I hope that through the mercy of God I have been brought to see my sins & submit to him who bled & died . . . for me.' "[4]

Tappan and Weld were soon fast friends. They were a study in contrasts. Tappan confessed that he could never be accused of wearing "a methodist garb, or having a sanctimonious glow." John Greenleaf Whittier later described what he considered an intellectual look about Lewis; actually, commerce and urbanity stamped his thin-lipped face with a certain flintiness. His blond hair was always neatly brushed. His face, washed in cold water, then rubbed vigorously with a crash towel, bore the coloration of an English schoolboy's. Weld, on the other hand, looked the part he actually played. Prone to mysticism, he sometimes lost himself in deep rumination, his swarthy face contorted by a scowl of concentration. His clothes never fitted, and his hair was long and unkempt. When he did turn his attention to the people around him, however, and discovered their problems, he radiated compassion.[5] It was the quality of his mind that marked him as one of the most gifted men of his day.

Outward appearance does not necessarily reflect inner convictions, for Tappan and Weld shared a faith in reform, an uncompromising hatred of "wrong principles," and a mutual love of revivals and Finney. Weld, however, sometimes criticized Tappan's severity. "It develops a peculiarity of your mind," he once had to say, "which you know you and I used to talk over when together years since—that is—a habit of coming to unfavorable conclusions about men on too *slight* grounds. . . ."[6] In spite of his fondness and respect for Tappan, Weld refused to join him in the New York free mission movement when invited to do so a few months after their meeting at Oneida. Instead, Weld limited their connection to long conversations about reform matters over his host's breakfast table, when he occasionally appeared in New York.[7] It was during these sessions that Tappan came to understand immediate abolitionism, although two years elapsed before he formally worked for the cause.

For most of 1832, Weld toured the countryside promoting Oneida's manual labor system, on behalf of which Tappan enthusiastically had founded a society in order to pay his expenses. Weld returned to New York in December, 1832, a firm abolitionist, having conferred with slaveholders and a tiny group of Garrisonians during his travels in the South and West. Arthur Tappan was most pleased to learn from him that Charles Storrs, president of Western Reserve College (later Western Reserve University, and then Case Western Reserve University) in Ohio, and Beriah Green and Elizur Wright, members of his faculty, had adopted Garrison's convictions. Storrs died a few months later; if he had lived and remained faithful to his principles, his college might have been the object of Arthur's munificence, which went instead to Oberlin Institute, not far from Western Reserve College at Hudson. Beriah Green was about Lewis Tappan's age; he was an intelligent, thoughtful orthodox minister and professor. Later, when George Washington Gale left to found Knox College in Illinois, Green assumed the direction of the Oneida Academy. The most dynamic and the youngest of the three was Elizur Wright, who taught mathematics. Like Green, he was from Connecticut, and he was as loyal to its traditions as his pious parents could have wished. He had already, when he was teaching school at Groton, Massachusetts, expressed his interest in the extraordinary conversion of Lewis Tappan from Unitarianism. Wright was to become one of Tappan's close friends in the early days of antislavery, sharing with him a fascination with the practical side of abolitionism—the publication of papers, the keeping of accounts, and office work, though he outshone Lewis as a writer and formulator of antislavery arguments. Arthur Tappan was aware that antislavery would have to make converts in the West; no likelier spot than the Western Reserve of northeast Ohio was available in which the task could be begun, since that area had mostly been settled by puritans from Connecticut. Arthur promised Weld that the little outpost at Hudson would receive his help *"in scattering light over the 'Reserve.'"*[8]

Unlike Storrs, Green, and Wright, Theodore Weld had not been influenced by Garrison's *Liberator*. Charles Stuart, an eccentric ex-major from the British India Army, had probably aroused Weld's interest in antislavery, since Stuart had long been associated with the English evangelicals before his arrival in western New York. Arthur Tappan hoped to bring Garrison and Weld together, writing Garrison that Weld, "a young man of very uncommon promise," ought to visit him in Boston. The proposal fell through, but Weld assured Garrison that their spirits were in harmony. While claiming ignorance of New England abolitionism, Weld assumed that it was

based upon that great bottom law of human right, that *nothing but crime can forfeit liberty*. That no condition of birth, no shade of color, no mere misfortune of circumstances, can annul that birth-right charter, which God has bequeathed to every being upon whom he has stamped his own image, by making him *a free moral agent*, and that he who robs his fellow man of this tramples upon right, subverts justice, outrages humanity, unsettles the foundations of human safety, and sacrilegiously assumes the prerogative of God; and further, tho' he who retains by force, and refuses to surrender that which was originally obtained by violence or fraud, is joint partner in the original sin, becomes its apologist and makes it the business of every moment to perpetuate it afresh, however he may lull his conscience by the vain plea of expediency or necessity.[9]

He had sounded the fresh idealism of the antislavery crusade.

Though pleased to find that Arthur Tappan "comes up to the mark, *just like himself*," Weld did not convince Lewis, in spite of their arguments. Tappan listened patiently and with interest, but he was momentarily entranced with helping the revivalist clergy work the miracle of personal conversion in the free mission enterprise. Weld did not give up, since he saw in Lewis just the sort of administrator who could make antislavery flourish as an organization, while leaving the ideas and rhetoric to the more intellectual leaders. Weld wrote to Elizur Wright that Lewis was "a glorious fellow. Sometimes perhaps a little presumptuous, but *very conscientious, highly intelligent,* and every whit as much moral courage as John Knox. If he gets fairly combustionized he will burn all before him."[10]

Although Tappan dated his conversion from a speech by Simeon S. Jocelyn that he heard in 1833, he actually owed his change of mind to Weld's persistence and the example that Arthur had begun to set before him. Still, Jocelyn's effort was a persuasive performance, appealing to Lewis' preferences for concrete information and religious instruction. Jocelyn concentrated on facts about the slave trade to the lower South, the absence of institutional and religious safeguards for the slave and his family, and the recent northern concessions to South Carolina in the settlement of the nullification controversy by means of a tariff reduction. Jocelyn warned that the southern opposition to the tariff was only an "entering wedge" for other means to protect slavery. "The scorpion whip of South Carolina dripping with the blood of the slave was shaken over Congress with mighty effect!" The southern slaveholders were alert to their interests, he continued, while the country had lost "$12,000,000" in revenue simply to appease "the monster" which had "struck the vitals of our republic." Characteristically, however, it took a riot to seal Tappan's commitment, although he had resolved to do his part for the cause by the beginning of summer, 1833.

In the meantime, Arthur Tappan had begun the *Emancipator,* an abolitionist journal, in the early spring. Charles Denison, the editor, was "an amiable, good & sometimes eloquent man," as Lewis once observed, but he had no flair for journalism. Furthermore, Arthur Tappan's abolitionism was still hesitant. Antislavery meant something less revolutionary-sounding to him than it did to Garrison. As Denison interpreted it, his employer's goal was that "the claim of property of men shall be forever and entirely set aside, BY THE OPERATION OF PUBLIC OPINION ON THE SLAVE LAWS UNDER ITS CONTROL." It was a wordy, ambiguous way of defining "immediate abolition," which was a crisp rallying cry, and typical of the *Emancipator's* plodding and uninspired style. Moreover, Tappan favored a transitional apprenticeship system, following the British pattern. "No restraint, actually indispensable to the welfare of the whole community, shall be removed," Denison promised. Nor did the paper attack slaveholders as sinners with the same virulence and conviction as did the *Liberator*. Persuasion was considered more effective than denunciation in winning over the Christian slaveholders upon whom Tappan's hopes of success rested. (Experience later taught the abolitionists to adopt Garrison's sterner measures.)[11]

By the fall of 1833, Arthur Tappan recognized that the time for action had come. By then he had taken several steps preparatory to the founding of an antislavery organization. Tappan paid for the printing and distribution of over seventy-six hundred *Emancipators*, which were sent to the northern clergy. Denison was jubilant; he wrote Elizur Wright that if Arthur Tappan's life were spared he would soon accomplish "moral wonders indeed." Moreover, Arthur Tappan had dispatched Garrison to England to obtain the blessing of British antislavery men. Also, he cut his last ties with the American Colonization Society by denouncing its supporters for condoning the export of "FOURTEEN HUNDRED BARRELS of the liquid poison" to Liberia. Other pamphlets, notably John Greenleaf Whittier's *Justice and Expediency*, were disseminated at his command, and Arthur arranged for Elizur Wright to come to New York in the fall as his antislavery secretary at an initial salary of five hundred dollars. (Wright was delighted with the prospect, since he was about to lose his position at the college because of the trustees' disapproval of his abolitionism.) In mid-June, Arthur wrote William Jay, son of the old chief justice, "Will you give me your opinion as to the expediency of forming an American Anti Slavery Socy? and of doing it now? The impulse given to the cause by the movements in England would, it appears to me, aid us greatly here."[12]

Judge Jay, a stalwart evangelical in spite of his Episcopalianism, wrote a lengthy reply. It exemplified the difficulty faced by any well-meaning moderate dealing with so explosive a question. Opposing Garrison's idea of immediate formation of a national society, Jay favored local organizations as a preliminary step. They should, he said, "be marked with great caution & prudence. Our Saviour when sending out his disciples, enjoined them to be, not merely harmless as doves, but also as wise as serpents." Garrison's New England Anti-Slavery Society had been unwise to admit a Negro member, for in so doing it aroused unnecessary suspicions in the South and North, Jay continued. Ignore but do not denounce the colonizationists, spell out limited political goals, and avoid interference with slavery in the South. Furthermore, Jay opposed making Negro suffrage in any state one of the goals and hoped that free Negroes would always be excluded from participation in the cause. In regard to freeing the slaves, he said, "It does not follow that because they are entitled to justice & humanity they are also entitled to political privileges. . . . Duty & policy in my opinion demand . . . that immediately on their emancipation they shall [not] be invested with the right of suffrage."[13] Even Arthur Tappan was not as circumspect as the ex-Federalist judge of Westchester County, but he did decide that a local effort was preferable to a national convention, while ignoring Jay's advice to exclude Negroes from participation.

Conferences followed with Joshua Leavitt, editor of the New York *Evangelist;* Elizur Wright; Peter Williams, Theodore S. Wright, and Samuel Cornish, three Negro ministers; William Goodell, editor of the *Genius of Temperance;* the Rev. George Bourne, editor of the anti-Catholic *Protestant Vindicator* and an early immediatist; and Denison of the *Emancipator.* When news of British emancipation of West Indian slaves reached America in September, these men agreed with Arthur Tappan that, in view of Britain's Parliamentary action during the summer, the moment was advantageous for starting a New York antislavery body.[14]

The abolition of West Indian slavery made a deep impression upon the United States. Great Britain was everywhere recognized as the leading power in the world, and its example aroused the admiration of northern humanitarians and the indignation of southerners. Yet an attempt to reproduce English success in the United States inflamed northern opinion as much as southern. New York City had become the chief port for cotton exports, and the city was filled with southerners on business and northern tradesmen with a stake in the products of slavery. Nor were white laborers sympathetic to a cause that could bring thousands of Negroes to compete with them for northern jobs.[15] Even before the little group of abolitionists announced publicly its intention to form the New-York Anti-Slavery Society, a newspaperman warned that the only way to cure the "phrensy of Garrison and Arthur Tappan" was by "cutting off their heads."[16]

It was unfortunate that Garrison's return from his visit with Wilberforce and Clarkson in England should coincide with the call for a new society. His anti-American remarks abroad fell on sensitive ears at home. In addition, the papers rehashed the old "church and state" theme. With rather un-Victorian bombast, James Watson Webb reprimanded those "who think it a marvelous proper occupation to sit at a window of a Sunday evening to watch the motions of fornication and sinners. . . . Such are the leaders in the crusade against the white people of the United States." Still smarting from Tappan's rebuke, colonizationists joined the general hue and cry, boasting that as soon as the abolitionists gathered at Clinton Hall they would shout them down.[17]

On the morning of October 2, the day of the announced inauguration of the new Society, Arthur Tappan had second thoughts. Fellow members of the Board of Trustees of Clinton Hall had censured him for leasing the premises for an abolitionist gathering, even though he had given more money to its construction than anyone else except John Jacob Astor. While Arthur favored delay, his brother insisted that plans proceed on schedule. Lewis suggested that Chatham Street Chapel be used instead, and the news was quickly passed by word of mouth. Meanwhile, James Watson Webb, John Neal, Ralph Gurley of the Colonization Society, and others posted notices urging "patriots" to assemble at Clinton Hall. When a large, angry mob reached the auditorium that evening, however, they found it deserted. Reassembling at Tammany Hall, the rioters were gaveled to order by Robert Bogardus, and a stream of invective from a succession of speakers whipped them to a frenzy.[18]

A short distance away, the abolitionists hurried through their business of adopting a constitution and electing officers, with Arthur Tappan, of course, chosen president. Just then, rioters were heard storming up the street. Someone had seen the abolitionists sneaking into the Chatham Chapel, and Bogardus had not been able to restrain a ragtag exodus from Tammany Hall. Cries of *"Garrison, Garrison, Tappan, Tappan, where are they, find them, find them"* filled the old theater.[19] (Garrison's whereabouts at this time is obscure; William Green, who was an antislavery merchant, or Arthur Tappan may have hidden him away, though Garrison claimed to have watched the crowd while posing as a spectator.)[20]

Quickly the reformers dispersed. Some retreated to a Sunday school meeting in an upstairs room, but policemen had to rescue them from bullies banging on the door. Down in the main lobby, the lights were out, but one tipsy rioter, with lantern and dagger, bumbled along after Arthur and Lewis. As the intruder passed, the janitor blew out his light, then slipped into the darkness, while the brothers fled out the back door unharmed.[21]

On the following day, some of the papers, notably Hale's *Journal of Commerce* and Evans' *Working Man's Advocate,* expressed mild regret at the disturbance, but other journalists were less reserved. In a style that only Garrison himself could equal, Webb announced that at last the city was safe from "this hugger-muggering, this packing together of a few straggling idlers, or malignant busy-bodies in the bar of a porter house," who misrepresented "the sentiments of the city." The fact that the New-York Anti-Slavery Society had been formed anyway disturbed him not a moment, for the riot had reduced the group "to the classical number of the fiddlers all in a row."[22]

Arthur Tappan replied to mob hysteria by signing a public address that set forth the aims of the Society and denounced mob violence in vigorous terms. While disclaiming any intention of arousing slaves to rebellion, the address did not mention all of those conservative principles that Jay had thought so necessary. Yet, mild in language and spirit, it was in pointed contrast to the violence that had just ended and consequently served as a useful precedent for future "disclaimers" following mob action.[23] So impressive was this announcement, which set forth the purposes of immediate abolition, that Robert Gurley had to admit that it was "working favorably for them in many minds."[24] Arthur Tappan's appeal, with its stress on British example and non-violent aims, was primarily directed to the "wise and good," the conservatives with whom he associated in evangelical affairs. Its defense of free speech and assembly was intended to attract this element, and to some degree it did impress, though not convert, them.

Garrison responded to the episode in his characteristic way, calling Webb "a cowardly ruffian" and William L. Stone, the colonizationist editor, "a miserable liar and murderous hypocrite." Garrison rejoiced in their accusation that abolitionists were the same evangelical party that urged Sabbath, temperance, and anti-vice reforms: "The question of slavery is a contest between light and darkness, justice and fraud, liberty and oppression, gospel truth . . . and the deceptions of the Devil and his servants. They have unintentionally defined the line of demarcation with the nicest accuracy [in calling us] the evangelical party."[25] Garrison's was also Lewis Tappan's interpretation of events; the two men were drawn together by a similar dissatisfaction with halfway proposals and caution. The contrast between "official" blandness and literary billingsgate, between the timidity of the *Emancipator* and the independence of the *Liberator,* was not to go unnoticed. Both, however, served their purposes. Arthur Tappan stood for responsible reform, but the ambiguity of his "immediatism" would have dwindled enthusiasm to a stifled yawn, while Garrison's recklessness easily might have become smothered in its own bombast. Without the aid of Arthur Tappan's money and prestige, abolitionism might not have included many of his distinguished friends, such as Jay and Gerrit Smith, who later joined the movement, and the merchants of his revivalist set. Without Garrison, there would have been a less vigorous and imaginative attack. His chief ability lay in goading the sluggish mass of well-intentioned citizens into taking a stronger antislavery position. Lewis Tappan perceived the importance of uniting the Garrisonians and the "respectable" element, and he served for a while as the bridge between them.

Garrison favored the immediate formation of a national society. Before committing himself, Arthur consulted with members of the Pennsylvania Abolition Society, one of the few pre-Garrisonian manumission groups to show interest in immediatism. Influenced by the riots and by the hesitations of the Quaker-led Philadelphia organization, Arthur postponed a convention tentatively set for October 29 until a more "efficient" time. Fearing that the initiative would be lost, Garrison and Lewis Tappan collaborated in persuading Arthur and his handful of merchant friends to agree to a date in early December.[26] Since the Quaker reformers of Philadelphia needed to be drawn more closely into the cause, the site chosen for the national convention was their city.

On December 4, 1833, sixty delegates gathered in Philadelphia, with Lewis Tappan representing the family while Arthur stayed at home. The sessions were so inspiring that the participants did not adjourn for meals; instead, they munched on crackers and drank cold water, a proper evangelical diet. One of the most memorable scenes for Lewis was Garrison's entrance with the Declaration of Sentiments, which he had finished after working all night. Tappan was just then giving a speech in which he called Garrison a man of boldness, imagination, and indeed prudence for following God's stern demands for righteousness rather than man's sinful desire for repose. Not all those present agreed with Garrison's point of view, by any means, but Tappan felt the Boston editor deserved a gesture of appreciation. Then the male participants joined in the solemn ritual of signing the Declaration, as momentous as Jefferson's, they thought.

The document to which Tappan attached his name was not a manifesto for bloody revolt or civil disruption. Garrison explicitly rejected "the use of all carnal weapons" by abolitionists or slaves, even though, he pointed out, the Founding Fathers had fought for freedom with the spilling "of human blood like water, in order to be free." He continued, "Their grievances, great as they were, were trifling in comparison with the wrongs and sufferings of those for whom we plead." One-sixth of the American population was nothing but "marketable commodities," without any means of security from the most brutal attacks "of irresponsible tyrants." For a country espousing the doctrine that all men are created in equality and holding to the tenets of the New Testament, slavery was more than a discrepancy; it was a national crime and a personal sin involving each one who condoned it. "Every man has a right to own his own body—to the products of his own labor—to the protection of the law—and to the common advantages of society," he asserted, in answer to charges that abolitionists were undermining the principle of property rights. It did not matter how long slavery had existed, for the principle of liberty was ageless and supreme, above all ungodly restraints. Therefore, the abolitionists were opposed to compensating slave-owners for what they ought never to have owned. If any person deserved remuneration, it was the slave. Garrison did, however, admit it to be true that the system was under state, not national, authority. Yet, he proposed efforts to end it wherever Congressional authority could be applied: in the territories and the Federal District; and (by means of the commerce clause) in interstate trade. After citing the pacific means by which the men of the free states were to abolish slavery and thus to put an end to the burden of their constitutional obligation to uphold it, he concluded:

We will do all that in us lies, consistently with this Declaration of our principles, to overthrow the most execrable system of slavery that has ever been witnessed upon earth . . . and to secure to the colored population of the United States, all the rights and privileges which belong to them as men, and as Americans—come what may to our persons, our interests, or our reputation. . . .[27]

He had merely expressed what many Americans one hundred and fifty years later would, at least theoretically, accept as the racial goal toward which the nation ought to press. Undoubtedly, the Declaration was fanatical talk as far as most southerners and northerners were concerned, but it was well within the structure of American ideals—in its references to the precedents established in 1776, in its careful admission of constitutional limitations, in its rejection of coercive means, and, above all, in its appeal to the Christian conscience. Abolitionism dealt with the weightiest of American problems, but, for most of its history, its advocates did not wander very far from the traditions of other, less difficult reform movements in our history.

The Tappan brothers held high positions in the new organization that emerged from the convention. As the most distinguished (certainly the wealthiest) of the abolitionists, Arthur Tappan received the presidency. Writing to Benjamin, Lewis Tappan commented, "They think rather better of A. T. than you seem to."[28] All members of the Executive Committee, to which Lewis was elected, were residents of New York City, a necessity in those days of slow travel. Moreover, Manhattan was the headquarters for most of the benevolent societies of the day. Garrison, secretary for foreign correspondence, was the only national officer for whom exception was made. Immediately, he informed his British friends of the formation of the American Anti-Slavery Society, and he received this endorsement in reply: "The excellent Constitution you have adopted, and the judicious choice of your officers, with that indefatigably devoted, great and good man, ARTHUR TAPPAN, as your President. . . , give assurance that you must conquer."[29]

The early days of antislavery were the purest and the best for the leaders of the movement, for all were united by a devotion to evangelical principles and to their humanitarian cause. Lydia Maria Child recalled in 1880 that "mortals were never more sublimely forgetful of self" than the antislavery men and women of the 1830's, whom the Holy Spirit safely guided through persecution and distress. "How quick the 'mingled flute and trumpet eloquence' of [Wendell] Phillips responded to the clarion-call of Garrison! . . . How wealth poured in from the ever open hands of Arthur Tappan, Gerrit Smith, the Winslowes, and thousands of others. . . !" During the brassy days of Chester Arthur and Blaine, such nostalgia was understandable.

Like all reform movements since the dawn of the modern epoch, abolitionism began with that unclouded faith that a new world was possible once the hearts of men were reached. "Let information be circulated," said Garrison, and Americans "cannot long act and reason as they now do." Although slavery had existed since the beginning of history, these reformers expected abolition to come within their own lifetimes. Elizur Wright, the new secretary of the Society, criticized his friends for thinking that slavery would only last another five years; "it may be," he said, "that I shall live long and still die before the happy jubilee comes, but come it will."[30] Unfortunately, the general optimism had its darker side, too. Once the institution was gone, the millennium that the abolitionists anticipated did not arrive. Their nineteenth-century concepts of society, economics, and the nature of man did not prepare them for the racial prejudice and violence that followed. Yet their shortsightedness served them well as a stimulus for risking their lives and careers in the 1830's to right the wrongs of American, and universal, history.

Hardened by business vicissitudes and shrewdly realistic by temperament, Lewis Tappan was no sentimentalist. Although an able speaker on occasion, he shared only vicariously the emotions of Theodore Weld, the British antislavery orator George Thompson, and Wendell Phillips when they addressed a steady succession of hostile crowds. Rather, he had to content himself with the routines of office management—snatching a moment to post an antislavery tract to an inquiring friend—and the time-consuming totaling up of columns of receipts and debits. Whittier described Lewis Tappan as "jaunty, man-of-the-world." Such an individual was not likely to have illusions about the antislavery "blessed" either. Privately, he gossiped that some delegates at Philadelphia "had no more religion than they ought to have, to say the least."[31] (He may have been referring to the Quaker delegates, since he had no use for the combination many saw in them of materialistic outlook and quietism.) Also, he scoffed at the timid ones who recoiled at the boldness of Garrison's Declaration of Sentiments.[32] Like all the original immediatists, Lewis had indeed become "thoroughly combustionized," as Weld had sensed he would a year before.

Beneath Lewis' crusty mannerisms, Elizur Wright found an ideal supervisor. Wright, who later proved his own business talents by becoming a brilliant life insurance actuary, had a mind "keen as a Damascus blade." At his dingy office on Spruce Street, he needed help in preparing mailing lists and establishing the routines of finance; Tappan, he thought, was just the type for this kind of enterprise. "Bro. L. T. is a most wonderful man for the dispatch of business, and truer than the needle to the pole," Wright confided to Weld, then at Cincinnati, "but perhaps his decision sometimes goes ahead of his judgment." Unfortunately, Lewis still owed his creditors too much money to tolerate a reformer's small stipend.[33]

Nonetheless, after the Pearl Street store was locked for the night, Tappan did almost as much as Wright himself. Whenever Lewis left his business duties, he would "write two editorials, attend a meeting of the American Antislavery Society's executive committee, step into [a] prayer-meeting and pray or deliver an exhortation," as a friend later recalled, "and wind up by sitting in a church session, and addressing a temperance meeting; all the time would be in a hurry, but never flurried, and would seem perfectly at home in each of these vocations."[34] When various editors and officers were absent, Lewis frequently took their places. For example, in the fall of 1834, he filled in for Leavitt at the *Evangelist*, for William Goodell, the *Emancipator*'s new editor, and for Wright at the office, all at the same time. There was little formality or division of labor at headquarters, but the bustle and chatter, the flow of visitors, the carting of pamphlets from the stock room gave the immediate appearance that antislavery was thriving.[35]

In wider view, despite the activity of Lewis Tappan and his friends national antislavery seemed to be slumbering, as if the very act of formation had exhausted all initiative. From Boston, Garrison complained in March, 1834, that he felt as if he were battling slavery by himself.[36] The trouble lay at the very heart of the movement, in the leadership Arthur Tappan gave the Society. As president and chairman of the executive committee, he was too self-conscious and reserved to command a large personal following or inspire others. Luckily for the shy New Englander, most other worthies who led evangelical societies were seldom more articulate or dynamic than he was, since they were supposed to represent the "respectability," not the vigor, of their causes. As long as he personally controlled the *Emancipator* it would continue to be soporific in spite of the journalistic experience of Goodell (and he was long-winded). Arthur Tappan could count on the support of two other wealthy merchants on the executive committee, William Green and John Rankin, both of whom had helped Lewis establish the Chatham Street Chapel. John Rankin owned a dry-goods store up the street from Arthur Tappan and Company, and Green, another Connecticut immigrant, was a real estate speculator. Often siding with these men was Abraham L. Cox, a doctor at New York Hospital on Broadway.[37] Although united in their loyalty to reform with the members whose entire profession it was to advance the cause—Wright, Goodell, and Leavitt—the businessmen and the physician had many interests to protect besides antislavery.

Unlike Lewis Tappan, Arthur and his merchant friends were rather suspicious of Garrison. During his trip to England, Garrison had managed his finances so haphazardly that he had confused the punctilious Arthur Tappan, loser in the muddle of loans. Already wary of Garrison's editorial style, which alienated their religious acquaintances, the committee refused to give him the funds he urgently requested in December, 1833. Excusing their decision, Abraham Cox wrote Garrison, "They have a kind feeling, but merchants are always exact & calculating in business affairs—and they have shown it in reference to whatever business has been before them."[38] Later, the committee relented, but the matter, small though it was, revealed Arthur Tappan's disapproval of Garrison's kind of reform, and it portended future trouble between the two allies.

Arthur Tappan also guided the financial policy of the Society along strict paths of economy. Liable for the debts of the unincorporated Society, he and the other wealthy patrons held expenses within the bounds of income as much as possible. Spartan himself, he expected frugality in others. Antislavery agents, as they were recruited, were expected to survive more on zeal than on a decent salary. A wise insurance against bankruptcy, the policy sometimes hindered flexibility and clipped initiative. Once, in 1836, Elizur Wright burst out in frustration, "Our friend A. T[appan] should be disabused of the idea that if he . . . and two or three others should fail to pay their notes at *three o'clock* some day, the cause of God's oppressed would fall through!" Even the devoted Lewis complained after one committee meeting that his colleagues were too "parsimonious."[39]

Not all the early difficulties with finance, a perpetual problem, were Arthur Tappan's fault. The times were skittish for both business and reform. Nonetheless, Arthur Tappan, Green, and Rankin proved exceptionally generous. According to Lewis, his brother donated three thousand dollars annually for the first few years, some of his gifts being hidden in private subsidies. The sum may not seem large, but it should be remembered that Arthur was probably still committed to projects antedating the abolition movement. Published records for the period from December, 1833, to September, 1834, show that Arthur Tappan gave $2,750; Rankin, $1,100; Green, $957; Lewis Tappan, $275 ($250 of the sum in September, when his financial status had improved); Abraham Cox, $100. The three largest givers accounted for thirty-seven per cent of the total budget, $13,000.[40] Just as antislavery got under way after the Philadelphia meeting, however, Andrew Jackson withdrew U. S. Treasury funds from the Bank of the United States. The result was panic on Wall Street and the beginning of an erratic course for the national economy.

The Tappan brothers, like General Jackson himself, were hard-money men with little fondness for banks and even less liking for credit, but, being businessmen, they disliked worrisome changes in financial policy. Lewis' prescription for rebuilding confidence was the restoration of a national bank, with proper safeguards carefully defined in the charter. Presenting his views to Benjamin, an ardent opponent of the Bank of the United States, he added genially, "If the Old General knows what I have written he will probably appoint Major Downing [a fictional political buffoon], myself, jointly, Sec. of the Treas. Therefore don't inform him."[41] It may have been heavy-handed, but the comment revealed a humorous streak in Lewis altogether absent in the melancholy Arthur. The crisis, however, compelled the resourceful Elizur Wright and his employers, the Executive Committee, to seek steadier supplies of funds among the growing rank and file of evangelical abolitionists in the interior. "Indeed," the secretary warned Amos Phelps, the first full-time agent in the field, "the idea that friend Tappan will do *all* the giving must be broken up."[42] Arthur Tappan and his committee established a type of religious program familiar to other benevolent societies. Antislavery agents, at first local volunteers, were to stir up discussion about the "SIN OF SLAVERY," particularly among religious country people. As chairman of the Agency Committee, the president instructed lecturers to "call on ministers of the gospel and other leading characters, and labor specially to enlighten them. . . . Ministers are the hinges of community, and ought to be moved. . . ." The Tappan regime encouraged the growth of auxiliary chapters throughout the North, the founding of pamphlet repositories, the holding of Monthly Concerts of Prayer for the Enslaved (on first Mondays), and the infusion of antislavery principles into other evangelical societies, clerical assemblies, and religious journals.[43]

In retrospect, this concentration upon the religious community may appear narrow, but in the early years, at least, the plan was the most likely to be effective. Few abolitionists, not even Garrison himself, would have quarreled at the time with the program. In harmony with his previous plan of action for missionary work, Arthur Tappan now set his heart upon two operations, the Valley project to cover the grass roots of evangelical growth and a local effort to win those middle-class churchgoers who supported and led the benevolent institutions in New York. Like the Rev. James Milnor, the Episcopalian evangelical, Arthur Tappan still had faith in "that grand moral machinery which the Spirit of Jehovah has put in operation. . . ."[44] He entrusted his Valley enterprise to Theodore Weld at Cincinnati and later to Finney at Oberlin. Lewis Tappan took charge of the local situation.

To recruit a loyal band of followers in the city, Tappan began with territory he knew best, the churches of the Third Presbytery, seat of Yankeedom in New York. With William Green, he organized a young men's society and a female chapter, drawing a highly active membership of evangelicals. Two Third Presbytery ministers also joined the movement, Henry G. Ludlow and Samuel H. Cox. The latter, a brother of Abraham L. Cox, who was on the Executive Committee, had Quaker, merchant, and Philadelphia origins. Like the anti-Catholic Reverend George Bourne, another early abolitionist of New York, Cox was a religious bigot, who turned against Quakerism as "Judas-like sorcery" and "infidelity in drab." With such leaders as Cox and Ludlow in the vanguard, Lewis Tappan's antislavery associates in the Third Presbytery linked New York City abolitionism to rural orthodoxy.[45] It would appear that many New York antislavery men and women were really transplanted country people.

The Tappan brothers' attempt to influence the national benevolent societies proved less successful, though it was more ambitious, than the work in the Third Presbytery. First and biggest target was the American Bible Society, favorite of the "Simon-pure blue" Presbyterians. Buttressed by Arthur Tappan's personal guarantees, the abolitionists voted at the May, 1834, anniversary meeting to give $5,000 toward a fund of $20,000 from which the Bible people were to supply the 460,000 slave families of the South with Holy Scriptures. This time Arthur Tappan received not the glad response he had come to expect but an unmistakable snub. The Bible Society did not re-elect him to its managerial board and refused his offer. Lewis Tappan made matters worse by tactlessly suggesting that the evangelicals should withhold their funds until the Bible group surrendered. At least one philanthropist was outraged; Gerrit Smith, a wealthy patron of the American Colonization Society, sniffed, "One Benevolent Society putting the screws of coercion on another!" He added that the incident simply furnished one more example of the abolitionists' "clamorous bigotry," a charge most evangelicals supported.[46] Apparently, Lewis Tappan's blunder helped delay Gerrit Smith's withdrawal from the Colonization Society. Evangelicals like Smith saw the Scripture scheme as an obviously Machiavellian device to embarrass the conservative management of the Bible Society and to publicize antislavery. Only two per cent of the 460,000 slave families contained members who could read. Though frustrated year after year in their attempts, the Tappan brothers never gave up hope of converting the Bible Society and other similar groups to their antislavery program.[47]

In the spring of 1834, Lewis Tappan organized a meeting that created a furor in the city and led to antislavery's first bid for national publicity. The antislavery week of May, 1834, was more exciting than any previous celebration of the evangelical front. Combining their spring shopping in the city with a pilgrimage, country people arrived in New York earlier, and stayed later, than usual. In a bid for the center of the stage at the Chatham Street theater, abolitionists boldly announced that they were presiding at the "funeral of colonization."[48] To prove the claim, Lewis Tappan arranged a special meeting at the end of the so-called "Holy Week." Thomas C. Brown, a Negro carpenter who had just returned from Liberia, agreed to a public interrogation on the wretched state of affairs there. Before a packed crowd at the Chatham Street Chapel, Lewis Tappan asked him a number of questions and received sensational but matter-of-fact replies about rum-drinking, slave-trading, and conditions of health and religion. Colonizationists present, including R. R. Gurley of the national Colonization Society, rudely interrupted and accused the two of collusion. The meeting finally broke up in a scuffle and an uproar, and the city press began another campaign against the abolitionists. Within a month, Lewis became as notorious locally as his brother. Newspapers declared that there was a "deep laid plan among these conspiring sectarians to bring us back to the settled gloom and superstitions of the dark ages. . . ."

It soon became apparent to both brothers that it was next to impossible to conduct abolitionism in the manner of a drawing-room prayer meeting. Even mild-mannered "un-Garrisonian" abolition was too strong a reform for New Yorkers to tolerate. An Irish-Catholic editor asked, "Why should the sable race of Africa, to whom the inscrutable wisdom of providence has denied the power of intellect . . . and the grace and whiteness of form, presume to enter the lists of human perfection with . . . superior grades of society . . . ?" (No matter how anti-Negro Irishmen were on other occasions, however, they apparently had less to do with the violence that soon erupted than did older groups of Americans.)[49]

Throughout the following month, the city seethed with antiabolitionist slanders circulated by the press. There had been an election riot in April, and the population was still in an excitable mood. Furthermore, unemployment was increasing rapidly, being estimated at one-eighth of the population in 1833. Fear of Negro competition in the labor market had as much to do with the opposition to antislavery reform as did the intermarriage issue. Nevertheless, racial mixing was a good excuse for indignation. William Green was supposed to have entertained Negroes for dinner in order to introduce them to his spinster daughters. Meanwhile, Samuel H. Cox had allegedly called Jesus Christ a black man from his pulpit, and H. G. Ludlow was said to have officiated at the marriage of a white woman and a Negro.[50] Prejudice, not disapproval of immediate abolition as such, was the real cause of the rioting that followed, in which Negroes, more than their white friends, were the victims of terrible pillage and destruction.

It was traditional for the fourteen thousand Negroes of the city to celebrate New York State Emancipation Day on the Fourth of July. On that date in 1827 the few remaining Negro slaves in the state became free, an extraordinary condition for their race among the geographic subdivisions of North America.[51] Each year, dressed in "outrageous costumes," they marched down the streets banging drums, blowing trumpets, and drinking rum and cider. To abolitionists as well as to the Negro religious leaders, the celebration was scandalous and disheartening.[52] In 1834 Lewis Tappan, as an alternative to that carousing, threw open the doors of Chatham Street Chapel for a special Negro service of commemoration on Friday the Fourth. Just as he completed a "forcible and impressive" reading of the Declaration of Sentiments to the mixed audience, a mob filled the galleries and began to hoot and stamp. When two choirs of Negroes and whites sang a new hymn from the always busy pen of John Greenleaf Whittier, a cascade of prayer books and epithets descended, but a squad of watchmen from the mayor's office arrived in time to prevent further disorder.[53]

Rumors continued to feed public passions; there were murmurs that proslavery merchants had ordered their porters and draymen to lie in wait for Lewis Tappan, "expressly to tar and feather" him.[54] On the evening of July seventh, a small congregation of Negroes occupied the Chapel, but the members of a group called the Sacred Music Society arrived for a rehearsal and ordered them to clear out immediately. Refusing to do so, the Negroes soon found themselves beseiged by rioters, who poured in from the streets, hurling benches down from the balconies.[55]

The sexton of the chapel ran breathlessly down the road to Tappan's new home on Rose Street, where Lewis was holding a Monthly Concert for the Enslaved. Quickly sending his friends away, Tappan rushed to the scene but found that the police had already scattered the mob. While he was inspecting the damage at the Chapel, Susan Tappan, her children, and three domestics heard a swelling crowd gathering on Rose Street, shouting for her husband to come out. Once again, Tappan hastened along the narrow streets, pushed his way through the mob "amidst a tremendous noise, mingled groans, hisses, and execrations," and slammed the door of his house behind him. A band of watchmen dispersed the rowdies outside.

On the following afternoon, with threats of further rioting in the air, Lewis Tappan took his family to Harlem Village, at the other end of the Island. William L. Stone, James Watson Webb, Mordecai Noah, and other editors printed their usual diatribes and commended the rioters for their civic spirit. Even the weather conspired against the abolitionists, for a blanket of hot, muggy air settled over the city. That night, a mob, led by a man on a white charger, returned to Rose Street.[56] It was a quiet neighborhood, mainly inhabited by solid mechanics and up-and-coming businessmen. Wheeling his horse at the lower entrance of the street, the leader pointed toward Lewis Tappan's home, opposite a neatly painted Quaker meetinghouse. With a roar, the vandals smashed open the door, poured inside, and began hurling the furnishings out of the windows. "Battenders" and "Huge Paws," the city's gangs of butcherboys and day laborers, did the actual dirty work, while "respectable" merchants and even a deacon or two watched and applauded them. His face hidden, Arthur Tappan stood aside, observing the proceedings. The toughs built a huge pile of bedding, pictures, furniture, and window frames in the center of the street. Soon, the shadows from the bonfire's glow danced grotesquely on the walls of the ruined house and the Quaker hall opposite. Outnumbered and thoroughly frightened by the size of the crowd, the night watchmen fled to their stationhouse and did not reappear until the worst was over. Then the crowd gave three cheers for Colonel Webb and left the scene as the flames died.[57]

The Tappans returned the following day. Brave and uncomplaining, Susan Tappan picked through her possessions. Later, her husband remarked proudly, "When my wife saw the large chimney glass (which we purchased 18 years ago and which I have often thought looked too extravagant) was demolished, she laughed and said, 'you have got rid of that piece of furniture that troubled you so much whenever we had prayer meetings in the room.' "[58] The *Courier* and *Enquirer* reported that only a window was broken while a group of gentlemen peacefully demonstrated. In order to advertise his ordeal, Lewis Tappan left his home unrepaired for the rest of the summer to serve as a "silent Anti-Slavery preacher to the crowds who will flock to see it."[59]

Callously, the city authorities reacted with an indifference that was ultimately as menacing to their own interests as to those of the abolitionists. Growing bolder, the rioters planned a similar fate for the Chatham Street Chapel, the office of *McDowall's Journal*, the homes of William Green, John Rankin, Samuel Cox, and Ludlow, and, above all, Arthur Tappan's store. In the face of the threat, the mayor, a Tammany Democrat named Cornelius Lawrence, belatedly placed the city under martial law and called up elements of the city militia. It was understood, however, that the soldiers were to deal leniently with rioters and were not to use their firearms under any circumstances. In the course of the night, a dozen Negro homes, one of the Manumission Society's African schools, and the Negro church of Peter Williams were gutted. Episcopal Bishop Onderdonk forced Williams to resign from the Anti-Slavery Society to placate the mob and to dissociate the denomination from malevolent radicalism. Under able tacticians, the rioters, often forewarned by squads of runners, escaped the slow-moving militia men and briskly took over sections of the city, particularly the Sixth Ward, the chief Negro area. Fighting off a cavalry attack behind barricades in front of Ludlow's church, one mob dismantled the pipe organ and then hurried off, leaving the soldiers and their horses still struggling through upturned wagons and barrels.[60]

Meanwhile, another band of marauders gathered in Hanover Square. Simeon Jocelyn, mingling in the crowd, heard someone mutter, " 'These Tappans . . . are always making trouble; they tried to get up Sunday mail laws. . . . *it is time they were stopped.*' " Inside his beseiged store Arthur passed out an estimated thirty-six stands of arms to his clerks and friends. As they listened to the thumps of an awning-post ramming against the door, Arthur Tappan gave the orders (as one clerk recalled): " 'Steady, boys. Fire *low*. Shoot them in the legs, then they can't run!' " Just then the mayor and a body of troops arrived.[61] The reformers' attachment to non-violence remained untested.

Mayor Lawrence had finally taken action, chiefly because rumor had it that the mobs were about to begin a general looting of houses and stores belonging to the wealthy. As long as Negroes and a few isolated white men were the targets, he had not cared. Overnight, the press came out staunchly on the side of law and order. "The military will *fire,* and the rioters will be swept down by the score, unless they cease to trample the laws and the Constitution under their feet," an editor warned. With the streets heavily patrolled by re-enforcements sent from Albany, the city finally simmered down after a week of near anarchy.[62]

For much of the summer remaining, Lewis Tappan was in Brookline with his family. It was painful for him to visit the city.

"In walking down town," he wrote Weld, "I could bear the *dignified* looks of colonization acquaintances, but the affectionate greetings of sympathetic friends almost overcame me." In a statement of his idealism, he concluded: "It is true I have advocated Anti-Slavery principles, [but I] have done nothing contrary to law or propriety, 'neither can the[y] prove the things whereof they accuse me'; but exercising the privileges of an American citizen I have contended earnestly for the doctrines of Immediate Emancipation, and still mean to do it come what will to my person, property, or reputation. The cause is a righteous one. It is, I believe, dear to the heart of the Savior."[63] His religious convictions had at last found form and meaning in the abolitionist cause, and this sense of commitment he would never lose.

Like the Clinton Hall riot, this incident provided Arthur Tappan with a chance to advertise abolitionism, the moderation of its leadership, and the malevolence of the enemy. He and John Rankin issued a placard the day after the attack on his silk store. It denied the newspapers' charges that abolitionists believed in racial "mongrelization" and wanted "to dissolve the Union or to violate the Constitution. . . ." Shortly afterward, another "disclaimer" from the Executive Committee reached the mayor's desk. This one repeated Tappan's denials and called for equal protection before the law. In its conclusion, the signers made a show of independence of spirit by pledging grandly "to live and die by the Constitution of our Society, and the Declaration of the National Anti-Slavery Convention." Some were disgruntled by the general tone of apology, all the same; Elizur Wright confided to Beriah Green that at the next rendezvous with "the honorable mob" abolitionists would not be so pusillanimous. "Besides, 'amalgamation' is too small a crime to be worth a *disclaimer*," he concluded with impatience. Gustave de Beaumont, Alexis de Tocqueville's fellow observer of the American scene, happened to reach the same conclusion. Tappan's apologetic notices, he reasoned, were just another example of the "tyranny" of majoritarian opinion in America.[64]

Immediately after the disorders, antislavery action came to a standstill. Lewis Tappan, William Green, Arthur Tappan, and others stayed out of town for most of the summer, while a skeleton force remained at headquarters under the threat of more riots. Unwilling to complain of the exodus, Elizur Wright announced that Arthur Tappan's "whole soul never seemed so enlisted."

120

Indeed, the merchant paid for the circulation of fifteen thousand *Emancipator Extras* before leaving for New Haven, perhaps partly because the sheet contained the disclaimer of amalgamationism and other protestations of his temperateness.[65]

In the long run, though, the riot helped the cause, if not the Negro homeowners and storekeepers picking through the ruins of their meager possessions. News of antislavery doctrine and the persecution of its white advocates spread throughout the nation. Little was said about the destruction in the Negro sections of town, but even the London *Times* reported the ransacking of "Louis" Tappan's house.[66] As James Gillespie Birney, a recent antislavery convert from Kentucky, remarked, the riots "will not deter a single friend worth having, and if I mistake not, they will alarm the considerate who have not been our friends, when they are thus brought to see in what danger the very principles of our government stand when brought in opposition to the principle of slavery. . . ."[67] The disorder also made a deep impression upon the leaders of New York society, and in equally dangerous times a year later they quickly rallied to curb excesses. In addition, the rioters had drawn abolitionists together under their "glorious leader," as Wright called Arthur Tappan.

The riotous summer became a time of re-dedication. In a letter to Weld, Wright described the spirit that prevailed at national headquarters. "The ferment here has been a severe trial to some of our wealthiest members, and considering that their business habits have necessarily given them a dread of popular agitation, it is astonishing that they have borne it so well. . . . Our hearts are wonderfully knit together." As if to underline the determination of the Tappans' Executive Committee to carry on without a pause, Wright continued, *"We want your list of names for the Valley."*[68] The secretary and the two merchant brothers were as much concerned with antislavery's growth in Ohio as in their own city.

Elaborate preparations, for which Arthur Tappan paid the bills, were made for the enterprise. He had already sent Lyman Beecher to Cincinnati, "The London of the West," and had guaranteed, for as long as he could afford it, to pay Beecher's salary as president of Lane Seminary. Next to Finney, Tappan thought of Beecher as one of the evangelicals' "best generals," who "should occupy the very seat of Western warfare. . . ." With Tappan paying their expenses, Weld and an eager band from Oneida Academy joined Beecher at Walnut Hills, which overlooked Cincinnati, the Ohio River, and the Kentucky slaveland beyond.[69] From this source at Lane, the Tappan brothers expected an antislavery tide to roll eastward.

NOTES

1. Finney to Weld, March 17, 1831, Weld MSS, Clements Library; LT to Mrs. Jonathan Bigelow, December 1, 1847, ltrbk.; LT to George Bond, December 27, 1833, George Bond MSS, BPL; New York *Evangelist*, June 18, December 17, 1831; *First Report of the Trustees of Oneida Academy* (Utica, 1828).

2. Josiah Bushnell Grinnell, *Men and Events of Forty Years* . . . (Boston, 1891), 30.

3. *Western Recorder* (Utica), May 18, 1830; Rochester *Observer*, May 12, 1831.

4. William Tappan to LT, January [?], 1832, in LT to BT, March 19, 1832, BT MSS, LC; Huntington Lyman to Weld, n.d. (1880's), Weld MSS, Clements Library; cf. Benjamin Thomas, *Theodore Weld, Crusader for Freedom* (New Brunswick, 1950), 25.

5. Quotation, LT to BT, March 19, 1832, BT MSS, LC; John Greenleaf Whittier, "The Antislavery Convention of 1833," offprint in Johns Hopkins University Antislavery Collection, Vol. 10, No. 12, 167; Thomas, *Weld*, 6–8; Grinnell, *Men and Events*, 27–28.

6. Weld to LT, May 21, 1836, Slavery Box II, New-York Historical Society.

7. Julia Tappan to Weld, August 30, 1886, Weld MSS, Clements Library.

8. LT to BT, March 19, 1832, BT MSS, LC; Huntington Lyman to Weld, n.d. (1880's), Weld MSS, Clements Library; Thomas, *Weld*, 33, 36, 37; Barnes, *Antislavery Impulse*, 32–33; Weld to Wright, January 10, 1833, and Wright and Beriah Green to Weld, February 1, 1833, in Barnes and Dumond, *Weld Letters*, I, 100, 105; AT to WLG, June 29, 1832, WLG MSS, BPL; *Abolitionist*, I (February, 1833), 29; Wright to his wife, April 9, 1833, Wright MSS, LC.

9. AT to WLG, December 12 and 21, 1832, WLG MSS, BPL; Weld to WLG, dated January 1, 1832 (actually, 1833), *ibid.*

10. Weld to Wright, January 10, 1833, Barnes and Dumond, *Weld Letters*, I, 99–100; LT to BT, January 8, 1833, BT MSS, LC.

11. *Emancipator*, May 18, June 15, July 13, 1833 (quotations); Leavitt in *National Anti-Slavery Standard* (New York), October 24, 1844; Charles W. Denison to Wright, March 15, 1833, Wright MSS, LC; Davis, "Emergence of Immediatism," 209–10, n. 2.

12. Garrison and Garrison, *Garrison*, I, 345 and n.; LT, "The Olden Time," n. 1, dated May 18, 1869, scrapbook; John A. Pollard, *John Greenleaf Whittier, Friend of Man* (Boston, 1949), 116–18; LT, *Arthur Tappan*, 165–67; Gurley to Philip R. Fendall, October 1, 1833, AT to Gurley, June 26, 1833, Joseph Tracy to Gurley, May 16, 1833, ACS MSS, LC; see also *Liberator*, July 6, September 14, 1833; *Emancipator*, May 1 and 8, June 1, July 24 and 30, 1833; AT to Lewis Laine,

March 26, 1833, *African Repository,* IX (May, 1833), 65–68; Wright to Elizur Wright, Sr., November 2, 1833, Wright MSS, LC; AT to Amos A. Phelps, September 12 and 19, 1833, Amos A. Phelps MSS, BPL; AT to William Jay, June 18, 1833 (quotation), William Jay MSS, Jay House, Mt. Kisco, N.Y.; Wright to Phelps [?], 1833, Weston MSS, BPL; Denison to Wright, March 15, 1833, Wright MSS, LC; Wright to Charles Backus Storrs, President, August 31, 1833, Frederick C. Waite MSS, Case Western Reserve University Library.

13. Jay to AT, June 24, 1833, Jay MSS, Jay House.

14. *Niles' Weekly Register,* September 21, 1833, announcement of British passage of the West India Bill; Wright to Green, June 7, 1833, Weston MSS, BPL.

15. Albion, *Rise of New York Port,* 256–59; Bernard Mandel, *Labor, Free and Slave: Workingmen and the Anti-Slavery Movement in the United States* (New York, 1955), 61 and *passim;* Joseph Rayback, "The American Workingman and the Anti-Slavery Crusade," *Journal of Economic History,* III (November, 1943), 152–63.

16. From the *Emancipator,* September 21, 1833.

17. John Neal, *Wandering Recollections of a Somewhat Busy Life* (Boston, 1869), 402, a dubious account; *Courier and Enquirer,* October 5, 1833; quotation from *Liberator,* October 12, 1833; John Neal to Gurley, October 2, 1833, Gurley to Fendall, October 1 and 3, 1833, ACS MSS, LC.

18. Nevins, *Hone's Diary,* I, 102; LT, *Arthur Tappan,* 169–71; *Liberator,* October 12, 1833; Wilson, *Rise and Fall of Slave Power,* I, 231–32; *Courier and Enquirer,* October 2 and 3, 1833; LT in New York *Evangelist,* November 16, 1833, in which he attacked Tammany Hall for being a temple for infidelity; Neal, *Recollections,* 402; Mott, *American Journalism,* 261.

19. *Liberator,* October 12, 1833.

20. Louis Filler, *The Crusade Against Slavery, 1830–1860* (New York, 1960), 63–64, n. 35; Garrison and Garrison, *Garrison,* I, 382; *Emancipator,* October 12, 1833, cites September 30, 1833, as date of Garrison's arrival; cf. Barnes, *Antislavery Impulse,* 54; *Courier and Enquirer,* October 19, 1833.

21. LT, *Arthur Tappan,* 169–71; *Liberator,* October 12 and 19, 1833; *Emancipator,* October 5, 1833.

22. *Courier and Enquirer,* October 5, 1833; *Liberator,* October 12 and 19, 1833.

23. For this address, see *Liberator,* November 2, 1833.

24. Gurley to Fendall, November 7, 1833, ACS MSS, LC.

25. *Liberator,* October 19, 1833.

26. *Emancipator,* October 26, 1833; quotation from *Liberator,* October 12, 1833; Leavitt in *National Anti-Slavery Standard,* October 20, 1844; Wright, Sr., to Wright, October 9, 1833, Weston MSS, BPL; Wright to Wright, Sr., November 2, 1833, Wright MSS, LC; Wright to Weld (circular), October 29, 1833, in Barnes and Dumond, *Weld Letters,* I, 117–19; LT to Amos Phelps, November 16 and 22, 1833, Phelps MSS, BPL; Wright to Green, November 26, 1833, Weston MSS, BPL; Edwin P. Atlee, D. Mandeville, Thomas Shipley, George Grisam, Committee, (copy) to AT, October 7, 1833, Pennsylvania Abolition Society MSS, Pennsylvania Historical Society.

27. Weld to Wright, Leavitt, and AT, November 22, 1833, in Barnes and Dumond, *Weld Letters,* I, 120; *Liberator,* December 14 and 21, 1833; *The Friend* (Philadelphia), December 14, 1833; *Emancipator,* December 12, 1833, January 4, 1834; Whittier, "Antislavery Convention of 1833," 166–69; May, *Recollections,*

84–85, 87–88; see also reminiscences in *Proceedings of American Anti-Slavery Society at Its Second Decade* (New York, 1854), 7–10, 28–31, 97; and *Proceedings . . . Third Decade* (New York, 1864), 6, 7, 25, 30–31, 34–35, and 43–44.

28. LT to BT, February 18, 1834, BT MSS, LC.

29. *Liberator*, April 12, 1834.

30. Lydia Maria Child to Theodore Weld, July 10, 1880, Weld MSS, Clements Library; Elizur Wright to his sister, September 16, 1834, in Philip Green Wright and Elizabeth Q. Wright, *Elizur Wright: The Father of Life Insurance* (Chicago, 1937), 77; *Liberator*, July 20, 1831.

31. LT to BT, February 18, 1834, BT MSS, LC; J. Miller McKim, in *Proceedings . . . Third Decade*, 37.

32. LT to Phelps, October 10, 1834, Phelps MSS, BPL.

33. Wright to Weld, February 20, 1834, in Barnes and Dumond, *Weld Letters*, I, 129; LT to George Bond, December 27, 1833, Bond MSS, BPL; Whittier, "Antislavery Convention of 1833," 168; see also Wright and Wright, *Elizur Wright*, 73.

34. Quoted by Wilson, *Rise and Fall of Slave Power*, I, 233–34.

35. LT to Phelps, October 10, 1834, Phelps MSS, BPL.

36. Wright to Beriah Green, March 8, 1834, Wright MSS, LC.

37. *Ibid.*, March 29, 1836; Wright to Phelps, December 31, 1833, March 3, 1834, Weston MSS, BPL; Charles W. Denison to WLG, January 14, 1834, WLG MSS, BPL; on Cox, see Henry Miller Cox, *The Cox Family in America . . .* (New York, 1912), 92.

38. Quotation, A. L. Cox to WLG, December 19 and 20, 1833, WLG MSS, BPL; AT to WLG, March 22, 1833, WLG MSS, BPL. It is doubtful that Garrison was deliberately dishonest, as Barnes implies (*Antislavery Impulse*, 56–57). LT to WLG, February 25, 1836, WLG MSS, BPL, is a letter which indicates that the Tappan brothers did not think that Garrison was anything worse than a poor businessman. There is no evidence to support Barnes's contention that WLG wanted a national antislavery society because he hoped for financial gain.

39. Wright to Weld, November 4, 1836, in Barnes and Dumond, *Weld Letters*, I, 347; diary, March 2, 1836.

40. The figures were published monthly in the short-lived *Anti-Slavery Reporter*. Leavitt in *National Anti-Slavery Standard* estimates that $15,000 came yearly from four individuals, a gross exaggeration. LT, *Arthur Tappan*, 175–76. An example of private subsidy was a $500 gift from AT to Beriah Green: Wright to B. Green, July 30, 1834, Wright MSS, LC, and Weston MSS, BPL.

41. LT to BT, March 4, 1834, BT MSS, LC

42. Wright to Phelps, August 8, 1834, Phelps MSS, BPL; see also Wright to Weld, June 10, 1834, in Barnes and Dumond, *Weld Letters*, I, 150.

43. Committee, LT, Wright, Rankin to Beriah Green (circular) on monthly concerts, etc., May 28, 1834, Wright MSS, LC; Wright to Phelps, June 20, 1834, Phelps MSS, BPL; and Commission to Theodore Weld, signed by AT, in Barnes and Dumond, *Weld Letters*, I, 124–25, with instructions that include quotation, 125–28. Cf. Barnes, *Antislavery Impulse*, 101–4.

44. See Dixon Ryan Fox, "The Protestant Counter-Reformation in America," *New York History*, XVI (January, 1935), 35.

45. Wright to Weld, December 31, 1833, in Barnes and Dumond, *Weld Letters*,

I, 122–23; Wright to WLG, April 13, 1834, WLG MSS, BPL; Cox, *Cox Family,* 91; Cox in *The Friend,* VII (April 4, 1834), 202.

46. *Emancipator,* May 13, 1834; quotations in *Liberator,* December 27, 1834.

47. For similar attempts in the peace, temperance, and mission societies, see *Emancipator,* May 13, 1834; on Bible Society, see *First Annual Report of the American Anti-Slavery Society . . . May 6, 1834 . . .* (New York, 1834), 33 (hereinafter *Annual Report*); Foster, *Errand of Mercy,* 201–2.

48. *Annual Report* (1834), 15; *Emancipator,* May 13, 1834.

49. *Liberator,* May 31, 1834, from *Courier and Enquirer;* New York *Evangelist,* May 24, 1834; *Annual Report* (1834), 34; quotation from Irish paper in Robert Ernst, *Immigrant Life in New York City, 1825–1863* (New York, 1949), 153; see also Mandel, *Labor, Free and Slave,* 66–67, 69.

50. *Liberator,* June 14, 1834, from *Courier and Enquirer;* New York *Spectator,* June 16, 1834; *Evening Post,* July 25, 1834; July, *Essential New Yorker,* 191–97, which has a vivid description of the mayoralty riot of April, 1834.

51. Leo H. Hirsch, Jr., "New York and the Negro, from 1783 to 1865," *JNH,* XVI (October, 1931), 391; Litwack, *North of Slavery,* 3n; see Linda K. Kerber, "Abolitionists and Amalgamators: The New York Race Riots of 1834," *New York History,* XLVIII (January, 1967), 28–39.

52. Hirsch, "New York and the Negro," 415; New York *Evangelist,* July 12, 1834.

53. New York *Evangelist,* July 13, 1834; *Liberator,* July 12, 1834.

54. *Liberator,* August 2, 1834, cites the rumor.

55. LT to Weld, July 10, 1834, in Barnes and Dumond, *Weld Letters* I, 153; *Liberator,* July 12, 1834, from the *Journal of Commerce.*

56. *Liberator,* July 12, 1834; *Evening Post,* July 12, 1834; New York *Evangelist,* July 12, 1834.

57. Picton, *Rose Street,* 5; LT, *Arthur Tappan,* 203–9; see also *Liberator,* July 12 and 26, 1834.

58. LT to Weld, July 10, 1834, in Barnes and Dumond, *Weld Letters,* I, 154; and Susanna A. Tappan to Julia and Susan Tappan (her daughters), July 12, 1834, in private collection.

59. LT to Weld, July 10, 1834, in Barnes and Dumond, *Weld Letters,* I, 155; LT, *Arthur Tappan,* 208; *Liberator,* July 19 and 26, 1834; see also New York *Times,* July 10, 1834.

60. Herbert Asbury, *The Gangs of New York: An Informal History of the Underworld* (New York, 1928), 39–40.

61. LT, *Arthur Tappan,* 222, 284; M. H. Mott to [?], July 19, 1834, Miscellaneous MSS file, New-York Historical Society.

62. *Liberator,* July 26, 1834.

63. LT to Weld, July 10, 1834, in Barnes and Dumond, *Weld Letters,* I, 154–55; Susan Tappan to her daughters, July 12, 1834, in private collection.

64. Beaumont is cited in Kerber, "Abolitionists," 35.

65. Wright to Phelps, August 20, 1834, Wright MSS, LC.

66. London *Times,* August 8, 1834.

67. James Gillespie Birney to Weld, July 26, 1834, in Barnes and Dumond, *Weld Letters,* I, 162.

68. Wright to Weld, August 14, 1834, in *ibid.,* 167.

69. Cross, *Beecher Autobiography,* II, 167, 181–83.

CHAPTER SEVEN

Oberlin and Boston

*D*uring *the latter part* of February and the early portion of March, 1834, Theodore Weld staged an eighteen-day "protracted meeting" on the subject of slavery at Lane Seminary. After one session, it was recalled, there was not "a dry eye in the Chapel."[1] Back in New York, Lewis and Arthur Tappan rejoiced at the news of Weld's success, and they published accounts of the antislavery "revival" in the *Emancipator* and *Evangelist*. A few of the participating students were southerners, who proved to be no less zealous in denouncing slavery than their northern friends. All of them pictured themselves in the "heroic role" of evangelical reformers. Like the Tappans and Weld, they were proper sons of Ezekiel, who intended to "rattle the bones, seemingly very dry, in the valleys of conservatism."[2]

Following the "Debates," as the prayer and sermon sessions were called, Weld and his abolitionist band put antislavery theory into practice. They established a "Lyceum" of elementary studies, an evening class in reading, three Sunday schools, a Bible class, and a lending library, all for the benefit of Cincinnati's Negroes. Impressed, Arthur and Lewis Tappan adopted the program as their own, sending out bundles of tracts, reading primers, clothing, and money. They also encouraged ladies' aid societies in New York to do the same. Out of Lewis Tappan's own pocket came the funds to transport several school teachers from the East, whom the students nicknamed the "Cincinnati Sisters." Moreover, Weld's activities in the Cincinnati slums were later to stimulate Lewis Tappan to undertake similar work for Manhattan Negroes. As there would be in New York during the following July, there was in Ohio "an outcry of unsanctified hearts," but the seminarians had not expected otherwise.[3]

Arthur Tappan was delighted with Weld's mission. Lane, he thought, was fulfilling his hopes of becoming a western citadel for his ideals. He had expected Lyman Beecher, zealous as the man was in the service of anti-Popery, Sabbatarianism, and temperance, to share Weld's enthusiasms for Negro work, but Arthur might have known better. A year before, at the outset of the Lane experiment, Arthur had learned that Beecher claimed to be an abolitionist and a colonizationist "without perceiving in myself any inconsistency."[4] A few words of timely warning from the New York merchant set Beecher straight for a while, and Beecher admitted a black student to the seminary to show his good faith and tolerance. Hence, it came as a shock to Arthur Tappan when the board of trustees threatened to expel Weld's company because of their "niggerism."[5] Beecher was not wholly to blame, since he spent the summer on a fund-raising tour of the East. Just before his return in October, the governing body, made up of local businessmen and conservative clergy, shut the doors on the unrepentant "Lane Rebels."[6] It was not just their abolitionism which shocked the board's sensibilities but their association with Negroes as partners, friends, and students, a breaking of the color line that violated social custom.

Upon reaching New York, Beecher hastened to the silk store to present the trustees' case in as favorable a light as possible. With him was the Rev. R. Y. Vail, who had first interested Arthur in the struggling school in 1830. There they found Lewis Tappan at his desk. A "volcanic excitement" was fast rising in Cincinnati, because the seminarians had acted "indiscreetly," Lewis Tappan quoted his old Boston friend as saying. Then Vail interjected some gossip: some Negro women of questionable character had been observed on the seminary grounds, in the escort of the students. Speaking from his own experience of the summer, Lewis Tappan replied that slander always accompanied an unpopular cause. Vail took the remark in stride but complained that Weld, who "could not be touched with a ten-foot pole," went his own way, unmindful of advice. Abolition was all very well, but men like Garrison, Beecher insisted, made it impossible for decent people to accept the movement. "Get rid of Garrison, & thousands will join. . . ," was his counsel. The comment made no impression on Lewis Tappan, but it may have planted a seed in the mind of his brother, to whom it was undoubtedly repeated. "If you, doctor, were a thorough Anti-Slavery man, how easy it w[oul]d be for you and Mr Weld to go on harmoniously," Lewis Tappan snapped.[7] The interview ended on this sour note, and Beecher found Arthur Tappan no less cool when he consulted him.

Actually, Lewis Tappan welcomed the decision of the Lane trustees, for he wrote to Amos Phelps, national antislavery lecturer in Massachusetts, that the "students will swing their packs, and be voluntary agents all over the country." But, Tappan continued, "as long as" Beecher and his friends "call slavery a 'wrong' thing, & dare not stigmatize it as a 'sin,' their adhesion would sink us to the bottom."[8] Both brothers were thoroughly disillusioned with the time-serving Beecher. In 1838, Arthur Tappan answered a friendly word from the president at Walnut Hills, "I thank you for the particulars respecting your Seminary and regret that I cannot feel any sympathy in the happiness you express in its present & anticipated prosperity." Although unhappy about Beecher's conduct, Arthur was aware of Beecher's campaign for reunifying the evangelical front on the slavery issue behind a program broad and vague enough to encompass conservative abolitionists and colonizationists alike, and he said nothing publicly against it at this time.[9]

In the meantime, Arthur sought a new site for his western seminary and his group of Oneida and Lane scholars, who wished to finish their studies before becoming "teachers in Israel." It cost him a thousand dollars, according to Weld, to hold the company together at the "Anti-Slavery Patmos," a boardinghouse on the outskirts of Cincinnati. During the summer, fall, and early winter of 1834, they performed a variety of charitable, religious, and social activities in service of Cincinnati's Negroes. Asa Mahan and John Morgan, two antislavery clergymen of Cincinnati, served them as a nucleus for the new seminary faculty. As the year came to a close, Arthur Tappan still had not found another location for them.[10] Then, in early January, a visitor paid a call.

The Rev. John Shipherd saw the world through rheumy eyes. As a young man he had accidentally taken a dose of saltpeter instead of epsom salts and had been nearly blinded as a result. Although energetic and inventive, Shipherd was a visionary. He thought of himself as an apostolic leader in the midst of the Western Reserve, where he had founded an impoverished colony of New England communitarians in the forests of Lake Erie's dismal clay flatlands. Desperately in need of aid, he had come east to induce Arthur Tappan to settle his school at Oberlin.

The merchant was agreeable. Foremost in Arthur's thoughts was his anticipation that the little colony could replace Lane Seminary as a center of religious reform. Moreover, it had been almost a Tappan family tradition to take an interest in northern Ohio settlement. At the turn of the century, Benjamin Tappan, Sr., in company with a group of Northampton investors, had bought lands on the Reserve. Unable to hold the properties long enough to realize a good profit, he had had to sell some of them to John Tappan and eventually the remainder to his son Benjamin, who took up residence first in Ravenna and then in Steubenville in order to oversee the investment. Over the years, Arthur had not had much to do with this side of family enterprise, but since John and Benjamin still controlled much of the town property in Ravenna, only two- or three-score miles from Oberlin, Arthur may have been encouraged to make his own contribution to the western reaches of New England expansion in an experiment more contributory to the spiritual needs of the area than his brothers' purely economic venture.

Oberlinites under Shipherd's guidance were already committed to "a life of simplicity, to special devotion to church and school, and to earnest labor in the missionary cause." But Arthur insisted that upon the framework of their covenant his own policies should be superimposed. He selected the fiery Asa Mahan, who had accompanied Shipherd from the West, as the first president of the college, while Charles Grandison Finney was to assume leadership of the theological department. Contrary to Shipherd's initial desires, Arthur Tappan and Finney required that the faculty, not the trustees, control the school.[11] Arthur guaranteed Finney's salary, as he had Beecher's, and the revivalist welcomed this arrangement. Still weak from a bout with cholera, Finney was attracted by the opportunity to return to country living, to renew old associations with Weld and the West, and to teach revival methods, although he promised to return to New York each spring to preach. (A little later, his friends financed the Broadway Tabernacle, a new building to replace Chatham Hall as his revival center.) Above all, Arthur and Lewis stipulated that "the broad ground of moral reform, in all its departments, should characterize the instruction in Oberlin."[12]

The last condition gave Shipherd a little trouble. The New England colonists at Oberlin and the trustees of the non-existent college there eyed the abolitionist scheme suspiciously and voted against it. Exasperated, Shipherd wrote back "to all the beloved in Jesus Christ. . . . I did not desire you to hang out an abolition flag or fill up with filthy stupid Negroes; but I did desire that you should say you would not reject promising youth who desired to prepare for usefulness. . . ."[13] The offer was too tempting; it was one of the few times in the 1830's when it paid to be an abolitionist. Finally, the townspeople and the trustees agreed; by the fall of 1835, the faculty and students had arrived.

Arthur Tappan took more interest in Oberlin than in any other project in his antislavery career. To one of the Oberlinites he wrote, "I think every nerve should now be strained by those who have embarked in the Oberlin enterprise to carry it forward to a gracious result. I have never felt more determined to use the ability God has entrusted me with than I feel in this case. . . ." There was some talk at Oberlin that nearby Western Reserve College was trying to woo Finney away. Fear of such a loss may have heightened Arthur Tappan's early interest.[14]

The amount of his donations for a single year proved Arthur's earnestness. In 1835 he contributed $7,251, and, in a joint arrangement with William Green and Isaac Dimond (a revivalistic New York jeweler originally from Connecticut), he lent the school $10,000 more.[15] Most of his funds were used in the construction of a four-story brick classroom and dormitory building. In dire need of housing, the students occupied it before the roof was finished. Because of Shipherd's mismanagement of the building arrangements, the structure was poorly built, and in heavy weather the upper stories groaned and swayed ominously. Drafty and poorly planned inside, the dormitory had to be abandoned within twenty years.[16] Unaware of these troubles, Arthur Tappan was pleased when the board of trustees named the new building Tappan Hall, though modesty forbade a display of his delight. "If you cannot fix on a better name," he wrote to Shipherd, "I do not object to your giving mine to the Hall, but I have no ambition to be immortalized in brick and mortar."[17]

Every aspect of the Oberlin Institute drew Arthur Tappan's interest, and he frequently offered friendly business advice. Like the typical college benefactor, he did not hesitate to express his views on how the campus ought to look. "There is a great defect in this particular in our eastern Colleges," he said, presumably with Yale College in mind. No friend of fussy architecture, Arthur thought that "good taste" and "chasteness" would have "a refining influence" on the development of students and would add immensely to "the enjoyments of life."[18]

Piety was, of course, to be Oberlin's watchword, as far as the merchant was concerned, but equally important to him was the fair treatment of Negro students. To help Finney spread the gospel, he and several friends bought a huge circus tent for seven hundred dollars. Until the First Church was built near Tappan Hall, the tent served as a prefabricated college chapel, which the seminarians raised and dismantled once a week for Finney's services. Hearing of its first use, Arthur Tappan felt "richly repaid." "May as great a harvest be gathered to the Lord from all our efforts at Oberlin, and to the Lord be ascribed all the glory," he prayed.[19]

Oberlin soon became the center of Western abolitionism. In the autumn of 1835, Weld arrived to give a series of lectures and to train the students as antislavery agents. During the summers of the 1830's, the college men taught school, preached in vacant pulpits, or lectured and distributed tracts, particularly in the antislavery cause. Except for some of the "Lane Rebels," few of its alumni of the thirties were ever famous, but Oberlinites spread an influence, "unseen & unsuspected," over the Western Reserve and in hundreds of Western communities.[20]

There was a certain eccentricity about the school's atmosphere. President Mahan called it an "ingenuous liberality," but it was not quite that. Dietary fads and other cures for the ills of humanity came and went. Among the institution's collection of "heresies," Mahan's and Finney's doctrine of Christian "sanctification in the present life" lasted longest, an appropriate philosophy for the earnest, humorless Oberlin temper. Arthur Tappan had endowed the college with something of his spirit along with his money. Some years later, Artemus Ward (whose satire on Oberlin must have especially pleased Abraham Lincoln, his great admirer) gave the popular view of the school's racial policies when he remarked that "on rainy dase white people can't find their way threw the streets without the gas is lit, there bein such a numerosity of cullerd pussons in the town." But, he concluded, "Oberlin is a grate plase. The College opens with a prayer and then the New York Tribune is read."[21]

Arthur Tappan was impervious to any slurs cast upon his favorite charity. He supported Oberlin because it represented the embodiment of all he held dear—spartan ruggedness, education, Christian piety, and world regeneration. Neither words nor actions, he told Shipherd, could fully express the depth of his feeling for the Institute. A more personal motive also played a part in his preoccupation with the college.[22] Eastern antislavery had not dealt kindly with him; in fact, events for which he was partly responsible heralded a dynamic change in the movement of which he was not the master. After the riots of 1834, few abolitionists commanded as much respect among their associates as he, for persecution always gives its victim a special authority in his own circle. Nevertheless, Arthur Tappan was shortly to jeopardize his power as well as the fortunes of the American Anti-Slavery Society in a poorly planned effort to curb what he thought was an excess of Boston zeal.

In the fall of 1834, evangelicals began to notice a difference between the abolitionism of Boston and that of New York. One religious journal noted that, though many antislavery men "have borne with Mr. Garrison's errors, in consideration of his services as a pioneer in the cause," they "have long lamented" his "reckless disregard of the courtesies of life and the precepts of Christianity. . . ."[23] Garrison was growing increasingly harsh toward the orthodox Calvinists of New England, and his attacks on slaveholders threatened any hope of a gradual spread of antislavery principles among Christians of the South.

True to his goals of gentlemanly reform, Arthur Tappan held the national society in strict rein and retained personal supervision of the *Emancipator*. He saw to it that there was no public commemoration of the founding of the New York City Anti-Slavery Society in October, 1834, an anniversary that might have provoked a revival of unpleasantness. When George Thompson, renowned for his radical oratory in favor of British abolitionism, arrived in the port in late September, 1834, a majority of the Tappan Committee "thought it imprudent to have a public meeting for him to address." Lewis opposed his merchant-colleagues' timidity, grumbling to Garrison, "If the cause is to advance . . . a bold stand should be taken . . . here, in Philadelphia, & Boston."

Even Elizur Wright, shortly to be New York's sharpest critic of slavery, fell under Arthur Tappan's sway. With surprising caution, he complained to Beriah Green, the new president of Oneida, "When I came here my plan was, not to start the *National Car* till we had got our team *harnessed.* But Garrison & the New Englanders prevailed, and the Car was set a-going by *hand* and now we are trying to 'tackle' while it is in motion—no easy matter!"[24] His brief attraction to Arthur Tappan's mild approach was understandable. It seemed to work.

Following the riots of July, William Jay, the Westchester aristocrat, openly joined the movement. Arthur Tappan's disclaimers had convinced him that the cause was in good, cautious hands. Always the legalist, Jay stressed the constitutional restraints that limited the aims of antislavery political action to the slavery and slave trade of the District of Columbia and the means to the presentation of conservatively worded memorials to Congress. Gerrit Smith, the millionaire colonizationist of western New York, was also "on the way over to Anti-Slavery," as he gradually despaired of the Liberian experiment. Furthermore, letters of encouragement reached headquarters from the South, especially from Alabama, Tennessee, and Kentucky, though the correspondents generally admitted that they were "afraid to own [antislavery principles] openly."[25] These signs of progress buoyed the hopes of Arthur Tappan and his friends.

Most encouraging of all was the capture of James G. Birney. Like Jay and Smith, the Danville, Kentucky, lawyer had not arrived at antislavery by reading the *Liberator.* Crossing the Ohio for clandestine visits to Lane Seminary, Birney adopted an antislavery creed through the influence of Theodore Weld, whom he had met two years before in Alabama. As a convert to Presbyterianism, Birney naturally identified himself with the Tappan wing of the party. He was a rich prize indeed. He had once been a slaveholder in north Alabama and a field representative of the arch-enemy, the American Colonization Society. When he published his first antislavery declaration during the summer of 1834, the Tappan brothers rejoiced. "I read it with tears of joy and gratitude. . . !" wrote Lewis.[26] Yet, Arthur Tappan hesitated to allow Birney to become a professional agent of the Anti-Slavery Society. As long as he resided in Kentucky, Birney's life would be in jeopardy; there was no point in inviting martyrdom, Arthur thought. Impatient to press on, Elizur Wright explained to Weld that nothing could be done for Birney until "Mr. A. T. according to the laws of his mind, which are somewhat anomalous, will be ready" to pay his share of Birney's salary. Finally, the president of the Society relented, but he insisted that Birney's connection with it remain surreptitious until he should leave Danville for the North.[27]

The more smoothly Arthur Tappan's courting of prominent philanthropists proceeded, the bolder he became in criticizing Garrison. It troubled Arthur to read in the *Liberator* a stinging denunciation of some respected individual whom he was at the time trying to win over by a display of persuasion and restraint. When Garrison, deep in financial trouble, once again applied for aid from New York, the committee refused him outright. "I vindicated him so far as I could," Lewis wrote to Garrison's companion, George Thompson, then visiting Boston. Arthur Tappan grew sterner as the year closed. If only the editor would write some "temperate essays" on the "inadequacy" of Liberia as a means of Christianizing Africa, he complained wistfully to Amos Phelps.[28]

Meanwhile, John and Charles Tappan exploited the friction by carrying forward the effort that Beecher had hinted was in progress when he had talked with Arthur and Lewis in New York City. The New England Tappans were prosperous, and particularly so John, who by this date belonged to the inner circles of Boston society. Both of them ardently supported religious orthodoxy, tract and temperance societies, and similar charitable activities. Charles, according to his sister-in-law Susan, was somewhat pompous. John was the more impressive and formidable of the two. Gustave de Beaumont, when visiting Boston with Alexis de Tocqueville, had said of John, "I declare I have never met anyone whose character and virtues inspired in me a more profound respect." A proud man, and certainly as stubborn as either Lewis and Arthur, John considered himself something of an expert on slavery. One of his closest friends was General John Hartwell Cocke, an aristocratic slaveholder with whom he had probably become acquainted as a consequence of their mutual interest in temperance. General Cocke was the owner of a handsome mansion called "Bremo," on the banks of the upper James in Fluvanna County, Virginia. Built with the advice of Thomas Jefferson, "Bremo" is perhaps the finest example of Southern Federalist architecture now remaining in private ownership.[29]

In the minds of John and Charles Tappan, their upstart younger brothers had no right to denounce a slaveholder like the good general, when no finer evangelical Christian could be found anywhere. It did not occur to these New Englanders that Cocke, a leading colonizationist, was one of the last of that breed of Southern liberals who were opposed to slavery. Yet, if John and Charles were not fully aware of the grim changes in the political climate of the South, so too were their aggressive New York brothers deceived. Abolitionists of all kinds, even Garrison, expected men of General Cocke's stature and Christian bearing to join their cause, just as James G. Birney recently had. In the spring of 1835 they were to launch a campaign specifically to attract others of this type, though their effort was awkward and in the end futile.

As early as the summer of 1831, the Boston Tappans, the Rev. T. H. Gallaudet, and other northern supporters of the Colonization Society had become disturbed by the ambiguities of its policy and sought a redefinition of its program. They particularly objected to forced deportation of free Negroes. "A crisis is approaching," Gaullaudet wrote R. R. Gurley, unless this and other changes were initiated. Three years later his prediction that *"very different mediums"* of action would soon be employed was being fulfilled in the columns of the *Liberator*. In July, 1834, Gallaudet renewed his appeal by sending to General Cocke a tentative plan for a new non-sectional society for the discussion of slavery and antislavery, and in the fall John Tappan announced to Cocke that some friends had banded together "to allay the rising spirits of the North & to convince those of the South that Slavery could not always exist & ought to come to an end as soon as it could be affected [*sic*] without injury to the white population." Involved in this effort, he said, were such trustworthy souls as Gerrit Smith, Dr. Justin Edwards, a temperance leader, and Courtland Van Rensselaer, a wealthy young missionary to the slaves of Virginia. The latter added his voice in appeal to Cocke, assuring him that "those abolitionists, who have united with Mr. [Arthur] Tappan only because they preferred violent measures to none at all" would quickly abandon Garrison and join the new movement. All these correspondents agreed that the "growing popularity of ultra-abolition" measures had filled them with anxiety and that "a rational plan of emancipation" must be forthcoming before "local and sectional prejudices" got out of hand. It was important, as Van Rensselaer asserted, however, that "a few Southern planters" take the initiative in founding the society instead of allowing northerners to be classified as the *"prime movers."*[30]

Presumably, Cocke replied to this hint with a certain caution, if not trepidation. He was already suspected of latent abolitionism in his neighborhood, not only because of his admiration for Yankee enterprises—canals, industries, and Bible societies—but also because he had openly denounced the hysteria that had gripped the southern states after the Nat Turner rebellion and had urged gradual emancipation, with state support, as a solution. Cocke declined to act himself. He probably encouraged his Boston friends to proceed without him, however, for shortly afterward they issued a call for the formation of "The American Union for the Relief and Improvement of the Colored People." Caustically and rather justly, Garrison called it "a soulless organization with a sounding title."[31]

One can almost sympathize with these conservatives who were seeking a painless way to resolve an agonizing problem. It is impossible to mourn the fate of those cotton and rice planters who hid behind a barrage of self-justification and coarse Negrophobia and reaped the rewards of their own short-sightedness. But Cocke represented the best fruit of Virginia aristocracy and Jeffersonian racial thought. Although he was undecided about his neighbors' contention that Negroes were inferior, Cocke was convinced that they were the possessors of immortal souls and that duty demanded that he help to save these souls. As for the four Tappan brothers, each in his way was attempting to create the kind of movement that would ultimately avoid the grave national calamity they all sensed otherwise lay ahead. The failure of this effort demonstrated the very complexity, and the tragedy, of American racial difficulties.

General Cocke and the Tappan brothers believed that a union of respectable leaders of society could at least begin the process of unraveling the cords of oppression that bound the slaves. Some historians claim that moderate reform was doomed because the nation lacked the institutional framework in which the play of ideas could operate freely to construct piecemeal remedies. This judgment is not wholly accurate, though admittedly American society was then less structured than that of England. The evangelical circle to which all these men belonged offered the kind of forum where matters of reform could be discussed. General Cocke, Chief Justice John Marshall, Judge John O'Neall of South Carolina, and other gentlemen who supported the Bible and mission agencies were in very close communication with their northern colleagues in these enterprises.[32] They met frequently at conventions in Boston and New York, at familiar vacation spots, and in the comfortable drawing rooms of Philadelphia, Washington, and Boston. Yet, convenient institutions and good intentions simply were insufficient to erase deep differences in racial and sectional attitudes.

Even if still more powerful and inclusive institutions had existed for the solution of national crises at this period, it is unlikely that the reform-minded leaders of the country's social and political life could have used them effectively. The four Tappan brothers illustrate the flaw in the conventional Yankee's understanding of how Negro freedom could be achieved peaceably. The New York Tappans relied upon even-handed, disinterested rebuke of slaveholders and upon appeal to the middle and upper classes of the North; the Boston Tappans depended upon polite persuasion of southern and northern dignitaries alone. While there were differences in emphasis between the two pairs of brothers, none of them disputed the importance of converting the southern "wise and good." All of the Tappans assumed that freedom was ultimately to be granted as a result of their example. Each of the brothers assumed that freedom was something to be bestowed by such men as General Cocke, who recognized Christian duty. They did not believe in revolutions from below. While this Christian elite was no better and probably no worse than the respectable classes in other periods of American history, it was neither talented, idealistic, united, nor farsighted enough to bring about an ending of slavery as the four Tappans envisioned that it would be accomplished. It was simply not in the nature of human affairs to expect the Jacksonian ruling class to lessen its own power by elevating the black man while sacrificing its southern members' power over him. The Tappans, but especially the Boston Tappans, were vain enough to think that they could convince the leaders of southern Christian society to do precisely that. The New York Tappans, however, were somewhat more flexible in their social views. They did not forget the influence and strength of the middle class of the North, a much broader portion of public opinion than the Whiggish aristocracy of North and South.

Yet it may be speculated that the owner of "Bremo" was in fact the kind of southerner Charles, John, Arthur, or Lewis would have been in Cocke's own circumstances. In other words, Cocke was a Christian compelled to face the moral issue not in a free state and among like-minded friends but in hostile territory and under a system of law that nearly prohibited him from giving his slaves the barest instruction in reading and writing, much more from offering them freedom on their own native soil. The Virginia planter and the four Tappans shared, too, a common sense of obligation to their subordinates, insisting that both Negro slave and merchant apprentice demonstrate moral worthiness, in an exercise of paternalism that permeated the two labor systems. Like the Tappans, Cocke tried to inculcate temperance, marital regularity, and all the other evangelical virtues into his charges.[33] He was moved by his regional conscience as they were by theirs.

The motives of John and Charles as they entered the quasi-colonizationist American Union movement are, however, somewhat more suspect than Cocke's. In August, 1834, the general asked Charles what his reaction was to being singled out as a fanatic because of the activities of his New York kinsmen. In reply, the Boston bookseller assured him that he "got along" with his "'hateful' name very well" when touring "different watering places" where southerners gathered, though there was always the chance of dangerous misunderstandings. Undoubtedly, the Boston brothers hoped by founding the "American Union for the Relief and Improvement of the Colored Race" to rescue the family name from the disrepute that Arthur and Lewis had brought upon it.[34]

They urged Arthur to visit them in Boston to look into the prospects of the new experiment as soon as he could. On January 14, 1835, he arrived, though too late to attend the Union's inaugural meeting. After a conference with his conservative brothers, Arthur visited the New England Anti-Slavery Society offices, where he found an assembly indignantly abuzz with talk of the American Union. Garrison, Amos Phelps, and George Thompson had ridiculed its "sort of beg-your-pardon" spirit when they attended its proceedings, and they freely aired their complaints to Arthur. The American Union was unrepresentative, with membership exclusively Calvinist, they pointed out. Its purpose was confined to doing something (no one was quite sure what) for northern free Negroes, and it said much too little of slavery. Throughout these reports, the merchant sat, glum and inscrutable.[35]

When Arthur did begin to speak, however, his displeasure with

Garrison became obvious. During a recent political campaign, the editor had supported the election of one or two candidates with satisfactory antislavery views. Moreover, Garrison had hinted at the need for a "Christian party" of nonsectarians. Arthur Tappan, always wary of political contamination of religious causes, had no desire to undergo another ordeal like the one to which Ezra Stiles Ely's Church and State party had subjected him during the Magdalen Asylum affair. He challenged the Society group to reconcile this political maneuvering with Garrison's own Declaration of Sentiments, which disavowed partisan purposes. The replies were not satisfactory to Arthur Tappan.[36]

When he returned to New Haven, Arthur wrote an endorsement of the new society for publication in Joseph Tracy's Boston *Recorder*. What could prevent the two national bodies from uniting "in every manner that religion and philanthropy can approve?" he asked. "Mr. Garrison," he declared, had the fault of using "severe and denunciatory language with which he often assails his opponents and repels their attacks."[37] Even Arthur's words smelled of the musty paternalism of his brand of Christianity.

It was now up to Garrison to make the next move. Wisely, however, the young man seemed to sense the feelings of the senior merchant as Arthur wavered almost publicly between conscience and convenience in the next few weeks. Even in private conversation Garrison remained tactfully silent; no editorials appeared to strike at the turncoat president of the parent society about to sell out to colonizationists in disguise. After all, Garrison's own position was well known. To threaten Arthur in the *Liberator* would only make matters worse. Yet, he must have asked himself if the New York merchant could be expected to follow him much longer anyway.

No broad social class, no individual property-owner, and above all, no privileged white Christian, Garrison had always insisted, could make a higher claim for justice before the bench of the God of History than the lowliest slave. It was Garrison's willingness to sacrifice the established, the known terrain of society, with its customary deferences to the "wise and good," for the forbidding seas of change that the Boston Tappans and their kind, both North and South, instinctively feared. In this curious confrontation in 1834, Garrison stood in the posture of a true revolutionary, placing the rights of the humblest of all Americans above the stability of society as a whole, and above the prerogatives of a Christian master like General Cocke. Garrison was asking Arthur Tappan to cut himself free of the past in a manner that neither John nor Charles nor the proud owner of "Bremo" could ever have brought himself to do, and to leap forward self-confidently toward racial equality. To make such a decision was to threaten the foundations of American security, as these gentlemen well knew.

Arthur Tappan was no match for the Boston "fanatic," whose sagacity, on this occasion at least, prevented a disastrous schism in the still-infant cause. Upon returning to New York City from New Haven some time later, the senior merchant found himself without a single supporter. Lewis, Garrison's collaborator throughout, had deftly seen to that, somehow gaining the tacit support of William Green and Abraham Cox, Arthur's friends on the executive board of the American Anti-Slavery Society. In addition, Lewis shrewdly applied a bit of pressure himself by frequently reminding his brother of Garrison's personal loyalty to Arthur and gratitude for old favors. More important, he wrote Garrison that he had read his remarks about the American Union, which "I should call AN ANTI-GARRISON SOCIETY, and for one, I cordially approve them. . . . Go on and prosper. . . . The Lord will be thy shield and buckler." Naturally, the Boston editor printed this endorsement next to Arthur's contrary testimonial to the American Union.[38] Lewis claimed that he did not wish to be placed in an "antagonistic position" with his brother but obviously hoped to embarrass Arthur just enough to make the implications of his position clear.[39] Would not Arthur's desertion of immediatism be a public repudiation of Lewis' sacrifice, the burning of his possessions?

The plan worked perfectly. At the next meeting of the Executive Committee of the Society no one spoke up for the Union. Arthur was mortified and perhaps a little perplexed by the cruel silence. In the end, he compensated for his brief deviation by pledging five thousand dollars to the Society, giving one thousand immediately and failing to attach his usual condition of matching funds. Garrison's crafty discretion also paid a handsome personal dividend. Arthur sent him a draft to cover all his current indebtedness.[40]

There was something forlorn about these gifts. Arthur put himself in the position of attempting to purchase the forgiveness, respect, and even affection of his associates. No one in those pleasantly conventional times mentioned this element of compromise, but Arthur's application of the balm of money became in this instance a pathetic attempt to speak through coin as a way of expressing his feelings of love and trust. If there is a psychological mechanism in the exercise of charity, then there is no act of giving, whether of money or self, that cannot be said to be motivated by personal considerations, however subtle or disguised, however compulsive or calculating. Rationally, Arthur surely knew that gold gives no ultimate security, and his religious beliefs reinforced this perception. The more gold that is dispensed, the more in a sense is demanded. And he must have perceived also that presents given "anonymously" are not anonymous to God. His sense of personal unworthiness drove him to extravagant charity, as all humankind may be driven to whatever magnanimity it can muster. It was Arthur's misfortune that his own mechanism of giving was too clearly revealed in the Union affair, and from this time forward Arthur's voice did not command the degree of respect in antislavery councils as it once had, though for the next few months he did manage to recoup something of his influence. Ironically, the money he presented to Garrison and the Society was employed in such a way as to ruin his fortunes and further decrease his reputation among men.

Lewis' victory over his Boston brothers was narrow, and there must have been elements of bitterness in it. To Garrison, Lewis spoke of the American Union as "a device of Satan," the sooner forgotten the better. He never revealed the extent of the antagonism to John and Charles he must have felt in this period of life. Yet it must have been only natural for him to burn a little inwardly whenever he remembered the days when all three of them were prosperous, happy family men of Boston and Brookline. Also, he may have recognized that they were deliberately trying to separate Arthur from his influence. Were they not tempting Arthur to regain his customary place in the tiny but powerful circle of national Christian benefactors, and by so doing challenging Lewis' right to membership? Whatever John and Charles might have thought, however, neither Lewis nor Arthur ever believed for a moment that their antislavery views really affected their standing, although proslavery individuals and organizations might claim to have expelled them. But Lewis surely resented his Boston brothers' effort to save Arthur from himself and from the influence of Lewis, whose impulsiveness, having already led to his self-imposed exile from Boston in 1828, now threatened Arthur's good name and perhaps even his financial ability to proceed with good works. If such thoughts crossed Lewis' mind at this time, he must have been profoundly relieved by Arthur's decision to seek the respect of his fellow abolitionists rather than that of the Christian elite. In old age, Lewis' feelings about John and Charles grew more benign. Until then, he was very sensitive on the few occasions he saw John, and their conversations sometimes erupted in heated bickering, though ending on the conventional note of brotherly affection. In a short time, the American Union was alive in name only. Gleefully, Garrison announced, "We will soon scatter to the winds this lofty but fragile fabric of persecution, pride and cowardice."[41] He was right, but the death of this feeble movement spelled the end of the influence of pious, nonsectional liberalism on slavery. When the officers of the American Anti-Slavery Society attempted by their own methods to reach the southern community leaders, abolitionism would not receive the polite hearing the Boston Tappans obtained from General Cocke.

As Arthur Tappan's flirtation with the Boston conservatives cost him his authority over national antislavery, he energetically turned to the pursuit of his Oberlin venture, leaving Lewis and the "professionals" to guide the New York committee. At once, they ordered Amos Phelps and George Thompson to conclude their lecturing in New England and to invade New York. In late February and early March, the British abolitionist spoke in the churches of the Third Presbytery. There were no ugly incidents, and he moved triumphantly on to Philadelphia, where he drew crowds of one thousand at a time.[42]

During the new burst of antislavery enthusiasm, the merchant William Green withdrew from the Executive Committee, and Simeon S. Jocelyn, at this time a missionary to New York Negroes, took his place in May.[43] Quietly, the "professionals" were assuming control. Meanwhile, Theodore Weld began his official career with the Society by organizing new antislavery chapters and conferring with Presbyterians at church conventions. In Kentucky, Birney was able to enlist some of his Presbyterian neighbors, but there were ominous signs of a coming gale in the South. In late April, a mob in Columbia, Virginia, assaulted General Cocke so fiercely that he was still nursing his cuts and bruises a month later. In the North, however, abolitionism was growing. Under the supervision of a band of recently hired agents a national network of auxiliary chapters developed. The total number of such fledgling associations by the time of the May, 1835, anniversary was over two hundred.[44]

When the delegates to the second annual meeting convened in New York City, Lewis Tappan presented a far-reaching goal for the Society. Unencumbered by the hesitations of his brother, he first suggested a budget of sixty thousand dollars for the coming year. More realistically, wiser heads reduced the sum to a still impressive thirty thousand dollars. The money was to finance a national pamphlet campaign, one of the most ambitious in evangelical history. As chairman of the publications committee, Tappan outlined for the delegates a renovation of antislavery literature. The headquarters would issue a series of four journals each month, one every week: first, *Human Rights,* a four-page sheet; second, the *Anti-Slavery Record,* embellished with wood-cuts; third, the *Emancipator,* demoted from a weekly but enlivened; fourth, the *Slave's Friend,* a "juvenile with cuts." These papers would be sent out to the leaders of communities all over the nation. At the end of his speech, the delegates enthusiastically pledged an initial $14,500 for the effort.[45]

As Lewis Tappan and the New York committee planned the operation, all abolitionists were to participate. A printed appeal went out to them to "come forward" with the means "to sow the good seed of abolition thoroughly over the whole country." The circular urged women to cover pincushions and workboxes with antislavery slogans and devices and to sell them for the great campaign. Children were asked to give their pennies "as they would if their own fathers and mothers were in chains and bleeding beneath the whip." Chapter leaders were first to send in the names of *"inquiring, candid, reading* men who are not abolitionists" to whom the new materials would be sent by direct mail and then to stand ready to distribute the literature to other citizens when it arrived.[46]

Lewis Tappan spent many hours in the feverishly busy atmosphere of the Anti-Slavery Rooms, assisting Elizur Wright with the publication of the first *Human Rights,* the liveliest of the series, and preparing the children's magazine himself. (His efficiency as an editor has never received much attention, but in fact it was impressive. He was intimately connected with the publication of a dozen newspapers and periodicals in the course of his life, and he contributed articles to at least three times that many both in the United States and abroad.) During this period, Tappan also aided R. G. Williams, the publishing agent, in handling the campaigns for funds and the paying of bills. Monthly costs rose to nearly one thousand dollars for printing alone, four times the sum expended on the lecture tours of salaried agents. Twenty-five to fifty thousand copies of each publication rolled off the presses every week.[47]

In keeping with the goal of nationwide coverage, the literature bore signs of a new spirit. Much of it was written with an eye to northern churchgoers and to Yankees generally "who support themselves in the good old-fashioned republican way of honest and honorable industry." The journals also reflected the sentimentalism of the age, for the *Slave's Friend* included such articles as "Lost Children Found," "The Little Blind Boy," and "The Poor Mother." Some columns were almost Garrisonian in their ferocity, denouncing slaveholding sinners and portraying in woodcuts the cruelties of the system. Lewis Tappan and Elizur Wright stated their purpose in the first number of what Elizur liked to call "Human *Wrights*": "If you wish to draw off the people from a mad or wicked custom, you must beat up for a march; you must make an excitement, do something that everybody will notice. . . ." There could be little doubt that antislavery literature would succeed on that score in the South, although no slaves or free Negroes were placed on the mailing lists. Even the whites included were primarily clergymen, national, state, and local officials, and other citizens of education and leadership.

Lewis Tappan and Elizur Wright had more in mind than mere "excitement" in spreading antislavery news below the Mason and Dixon Line. In the same issue of *Human Rights*, they reasoned that obstinate slave owners "will find a feeling against which they cannot stand." Resistance to abolition would prove hopeless, because world opinion and southern manumissionists themselves would constantly rebuke the shrinking number of proslavery loyalists. Antislavery was apparently to progress by means of social coercion, although the abolitionists had a milder name for it, "moral suasion."

Browbeaten, ostracized from Christian fellowship, gradually restricted by state and federal laws, slaveholders would surrender peaceably—or so the two reformers promised. They admitted that "some will rave and scold and threaten. Some, in their rage, will draw closer the cords and ply the lash more cruelly." But violence would prove to be only a passing phase because repentant masters "will liberate their slaves" to ease themselves "of an intolerable [moral] burden." Such was the rationale of one of the first large-scale American reform campaigns.[48] Lewis Tappan and his friends fully exploited the modern innovations that made their effort possible—the steam press, cheap and efficient; the concept of a national network of associations for spreading the message; the relatively cheap and rapid transportation available through the federal postal system. Lewis Tappan's experience in the evangelical movement prepared him well for the enterprise. Romantic as his goal of instant conversion of his enemies may appear, one must remember that few other propaganda attempts have been any less so.

By mid-July the first shipments of materials were ready. Great bundles of papers, numbering 175,000 separate items, piled up in the New York City post office, awaiting delivery to hundreds of communities over the nation. Before the Society's next anniversary, in May of 1836, Lewis Tappan's publications board issued over a million impressions of antislavery pieces.[49] This effort was to change the nature of the movement. Thereafter, antislavery, no longer inhibited by Arthur Tappan's caution, was a subject no American could ignore.

NOTES

1. George Clark to Weld, October 10, 1834, Weld MSS, Clements Library; Thomas, *Weld*, 71.

2. Grinnell, *Forty Years*, 30, 37. A history of Lane Seminary's antislavery troubles is in New York *Evangelist*, January 10, 1835; see also Weld to LT, March 18, 1834, in *Liberator*, April 12, 1834; *Emancipator*, March 25, April 22, 1834; Sydney Strong, "The Exodus of Students from Lane Seminary," *Ohio Church History Society Papers*, IV (1893), 1–16.

3. Huntington Lyman, fragment, n.d., Weld MSS, Clements Library; *Liberator*, April 12, 1834; see also Weld to LT, March 18, 1834, in Barnes and Dumond, *Weld Letters*, I, 132–35; Robert S. Fletcher, *A History of Oberlin College from Its Foundation through the Civil War* (Oberlin, 1943), I, 154–55; LT, *Arthur Tappan*, 236.

4. Cross, *Beecher Autobiography*, II, 242–43; *Spirit of the Pilgrims*, VI (1833), 299–402, 569 ff.; see also AT to Amos Phelps, September 19, 1833, Phelps MSS, BPL; Huntington Lyman, in W. S. Ballantine, ed., *The Oberlin Jubilee, 1833–1883* (Oberlin, 1883), 66.

5. Huntington Lyman to James Thome, August 17, 1834, Robert S. Fletcher File, Oberlin College Library; Cross, *Beecher Autobiography*, II, 243.

6. Lyman Beecher to Weld, October 8, 1834, Barnes and Dumond, *Weld Letters*, I, 170–73, with fn.; Fletcher, *Oberlin*, I, 157–58; Thomas, *Weld*, 75–77.

7. LT to Weld, September 29, 1834, Slavery MSS, Box II, New-York Historical Society.

8. LT to Phelps, October 10, 1834, Phelps MSS, BPL.

9. Quoted by Fletcher, *Oberlin*, I, 164; LT, *Arthur Tappan*, 233.

10. LT, *Arthur Tappan*, 236–37; S. Wells to Weld, January 8, 1835, Barnes and Dumond, *Weld Letters*, I, 192; Fletcher, *Oberlin*, I, 173.

11. Fletcher, *Oberlin*, I, 58–116; on founding of Oberlin, see Shipherd to Fayette Shipherd, February 16, 1830; Shipherd to Keep, December 13, 1834, Shipherd, "pastoral letter," January 28, 1835, autograph file, "Shipherd," Oberlin College Library; Shipherd to N.P. Fletcher, December 15, 1834, treasurer's office file, Oberlin College; Asa Mahan, *Autobiography, Intellectual, Moral, and Spiritual* (London, 1882), 190–94; quotation from Page Smith, *As a City upon a Hill: The Town in American History* (New York, 1966), 47. Smith clearly indicates the influence of New England culture upon frontier settlement, but he errs in implying that bigotry and intolerance were characteristic of Yankee puritans alone. On the Tappan investments, see Portage County Tax and Property Records, Kent State University Library (data supplied by Robert Gould).

12. LT to J. J. Shipherd, May 5, 1835, photostat, LT MSS; Charles Grandison Finney, *Memoirs* (New York, 1876), 332–35; Shipherd to Board of Trustees, January 19, 1835, treasurer's office file, Oberlin College; Finney to Stanton and Whipple, January 14, 1835, Finney MSS, Oberlin College Library; Fletcher, *Oberlin*, I, 177–78.

13. Shipherd to Board of Trustees, January 14 and 28, 1835, treasurer's office file, Oberlin College; see also vote of the colonists, December 31, 1834, miscellaneous file, Oberlin College Library.

14. AT to John Keep, May 6, 1835, autograph file, "Arthur Tappan," Oberlin College Library (quotation); see also AT to Shipherd, May 6, 1835, treasurer's office file, Oberlin College.

15. AT to Shipherd, May [n.d.], May 6, June 16, October 1, 1835, AT to Levi Burnell, October 6, December 25, 1835, treasurer's office file, Oberlin College.

16. Fletcher, *Oberlin*, I, 187–88, and II, 596; see also AT to Levi Burnell, October 6, 1835, treasurer's office file, Oberlin College.

17. AT to Shipherd, June 10, 15, 1835, and July 25, 1835, autograph file, "Arthur Tappan," Oberlin College Library.

18. AT to Shipherd, June 15, 1835, *ibid.*

19. AT to Shipherd, October 1, 1835, treasurer's office file, Oberlin College; Finney MSS of "Memoir," 675, Finney MSS, Oberlin College Library; Mrs. Lucretia Smith, 1883 reminiscence, Fletcher MSS, Oberlin College Library; "Interview with Pres. Fairchild," January 4 and 5, 1894, 55–56, Oberlin Collection, Oberlin College Library.

20. "Fairchild Interview," February 7, 1894, 82, and February 23, 1894, 94–98; Thomas, *Weld*, 97.

21. Fletcher, *Oberlin*, I, 233; *The Complete Works of Artemus Ward* (London, 1910), 59–61; Julius O. Beardslee to Ezra H. Beardslee, September 10, 1835, Fletcher file, Oberlin College Library.

22. AT to Shipherd, May [n.d.], 1835, treasurer's office file, Oberlin College.

23. Lowell *Observer,* quoted in *Liberator,* September 20, 1834.

24. LT to WLG, October 7, 1834, WLG MSS, BPL; LT to Weld, September 29, 1834, Slavery MSS, Box II, New-York Historical Society; Wright to B. Green, September 19, 1834, Wright MSS, LC.

25. Wright to B. Green, March 3, 1834, Wright MSS, LC; Wright to Phelps, October 7, 1834, Wright MSS, LC; see also Weld to Birney, May 28, 1834, Dwight L. Dumond, ed., *Letters of James Gillespie Birney, 1831–1857* (New York, 1938), I, 113; Tuckerman, *Jay,* 57.

26. Quoted by Weld, August 25, 1834, in Dumond, *Birney Letters,* I, 130.

27. Quotation, Wright to Weld, August 14, 1834, Barnes and Dumond, *Weld Letters,* I, 166–67; Weld to Birney, September 4, 1834, *ibid.,* I, 132–33; Wright to Phelps, August 20, 1834, Phelps MSS, BPL.

28. *Liberator,* May 24, 1834; LT to George Thompson, January 2, 1835, WLG MSS, BPL; AT to Phelps, January 17, 1835, Phelps MSS, BPL.

29. Beaumont quoted by George Wilson Pierson, *Tocqueville and Beaumont in America* (New York, 1938), 363n.

30. T. H. Gallaudet to General John Hartwell Cocke, July 18, 1834; R. R. Gurley to Cocke, September 14, 1834, with enclosure of Gallaudet to Gurley, July 21, 1831; Courtland Van Rensselaer to Cocke, November 25, 1834—all in John Hartwell Cocke MSS, Shields Deposit, Alderman Library, University of Virginia (hereinafter, Library, UVA); Cocke to Mrs. Louisa Cocke, December 13, 1831, "Bremo" Deposit, Library, UVA; John Tappan to Cocke, October 24, 1834, Cocke Deposit, Library, UVA.

31. *Liberator,* January 17, 1835; Garrison and Garrison, *Garrison,* 470; Staudenraus, *African Colonization Movement,* 231.

32. Elkins, *Slavery,* Chapter IV.

33. Martin Boyd Coyner, "John Hartwell Cocke of Bremo," Ph.D. dissertation, University of Virginia, 1962, *passim.* Cocke wrote in his diary, "While I protest against holding slaves being a Sin under all circumstances I am equally fixed in the opinion that no sanction can be brought from the Bible for defending American Slavery interminably" (diary, July 8, 1851, Shields Deposit, Library, UVA).

34. Charles Tappan to Cocke, September 2, 1834, Cocke Deposit, Library, UVA.

35. Garrison and Garrison, *Garrison,* I, 470–71.

36. *Liberator,* November 8 and 29, December 20, 1834, January 24, 1835.

37. *Liberator,* January 31, 1835, reprint from Boston *Recorder.*

38. Elizur Wright to B. Green, March 7 and 19, 1835, Wright MSS, LC; Wright to Weld, March 16, 1835, in Barnes and Dumond, *Weld Letters,* I, 210; Henry Benson to WLG, February 25, 1835 and LT to WLG, February 5, 1835, WLG MSS, BPL; *Liberator,* January 31, 1835.

39. LT to WLG, February 5, 1835, WLG MSS, LC.

40. See citations in footnote 38.

41. *Liberator,* February 7, 1835.

42. Wright to Phelps, January 22, February 9, 1835, Phelps MSS, BPL; Minutes, Agency Committee, for January 22, 1835, BPL; *Liberator,* March 7 and 21, April 4, 1835; Wright to Green, March 7, 1835, Wright MSS, LC; John L. Myers, "The Beginning of Anti-Slavery Agencies in New York State, 1833–1836," *New York History,* XLVIII (April, 1962), 149–81.

43. Myers, "Beginning of Anti-Slavery Agencies," 149–81; Garrison and Gar-

rison, *Garrison*, I, 483n; S. S. Jocelyn appointed to Agency Committee, May 20, 1835, Agency Minutes, BPL.

44. *Annual Report* (1835), 83–87, Birney's report, 4–11, 76–82; Thomas, *Weld*, 92–99; Myers, "Beginning of Anti-Slavery Agencies," 167, 170–71; Coyner, "Cocke," 350–51.

45. *Annual Report* (1835), 30; *Emancipator*, June 8 and 16, 1835; *Liberator*, May 30, June 20, 1835; and Boston *Recorder*, May 22, 1835.

46. Quotations from *Emancipator Extra*, June 16, 1835, and Wright to Weld, June 10, 1835, in Barnes and Dumond, *Weld Letters*, I, 225; *Liberator*, June 20, 1835.

47. LT, "Chronological Resume," 1835; Wright to Weld, September 16, 1835, in Barnes and Dumond, *Weld Letters*, I, 231; Wright to his parents, July 20, 1837, Wright MSS, LC. The dozen include *Christian Register* (Boston), 1825–26; *Journal of Commerce*, 1828–29; New York *Evangelist*, 1831–35; *Slave's Friend*, 1835–37; *Emancipator*, 1834–37; *Human Rights*, 1835–36; *American and Foreign Anti-Slavery Reporter*, 1840–50; *Union Missionary*, 1844–46; *American Missionary*, 1846–65; *National Era*, 1848–52; *Independent*, 1861. Dates are approximate periods of Tappan's intimate connections with these publications. See also Henry B. Stanton, *Random Recollections* (New York, 1887), 267–68.

48. Wright and Wright, *Elizur Wright*, 105–6. Cf. Barnes, *Antislavery Impulse*, 62–63; see also E. Wright to Jay, August 21, 1835, William Jay MSS, Jay House, Mt. Kisco. All the above quotations are from *Human Rights*, July, 1835, and from *Slave's Friend*, August, 1835.

49. *Annual Report* (1836), 35, 76–77.

CHAPTER EIGHT

The Great Postal Campaign

The New York riots of 1834 may have acquainted Lewis Tappan with the violence of American racism, but he and his friends were nonetheless caught by surprise by the unanimity of the southern reaction to their propaganda in the following year. Opposition was expected and, to a degree, sought in order to advertise antislavery principles, but the southerners' universal abhorrence of abolitionism doomed the strategy of moral suasion —a strategy that underlay the postal campaign.

On the evening of July 29, 1835, a group of Charlestonians broke into the U.S. Post Office and hauled off a number of mail-bags, which had just arrived from New York City by the fort-nightly packet. The thieves considered themselves as patriotic and virtuous as the "Indians" who dumped tea into Boston harbor in 1775; the real criminals were the Tappan brothers. On the following evening, three thousand Charlestonians gathered on the parade grounds to watch effigies of Arthur Tappan, Garrison, and Samuel H. Cox strung up on a mock gallows. Then, on the signal of a balloon's ascent, a match was put to the abolitionist papers piled underneath.[1]

During the following week, Charleston conducted its affairs with the same urgency a sudden military invasion might have created. Merchants, ministers, and nullification aristocrats, such as General Robert Y. Hayne and William F. Colcock, organized public protest meetings, issued circulars to warn the state's post-masters, formed a committee to inspect the mails, and passed resolutions against the "fanatics and incendiaries."[2] With the memory of South Carolina's isolation during the nullification crisis still fresh, it was recognized that full co-operation from the federal government, at least some northern states, and other southern states would be essential. The editor of the *Southern Patriot* and the leaders of the Charleston rallies asked the postmaster general to overlook the southern violation of the mails, since it conformed to the "spirit of the Constitution," if not the letter, and to see that there was no further abuse of the postal system by the abolitionists.[3] Editorials and resolutions at the public meetings demanded northern apologies, pledges of reform, and complete suppression of abolitionism. Hitherto, the South had considered antislavery more a future than a present danger, but suddenly fears of national intervention were alive, and forecasts of disastrous consequences filled the newspaper columns. "The indications are that the South is unanimous in their resistance," warned John C. Calhoun, "even to the extent of disunion, if that should be necessary to arrest the evil."[4]

Even though northern response fell short of southern hopes, the South was more united on this issue than it had been on the nullification question only three years before. Torchlight parades, vigilance committees, speeches, and resolutions reassured southerners that Yankee subversion would not destroy their way of life without broad resistance. Community spokesmen fulminated in press and pulpit against "the extensive conspiracy," this "new emission of mischief," "the Abolitionists' pandemonium of New York," and the Yankee "banditti" and "desperadoes." A clergyman of Virginia warned his Presbytery, "If there be any stray goat of a minister among you, tainted with the blood-hound principles of abolitionism, let him be ferreted out, silenced, excommunicated, and LEFT TO THE PUBLIC TO BE DISPOSED OF IN OTHER RESPECTS." Legislators passed new laws and urged the enforcement of old ones to police the free Negroes, who were the chief objects, they claimed, of the postal effort.[5]

Southerners were convinced that the abolitionists would stop at no limit of decency or ingenuity to spread their message. Rumors raged through the countryside. A Norfolk paper, for instance, claimed that agents in New York were handing out *Human Rights* to children of southern visitors "as 'something pretty for them to read,'" in the hope that they would pass the journal along to their Negro mammies back home.[6]

While some gentlemen still believed that the movement was small enough to handle by quick suppression, others saw a deeper meaning in the mail campaign. The editor of the *Southern Patriot* of Charleston declared that it was an outgrowth of "a subterranean stream of evil . . . working its way imperceptibly from the interior towns and villages to the sea ports." A Georgia slaveholder wrote in the New York *Spectator,* "The present movements, of themselves, are nothing. It is only in their progress that they may do mischief, but the zeal of Garrison, the wealth of Tappan, and the talents of Cox . . . will do much." A committee of the South Carolina legislature pointed out that it was not very likely that a slave rebellion, stirred by Yankee abolitionists, could succeed, but southern peace of mind was the real concern. So long as northern fanatics were known to be spreading their "lies," southern whites lived in "perpetual panic," even though "the real danger can be long deferred." In demanding censorship laws in the free states, therefore, slaveholders were attempting to prevent their exclusion from civilized society and to protect their feelings of well-being.[7]

In the midst of this ferment, Arthur Tappan tried to carry on his business and philanthropy as usual, but he had to bear the brunt of the reaction which his brother's publication effort evoked. Frequently in times of crisis, hatreds focus upon a single individual who comes to symbolize all that is thought evil. Rather than William Lloyd Garrison, for a short period that enemy was, ironically, Arthur Tappan. He heard his name cursed on the streets as he passed, found former friends turning away when he approached, and read bristling editorials about himself in the local press. James Watson Webb, his fury still unabated, played upon the prejudices of those who feared any signs of white liberality and Negro prosperity: "The air," he observed, "in all our public conveyances is poisoned with the rank effluvia of . . . aromatic damsels, who . . . always challenge the favorite seats . . . dressed in silks obtained from the munificence of Arthur Tappan."[8] For the first time in the Tappans' experience, however, the real danger was not from local bullies but from the South.

Although antislavery friends reassured him, Arthur may have felt a certain twinge of fear upon reading of the various demands for his extradition to face southern charges of fomenting slave rebellion. With a perverse kind of logic, the Richmond *Whig* denounced a New York journalist for defending Tappan's right to speak: "The scoundrel who set a whole country aflame and subjected innocent men to the lash ought by all means to enjoy unmolested security!"[9] In the *Evening Post*, there was an account of a meeting in Norfolk that called for public donations to buy "the heads of Garrison, Tappan & Co."[10] In East Feliciana, Louisiana, another rally pledged a $30,000 reward for Tappan's delivery on a New Orleans wharf, and the Rev. J. C. Postell of South Carolina raised the bid to $100,000 if La Roy Sunderland, a Methodist abolitionist editor, "and old Arthur Tappan come out to the South this winter. . . ." When asked about these tempting prizes, Arthur is said to have replied in a rare but brave moment of humor, "If that sum is placed in a New York bank, I may possibly think of giving myself up."[11]

Lewis also had his share of abuse. Boys hooted at him on the street, and like his brother he was insulted by strangers. Lewis took the excitement and danger in stride, writing John Shipherd at Oberlin, "My house has been named in a handbill signed *Judge Lynch,* as a mark of popular fury. But hitherto the Lord has preserved us, & blessed be his holy name!"[12] Later, in 1836, he opened a package containing a Negro's ear, with a note enclosed recommending it for his "collection of natural curiosities."[13] Threats of this kind simply added to the publicity of antislavery. As the August, 1835, issue of *Human Rights* asserted, "Nothing is really anti-abolitionist, but apathy."

Insults were harmless enough, but there was a danger of a violence greater than the previous New York tumults. Seven thousand southern visitors were estimated to be in the city. Philip Hone confided in his diary that "the least spark would create a flame in which the lives and property of Arthur Tappan and his associates would be endangered." According to one abolitionist, someone at the Merchants' Exchange, just across the street from Arthur Tappan & Co., announced a bid of $5,000 for his head.[14]

Not long before the postal effort began, Arthur Tappan had moved his residence from the city to fashionable Brooklyn Heights, overlooking the East River and harbor. Commuting regularly by ferry, he could easily have been murdered or captured at any time. If rumors had the slightest truth, assassins were indeed skulking about. It was said that ruffians from Savannah, out for the rewards, had a pilot boat ready to carry him off. According to the impressionable Lydia Maria Child, then staying in Brooklyn, "Private assassins are lurking at the corners of streets to stab Arthur Tappan. . . . 'Tis like the times of the French Revolution, when no man dared trust his neighbor."[15] The mayor of Brooklyn thought the danger real enough to patrol at night in front of Tappan's house himself, at the same time stationing a relay of men at the Brooklyn Navy Yard in case military force became necessary.[16]

The riots of 1834 had provided the Tappans with some unexpected protection the following year. City officials and the more responsible editors wanted no repetition of lawlessness. James Watson Webb, however, carried on in his usual vein, warning that men who could start a society to suppress prostitution and "end by advocating promiscuous intercourse and unlimited concubinage!" could also pretend "a zeal for the unhappy negroes," even though the reformers' path led "to discord, and to civil war, with all its kindred horrors of rape, sack and slaughter." The reply that antislavery men gave to such charges was standard throughout the antebellum years: "Abolitionists are probably as fond of the Union as a slaveholder; but not of a Union to oppress the poor. If this Union is severed, *Slavery* will be the blame for it."[17] In spite of these hot words on both sides, there was no violence. When an antiabolitionist meeting was held in Battery Park at the end of August, the speeches were comparatively mild and unprovoking. In frustration perhaps, Webb added in an article about a reported attempt to kidnap Arthur Tappan, "'Keep a look out, Arthur—a large reward is offered for you—before you are aware, you may be boxed.'"[18]

Abolitionist reaction to threats of violence and reprisal was uniformly courageous, but most admirable of all was the attitude of Arthur Tappan, on whom the pressures were the greatest. With genuine self-effacement, he cared less about his personal safety than about antislavery and his ability to sustain it. He gave another $1,750 to the Society during the summer, but a warning went to Oberlinites to expect little in the future from Arthur Tappan.[19] Shipherd, who had already drawn heavily on the New York account without the merchant's approval, was badly shaken by the news and wrote Arthur Tappan for reassurance. Shipherd's relief was probably profound when he read the reply: "The drafts you speak of as *to be* drawn will be duly honored if my life is spared . . . and we begin to feel that the danger is passing over."

Yet, Arthur had to admit, "If I had foreseen the storm that was gathered around my head I should not have dared to assume the responsibilities I did for your Institution. It was wisely ordered that I had no expectation of such an event." For a man perpetually suffering from nervous tension, Arthur's steadiness of purpose was impressive. Rather than calling attention to his own peril, he told Shipherd, "The Lord has hitherto preserved me and my dear brethren of the Executive Committee from the band of assassins who have been hovering around our steps. . . ."[20]

Lewis Tappan, on the other hand, drew real pleasure from his defiance of danger. With obvious relish, he told one abolitionist, "The Gov[ernor] of Georgia calls us monsters."[21] Probably without consulting his brother or the other abolitionists, Lewis published a letter addressed to a South Carolina vigilance committee. It concluded with the boastful words, "We will persevere, come life or death. If any fall by the hand of violence, others will continue the blessed work." According to a local paper, Manhattan was ready to give Lewis a second lesson in public manners.[22] To such threats as this, he retorted, "The Lord, we trust, will overrule this 'madness of the people' to the promotion of this blessed cause, & the glory of his name."[23] Of all the New York abolitionists, Lewis Tappan's response was most like that of the Garrisonians.

None of the abolitionists was willing to give up his principles to escape danger, but the Boston faction positively exulted in the crisis. " 'Catch a fish before you cook it,' " jeered David Lee Child. "If Arthur Tappan's blood should be shed the fate of oppression if not of oppressors (much as we might wish to save them) would be sealed in this country."[24] Meanwhile, Garrison poured out scathing articles, indicting particular proslavery editors and clergymen for spreading "LIES of the hugest dimensions, of the most malicious aspect, and of the most murderous tendency." On October 21, a mob led the plucky agitator, serene and sometimes smiling, through the streets of Boston with a noose around his neck. Garrison, like Arthur and Lewis, was a victim of the uproar over the postal effort, but added to the heat of that controversy was the presence in the Boston vicinity of George Thompson, the British agitator who shared Garrison's gift for causing a ruckus wherever he went. After his exciting brush with immortality, Garrison welcomed Lewis and Arthur to the grand fraternity of martyrs. "You and your much devoted brother," he wrote Lewis, "are . . . liable to be abducted by blood-thirsty men. . . .I rejoice that you are thus counted worthy to suffer. . . ." It was a time of abolitionist glory.

Arthur Tappan shared Lewis' and Garrison's expectation of an antislavery awakening, but he did not delight in the present opposition. After all, the postal campaign was not his idea, even though most of his donations were spent on it. It was all very well for Garrison and Lewis Tappan to sigh that the "burdens of the cross" were "light to bear in these modern days."[25] Garrison was too poor to be brought to heel by economic reprisal. His business, in a sense, depended upon southerners' hostility, while Arthur's relied upon their goodwill. Financial martyrdom was hardly the usual prelude to beatification.

The publicity that descended on the firm turned out to be a financial bonanza at first. Country tourists and local residents came in to stare at Arthur Tappan as he sat at his desk. No doubt the Yankee clerks were wide awake enough to press sales upon the visitors, and Lewis had just the things to catch their eye—silk prints depicting "The Poor Slave," in four poses, suitable, perhaps, for employment as a purse covering or lamp mat. There were also "handsome" plaster mannikins of slaves in chains for only fifty cents apiece. More utilitarian were antislavery wax-sealers and children's pocket handkerchiefs bearing the "Teetotallers Temperance and Anti-Slavery Pledge." The company happily reported in the *Liberator* that cash sales in August and September topped all records for the fall season.[26]

The South, meanwhile, was preparing an economic campaign against the firm. It opened at Charleston, whose dry goods dealers had grown accustomed to ordering goods from Arthur's company. At a meeting in early August, R. J. Moses urged storekeepers to halt their trade with the Tappans. The movement quickly spread. It must have been one of the first organized attempts to bankrupt a national business because of its owners' political and moral convictions. In Nashville, the vigilance committee ordered merchants to stop purchases at once.[27] The editor of the Petersburg, Virginia, *Constellation* applauded the movement: "Strike at the root of the evil, fellow-citizens of the South! It is *you* who have enriched these miscreants. . . . We ought to wear nothing bought of the Tappans, or suffer it to be worn in our families. . . ." Southern citizens' groups warned visitors to New York not to stop at 122 Pearl Street. It took special courage for a southern lawyer to take Arthur Tappan's case against a delinquent Georgia debtor.[28]

Faced with the example of southern reaction to Arthur Tappan's antislavery views, other New York merchants grew increasingly worried. In late August and September, 1835, a non-importation movement against the whole city was discernible. Southern papers demanded the transfer of commerce to Philadelphia, where a protest rally had resolved to press for state censorship laws against antislavery. Abolitionists, of course, ridiculed the southern economic plan, but the threat was enough to excite the fears of New York businessmen.[29]

Delegations from the Chamber of Commerce and city dignitaries solemnly trooped into the store to reason with Arthur. According to Lewis, they pointed out that Arthur's chief duty was to his creditors, who would bear the ultimate effect of a change in his fortunes. Moreover, his course might soon bring ruin upon all those law-abiding, earnest members of the business community who depended on the southern trade. And why not let the South solve its own problems? After a moment's hesitation, the merchant replied, "You demand that I shall cease my antislavery labors. . . . *I will be hung first!*" A friend remarked admiringly, "That man has the spirit of a martyr!"[30] Arthur Tappan realized that his reply might put an end to his philanthropy, in spite of all the accolades he received from sentimental reformers. More to the point was William Green's rather dry comment, "It will be surprising if the banks do not try to cripple A. T. & Co."[31]

Economic sanctions take time to succeed, and the South was in a hurry. Editors demanded the extradition of leading abolitionists to stand trial in the South. A Virginia county grand jury indicted the entire Executive Committee. At Columbia, South Carolina, the state attorney-general received a number of petitions urging a trial for Arthur Tappan and the others. The Governor of Alabama demanded the extradition of R. G. Williams, the Society's publishing agent, whose name was the only one to appear on any of the publications. "Authur Tappan," fumed the governor, "and the infuriate demoniacs have never acquired any considerable notoriety until this opposition [in the South] commenced." The Tappans could hardly have agreed more heartily with his diagnosis. Needless to say, Governor William L. Marcy refused to honor any of these efforts to lay hands upon the New York abolitionists.[32]

The extradition attempts began to influence many in the North who formerly had been antagonistic to abolitionism, a shift of sentiment Lewis Tappan hoped to encourage. He urged William

Jay to draw up a legal manifesto, pointing out the irrationality and danger of southern demands. With good reason, Jay refused, on the grounds that public opinion was already rising in favor of the abolitionist case. A number of northern papers defended the right of free speech, including the New York *American* and William Leggett's *Evening Post*. Even Charleston's *Southern Patriot* called efforts to bring Arthur Tappan to southern justice a useless gesture.[33]

Antislavery sentiment, although moderate and circumscribed, quietly developed as the controversy wore on. Philip Hone, the urbane New Yorker who had no sympathy for evangelical causes, remarked, "I do not choose to surrender the power of executing justice into the hands of slaveowners of South Carolina." It was a common opinion. Moreover, the numerous antiabolitionist rallies in the North fell short of southern expectations. Only in Philadelphia was there much support for censorship of abolitionist literature, while in New Haven and Lowell, Massachusetts, citizens publicly condemned southern belligerence.[34] Another "disclaimer," written by Judge Jay and signed by Arthur Tappan, set forth the dangers to white liberty that censorship posed. It also asserted that the Executive Committee had not tried to reach free Negroes and that the members of the Society were peaceful men and women who honored the Constitution, including the slavery clauses. Denying any partisan ambitions, the disclaimer reaffirmed abolitionist faith in moral suasion rather than physical force, and it defined abolitionist political aims as the repeal of slavery in the District of Columbia by Congressional action. Elizur Wright reported that "none but the determined pro-slavery presses fail to speak of it as a candid, firm and honorable, if not convincing document." Faced with the examples of abolitionist moderation on the one hand and southern intransigence on the other, many were brought to see that more was at stake than simply the right of a few men to use the post offices. Both Hezekiah Niles of Baltimore and James Gordon Bennett of the New York *Herald* admitted that the South had gone too far and that a reaction was setting in.[35] Abolitionists were pleased with the change in antislavery fortunes in spite of the continued threat of violence. Perhaps the original goals of converting the southern intelligensia through tracts and woodcuts had failed, but publicity had also been a purpose, and that the abolitionists received in abundance.

157

While abolitionism withstood the fierce reaction that the postal campaign aroused, there were ominous consequences as well. In spite of the New York committee's reiterations of its peaceful designs, antislavery efforts were inadvertently helping to unleash forces of violence beyond normal control. For the reformers, of course, every evidence of proslavery disorder confirmed their opinion of the nation's guilt and blindness. In an impassioned, bitter passage Theodore Weld spoke of the hidden terrors that abolitionists had uncovered in the American soul—terrors so like those that scourged another empire of centuries before:

The empty *name* [of freedom] is everywhere,—*free* government, *free* men, *free* speech, *free* people, *free* schools, and *free* churches. Hollow counterfeits, all! FREE! It is the climax of irony, and its million echoes are hisses and jeers, even from the earth's ends. FREE! *Blot it out.* Words are the signs of *things.* The substance has gone! Let fools and madmen clutch at shadows. The husk must rustle the more when the kernel and the ear are gone! Rome's loudest shout for liberty was when she murdered it, and drowned its death-shrieks in her hoarse hussas. She never raised her hands so high to swear allegiance to freedom, as when she gave the death-stab, and madly leaped upon its corpse! and her most delirious dance was among the clods her hands had cast upon its coffin! FREE! The word and sound are omnipresent masks, and mockers! An impious lie! unless they stand for free *Lynch Law,* and free *murder*; for they *are* free.

The occasion of these words, addressed to the Philadelphia abolitionists, was the near completion of the Pennsylvania Hall for Free Discussion (it was soon to be destroyed by a mob), but Weld also composed this lamentation in memory of the murdered Elijah P. Lovejoy, shot in 1837 while defending his antislavery press in Alton, Illinois.[36] Abolitionists had reason to be skeptical about the American boast of liberty.

Nevertheless, even the victims of persecution were not themselves completely free from the climate of hostility that their oppressors generated. Ironically, before his death Lovejoy, who was a controversial, passionate man, was not in good favor with some of the more pacifistic abolitionists. Sarah Grimké had written Weld, "And E. P. Lovejoy keeping arms in his office! Truly I fear we have yet to learn the lesson 'Trust in the Lord'. . . . Surely posterity will brand us hypocrites. The slave must not raise his hand against his oppressor, but we are at liberty to revenge our wrongs. Oh consistency where art thou?" Only a few months later, when news of the Alton tragedy arrived, abolitionists quietly forgot that Lovejoy himself had added fuel to public passion by relying on the protection of guns. Like John Brown many years later, he was immediately transfigured into a Christian martyr— the first white man to earn this distinction in the antislavery cause. Only the gentle Grimké sisters, Samuel J. May, William Lloyd Garrison, and a few other non-resistants expressed their doubts about the "dangerous precedent" that Lovejoy had set "in the maintenance of the cause. . . ."

After an emergency meeting of the Executive Committee, it was resolved to exploit the shock and chagin of the northern public as quickly as possible. Lewis Tappan organized a well-attended memorial service for Lovejoy in the Broadway Tabernacle. Perhaps it was quite appropriate that the Society should issue a special forty-thousand-copy edition of *Human Rights,* giving all the unhappy circumstances surrounding the events in Alton and that the office stationery should bear at the top the inscription: "LOVEJOY the First MARTYR to American LIBERTY. MURDERED for asserting the FREEDOM OF THE PRESS. Alton Nov. 7, 1837."[37] The movement was drifting away from its original premises and approaching the corrosive mood that was so prevalent throughout the land.

There were other signs of a fearful tension in the nation in the 1830's, the results of which the abolitionists were not alone to experience. In St. Louis, a mob chained a free mulatto to a tree and burned him alive because he was thought to have murdered a white man. In Mississippi, lynch law threatened to unravel the social fabric. "Never was there an instance of more extraordinary or even maddening excitement amid a refined, intelligent and virtue loving people than that which I had the pain to witness in the counties of central Missisippi in the summer of 1835," recalled Henry S. Foote, a level-headed politician of the state. Because of a supposed plot of insurrection among the slaves, an odd assortment of "steam doctors," gamblers, slaves, free Negroes, and ordinary bystanders were put to death by lynchers on the excuse that the jails were too insecure and the danger too great to await the proceedings of trials.[38]

World opinion was perplexed by these events in a country regarded by many as the hope of civilization. In an address to

Tory leaders at Tamworth in the summer of 1835, Sir Robert Peel spoke of the wild mobocracy into which American institutions were plunging. His "bare catalogue of enormities," which included "acts of aggression" between citizens of Ohio and Michigan and extended to the summary hangings in Vicksburg and Livingstone, Mississippi, was sufficient he said, to cast doubts about the vaunted happiness of the United States. Englishmen ought to ponder these signs, he concluded, before launching further into electoral reforms.[39]

In this country too, there were expressions of fear for the safety of the Republic. The young Whig attorney Abraham Lincoln told a Springfield audience, "I hope I am over wary; but if I am not, there is, even now, something of ill-omen amongst us. I mean the increasing disregard for law which pervades the country; the growing disposition to substitute the wild and furious passions, in lieu of the sober judgment of Courts; and the worse than savage mobs, for the executive ministers of justice." Like the conservative leaders of England, he wondered whether, "if destruction be our lot, we must ourselves be its author and finisher." As for abolitionism, he added, its merits and its wisdom could not be decided upon the basis of "the interposition of mob law. . . ."[40] But wise or not, the Tappans' crusade was affected by the violence which was nurtured in part by the antislavery movement itself, even though the abolitionists had not planned it that way. Lewis' and Arthur's generation was unwittingly preparing the next for a militancy that went beyond Lovejoy's death in defense of his Presbyterian journal and beyond the exploitation of that tragedy by the national antislavery leaders. Yet the fault lay not in the movement itself, for the failure of the nation as a whole to recognize its institutional complicities with inhumanity of various kinds was of greater moment than the actions of this group of reformers.

In the face of these indications of lawlessness, thoughtful moderates on both sides of the Potomac were becoming aware of the dilemma that Garrisonian agitation and southern reaction were forcing upon them, even though the mass of people were still generally indifferent to problems not directly affecting them. Writing an evangelical friend, a Virginian summarized his forebodings in this manner: "When I think of the myriads of . . . papers . . . from the prolific press in New York . . . diffusing at once delusion and bitterness through the North, and exasperation through the South; of *our own imprudences* in offering rewards for Tappan . . . , of our *lynchings* and excessive irritability through-out this whole season of agitation, how is it possible to avoid fearing the worst?" Except for their battle cry of "repent, repent," the abolitionists had no answer for him, no plan for satisfying the claims of all. They did not consider it their task to offer one; their duty was simply to arouse the nation to the fact that a problem existed. No wise men appeared at this point to propose an imaginative scheme of gradual emancipation, for even the Founding Fathers had found it necessary to avoid the issue at a juncture much more appropriate for its consideration some forty-six years earlier. The avenue to peaceful solution, perhaps never wide, was rapidly closing.[41]

After the postal controversy began, antislavery agents could no longer operate with any assurance of safety in the South. James G. Birney was expelled from Kentucky in October, 1835, and Amos Dresser, a Lane and Oberlin seminarian, was publicly whipped at Nashville for carrying an *Emancipator* in his luggage. On August 17, Dr. Reuben Crandall, brother of Prudence Crandall, was thrown into jail in Georgetown, D.C., for "circulating Tappan, Garrison & Co's papers. . . ." In New Orleans, a group called the Louisiana Constitutional and Anti-Fanatical Society was organized with a proposed budget of one-half million dollars to counteract the effects of Yankee agitation.[42]

In the North, widespread hostility developed too. Leonard Woods, Jr., editor of a Presbyterian journal in New York, declared that the "radicals" were "*justly liable to the highest civil penalties and ecclesiastical censures.*" The wedge between conservative churchmen and the evangelical abolitionists was being driven deeper into the country's religious system. Nor was Birney welcomed as a refugee when he set up his *Philanthropist* in Cincinnati. Instead, a mob hurled his press into the Ohio, while elsewhere in the state Weld met fierce antagonism during his antislavery tour. In late August a Philadelphia mob discovered antislavery materials on a wharf awaiting southern shipment, carried them to a steamboat, and dumped them in the middle of the Delaware. On October 21, within a few hours: the mayor of Boston put Garrison in the jailhouse to save him from the howling mob; Henry Stanton was attacked in Newport, Rhode Island; Lewis Tappan and Gerrit Smith were hounded in Utica at a gathering of the New York State Anti-Slavery Society. Grimly, Lewis worked out the precise times it took Satan to travel between

these places to rouse the opposition.[43] In spite of abolitionist protests, Amos Kendall, postmaster-general, virtually endorsed state
postal inspection. Even in New York, S. L. Gouveneur, the local
postmaster, requested antislavery men to give up the campaign
voluntarily in the public interest.[44] While formally refusing, Arthur
Tappan did see to it that the Executive Committee made no
further attempts to reach the South directly.

What had the abolitionists actually done? They did not urge
slave rebellion; they had committed no seditious act; their means
were peaceful. Benjamin Tappan, while still aloof from the cause,
wrote Lewis, "The course pursued by the abolitionists invites
aggression & gives free course & impunity to crimes which are
shaking the foundations of the Republic." They should take up
arms against hostile mobs, he said, as "our fathers" did. But the
abolitionists, rejecting a policy of overt violence, yet achieved an
important result—they exposed the South's unwillingness to accept
any alteration of the institution of slavery. "Our opposers," said
R. G. Williams, "took the wrong course to accomplish their purpose. Instead of putting us down, they put us and our principles
up before the world—just where we wanted to be."[45]

Lewis and Arthur Tappan were always to consider the religious
groups of the country the proper targets of their program. Indeed,
most of the literature sent out had been directed to clergymen
and such prominent laymen, North and South, as General Cocke
(who at least had the courtesy to save his copy of the *Anti-Slavery
Record*). Yet the postal campaign carried the question beyond
the province of religion. Abolitionism began its political phase at
the next session of Congress in December. In his annual message,
Jackson, that alleged champion of American liberty, requested the
passage of a national censorship law to prohibit the dissemination
of dangerous writings. Fearing federal interference in any phase
of the dispute, Calhoun proposed a state-controlled measure.
Neither plan, however, had much support, for few politicians,
even those from the South, really wanted to grasp the nettle at
all. Besides, censorship could lead to the suppression of any political literature with which the current administration disagreed.[46]
Once abolition was recognized and debated on the floor of Congress, however, it was difficult to prevent further discussion. John
Greenleaf Whittier, Joshua Leavitt, and Theodore Weld kept the
political pot boiling for several years with a petitions campaign.
Beginning in 1836, John Quincy Adams, defying the bipartisan

passage of "gag" rules, steadfastly introduced antislavery memorials to a distracted House of Representatives. Moreover, on a state level, legislatures throughout New England held hearings at which abolitionists were invited to state their opposition to restrictive postal laws, giving them a new platform from which to speak.[47]

Within the movement itself, the postal controversy led to a proliferation of antislavery societies—from two hundred in May, 1835, to five hundred twenty-seven the following year. R. G. Williams reported that fifteen thousand people had bought subscriptions to the Society's publications during the same period, a rate of growth, he said, unparalleled in the history of American reform.[48]

The Tappans played their part in these developments, but they did not attend state legislative sessions, lecture to crowds and form new societies, or spend hours with Adams planning Congressional strategy. Their task was to supervise the growing movement, set policy, and aid the missionaries in the field with funds, information, and materials. It was their work in the postal campaign that had made possible the sudden growth of the cause— Lewis with his writing and management and Arthur with his financial support. After the controversy of 1835, the public was aware of abolition doctrine and the issue of free speech that accompanied it. In depth of effect, few abolitionist efforts could match it.[49] As Elizur Wright pointed out, proslavery response "has done more than could have been by the arguments of a thousand agents to convince the sober and disinterested" of slavery's crime. Abolitionists had fought their way to northern attention—and to toleration. The southern *cordon sanitaire* made it impossible for them to reach the southern evangelical slaveholders and community leaders, but motions were being created that would bring freedom to the slaves nonetheless. The very success of the postal campaign transformed the nature of antislavery, a change of which neither Arthur nor Lewis, faced with financial troubles as well, approved.

NOTES

1. Charleston *Southern Patriot*, July 29, August 1, 1835; *Liberator*, August 15, 1835; *Pennsylvania Reporter and Democratic Herald* (Harrisburg), August 14, 1835, article from New York *Evening Star*.

2. *Southern Patriot,* August 3, 4, 10, and 11, 1835; *Proceedings of the Citizens of Charleston, on the Incendiary Machinations Now in Progress against the Peace and Welfare of the Southern States, Published by Order of the Council* (Charleston, 1835).

3. *Southern Patriot,* August 4 and 10, 1835; New York *Evening Post,* August 8, 1835.

4. *Southern Patriot,* August 4, September 30, 1835.

5. *Southern Patriot,* August 4, 1835; Norfolk *Beacon* in *Liberator,* August 15, 1835; Richmond *Enquirer* in *Liberator,* August 22, 1835; Rev. Robert N. Anderson of Hanover, Pa., in William Goodell, *Slavery and Anti-Slavery* . . . (New York, 1853), 411.

6. Quotation in *Liberator,* August 15, 1835; *Southern Patriot,* September 3, 1835; Norfolk *Herald* in *Southern Patriot,* August 3, 1835; Eaton, *Freedom of Thought,* 126–29, and "Censorship of the Southern Mails," *American Historical Review,* XLVIII (January, 1943), 267–68, 274–75; New York *Evening Post,* September 6, 1835; Nashville *Banner and Whig,* August 14 and 17, 1835.

7. New York *Spectator,* August 14, 1835; William W. Freehling, *Prelude to Civil War: The Nullification Controversy in South Carolina, 1816–1836* (New York, 1965), 344–45, quotes from this report.

8. *Morning Courier and New York Enquirer,* August 3, 1835.

9. Quoted in New York *American,* September 14, 1835.

10. New York *Evening Post,* August 29, 1835, from Baltimore *Chronicle.*

11. LT, *Arthur Tappan,* 264–65; *Louisiana Journal* in *Niles' Weekly Register* (Baltimore), October 3, November 14, 1835; Goodell, *Slavery and Anti-Slavery,* 410–11, 412.

12. LT to Shipherd, August 19, 1835, miscellaneous MSS, Oberlin College Library; "Index to Narrative of L. T."

13. *Emancipator,* December 8, 1836.

14. Nevins, *Hone Diary,* I, 173; Tuckerman, *Jay,* 67; see also Lydia Maria Child to Mrs. Ellis Gray Loring, August 15, 1835, *Letters of Lydia Maria Child* (Boston, 1883), 15–16; *Courier and Enquirer,* September 1, 1835; *Liberator,* August 22, 1835.

15. LT, *Arthur Tappan,* 245; L. M. Child to Mrs. Loring, August 15, 1835, *Child Letters,* 15; D. L. Child to WLG, September 29, 1835, WLG MSS, BPL; William Green to Finney, August 28, 1835, Finney MSS, Oberlin College Library; Henrietta Buckmaster, *Let My People Go* (New York, 1941), 87; AT to Shipherd, September 15, 1835, autograph file, Oberlin College Library.

16. LT, *Arthur Tappan,* 249–50.

17. *Courier and Enquirer,* September 24, 1835; *Human Rights* (New York), September, 1835.

18. *American Spectator* (New York), August 28, 1835; *Courier and Enquirer,* August 26, 27, 28, September 1 and 5 (quotation), 1835.

19. Green to Finney, August 28, 1835, Finney MSS, Oberlin College Library; *Human Rights,* September, 1835.

20. AT to Shipherd, September 15, 1835, autograph file, Oberlin College Library; Green to Finney, August 28, 1835, Finney MSS, Oberlin College Library; LT to Shipherd, August 19, 1835, miscellaneous MSS, Oberlin College Library.

21. LT to Phelps, November 14, 1835, Phelps MSS, BPL.

22. *Niles' Weekly Register* (Baltimore), September 12, October 5, 1835; LT to Jay, October 5, 1835, Jay MSS, Jay House, Mt. Kisco.

23. LT to Shipherd, August 19, 1835, miscellaneous MSS, Oberlin College Library.

24. D. L. Child to WLG, September 29, 1835, WLG MSS, BPL.

25. WLG to LT, December 17, 1835, both quotations.

26. LT, "Chronological Resume," 1835; *Liberator,* November 21, 1835; *Emancipator,* August, 1835.

27. *Southern Patriot,* August 1 and 4, 1835; *Courier and Enquirer,* August 11, 1835; *Liberator,* August 15, 1835; Nashville *Banner,* August 24, 1835; see also Green to Finney, August 28, 1835, Finney MSS, Oberlin College Library.

28. Quoted in *Courier and Enquirer,* August 11, 1835; LT, *Arthur Tappan,* 244, 265.

29. *Niles' Weekly Register,* October 3, 1835; see Philip Foner, *Business and Slavery* (Chapel Hill, 1941), for study of North-South economic tensions.

30. LT, *Arthur Tappan,* 269–70.

31. Green to Finney, August 28, 1835, Finney MSS, Oberlin College Library.

32. Quotation from Thomas M. Owen, "Alabama's Protest Against Abolitionism," *Gulf States Historical Magazine,* II (July, 1903), 28–32; see Richmond *Whig* in New York *Evening Post,* October 12, 1835; *Southern Patriot,* October 12, 1835; R. G. Williams to William Jay, October 30, 1835, Jay House, Mt. Kisco; Albany *Daily Advertiser* in New York *Evening Post,* August 29, 1835.

33. *Southern Patriot,* October 2, 1835; Wright to Phelps, September 4, 1835, Phelps MSS, BPL; Tuckerman, *Jay,* 75–76; extracts in *Niles' Weekly Register,* October 3, 1835; New York *American,* August 19, September 14, 1835; *Courier and Enquirer,* September 15, 1835, quoting from *Journal of Commerce;* LT, *Arthur Tappan,* 250–51; New York *Evening Post,* August 8, 9, 12, and 26, 1835; see also New York *Spectator* (country edition of *Commercial Advertiser*), August 17, 1835.

34. Nevins, *Hone Diary,* I, August 13, 170–71, August 26, 172–73, and September 15, 1835, 177; *Emancipator,* October, 1835; New York *American,* September 14 and 18, 1835; Rochester *Democrat* in *Southern Patriot,* September 2, 1835.

35. Wright to Phelps, September 4, 1835, Phelps MSS, BPL; LT, *Arthur Tappan,* 246–47; Nye, *Fettered Freedom,* 60; Tuckerman, *Jay,* 56–69, 73; *Niles' Weekly Register,* October 3, 1835.

36. Weld to S. Webb and Wm. H. Scott, January 3, 1838, Barnes and Dumond, *Weld Letters,* II, 511–12.

37. Sarah and Angelina Grimké, September 9, 1837, *ibid.,* I, 447–48; Garrison quoted from *Liberator,* by Garrison and Garrison, *Garrison,* II, 190. Garrison denied that Lovejoy was a "*Christian* martyr. He died like Warren, not like Stephen." Merton L. Dillon, *Elijah P. Lovejoy: Abolitionist Editor . . .* (Urbana, 1961), 177, for last quotation; Samuel J. May in *Emancipator,* February 8, 1838.

38. Quoted by Eaton, *Freedom of Thought,* 97; Roy P. Basler, ed., *Abraham Lincoln: His Speeches and Writings* (New York, 1962), 76–85.

39. London *Times,* September 5, 1835.

40. Basler, *Lincoln: Speeches and Writings,* 77, 81.

41. Reprinted in *Emancipator,* May 26, 1836.

42. Arthur F. Hopkins to Birney, August 15, 1835, Dumond, *Birney Letters,* I, 237–38; Birney to Joseph Healy, October 2, 1835, *ibid.,* I, 249–51; Amos Dresser, *Personal Memoir Narrative of the Arrest, Lynch Law Trial, and Scourging of*

Amos Dresser at Nashville, Tennessee, August, 1835 (Oberlin, 1836); Nashville *Banner,* August 10, 1835; *Liberator,* August 22, 1835; New York *Evening Post,* September 6, 1835; *Southern Patriot,* August 22, September 3, 1835; LT, *Arthur Tappan,* 165; New York *American,* September 10, 1835; Betty Fladeland, *James Gillespie Birney, Slaveholder to Abolitionist* (Ithaca, 1955), 139–44.

43. Thomas, *Weld,* 100–9; Stanton, *Random Recollections,* 51–52; Leonard Woods, quoted by Goodell in *Slavery and Anti-Slavery,* 409; see also Bertram Wyatt-Brown, "The Abolitionists' Postal Campaign of 1835," *JNH,* L (October, 1965), from which this chapter is largely derived; E. P. Atlee to Wright, August 28, 1835 (copy), Pennsylvania Abolition Society MSS, Pennsylvania Historical Society.

44. New York *Evening Post,* August 12, 1835; New York *Spectator,* August 17, 1835; S. L. Gouveneur to AT, AT to Gouveneur, August 7, 1835, etc., reprinted from *Commercial Advertiser* by *Southern Patriot,* August 20, 1835.

45. In *Emancipator,* November 14, 1836; BT to LT, August 14, 1836, BT MSS, Ohio Historical Society.

46. Eaton, "Censorship of Southern Mails," 272–73; see "Protest of the American Anti-Slavery Society," *A Collection of Valuable Documents . . .* (Boston, 1836); Nevins, *Home Diary,* I, August 13, 1835, 170–71; *Emancipator,* September, 1835; *Anti-Slavery Record* (July, 1835), Cocke Deposit, Library, UVA; Freehling, *Prelude to Civil War,* 340–48.

47. Dumond, *Antislavery,* 208–11.

48. Williams in *Emancipator,* November 14, 1836; C. C. Burleigh in *ibid.,* March 16, 1837; see also *Friend of Man,* June 30, 1836; *Second, Third, and Fourth Annual Reports of the American Anti-Slavery Society* (New York, 1835, 1836, 1837), 37, 99, and 140 respectively.

49. Cf. Barnes, *Antislavery Impulse,* 62–63, 100–4, who takes the opposite view of the campaign, claiming that it "was disastrous from the very beginning."

CHAPTER NINE

Jehovah's Fire

L eather buckets, hand-pulled and horse-drawn engines, quarrelsome companies of volunteers, and crude, defective apparatus—these comprised the Manhattan fire-fighting system. To make matters worse, buildings, a majority constructed of wood, huddled close together—patroon's mansion next to bawdy house, countinghouse next to slum tenement. Refuse, shavings, packing paper, and other tinder drifted on the wind. In 1836 New York installed its first central conduits, but wells of uncertain sanitation and "tea water" pails hawked by street boys at two cents each were the main sources of water in 1835.[1] It was not a wonder that, next to poor policing and the cholera, fire was the city's greatest problem.

Arthur Tappan considered himself luckier than most merchants on Pearl Street, for near his store stood the engine house for Oceanus Company No. 11, one of the oldest and finest volunteer units in the city. Moreover, Hanover Square's single hydrant was only a few paces away from the entrance to his store, and the building itself was made of thick Maine granite, a natural fire wall.

On December 16, 1835, the temperature dropped to zero. Water froze in pipes and cisterns, and a gale howled mercilessly through the lanes of lower Manhattan. At the Anti-Slavery Rooms on

Spruce Street, Arthur and Lewis sat in session with their committee after supper, discussing Andrew Jackson's Annual Message and how to exploit its antiabolitionist demands. At about nine o'clock, excited voices, the noise of running feet, and the fierce clanging of fire bells gave warning that somewhere in the business district a blaze had broken out. Hurrying south with the crowd along Pearl Street, the abolitionists could see that Comstock and Andrews, a dry-goods house off Hanover Square on Beaver Street, was red with fire, while the gusts of wind fanned the flames in all directions.[2]

The Tappans arrived in the tiny plaza just as the store next to theirs caught fire. Luckily, the senior partner had recently placed boiler-iron shutters on his windows as a protection against mobs, giving the partners an hour's grace to clear the inside. At once Lewis Tappan organized volunteers, most of them Negroes, to haul out goods and furniture through the rear entrance.[3] Meanwhile, Arthur pulled out one-half million dollars' worth of promissory notes from his fire closet, and a clerk carried them off to safekeeping. (Most of Lewis Tappan's personal files remained inside the safe to burn to cinders.) By the time the heat became unbearable, the Negro helpers had removed two-thirds of the valuable stock to another warehouse. Without their tireless energies, the Tappans would have suffered total disaster.[4]

On the following day, the flames were still blazing; not until noon were demolition teams finally able to halt the fire's progress. By then, however, fifty-two acres of the business district lay in ruins. Five to seven hundred buildings and thousands of tons of goods, worth an estimated eighteen million dollars, had been destroyed.[5]

Weary, numb with cold, and worried that their employment had been consumed along with the place of it, the clerks sat down to breakfast at dawn with their employers. Arthur did not have much to say to them, except "We must rebuild immediately." At once the staff responded—one went off to fetch an architect, while the rest fitted out temporary quarters with counters and trays and picked through the jumbled crates to separate the salable from the ruined. At noon, the *Journal of Commerce* carried Arthur Tappan's notice that his store was open for business as usual "by the blessing of God" and that plans were under way for construction at the old site. By mid-afternoon, workmen began clearing the still warm rubble, while passers-by watched in amazement.[6]

For a short time, Arthur Tappan became almost a popular figure, for he caught the admiration of a dejected community still stunned by the disaster. One insurance company executive observed that God must also have been impressed. If Arthur Tappan, he exclaimed, "should undertake to rebuild his store in 20 days," as Leavitt had reported, "I will be bound there would be 20 days of good weather."[7] Even the abolitionists were allowed to share in the general good feeling which prevailed while the crisis was fresh in everyone's mind.

As usual, the evangelicals saw God's handiwork in calamity. Lewis Tappan assured Gerrit Smith that it was a "rebuke to our covetousness & other sins. . . ."[8] Theodore Weld imagined that it was a herald of Judgment Day itself, and he wrote Lewis, "This awful calamity which has whelmed the queen city of the Land seems to me so like Jehovah's voice, its last warning spoken in articulate thunder over the sealed ear of a besotted people drugged by its sins into the sleep of death. . . ."[9]

The Tappans took a more hopeful view, but the store was in deep trouble nonetheless. Merchants seeking goods lost in the confusion during the fire found twenty thousand dollars' worth of their merchandise in Arthur's warehouse on Beaver Street. Worse still, his insurance firms went bankrupt under the deluge of claims. It was difficult to collect even a fraction of the amount due. Lewis reported in his diary, "Very busy visiting Insurance offices, & had my patience tried. Kept cool."[10] A rumor traveled about the antislavery circuit that the brothers had been solely insured by solid Boston firms, because local offices had refused them in view of the danger from mobs; but that was only wishful thinking. Lewis Tappan estimated that the business had lost forty to fifty thousand dollars.[11]

Actually, Arthur Tappan's circumstances were much worse than he would admit. Because of the almost complete loss of his southern trade, he had been forced to sell his goods on long-term credit while maintaining his old prices.[12] At the same time, his own credit needs could be satisfied only at rates of twenty-five to thirty per cent, the tariffs of an increasingly tight money market. When the Rev. John Shipherd visited New York in the spring to raise money for Oberlin, he got nothing from Arthur Tappan. Sorrowfully, he wrote home that the brothers "are obliged to get their paper discount at the Bank almost daily, & less cash comes in from the country than they expected."[13]

Dreams of quick profit-taking replaced the senior merchant's religious fancies at his desk. Henry Dana Ward, who had recently achieved a certain notoriety in helping to publicize the absurd story of Maria Monk, an "escaped" novitiate from a Canadian nunnery, urged him to invest in a tool- and brick-making process invented by Thomas Harvey. Lewis Tappan had no objections to Ward's anti-Papism, but he certainly mistrusted his business transactions. Bluntly, Lewis advised Arthur to stick to silk-trading, which he knew something about. Besides, he said, they had not "leisure eno[ugh] to cultivate our minds for the good of our souls," and greed was the Devil's handmaid.[14] While apparently successful in cooling Arthur's enthusiasm for this scheme, Lewis did not learn about his brother's heavy speculations in real estate until too late.[15]

Poor business made for poor tempers at the once-humming Pearl Street store. Lewis lashed out at clerks' trifling over the books of accounts and reading and gossiping during office hours. Generally, he "felt sorry" afterward, he said, "when I considered how hard & how cheerfully they worked for us." Sometimes he apologized personally, remembering that lack of customers gave them little else to do. "May the Lord restrain my ill-temper," he prayed in his diary.[16] Suffering from a particularly heavy attack of migraine headaches, Arthur took his family on a lengthy vacation in the summer of 1836, only to find business still languishing on his return in the fall.[17]

Never one to waste a moment, Lewis Tappan took advantage of the slack to increase his activities at antislavery headquarters. After planning and managing a successful anniversary meeting for the Society in May, 1836, he assisted in the reorganization of headquarters.[18] The offices were transferred to more "commodious" spaces on Nassau Street, where most of the other evangelical societies were centered. John Greenleaf Whittier, the sickly poet, joined the staff to head the petitions campaign. At one time Whittier had expected to earn fame as a politician of the Henry Clay school, but his health and a curious, introspective temperament had prevented him. In the petitions effort and in antislavery work in general he, like Lewis Tappan, had discovered a way to reconcile the conflicts of personal ambition, desire for power, and the contrary striving for religious satisfaction. To help Whittier with his management of the petitions work, Theodore Weld arrived in

July, 1836. He was soon busy, as Elizur Wright reported, "rummaging, or, as he says, wazzling among old speeches in Congress &c for *facts*" regarding slavery and previous memorials to Congress. Henry B. Stanton took charge of fund-raising.[19] Meanwhile, William Goodell, who, Wright said, was "too prolix. . . . for a hebdomadad," left for Utica to edit Gerrit Smith's *Friend of Man*, and Amos Phelps, a Boston antislavery agent, recast the *Emancipator* as a weekly paper. Phelps later became Lewis Tappan's closest friend, sharing his views about religious antislavery.[20] "Weld, Whittier, Stanton, Wright—what a pestilent, dangerous clump of fanatics all in our little room plotting freedom for slaves!" exclaimed Elizur Wright.[21]

Supervision of publications devolved upon Lewis Tappan, but the work had less significance than the Agency Committee under Arthur's charge. The living word replaced the written as the means to reach "the *country* places," for the theory was, as Elizur Wright put it, "The great cities we cannot expect to carry till the country is won."[22] Worried about his business, Arthur was really no more than a figurehead; Theodore Weld did most of the selecting and training of the lecturers. Since he had more time to spare, Lewis co-operated with Stanton in planning new ways of collecting funds, an onerous and thankless job during the bleak days before the crash of 1837. The founding of state societies was supposed to make the task easier and more productive. Instead, Lewis discovered that the auxiliary chapters wanted to retain the money raised in their territories for their own purposes. Such schemes as the "cent a day" plan for children and a quarterly collection in areas recently covered by the advance guard of lecture agents were not successful. They were replaced with complicated systems of dividing funds with state society leaders, but regional rivalries and constant bickering among agents, chapters, and national headquarters hindered the growth of the national treasury.[23]

Tappan believed in central direction for the movement, but he was undiplomatic in making his case. He reprimanded the Rhode Island Anti-Slavery Society members for mishandling campaign funds, consuming more money from headquarters than they gave in return, preferring local to national agents, and neglecting the state's free Negroes and their needs. It was a well-deserved criticism, but Henry Benson and other state leaders were furious.[24]

Amos Phelps, whose experience in the field gave him authority to gauge its effect, was worried about Tappan's lack of restraint in handling the local societies. He warned Tappan that he was wearing out antislavery ground just as repeated cotton plantings destroyed the soil's fertility. When Tappan went to abolitionist conventions, he ought to be less impulsive. "You and Stanton," he said, "have too much fun—tell some rather large stories . . . & sometimes make a real 'bore' of the matter." Tappan accepted the criticism gracefully.[25] On the whole, he performed a difficult assignment well.

Abolitionist techniques of agitation had by now reached their fullest development. From this time until the Civil War, there was to be a constant repetition of the same themes by the same methods—pamphleteering, petitions, conventions, speeches, and sermons. Historians have stressed the work of the major figures —Garrison, Weld, Phillips, and Gerrit Smith—and the riots, wranglings, and other colorful episodes, but on another plane a change was taking place. Lewis Tappan was as essential to the Society on that less conspicuous level as any of the public leaders. To illustrate: the scene was the first meeting of the Chatham Street Chapel Juvenile Anti-Slavery Society, on August 14, 1836. Solemn parents sat in rows of chairs against one wall of the lecture hall; young wives loosened their bonnet strings; husbands perspired in bulky suits. Opposite them were their girls and boys, none over fourteen, squirming in stiff-backed seats. Between the two rows of listeners stood Lewis Tappan, who enjoyed nothing more than addressing a crowd such as this, for his language could be simple, direct, and unself-conscious. "May all the dear children in this congregation," he said, "all the children in the land pity the poor slaves! They are naked and hungry; they are kept in ignorance and sin; they are heathens in a Christian land. . . . Do any of my young friends ask, what can I do? I answer, you can read the *Slave's Friend;* you can ask your playmates to do the same; you can pray God *to break the rod of the oppressor and let the oppressed go free!*"[26]

The event was a typical one for him, and typical in antislavery efforts everywhere. The rural plainness of the scene, the moral chords he played, the youth of the audience, were all in harmony with the age. In thousands of communities across the North, this event was re-enacted. A Sabbath schoolroom, a church pulpit, a picnic, or a neighborhood gathering served as the places and occasions of antislavery lectures. The work of Weld and the "Seventy," Garrison's editorials, and the murderous forays of Kansas free-soilers did not fully account for antislavery growth. While such efforts were important, the majority of abolitionists were like Lewis Tappan—part-time workers who seldom missed an opportunity to express their views, and ministers and laymen who only occasionally converted a religious meeting into an antislavery discussion. Tappan was aware of the need to stir this vast audience. It was particularly important, he thought, to reach the Sunday-school-age children and to instill in them a perfect hatred of southern slavery and all other forms of wrongdoing. They might be called upon to complete what their fathers had only begun. "For one, I hope all the children of our Sabbath schools," Lewis said, "will come out against every sin, be young moral reformers indeed, and say of all kinds of wickedness—*Think not, taste not, handle not.*"[27]

Lewis also recognized the value of enlisting the women, although their role was circumscribed according to the customs of the time. Susan was too busy with domestic duties to join him in many of his projects, but she and Julia, the eldest daughter, attended the first female abolition convention in Philadelphia in 1837. They also distributed petitions to free District of Columbia slaves, made items for the popular Anti-Slavery Bazaars, and corresponded with Maria Weston Chapman's circle in Boston. The Tappan family did not approve of Angelina and Sarah Grimké, who spoke before "promiscuous assemblies" of men and women. Though fond of the Quaker sisters, they drew the line at this flouting of tradition, which raised a furor among the orthodox Calvinists of Massachusetts. Julia, for instance, thought that female "delicacy of feeling" forbade competition with men. Likewise, Tappan agreed with Elizur Wright, who exclaimed, "The tom turkies ought to do the gobbling. . . ."

In defiance of such views, the Grimkés had launched what became a crusade for "Women's Rights," a "tin-kettle" tied "to the tail of antislavery" but one that Garrison and other Massachusetts radicals felt had a place in reform efforts.[28] In spite of Garrison's growing interest in this cause, Lewis Tappan hoped the whole question would be solved when Angelina married Theodore Weld. On hearing the news of their engagement, he congratulated Weld for rare "moral courage!" Weld was either too solemn or too much in love to understand the awkward remark.[29] In due course the sisters did retire from the antislavery speaking circuit; the cause seemed to make its way without noticeable effect.

After the spring of 1836, the very existence of the firm of Arthur Tappan and Company was in serious doubt. Credit was growing harder to find at any rate of interest, the English factors were growing worried, and country tradesmen were forwarding their regrets instead of their arrears. A trickle of bankruptcies in the city had become a flow, and "things" on Wall Street looked "rather queer," as one importer expressed it. In the face of the looming financial threat, Lewis Tappan hurried to Philadelphia for a conference with Nicholas Biddle, president of the Bank of the United States. Biddle generously offered the firm one hundred and fifty thousand dollars, but, when Lewis returned to New York with the news, Arthur had to tell him that the amount was only a fraction of what he needed. Another trip to Biddle's office proved futile, for he had problems enough of his own, as he prepared to shut down the B.U.S. and open a private bank. Shortly afterward, an "adroit" thief stole thirty-five hundred dollars from the youngest clerk, who was on his way to the bank to deposit the sum. Arthur Tappan did not even reprimand him—there was no point, since the end was only a few days away. At the end of April the Liverpool steamer arrived, bringing the black news of heavy demands from the firm's British creditors. On May 1, 1837, Arthur Tappan had to announce his suspension of payments to a stunned public.[30] When it was revealed that he owed one million, one hundred thousand dollars, the sum seemed almost incredible.[31] Few merchants even grossed that much in a year of heavy trading.

Most surprised of all were the evangelicals, who thought that even if God brought economic ruin on the rest of the nation, His chosen would be spared. "I am loath to believe it," cried an Oberlin professor. Israel Clark, a New York merchant, wrote Finney,

Truly the Lord seems to shake terribly the earth. Today a concern has stopped that I had hoped and tried to pray might be spared—Arthur Tappan & Co.—But the Lord sees not as we see & the event assures us that there are wise & good reasons for it or it would not have been so. It will produce a deeper sensation all over the country than would have remitted from the failure of any other mercantile firm.

From the other end of the religious spectrum came the comment of a New York wag, "Arthur Tappan has failed! Help him all ye niggers!"[32]

Whatever power remained to the merchant in antislavery circles vanished as his prosperity did. His prestige was not publicly impaired, but his vote in Executive Committee carried no authority thereafter. He continued to preside at antislavery gatherings, as Lewis put it, "with unusual self-control and dignity amid the exciting scenes," but his time and energy were mostly given to the reparation of his losses. True to his principles of Christian merchandising, he cut his expenses to the bone, moved into a boardinghouse, and scraped up every resource at his command. Creditors recognized his good faith, renegotiated their loans, and allowed him to remain in business. With silent fortitude, he did not rest until he had repaid all his outstanding obligations eighteen months later, including the extra charges of accumulated interest.[33] It was an amazing feat in view of the rapidly worsening state of the economy following the crash of May, 1837.

Although he did not say so at the time, Lewis Tappan was nettled by his brother's failure to tell him about the true state of the company prior to the final disaster. It seems obvious that he was thoroughly devoted to Arthur: he always asked for God's blessing on Arthur's birthdays; he defended Arthur against the criticisms of antislavery hotheads at headquarters. Nevertheless, the senior partner had not confided in Lewis or taken his advice in financial dealings. Before the month following the suspension had passed, Lewis decided to leave the debt-ridden firm and take up an antislavery agency, but James Birney, then in New York for the annual national convention, discouraged him from doing so. "He expressed great confidence in me," Tappan noted in his diary, "but had some doubts whether in the present situation of AT & Co's affairs my separation would be judicious."[34]

Tappan would have been unwise to leave the company at this point, for during 1837 the national society steadily declined in power and resources. With a wife and seven children to support, Lewis could not afford to depend on the pittances of the professional reformer. Financial stringency, however, did not worry him as much as the shortcomings of abolition itself. Chief among its weaknesses, he thought, was the movement's division over the matter of race.

Abolitionists agreed on the sin of slaveholding, but they were in some dispute over the proper way to treat free Negroes. Prejudice ran so deep in the American character that even these reformers were not immune from its effect. Arthur Tappan cannot be accused of outright racial intolerance, but there was clearly some ambivalence in his feelings. Shortly before the July riots of 1834, he saw Samuel Cornish, an almost-white Presbyterian clergyman, standing outside the Laight Street church of Samuel H. Cox. Together, the two men walked in and sat in the merchant's pew. The incident created an uproar; some church members even threatened to resign their memberships. Never again was Arthur Tappan seen in public places with a Negro, unless on business connected with the cause. Many years later, he defended his policy of distinguishing between emancipation and racial mixing:[35]

Though I advocated the sentiment that as Christians we were bound to treat the colored people without respect to color, yet I felt that great prudence was requisite to bring about the desired change in public feeling on the subject; and therefore, though I would willingly, so far as my own feelings were concerned, have *publicly* associated with a well educated and refined colored person, male or female, I felt that their best good would be promoted by refraining from doing so till the public mind and conscience were more enlightened on the subject.

Arthur Tappan was perhaps more representative of the rank and file of the party than he at first may appear. Yet the judgment he made may be accurate enough. Anti-abolitionism in the North owed much more to antiracial feelings than to outright approval of the slave system. In most minds there was no contradiction between deploring southern custom and fearing Negro mixing at home. Moreover, abolitionists, influenced to some degree by the swirl of racial animosity around them, had to consider the effect of their own actions on the Negro communities they tried to serve. Lewis Tappan had lost his possessions in 1834, but he could afford to replace them; presumably, Peter Williams, whose Episcopal mission was destroyed, had few resources to command for its rebuilding. Such thoughts passed through Tappan's mind when he wrote, "As [Christ]ians—and [Christ]ian abolitionists [—] will not tolerate my associating with my colored brethren in a white man's ch[urc]h it seems my duty to unite with a colored ch[urc]h. But will it not invite insult to my col[ore]d brethren?"[36] Both brothers were aware of white intolerance and Negro vulnerability, but Lewis' attitude of non-discrimination was certainly a minority opinion among Yankee evangelicals generally, and even among the thousands already convinced of the criminality of slavery.

As early as 1834, Lewis Tappan commented on the relation between the principles of emancipation and racial equality. When Lyman Beecher told him that such social contacts with Negroes as Theodore Weld encouraged in Cincinnati would lead to promiscuity and mongrelization, Lewis bluntly replied, "In a thousand years probably all the inhabitants on this continent would be of one color, neither black nor white (both being exotics) but copper colored, the original color of this climate. That is, if emancipation takes place. By the present system of bleaching," he added scornfully, "the blacks will disappear sooner."[37] Amalgamation was an academic matter to him, hardly worth discussing. He was not concerned by white and black intermarriage—though he would have insisted that the partners had to be of the same religious persuasion!

The issue arose again with the other great leader of the evangelical faith, Charles Grandison Finney. After Finney had left for his Oberlin duties, Lewis Tappan arranged for a distinguished Negro to serve on the board of trustees of the Chatham Chapel. In addition, he launched a vigorous campaign to abolish "nigger heaven," the upper galleries where black members were seated. When Finney returned in the spring of 1836, he immediately vetoed these measures, over Tappan's irate protests. The dispute ruined the congenial atmosphere Finney required for saving the fallen, and Tappan gloomily surmised that "God's blessing in this ch[urc]h is withheld because the minister & the ch[urc]h have not done their duty in reference to people of color."[38]

When a rumor circulated that Finney had segregated colored students from white at Oberlin, even Arthur Tappan was aroused, and called on him to explain his actions. His defense rested on a distinction between slavery (an "unblushing wrong") and a "constitutional" distaste for black people which did not "necessarily deprive any man of any positive right." Hoping to play on Arthur's conservative instincts, Finney added that, while Lewis was "one of our most talented & efficient laymen," with "uncommon executive talents," he had "to say that[,] in a great excitement when a question requires moderation & the utmost extent of Christian meekness[,] forbearance & candor," he preferred Arthur "as a

177

counselor & leader to him." So-called racial prejudice was only a "collateral point"; let us work together, denounce "the sinfulness of slavery & the duty of immediate emancipation; & for the time being, refuse to be led into controversy. . . ." As for his people in the free missions—they loved Negroes, but only would not worship with them in the same pews. Finney ended by insisting that he was as good an abolitionist as anyone else.[39] Undoubtedly, he was not far from the truth as far as the ordinary antislavery men were concerned.

Shortly afterward, some of Finney's laymen established the Broadway Tabernacle, a new center for revivals, bigger and more solidly built than the Chatham Street Chapel. Finney retired to Oberlin after a year of association with the new church, and the conservative elders passed over his assistant, George Duffield, an abolitionist, and selected the proslavery Joel Parker as Finney's successor. Having transferred his membership to the Tabernacle, Tappan not only protested Parker's appointment but also tried to found an abolition society open to white and black communicants. Parker had him excommunicated without even citing the charges. After further controversy in the Third Presbytery and Synod, the General Assembly of the Presbyterian Church reversed the decision at its convention in 1839, but Tappan never returned to the Tabernacle.[40] By then the entire free church system had collapsed, bankrupt from depression, debt, and the loss of Arthur Tappan's support and torn with strife over the "amalgamation" issue.[41] The question at stake was not simply antislavery but racial equality in the churches; one problem exacerbated the other.

It was a sore disappointment to Lewis Tappan that the results of evangelism in New York had disintegrated within a decade. The various missions of the Third Presbytery either merged with each other and separated from Presbyterian discipline, becoming independent Congregational churches, or else disappeared, their distinctive reform character thoroughly lost. "After many years of toil and suffering," Tappan told a young evangelical of Philadelphia, "I am reluctantly brought to these conclusions—to this low estimate of the steadfastness of a majority of professed Christian abolitionists—and to the painful necessity of laboring to elevate people of color rather than bring white people to right conduct towards their colored brethren."[42] Thereafter, he worked with a small group of friends in conducting mixed Sunday school classes, independent of regular church affiliation; he also co-operated with

Negro pastors, attended their churches, and, of course, helped their independent work with fugitive slaves.[43] Every so often he experimented by returning to white parishes, only to be discouraged once more by the moral failures of his fellow Christians; circumstances, not desire, forced him to accept segregation in the American church system.

Matters were not much better in the American Anti-Slavery Society itself. William Green, John Rankin, and William Jay (also a member of the Executive Committee) preferred to see the Society as a white endeavor.[44] When Lewis Tappan suggested Theodore S. Wright, a Negro Presbyterian minister, as a speaker at the anniversary meeting, Jay threatened to resign. He argued that neither the public nor abolitionists themselves were ready for so revolutionary a step.[45] Overruled and disheartened, Tappan was, for one of the few times in his life, thoroughly depressed, for he held Jay in high esteem. "When the subject of acting out our professed principles in treating men irrespective of color is discussed," he wrote afterward, "heat is always produced. I anticipate that . . . if ever there is a split in our ranks it will arise from collision on this point."[46]

If the rank-and-file abolitionists were only somewhat more tolerant than other Americans in their attitudes toward racial equality, in time the leadership of the movement took a more liberal view. Conservatives, like Rankin and Green, finally left the Society or else, like Jay, modified their convictions to some degree. One suspects, however, that even the most earnest of reformers could hardly escape all the racial animosities of American society, try as he might, and there remained an ambiguity about racial equality that was not present in "immediate abolition." When Lewis rode from Philadelphia to Harrisburg for a state convention meeting in 1837, he reported in the *Emancipator* that his white companions defied the other white railroad passengers by sitting with the Negro delegates. When it came to dining in public, however, some of the whites proved more squeamish and moved to separate tables.[47]

In addition, the nineteenth-century reformer had to cope with his impulse toward paternalism. Certainly the Tappans, raised upon autocratic principles and practicing them in their store, had trouble in treating uneducated people, white or black, as social equals. So few Negroes at that time met their high standards of conduct and literacy that a conscious effort had to be made not to confuse social and economic deprivations with racial inferiority. Speaking of David Ruggles, treasurer of the New York Vigilance Committee for aiding slaves, Lewis Tappan wrote, "Like most every colored man I have ever known, he was untrustworthy about money matters. I do not accuse him or others as deficient in integrity, but no regular account appears to be kept of moneys received or paid."[48] To merchants well versed in the complexities of bookkeeping, undoubtedly Ruggles and other Negroes seemed inept. The Tappans did not employ Negroes as clerks. When Jekiel Beman, a black minister, once asked the brothers to hire a Negro clerk in the store, Lewis replied evasively, "When business revives, if one can find a colored young man of good education, principles, and capacity who has some experience in Bookkeeping or as a Salesman, we should be glad to receive him into our store."[49] Few Negroes could meet such qualifications; and if any had been hired, their presence behind the counter would have been extremely dangerous to the silk firm, already near extinction because of the antislavery cause. Still, the Tappans' failure—in good times as well as bad—to hire any Negro above the level of porter remains a matter of record.[50]

Although more enlightened than many of his colleagues about Negro relations, Lewis Tappan was as blind to the complexities of slavery as many other abolitionists. Some antislavery authors showed remarkable sophistication in the handling of social criticism and argumentation. While Lewis Tappan appreciated such impressive efforts, his own pieces, most of them designed for the average churchgoing reader, were hardly exceptional in concept or presentation. He dwelt upon the gruesome and patently sentimental aspects of the system with an absoluteness of distinction that was wholly in keeping with his kind of religious faith. Once he invited a runaway slave to lecture to his mixed Sunday school class. The Negro described his experiences in moving words. Particularly effective was his account of watching his sister whipped to death to gratify the pleasure of her master. Afterward, an old Negro woman, weeping quietly, pressed forty dollars into the speaker's hands. Tappan wrote up the episode in the *Emancipator* under the title, "A Touching Scene."[51] The scene *is* touching; the slave's tale may be true. But of environmental influences, political realities, economic forces, and degrees of cruelty or kindness it says nothing.

Sunday school simplicities had their place in antislavery literature because melodrama is the stuff of popular agitation. Yet, like so many other abolitionists, Tappan became a victim of his own propaganda. The South assumed for him monstrous proportions. Cart-whip lashings and other enormities, some gleaned from southern papers themselves, were not just grist for the abolitionist mill; they constituted a large portion of what many of the reformers knew about southern race relations. The Negro was their "noble savage," as the Indian had been for the Augustan age. Not until the Civil War was there a genuine confrontation between the white evangels and the ex-slaves. Until then, the latter were seen either as victims of outrage, like Tappan's Sabbath orator, or as black moral giants, like Frederick Douglass. The making of such stereotypes may have advanced the cause, but it had the collateral effect of creating a veil of falsehood that would obscure relations between the races in the future.

Still, the abolitionists were right in their aim, though they were also banal. Moreover, they were the first in modern history to find the source of the human condition in the environment rather than in the inferiority or malevolence of any race or individual. In spite of Tappan's unsophisticated, sentimental, and abstract view of slavery, he contributed to the progress of that concept.

NOTES

1. Grinnell, *Forty Years,* 24; Picton, *Rose Street,* 3; Waylen, *Ecclesiastical Reminiscences,* 2; Fowler, *Tour of New York,* 22, 221–22; Dodge, *Old New York,* 27; Martha J. Lamb and Mrs. Burton Harrison, *History of the City of New York: Its Origin, Rise, and Progress* (New York, 1896), III, 377–78.

2. William L. Stone, *History of New York City* (New York, 1868), 226–33; LT, *Arthur Tappan,* 272–73; *Southern Patriot,* December 24, 1835; *New York Observer,* quoted by Boston *Recorder,* December 25, 1835; *Niles' Weekly Register,* December 26, 1835; *Emancipator,* January, 1836; Kenneth Holcomb Dunshee, *As You Pass By* (New York, 1952), 58–62; C. Foster, *An Account of the Conflagration . . .* (New York, 1835?).

3. LT, *Arthur Tappan,* 275, 278–79; Boston *Recorder,* December 25, 1835.

4. Boston *Recorder,* December 25, 1835; LT, *Arthur Tappan,* 274–75, 278; LT to WLG, February 26, 1836, WLG MSS, BPL, and LT to Shipherd, March 16, 1836, treasurer's office file, Oberlin College; Stone, *History of New York,* 228.

5. LT to Gerrit Smith, December 21, 1835, Gerrit Smith Miller MSS, Syracuse University Library; Lamb and Harrison, *History of New York,* III, 725–26; Rodman Gilder, *The Battery* (Boston, 1936), 173–74; *Niles' Weekly Register,* January 9, 1836. Estimates of the damage varied, but eighteen million dollars was a figure generally accepted.

6. LT, *Arthur Tappan*, 276–78; *Journal of Commerce*, December 17, 1835.

7. Joshua Leavitt to Phelps, December 26, 1835, Phelps MSS, BPL.

8. LT to Smith, December 21, 1835, Gerrit Smith Miller MSS, Syracuse University Library.

9. Weld to LT, December 22, 1835, Barnes and Dumond, *Weld Letters*, I, 248; see also Jocelyn to Henry E. Benson, December 21, 1835, WLG MSS, BPL.

10. Diary, February 24, 1836; *Niles' Weekly Register*, January 9, 1836; LT, *Arthur Tappan*, 274; *An Account of the Conflagration at New York City* . . . (New York, 1836), 52.

11. LT, *Arthur Tappan*, 277; George Whipple to "Corresponding Secretary of Oberlin Institute" [Burnell], January 8, 1836, treasurer's office file, Oberlin College; *Hampshire Republican* quoted by *Liberator*, February 6, 1836; *Liberator*, May 28, 1836; cf. Barnes and Dumond, *Weld Letters*, I, 247n.

12. LT, *Arthur Tappan*, 279; see Ellis Gray Loring letterbook, 1837–41, Houghton Library, Harvard, letters to AT, dated October 25, November 24, December 10, 1840; see also LT to AT, October 5, 1838, copy, LT MSS, LC.

13. Shipherd to Burnell, April 26, May 9, 1836, treasurer's office file, Oberlin College; see also Henry Cowles to Alice Cowles, January 31, 1836, Henry Cowles MSS, Oberlin College Library.

14. Diary, March 18, 1836, and March 22, 23–25, 1836.

15. LT, *Arthur Tappan*, 296–97.

16. Diary, April 22 and 29, August 13, 1836.

17. *Ibid.*, August 27, September 12, 1836; LT to Burnell, September 12, 1836, treasurer's office file, Oberlin College; LT, *Arthur Tappan*, 401.

18. *Liberator*, May 14, 1836; *Voice of Freedom* (New York), May, 1836; *Emancipator*, May 19, 1836.

19. Pollard, *Whittier*, 160; Perry Miller, "John Greenleaf Whittier: The Conscience in Poetry," *Harvard Review*, II (Winter-Spring, 1964), 8–24; Samuel T. Pickard, *Whittier as a Politician, Illustrated by his Letters to Professor Elizur Wright, Jr.* (Boston, 1900), 3, 5; office relocation in *Emancipator*, April 13, 1837, *Friend of Man*, March 15, 1837; the staff consisted of four full-time agents and three to four assistants, a large number for a benevolent society—see Lydia Maria Child to Ellis Gray Loring, February 28, 1842, personal miscellaneous letters, New York Public Library; Thomas, *Weld*, 120–21; Barnes, *Antislavery Impulse*, 104–8; diary, July 7, 1836; on Stanton, see Wright to parents, July 31, 1836, Wright MSS, LC.

20. Elizur Wright to Phelps, February 9, 1836, Wright MSS, LC; see LT to Phelps, February 24 and 28, 1836, Phelps MSS, BPL; Dumond, *Antislavery*, 179; WLG to LT, February 12, 1836, WLG MSS, BPL; Wright to B. Green, January 13, 1836, Wright MSS, LC.

21. Wright to parents, July 20, 1837, Wright MSS, LC.

22. Wright to parents, July 31, 1836, *ibid.*; see the Agency Committee Minutes, November 17, December 7, 1837, BPL; *Human Rights*, "Hints on Anti-Abolition Mobs," reprinted in *Friend of Man*, August 4, 1836.

23. LT speech at Rhode Island Anti-Slavery Society, *Liberator*, November 19, 1836; *Emancipator*, May 25, July 7, December 29, 1836; LT, circular, June 26, 1837, WLG MSS, BPL.

24. LT in *Friend of Man*, November 24, 1836.

25. Phelps to LT, December 28, 1837, and LT to Phelps, December 27, 1837, Phelps MSS, BPL.

26. *Slave's Friend,* II, No. 5, Whole No. 17, 1836, with woodcut of scene.

27. Emerson Davis, *The Half Century* . . . (Boston, 1851), 160–61; LT in *Friend of Man,* November 24, 1836; *Slave's Friend,* III, Whole No. 20, 1836.

28. Julia Tappan to Anne Weston, July 18, 1837, Weston Family MSS, BPL; *ibid.,* July 12, 1837; *National Inquirer* (Philadelphia), July 8, 1837; William Smeal to Wright, August 22, 1837, Wright MSS, LC; Sarah and Angelina Grimké to Weld, November 30, 1837, Barnes and Dumond, *Weld Letters,* I, 487; Wright to Phelps (quotation), July 11, 1838, Phelps MSS, LC; Julia Tappan to Sarah Grimké, n.d., 1869, Weld MSS, Clements Library.

29. Weld to Angelina Grimké, April 13, 1838, Weld MSS, Clements Library.

30. LT, *Arthur Tappan,* 279–81; quotation by Daniel James in Lowitt, *Merchant Prince;* Dodge, *Old New York,* 73; William Dawes to Burnell, April 22, 1837, treasurer's office file, Oberlin College; Hubbard *Autobiography,* 7–9.

31. LT, *Arthur Tappan,* 281; Nevins, *Hone Diary,* II, 254.

32. Dawes to Burnell, April 12, 1837, treasurer's office file, Oberlin College; Israel Clark to Finney, May 1, 1837, *ibid.;* Allan Nevins and Milton Halsey Thomas, eds., *Diary of George Templeton Strong, Young Man in New York, 1835–1849* (New York, 1952), I, 62; see also Alfred Smith to Burnell, May 12, 1837, typescript, and L. A. Spaulding to Burnell, May 9, 1837, typescript, Fletcher file, Oberlin College Library; New York *Evangelist,* quoted by *Liberator,* May 12, 1837.

33. LT, *Arthur Tappan,* 176, 294–96.

34. Diary, May 23, 1837; see also *ibid.,* May 22, 1836, May 22, 1838, May 22, 1839.

35. AT to A. F. Stoddard, August 27, 1863, LT, *Arthur Tappan,* 200–02.

36. Diary, February 25, 1836.

37. LT to Weld, September 29, 1834, slavery MSS, Box II, New-York Historical Society; see also LT in *Emancipator,* September 8, 1836.

38. Diary, February 25, March 5, 1836, March 14, 1836, quotation.

39. Finney to AT, April 30, 1836, Finney MSS, Oberlin College Library; Cole, "Free Church Movement in New York City," 193–96; on Finney's pietism, antislavery, McLoughlin, *Modern Revivalism,* 107–12.

40. LT to Phelps, January 9, 10, and 15, 1839, Phelps MSS, BPL; L. Brown to Finney, January 28, 1839, Finney MSS, Oberlin College Library; David Hale, *Facts and Reasonings on Church Government, Report of a Discussion Held at a Meeting of the Broadway Tabernacle* . . . (New York, 1839), a copy located in New-York Historical Society; see also C. Bruce Staiger, "Abolitionism and the Presbyterian Schism of 1837–1838," *MVHR,* XXXVI (December, 1949), 391–414.

41. Nichols, *Broadway Tabernacle,* 71–72; Jonathan Greenleaf, *A History of the Churches, of All Denominations in the City of New York* . . . (New York, 1846), 142–44, 166, 171–81; Samuel D. Alexander, *The Presbytery of New York* . . . (New York, 1887), 101 ff.; LT to Burnell, March 2, June 3, July 10, 1840; AT to Burnell, February 20, 1840, E. W. Chester to Burnell, July 27, 1840, George Whipple to Burnell, June 5, 1840, Burnell to AT & Co., June 22, 1840, treasurer's office file, Oberlin College.

42. LT to Hastings, April 11, 1841 (photostat), LT MSS, LC.

43. See LT, *Caste: A Letter to a Teacher among the Freedmen* (New York,

1867), 1; LT, remarks at New York Vigilance Committee meeting, November 21, 1836, *Emancipator,* December 15, 1836; William Still, *The Underground Railroad* . . . (Philadelphia, 1872), 681–88; LT in *Emancipator,* October 6 and 13, 1836; P. P. Stewart and R. E. Gillett (LT's Sunday school teachers for Negro children) to Burnell, January 28, 1837, treasurer's office file, Oberlin College; diary, February 24, 1836, November 8, 1840, and scattered entries and newspaper clippings in the diary, after February, 1836.

44. Green to Finney, August 28, 1835, September 26, 1836, Finney MSS, Oberlin College Library, and Green to Shipherd, September 9, 1835, treasurer's office file, Oberlin College; on Rankin, see LT to Weld, March 15, 1836, Barnes and Dumond, *Weld Letters,* I, 276–77.

45. Diary, April 6, 1836, and LT to Weld, March 15, 1836, Barnes and Dumond, *Weld Letters,* 276–77.

46. Diary, April 6, 1836.

47. *Emancipator,* February 9, 1837; *Philanthropist* (Cincinnati), February 10, 1837; *Pennsylvania Intelligencer* (Harrisburg), February 2, 1837.

48. LT to Gerrit Smith, January 4, 1839, Gerrit Smith Miller MSS, Syracuse University Library.

49. LT to Jekiel C. Beman, January 6, 1840, ltrbk.

50. *Twelfth Annual Report of the American and Foreign Anti-Slavery Society* (New York, 1852), 29–30; Litwack, *North of Slavery,* 229.

51. LT in *Emancipator,* October 13, 1837.

CHAPTER TEN

Antislavery Schisms

It had always mystified Lewis Tappan that William Lloyd Garrison had never proclaimed his submission to Christ and joined a church. In fact, Tappan was unable to overcome his suspicion of anyone who was not a professed evangelical. While others, such as Elizur Wright, began to think that revivalism spawned too much "cant," and even William Jay criticized the *Emancipator* for supporting "pure wine" and other irrelevancies, Lewis Tappan remained rigidly and self-consciously true to his conversion of 1827. He had committed himself too deeply to orthodoxy ever to admit that any portion of the creed was defective. Characteristically, he vainly protested the appointment of Samuel J. May as an official agent of the abolition society. After all, May was a Unitarian, and the cause, according to Tappan, ought to be confined to "pious men" only. In addition, Lewis had little use for Quakers, except for the gentle Whittier and a few English Friends whom he later knew. Lewis naturally worried about the safety of Garrison's soul, though they agreed about matters non-theological. In November, 1835, he wrote Amos Phelps, "I pray that br Garrison may have grace to show the sanctifying influence of affliction upon his heart. Will you not have a faithful conversation with him on the subject of personal religion?"[1]

Some months later, Tappan was further aroused by an editorial in the *Liberator* in July, 1836, which condemned "pharisaical" Sabbath-keeping. In quick reply, Tappan wrote Garrison that his "wanton spirit" was likely to "foment jealousies and contentions, and cause divisions in the anti-slavery ranks."[2] In the fall, Tappan invited Garrison to visit New York, expenses fully paid, so that they could talk things over and Garrison could watch Weld whipping up the fervor of his class of lecture agents. Glad of the holiday, Garrison brought his family along, and his "warm-hearted friend" treated him with much generosity. Garrison was especially appreciative because the trip allowed him to meet the agents before they left on their lecture tours and to dispel any "prejudices" they may have entertained about his being "a great stumbling-block" to the movement. Tappan genuinely liked and admired Garrison, certainly more than any other national officer did, but he was sorry to learn that his guest no longer believed in family prayer, church attendance, or the usefulness of a regular clergy.[3] It was the first inkling Tappan had of a new spirit abroad in New England antislavery.

In the spring of 1837, Garrison fell under the influence of John Humphrey Noyes, as strange a wanderer in the "Burned-Over District" of western New York as any in that spiritual seedbed. Carrying the doctrine of free will much further than did Nathaniel Taylor, with whom he had once studied at Yale, Noyes professed complete human freedom in self-development and total security from sin. Elizur Wright gossiped that, after his conversion to "'holiness,'" Noyes "lay dead *drunk* in this city for several days— by way of showing the *perfection* of his *flesh.*"

Straitlaced as ever, Garrison did not succumb to Noyes's "Gospel liberty" of "*gin slings!*" or to his concept of free love (sometimes called spiritual wifery) but did absorb his anti-institutionalism, belligerent pacifism, and high-sounding logical absolutes. In March, 1837, Noyes warned Garrison that America, "a country which, by its boasting hypocrisy, has become the laughing-stock of the world, and by its lawlessness has fully proved the incapacity of man for self-government," was "ripe for a convulsion like that of France. . . ." While irreligion swept France into revolution, Noyes continued, America was destined to be overthrown by the Bible, by the antislavery movement, and by other social and ethical reforms. Unless Garrison and his friends followed the Biblical injunction, "'Come out of her, my people, that ye be not partakers of her sins and of her plagues,'" Noyes concluded, a "UNIVERSAL EMANCIPATION FROM SIN" would never be accomplished in the United States. Garrison was converted to this creed rather than to the faith of Lewis Tappan. He repeated in the *Liberator* Noyes's slogan: "*My hope of the millennium begins where Dr. Beecher's expires—viz.,* AT THE OVERTHROW OF THIS NATION." Soon the whole range of perfectionist ideas appeared in profusion in the columns of the *Liberator,* often in articles written by national agent Henry C. Wright, already suspect to the New York committee for having vehemently defended the Grimké sisters' lecture tour.[4]

As a philosophical system, Garrison's conceptual fads made no logical sense at all, but, with Yankee ability to turn absurdities to good advantage, he fashioned perfectionism into an effective tool for immediate emancipation. Garrisonians claimed that churches and even human government itself obstructed progress toward absolute purity, and specifically toward abolitionism, among the forms of it. They denounced all varieties of coercion and military measures, from the act of carrying a militia rifle to capital punishment and jails. In effect, Garrisonian perfectionism was a rejection of history and a rebellion against religious traditionalism. Refreshingly iconoclastic, the doctrine included, after 1842, a thorough denunciation of the Constitution and later a demand for a northern confederacy, politically and morally separated from the sins and from the allegedly un-American values of southern society. In spite of its radicalism, however, Garrisonianism remained true to its commitment to non-resistance, a position that was later challenged by hot-eyed abolitionists in the 1850's.

From his lofty perfectionist perch, Garrison was enabled to leap upon any human folly with unlimited freedom for self-righteous invective. The heroes of the Revolution came under attack for evading moral duty by writing slavery into the Constitution; churches had recrucified Christ by allowing slaveholders to take communion; political parties had surrendered moral courage in behalf of corrupt self-interest; and society as a whole was criminally responsible for both overt and subtle violence against the weak and defenseless Negro. Only by renouncing malevolent institutions and with them oath-taking and political office-holding, voting and religious affiliation, could a man be faithful to God and bring about His kingdom on earth. Garrison anticipated that withdrawal of the righteous from impure society could result in the transformation of America, or at least the northern states, into a new paradise. This form of philosophical segregation was meant to be more a state of mind than a new political arrangement, for Garrison never urged civil disobedience—a refusal to pay taxes, serve in the military forces, or use the ordinary agencies of government. As a result, there was a hidden conservatism in his system that escaped most of his contemporaries of the 1830's and 1840's but gradually was revealed when more radical plans of action were proposed in the 1850's.

Although Garrison claimed to represent the true spirit of Gospel Christianity, he was in fact assisting a long-term trend toward the secularization of American idealism. Since American political and religious institutions seemed to be impervious to change by the ordinary processes, he moved simultaneously in two paradoxical directions. The first was toward a kind of utopian Christianity similar to previous "come-outer" movements that had once arisen during the European Reformation. In this connection it is interesting to note that Garrison earned the support in the 1840's and 1850's of such groups, as one observer from the backwoods of Pennsylvania reported to Lewis Tappan, as "the Old Side Covenanters" who were "the descendants of those Scotch Covenanters immortalized by their contest with the Stewarts [*sic*]." Like the Garrisonians, these odd Pennsylvania dissenters refused to take oaths or vote in elections, and slaveholders were not admitted to fellowship.

The second direction, which proved the more powerful, was toward a reform philosophy that replaced old orthodoxy with a reliance upon man's rationality, not God's sovereignty or the Holy Spirit acting through the revival experience. This new evangelism honored the god of human progress while castigating all compromises in religion and politics. The combination of the old and new gained Garrison the loyalty of the antislavery Hicksite Quakers of Philadelphia. In keeping with the earliest tenets of their faith, they too refused to take oaths, but they also found that Garrison's rejection of narrow Christian conventions, including the denial of feminine equality with men, paralleled their own displeaure with traditional Quaker restrictiveness and conservatism.[5]

In Boston, where Unitarianism had prepared the intelligentsia for a liberalism of a somewhat more intellectual character than that of his Hicksite allies, Garrison gathered a small band of followers with unusual gifts and youthful vitality. It included

Edmund Quincy, Maria Weston Chapman, her sisters Anne and Deborah Weston, Wendell Phillips, and, as friends if not disciples, Theodore Parker and Thomas Wentworth Higginson. In contrast to these generally high-born men and women, some of the bearded wonders of the day also responded: Parker Pillsbury, S. S. Foster, C. C. Burleigh, and James Boyle—a colorful set with a contentious spirit that surpassed Garrison's.

The Garrisonians were not a disciplined sect by any means. Some, like the wealthy Francis Jackson, Samuel J. May, Lydia Maria and David Child, and Ellis Gray Loring, seemed more enchanted with their leader's personality than his theories, while others, like Henry C. Wright and Adin Ballou, entertained dreams of a utopia that even exceeded Garrison's, for he was actually more concerned with the cancerous society of here and now than with the details of a new world order.

First to sniff the change in the antislavery winds of Massachusetts were the orthodox clergy, who feared the rise of a "speculative antinomianism" far more liberal than that of previous anti-Calvinists. In June, 1837, Nehemiah Adams, a prominent Congregational minister, and several other conservative clergymen wrote a so-called "Pastoral Letter" that was read from many pulpits about the middle of July. The document deplored Garrisonian agitation, which allegedly encouraged disrespect of the clerical office, and it also disapproved of the "unnatural" presumptions of such advocates of women's rights as the Grimké sisters. Then, a few weeks later, the Reverends Fitch and Towne, who had had a short connection with the American Anti-Slavery Society, and three other divines published *The Appeal of Clerical Abolitionists on Antislavery Measures.* Like the "Pastoral Letter," this piece, a later "Clerical Appeal" signed by the Rev. James T. Woodbury, and another "Appeal" from the Andover Seminary faculty, were challenges—and not altogether temperate ones—to Garrison's leadership. At once, Garrison retaliated by condemning the nation's clergy as "blind leaders of the blind, dumb dogs that cannot bark, spiritual popes—that . . . love the fleece better than the flock. . . ." As a self-proclaimed martyr to a Calvinist suppression equaled in vigor only by the Spanish Inquisition, he called on national headquarters for unqualified support.[6]

Writing to Lewis Tappan, his friend in past disputes with the New York committee, Garrison asked, "Does it indeed not concern the Parent Society, that five clergymen, professed abolitionists, have publicly impeached . . . its 'leading' advocates?" Defending the policy of silence that had prevailed since the issue had arisen, Lewis Tappan replied in a friendly but evasive way. After all, the Executive Committee was too busy to undertake the arbitration of personal and local affairs, and besides, Garrison had been offensive to Fitch and company, who "come up to the average abolitionism of the day." To reject them was to reject the rank and file of the American Anti-Slavery Society. Garrison concluded that the New Yorkers "would be glad, on the whole, to see me cashiered, or voluntarily leave the ranks." He was right, and as events unfolded he was justified in boldly extending his attack to include the leadership of the Society itself.[7]

While remaining publicly neutral, Lewis Tappan and the Executive Committee were preparing to free antislavery doctrine from Garrison's heresies about war, women, and social institutions. They drew James G. Birney from Cincinnati with the object of reinforcing headquarters "as the strongest center of confidence and attraction" in antislavery. Lewis Tappan assigned Amos Phelps to organize the clerical abolitionists in Massachusetts into a new group loyal to the New York committee.[8] The first test of strength occurred in neighboring Rhode Island.

Tappan, Birney, and Henry Stanton took the steamer to Providence for the annual meeting of the state antislavery society. All was outwardly pleasant until Garrison himself arose to offer a resolution censuring the "Clerical Appeal." "Think of his introducing it!" Tappan exploded, "a party concerned and not a member of the [Rhode Island] Society!" Still more astounding was the fact that the resolution passed handsomely.[9] The Boston faction seemed to have greater strength than Tappan imagined.

Garrison had earned respect in reform circles for his unbridled independence. Elizur Wright later complained that Garrison had "gone down to the bottom of government and 'Priestcraft,' and the only way he can *consistently* do anything at all for the abolition of slavery is by undermining the whole fabric of social relations." Wright missed the point. A quiet alienation from politics and society would have been most ineffective, and Garrison did not intend to be quiet. His revolutionary call was for a renovation of American attitudes about race, slavery, and war and for a drastic, soul-searching appraisal of the nature of American destiny —exactly the kind of appeal his followers needed for inspiration. Revivalism had skidded with the prices on Wall Street in 1837, and a number of reformers were tired of being harangued about travel on Sunday and other causes petrified in the sterile climate of benevolent societies. Neither Taylor's compromised Calvinism nor Unitarian formality satisfied them, for they promised only a dreary world of conformity in which the individual soul would have no room for self-expression. The Garrisonians, moreover, were restive under the unimaginative leadership of New York— long on administration, short on ideas. The postal and lecture campaigns had exhausted their vigor, while the petitions campaign had become a mostly local effort. Abolitionism was in danger of being smothered by institutional bureaucracy and narrow concepts. It was not enough to woo ministers and Finney's revival converts and to print up sermons and antislavery Sunday school materials. There were hundreds of thousands of Negroes being born and buried under the grim shadow of slavery. The cause required a new beginning and a broadening of its base of power beyond evangelical limits.

Lewis Tappan reacted to insurgency in the manner most administrators would, first seeking a way out while remaining "neutral" and open-minded officially but steadily being driven into the arms of liberal-talking, well-meaning preservers of the existing order. He tried to calm the outraged feelings of the Fitch and Woodbury camp, but his conferences with them only stepped up the criticisms of the Garrisonians, thereby drawing him closer still to the orthodox.[10] During 1838 and 1839, the bickerings and intrigues smoldered steadily, and the Tappans' committee gradually lost its control over the situation. Garrisonians gained strength from closer communications with radical Quaker elements, while state antislavery societies vigorously demanded and gained more financial autonomy.[11] After one of Tappan's unsuccessful efforts to patch things up in Boston, Henry Chapman blurted to Henry Stanton, "By G-d, your committee at New York are what I call d--n small coffee!" On hearing of Chapman's profanity, Tappan threw up his hands, now firmly convinced that the devil himself had joined the Garrisonian infidels.[12] The May, 1839, antislavery meeting in New York promised to be stormy.

As usual, abolitionists flocked to the convention, expecting an exciting session. At the opening meeting, Lewis Tappan made his first and only major address to the Society, speaking before an assembly of five thousand in the cavernous Broadway Tabernacle. In one hand he held a brace of slave whips and in the other a specimen bowie knife with the inscription "Death to Abolitionists" on the blade. In keeping with the sensationalism of his props, his theme was the complicity of the North in the sins of the South. Brandishing them as he walked the platform, he declared that they were illustrations of the subserviency of northern merchants and manufacturers as well as examples of the "murderous spirit of slaveholders. . . ." Laying the exhibits aside, Lewis then argued that northern clergymen were no better, referring to a Presbyterian minister of New York City who had recently separated an emancipated mother from her slave child and had exclaimed with a sneer that he did not care what happened to the "brat." Roaring with indignation, the crowd yelled, "Give us his name," while Arthur Tappan pounded his gavel to restore order.[13] Lewis refused to say who it was, but he turned rather conspicuously to Joel Parker, pastor of the Broadway Tabernacle, with whom he then was contending for control of the Third Presbytery. With blistering effect, he condemned Parker for his proslavery attitudes. Shaking with rage, Parker rose from a seat in the gallery to hurl counter-charges, but Tappan turned suavely to other points before Parker gained the crowd's attention. Even Oliver Johnson, Garrison's co-editor on the *Liberator*, momentarily forgot his bias and called the performance electrifying.[14] Still, Tappan's success on the rostrum could not hide the fact that the national Society was in deep trouble.

At the business meeting on the same day, Tappan and Birney showed appalling ineptitude in parliamentary maneuvering, while Garrison, seldom remembered for political skill, was as wily in gathering support as Henry Clay himself. One of the chief questions was the right of women to vote. Theodore Weld, Gerrit Smith, and other prominent figures were not opposed to the idea. Tappan and Birney, however, feared that Garrison's faction would be able to make more use of the enlarged franchise than their group of conservatives. Political convenience combined with their traditional notions of the role of women to determine their stance. The convention granted the ladies their rights, but Tappan rustled up a "protest," obtained the signatures of his friends to it, and presented it to the convention, compounding his tactical error with a show of petulance.[15] He was convinced that most abolitionists throughout the country were radical only on the slavery question, not on such tangential matters as women's rights. Undoubtedly he was correct, but if he had surrendered this point gracefully he might have gained more allies than he lost, at least among those Society members dedicated enough to attend the annual meetings. It was not many years, after all, before women were voting in some school and church elections. Besides, Susan and Julia Tappan and their friends could perhaps have provided the margin of victory on matters more seriously affecting the central committee. As it was, Birney's motion to condemn "No-Government" and "Non-Resistance," the twin Boston heresies, failed to carry. Playing on the miscalculations of the New Yorkers, Garrison also mustered a resounding defeat of the committee's proposed changes in financial arrangements with the state societies. As a result, an unworkable system of voluntary contributions to national headquarters from local chapters continued in effect. Having lost control of the purse, the Executive Committee lost control of the movement. Alone among the chief antislavery contenders, Garrison returned home after the May anniversary with "as light a heart as he brought."[16]

The Tappans' intolerance in religious affairs was one of the many handicaps under which the central office had to function. "I sometimes fear," Lewis wrote Gerrit Smith, "we have greatly erred in associating with ungodly men in the Anti S. enterprise."[17] All that interested the brothers at this point was church action, while others were growing weary of the restrictions this policy imposed. Garrison's philosophy was not really popular, but at the crucial meeting in 1839 he was allowed to play on the divisions within his opponents' camp. Gerrit Smith, for instance, though always friendly toward Garrison, did not separate himself entirely from the Tappanites; but he wanted to see some experimentation in political abolition. The old method of questioning candidates about antislavery had not been very effective; Whigs and Democrats either made vague promises, quickly forgotten, or ignored the issue of slavery altogether. Associating himself with Myron Holley and Alvan Stewart, veterans of the Anti-Masonic crusade a few years before, Smith, along with Henry Stanton, Elizur Wright, and Joshua Leavitt, began agitating for third-party action. As this movement gained force, Tappan stood out uncompromisingly for the old policies—questionnaires, petitions, and church prayers for better rulers. Politics, he insisted, corrupted even the best reformers, while patience and faith would eventually triumph. By isolating himself from the talented leaders entering the Liberty party, as the group was later called, Tappan could rely on the support only of Amos Phelps, William Jay, brother Arthur, the Methodists LaRoy Sunderland and Orange Scott, the Baptist Duncan Dunbar of New York City, and other church-minded men.[18] For many other abolitionists, moral witness was no longer exciting or promising enough.

Tappan was depressed by this turn of events, but, convinced that all his critics were wrong, he spent 1839 and early 1840 dismantling the old antislavery Society and trying to found a new one. First, he experimented with a plan based on the centrally directed American Board of Commissioners for Foreign Missions. Evangelicals, however, recognized that the country was too large, transportation too slow, and democratic procedures too diffuse for rigid, centralized direction. Moreover, as Ellis Gray Loring pointed out, "Great Revolutions, civil or military, are not to be wrought by 'Boards of Commissioners!' "[19] Tappan and Duncan Dunbar did form a local chapter with thirty members from New York churches, but the movement died on its feet.[20] Then Lewis heard about the formation in 1839 of the British and Foreign Anti-Slavery Society, which was designed to revive the languishing cause there. Led by Joseph Sturge, a Quaker corn merchant from Birmingham, it was made up of Dissenters and Broadchurchmen with the same religious views that Tappan and his friends held. As it turned out, this organization would serve as the model for the new association once the evangelicals departed from the old.[21]

Meanwhile, the American Anti-Slavery Society was "limping along," debt-ridden and divided. Even the *Emancipator* was broadcasting appeals for third-party action. Joshua Leavitt and Tappan fought constantly over its editorial policy, Tappan maintaining that the official Society organ must reflect the traditional and official plurality of the Executive Committee, Leavitt refusing to accept such legalistic instructions. All last-minute efforts to resuscitate the Society by calls for unity and additional funds failed to rally much wholehearted support for the central committee, while the Garrisonians "seemed to enjoy" the muddle in New York, ridiculing political action and calling the national officers "incompetent." They were ready to assume control as soon as opportunity permitted. The Tappanites knew it and sorrowfully prepared for the worst.[22]

Shortly before the annual conclave in 1840, Lewis Tappan and S. W. Benedict, the publishing agent, persuaded the Executive

Committee to assign the entire stock of tracts and pamphlets to them as "Trustees." The committee then instructed the two agents to sell the property to meet the Society's debts, amounting to about $8,000. Actually, the materials could not be easily unloaded on a market already saturated with antislavery literature. After many months of discouraging effort, Tappan sadly discovered that $3,400 worth of bills still remained unpaid, although the entire stock had been sold or virtually given away. Tappan and other members of the Executive Committee had to dip into their own pockets to pay off these obligations. Complicating matters still further was a committee decision to send Birney and Stanton to London. A strong delegation at Joseph Sturge's World's Anti-Slavery Convention was thought essential if the old committee's case was to obtain a favorable hearing before British friends of the cause. While the eight hundred dollars necessary for the expedition was raised privately from among members of the committee, the decision to dispatch two Society agents when the state of the official treasury was so poor gave an unfortunate impression about the alleged bankruptcy of the Society. It could be justly asked how so large an outlay could be quickly collected when these same benefactors claimed embarrassment about the Society's more pressing obligations? Indeed, these seemingly contradictory actions, hastily and perhaps carelessly devised, exposed the New York leaders to the charge of fraud and thievery—"mere swindling," Wendell Phillips called it.

As if these decisions were not already troubling enough, the Tappan committee, to prevent the *Emancipator* from falling into "the hands of their successors of different principles," as Lewis himself later admitted, transferred the paper to a subsidiary antislavery chapter in New York City, the leaders of which agreed to assume all of its debts. Thus the American Anti-Slavery Society was left without an official newspaper or press. Even the Society's records and correspondence were put into storage somewhere, to be lost forever, and the office furniture was removed, some of it ending up in Tappan's study at home. All these actions—the transfer of the Society's property, the funding of Birney's and Stanton's trip, the reassignment of the *Emancipator*—were accomplished before the fateful anniversary meeting of the Society. This liquidation of property was a calculated attempt to render the organization valueless and practically extinct, simply to frustrate Garrison's well-known plans to take it over. The excuse was that the Bostonians had intimated that they would not accept any liabilities incurred prior to the anniversary meeting.[23]

Both the Garrisonians and the Tappanites were culpable in this chaotic situation. Legally, the Executive Committee members were personally liable for all debts, since the organization was unincorporated. Morally, however, the selection of trustees and the disposition of all property, including the *Emancipator*, ought to have been brought before the convention for the decision of the members. While the Society's constitution did not require such action, a compromise of some sort could probably have been reached. As it was, internal politics rather than a just settlement of the dispute determined the actions of Lewis Tappan, who engineered most of these transactions. Not a thought was given to the long-range effect that they might have on the antislavery public or on the feelings of mutual confidence among the leaders.

The Garrisonians were blameworthy, too. They charged that Tappan and Benedict made handsome profits from the sale of the Society's literature, which, they erroneously claimed, was valued at eighteen thousand dollars. This accusation and others of an equally outlandish nature were simply distortions without foundation. Yet the Bostonians had reason to be antagonized, for they represented a force in the movement too important to be wholly ignored on questions concerning the very existence and functioning of the American Anti-Slavery Society.[24]

Not all evangelicals agreed with Tappan that the association ought to be surrendered to the Garrisonians without a fight. It is true that many were bored and perplexed by the indiscriminate charges and countercharges of both factions while there were much more imperative issues regarding slavery to be dealt with. But some antislavery reformers who belonged to the Tappan faction determined to carry their point of view to the convention floor in New York. In Massachusetts, Amos Phelps scoured the countryside for delegates to back the Executive Committee, and in Philadelphia Samuel Hastings and other Presbyterians readied a similar group that would attend if Tappan paid the cost of transportation. "Abolitionists generally," Hastings warned Lewis, "*love* the Am Soc and it will go hard with many to consent to a change. . . ." Tappan and his friends were too busy disbanding the Society to give these efforts much attention. Nonetheless, a very large number of faithful evangelicals appeared in New York, ready for battle and expecting a close fight.[25]

The whistle of the steamer *Rhode Island* announced the arrival of the Garrisonian forces in New York harbor on May 11, 1840. John A. Collins, Garrison's chief organizer, had chartered the vessel and loaded it down with ladies and gentlemen of both races from all corners of New England. Meanwhile, Henry C. Wright, Lucretia Mott, and other leaders from Pennsylvania arrived with a large delegation of Hicksite Quakers to supplement the New England contingent. Gaily they all trooped off to St. John's Hall, their dormitory-hotel (fifty cents a day). James Gordon Bennett's *Herald* made fun of the encampment, with its piles of bags, boxes, bedding, pots, and pans—and its amalgamation quackery—but nothing discouraged the visitors.[26] Over a thousand abolitionists descended on the city, cramming the Fourth Free Church to the bursting point at the opening meeting. Dreading "a recurrence of the scenes witnessed last year," Arthur Tappan failed to appear to preside but instead sent in his letter of resignation.[27] Obviously, there was still some confusion about what the evangelicals should do; Arthur had vanished, but Lewis was very much in evidence on the convention floor, rallying his faction as if he intended to fight down to the wire.

Events moved quickly. Garrison's close associate, Francis Jackson, was elected to fill the chair, conveniently vacant by Arthur's absence, and Garrison's slate of candidates won seats on the convention's business committee. Generously, Garrison had nominated Lewis Tappan and Amos Phelps for places on this committee, but included with them was Abby Kelley, a contentious feminist. On her selection the real test of strength was made. By a vote of 557 to 451, Miss Kelley won, amid the cheers of Garrison's forces. Giving four reasons why it was immoral for a lady to sit behind closed doors with gentlemen, Lewis Tappan resigned from the committee and departed, while Phelps, who shortly followed him, made a speech condemning the "packing" of the convention. In fact, both sides had "packed" the hall; Garrison was simply more efficient. Furthermore, there were no clear rules concerning the seating of delegates. Apparently all members who came could vote.[28]

That evening, thirty leaders gathered with Lewis Tappan at his house, where he read them a constitution he had drafted some weeks before. On the following day, the clericalists adopted it, forming the American and Foreign Anti-Slavery Society and electing Arthur Tappan president. Women were explicitly denied the right to vote (the old constitution had not been so specific on this point). Nor was there to be any swerving from moral suasion to third-party action in the "new organization," as the Garrisonians called it. Later in the week, three hundred clergy and laymen convened in the basement of the Fourth Free Church, while overhead the Garrisonians exulted in their easy triumph. As if to pierce the ceiling with a holy racket, the Tappans and their friends bellowed hymn no. 187 from *Freedom's Lyre*: "Lo! what an entertaining sight/Are brethren who agree."[29]

But no amount of fervent singing could keep up the spirits of the new enterprise. Missing from the assembly that afternoon were some of the biggest names in antislavery circles—Gerrit Smith, Alvan Stewart, Elizur Wright, the Grimkés, and Theodore Weld. His voice ruined from overuse, Weld was later to retire altogether from antislavery work. Furthermore, he disapproved of the new Society's conservatism on the matter of women's rights, a cause still dear to his wife and sister-in-law. Annoyed that the Tappans refused to join the Liberty party, Gerrit Smith, Stewart, and Wright were also skeptical of the new venture. Many others hesitated, as even Lewis had to admit, because they imagined that "the two armies intend waging a fierce conflict" that could only weaken the cause. "What a tremendous wrong has been done by the faction that have rendered anti-slavery organizations so odious in the community," he wrote Phelps.[30] Certainly Garrison's new ideas alienated many, but the intrigues of the Tappanites had hardly promoted much confidence in the New York leadership.

The new Society began as a museum of old abolitionists, not as a living organism. Many chapters dissolved rather than associate with either sect, leaving the "new organization" with fewer assets and a smaller active membership than even the Garrisonians mustered.[31] What little was done through this agency was performed by Lewis Tappan or by his close friend William Jay. Whenever Tappan could raise the funds or find the time, he wrote the *American and Foreign Anti-Slavery Reporter*, as dreary a publication as ever came from an antislavery press. Its imperfections were not his fault, however; he simply lacked the time and money to do the job well. All efforts to find a regular editor and secretary failed. Some years later, the Society published William Jay's *An Address to the Non-Slaveholders of the South*, perhaps one of the better antislavery documents. Jay argued that poor whites ought to resent a system that kept them in bondage to the slaves' overlords, and he stressed that modern technological advances rendered slavery obsolete and even retrogressive. The document served as precedent for Hinton Helper's later *Impending Crisis*, which created a sensation in the South by repeating this line of reasoning.[32]

The basic intent of the new group was to foster international accord on slavery matters, but the concept was too peripheral to the eradication of the domestic evil to arouse much popular interest. Though diverging in their emphasis on internationalism in antislavery, both the Tappanites and Garrisonians competed fiercely for British approbation. For instance, Garrison, the Philadelphia Quaker Lucretia Mott, Wendell Phillips, and other friends arrived in London in June, 1840, for the World Anti-Slavery Convention, hoping to enlist the kind of backing Garrison himself had obtained in 1833. Instead, they discovered that Birney, Stanton, and Leavitt had already converted Sturge, Thomas Clarkson, the Buxtons, and other leaders to their views. In addition, the British were cool toward so radical a measure as seating the Garrisonian ladies as regular delegates in the convention hall, and Garrison conspicuously took a seat in the spectator's gallery next to Lady Byron.[33] In later years, however, the Bostonians attracted some English support by virtue of the oratorical efforts of George Thompson and of a certain swell of sympathy that had resulted in the formation of pro-Garrison societies, particularly in Glasgow, Dublin, and Bristol.

The Tappan-Garrison squabble in Great Britain and at home was only a sub-plot in this *opéra bouffe*. Almost forgotten in the uproar was the "common enemy" of slavery. Tappan admitted that the cause had suffered from these divisions, but he placed most of the blame on Garrison and the residue on the political activists who tried unsuccessfully to harness his American and Foreign Anti-Slavery Society to their Liberty party wagon.[34]

Though they created despondency and bitterness, the cause in general gained more than it lost by these divisions. Each wing of the movement could pursue its aims independently, while antislavery sentiment grew year by year. Garrison's clique remained small but very noisy; the American Anti-Slavery Society served mainly as a springboard for his radical ideas. It was just as well that the Tappan brothers had surrendered the organization to him, for, with the exception of a few weeks during the postal effort of 1835, the public mind had always identified the Society with Garrison, not with its national officers. No other organization would ever capture that spirit of implacable hostility to slavery that characterized the parent Society, and no one could ever match Garrison's symbolic role as the spokesman of the American conscience, at least until John Brown appeared.

The evangelicals who had supported the cause up to this point, numbering somewhere between one hundred thousand and one hundred and sixty thousand,[35] continued to exert an influence in the national churches and political parties that was independent of formal organization. Lewis Tappan soon discovered that the American and Foreign Anti-Slavery Society could never reach them or stir their spirits. It took six years for him to found an association that could attract a sizable number of them. The origin of that organization, the American Missionary Association, was the outcome of a most bizarre affair of murder, mutiny, and African slavery. In his association with it, Tappan proved himself not only an impressive manipulator of public opinion but also an able student of American law.

NOTES

1. E. Wright to James R. Wright, October 10, 1837, Wright to B. Green, December 15, 1838, Wright MSS, LC; William Jay in *Emancipator*, June 8, 1837; LT to Phelps, November 14, 1835 and December 27, 1837, Phelps MSS, BPL; Tuckerman, *Jay*, 84; Jay to LT, August 22, 1836; LT to Weld, February 2, 1837, Box II, slavery MSS, New-York Historical Society; LT in *Emancipator*, February 9, 1837.

2. LT, letter, August 5, 1836 in *Liberator*, September 3, 1836; Garrison and Garrison, *Garrison*, II, 107–14; LT to G. Smith, September 5, 1836, Gerrit Smith Miller MSS, Syracuse University Library.

3. LT to Birney, November 17, 1837, extract of letter in William Birney, *James G. Birney and His Times* (New York, 1890), 296–97; WLG to Henry E. Benson, December 23, 1836, in Garrison and Garrison, *Garrison*, II, 114–17.

4. Garrison and Garrison, *Garrison*, II, 145–52, including Noyes to WLG, March 22, 1837; Wright to Phelps, October 20, 1837, Phelps MSS, BPL; Cross, *Burned-*

Over District, 245–49; Walter M. Merrill, *Against Wind and Tide: A Biography of Wm. Lloyd Garrison* (Cambridge, 1963), 133–34; LT to Phelps, August 22, 1837, Phelps MSS, BPL; *Liberator*, June 30, 1837; Wright to his parents, August 9, 1837, Wright MSS, LC.

5. Arthur Bradford, Darlington, Pa., to LT, July 1, 1852; Robert W. Doherty, *The Hicksite Separation: A Sociological Analysis of Religious Schism in Early Nineteenth Century America* (New Brunswick, 1967), 82–88; see Lucretia Mott's discussion of the relation of old Quakerism to contemporary liberality: Cromwell, *Lucretia Mott*, 109–110. On Garrison and non-resistance, its radicalism and conservatism, see Ernest Crosby, *Garrison, The Non-Resistant* (Chicago, 1904); Guy F. Hershberger, *War, Peace, and Nonresistance* (Scottdale, Pa., 1946), 215–18; Staughton Lynd, ed., *Nonviolence in America: A Documentary History* (Indianapolis, 1966), xxiv–xxix; and Bertram Wyatt-Brown, "William Lloyd Garrison and Antislavery Unity: A Reappraisal," *Civil War History*, XIII (March, 1967), 5–24.

6. *Liberator*, August 18, 1837; for the series of clerical protests, see reprints in *ibid.*, August 11 and 25, September 1 and 8, 1837, and *New Spectator* (Boston), August 2, 1837; Irving Bartlett, *Wendell Phillips, Brahmin Radical* (Boston, 1961), 64–65; cf. Hazel Catherine Wolf, *On Freedom's Altar: The Martyr Complex in the Abolition Movement* (Madison, 1952), 27–29; Goodell, *Slavery and Anti-Slavery*, 461.

7. Quotation, WLG to G. W. Benson, September 16, 1837, in Garrison and Garrison, *Garrison*, II, 162; cf. Dumond, *Antislavery*, 283; WLG to LT, September, 13, 1837; LT to WLG, September 21, 1837, WLG MSS, BPL.

8. Goodell, *Slavery and Anti-Slavery*, 458; Wright to Birney (quotation), August 14, 1837, Dumond, *Birney Letters*, I, 144; Birney to LT, July 29, 1837, *ibid.*, 399, 401; August 23, 1837, *ibid.*, 417–24; September 14, 1837, *ibid.*, 424–25; see also Stanton to Birney, August 7, 1837, *ibid.*, 404–12; September 1, 1837, *ibid.*, 420–24; LT to Phelps, August 22, 1837, Phelps MSS, BPL; but contrast impressions of these letters with official neutrality as found in Wright's letter to *Emancipator*, reprinted in *Liberator*, September 1, 1837.

9. LT in *Emancipator*, November 16, 1837; quotation, LT to Birney, November 17, 1837, Birney, *Birney*, 295–96.

10. E. Wright to Phelps, January 22, 1839, Wright MSS, LC (quotation); on the dangers of too close an identification with Massachusetts clericalists, advice probably ignored, see Wright to Phelps, October 20, 1837, Phelps MSS, BPL, and Phelps to LT, December 18, 1837.

11. Diary, May 8, 1838; LT to Birney, November 17, 1837, Birney, *Birney*, 295–96; *Liberator*, May 18, 1838; *Annual Report* (1838), 12; LT to G. Smith, October 13, 1836, January 4, 1839, Gerrit Smith Miller MSS, Syracuse University Library; Wright to Green, December 15, 1838, Wright MSS, LC. Income of national society was not commensurate with its growth in numbers: it was $29,071.32 in 1836–37, *Annual Report* (1837), 30; $32,534.64 in 1837–38, *ibid.* (1838), 43; $27,090 in 1838–39, *ibid.* (1839), 50; as a result most agents were dismissed—see Agency Committee Minutes of Meetings, 1838–39, BPL; and LT in *Emancipator*, clipping [n.d.], in diary, July 16, 1838.

12. *The True History of the Late Division in the Report of the Executive Committee of the Massachusetts Abolition Society* (Boston, 1841), 36; LT's reaction to Chapman's remark in LT to G. Smith, March 8, 1839, Gerrit Smith Miller MSS, Syracuse University Library; see also *ibid.*, March 30, April 12, 1839; Anne Weston

to Deborah Weston, March 23, 1839, Weston Family MSS, BPL; Maria Weston Chapman, *Right and Wrong in Massachusetts* (Boston, 1839), 136; *Liberator,* March 2, 9, and 29, 1839; see also "The Address of the Boston Female Anti-Slavery Society" in *Liberator Extra* [n.d.], 1840.

13. *Liberator,* May 10, 1839; LT in *Emancipator,* quoted by *Liberator,* June 23, 1837; see also N. Southard to Wright, July 14, 1837, Wright MSS, LC; speech reprinted in *Annual Report* (1839), 19–22.

14. *Liberator,* May 10, 1839.

15. *Annual Report* (1839), 28–49; cf. Dumond, *Antislavery,* 283–84.

16. Garrison and Garrison, *Garrison,* II, 296–99; *Annual Report* (1839), 28–49; cf. Barnes, *Antislavery Impulse,* 158–60; Goodell, *Slavery and Anti-Slavery,* 462–63.

17. LT to G. Smith, May 15, 1839, Gerrit Smith Miller MSS, Syracuse University Library.

18. Cross, *Burned-Over District,* 116–22; Wilson, *Rise and Fall of Slave Power,* I, 547; Elizur Wright, *Myron Holley: and What He Did for Liberty and True Religion* (Boston, 1882), 172, 243, 252, 256–60; Fladeland, *Birney,* 178–82; Luther R. Marsh, *Writings and Speeches of Alvan Stewart, on Slavery* (New York, 1860), 21–27; LT to G. Smith, March 24, 1840, ltrbk.; New York *Commercial Advertiser,* November 1, 1839; LT in *National Intelligencer* (Washington), June 1, 1840.

19. Letter to editor, *Emancipator,* quoted by *Liberator,* May 8, 1840; see also WLG to Elizabeth Pease, November 6, 1837, in Garrison and Garrison, *Garrison,* II, 183, for loss of faith in this approach; also E. Wright in *Massachusetts Abolitionist* (Boston), March 19, 1840.

20. LT to Samuel Hastings, January 12, 1839 (photostat), LT MSS, LC; *Address to the Churches of Jesus Christ: By the Evangelical Union Anti-Slavery Society of . . . New York . . .* (New York, 1839), 53–54; LT to Gamaliel Bailey, October 24, 1839, LT to G. Smith, November 18, 1839, LT to Loring, November 20, 1839, ltrbk.; LT to William McKee and others, December 11, 1839 (photostat), LT MSS, LC; a printed circular of McKee and Hastings, December 6, 1839, Phelps MSS, BPL; LT to John Scoble, December 10, 1839, Annie H. Abel and Frank Klingberg, eds., *A Side-Light on Anglo-American Relations . . .* (Lancaster, Pa., 1927), 63.

21. *British and Foreign Anti-Slavery Reporter, January* 15, 1840, 102–12; Abel and Klingberg, *Side-Light,* 3, 10–11; Birney to Phelps, August 8, 1839, in Dumond, *Birney Letters,* I, 497–98.

22. LT to Birney, January 23, 1840, to G. Smith, February 5, March 13, 1840, to Seth Gates, March 21, 1840, ltrbk.; Hastings to LT, March 25, 1840 (photostat), LT MSS, LC; *Liberator,* May 15, 1840; reprint from *Friend of Man* (Utica), which indicated that Garrison's plans were no secret.

23. See Joshua Leavitt in *National Anti-Slavery Standard* (New York), October 24, 1844; LT to Maria Waring, Dublin, Ireland, May 14, 1847, WLG MSS, BPL (quotations); Garrison and Garrison, *Garrison,* II, 343n (Phillips' quotation); LT and S. W. Benedict, printed circular, July 21, 1841, Gerrit Smith Miller MSS, Syracuse University Library.

24. *Liberator,* May 1 and 15, 1840; *Ninth Annual Report of the Mass. Anti-Slavery Society . . .* (Boston, 1841), 49–50, appendix, xvi; *Eleventh Annual Report . . .* (Boston, 1843), 67–68; Edmund Quincy, *An Examination of the Charges of Mr. John Scoble & Mr. Lewis Tappan against the American Anti-Slavery Society*

(Dublin, Ireland, 1852); Quincy in *National Anti-Slavery Standard,* September 19, October 24, November 7, 1844; Goodell, *Slavery and Anti-Slavery,* 464–65n; Fladeland, *Birney,* 193; John Jay to "editor, National Anti-Slavery Standard," n.d., 1841, Jay MSS, Columbia University Library.

25. Hastings to LT, March 25, April 14 and 29, 1840 (photostats), LT MSS, LC; see also George Storrs in *Emancipator,* February 27, 1840; Lydia Maria Child to Loring, May 7, 1840, miscellaneous personal letters, New York Public Library; *Massachusetts Abolitionist,* June 18, 1840; *Philanthropist,* May 19, 1840.

26. Samuel J. May to WLG, May 18, 1840, WLG MSS, BPL; *Liberator,* May 22 and 29 (quotation from New York *Herald*), 1840; see also *Massachusetts Abolitionist,* May 21, 1840; Garrison and Garrison, *Garrison,* II, 346–48.

27. Anne Weston to Maria Chapman, May 13, 1840, Weston Family MSS, BPL; diary, May 13, 1840; *Liberator,* May 15, 1840, and *Philanthropist,* June 16, 1840.

28. Thomas, *Liberator,* 290; Garrison and Garrison, *Garrison,* II, 348 and note. Thomas (p. 289), Barnes (*Antislavery Impulse,* pp. 169–70), and Dumond (*Antislavery,* p. 285) have taken a generally severe view of Garrison's packing of the assembly and the consequent *"coup d'état."* They do not account for the ability of Garrison to muster such loyal support as that which he gained from the textile town of Lynn, Massachusetts.

29. Diary, May 13, 1840; *American and Foreign Anti-Slavery Reporter,* June, July, 1840.

30. LT to Weld, May 26, 1840, LT MSS, LC; LT to G. Smith, April 27, 1841, June 15, 1842, Gerrit Smith Miller MSS, Syracuse University Library, and March 13, 1841, American Missionary Association MSS, Fisk University Library (hereinafter, AMA MSS, Fisk); Thomas, *Weld,* 214–24; LT to Weld, May 26, 1840, ltrbk., in which LT confessed that the "woman question" was only one of the many complaints against Garrison. Weld, however, remained convinced that power, not principle, was behind the struggle, which had degenerated into a conflict between personalities. See also, Jay to James C. Jackson, June 8, 1840, Jay MSS, Columbia University Library (he was more squeamish about the woman question than LT); LT to Phelps (quotations), June 20 and 25, 1840, Phelps MSS, BPL.

31. *Liberator,* May 22, 1840, on Pittsburgh antislavery; Hastings to LT, May 25, 1840, on dissensions in eastern Pennsylvania; L. Blanchard to Henry Cowles, August 4, 1840, Cowles MSS, Oberlin College Library, on troubles with James Boyle, a Garrisonian; see also, on Ohio, *Massachusetts Abolitionist,* June 18, 1840, and *Philanthropist,* June 9, 1840.

32. [William Jay], *Address to the Non-Slaveholders of the South on the Social and Political Evils of Slavery* (New York, 1843); Dumond, in *Antislavery,* 287–89, and in *A Bibliography of Antislavery in America* (Ann Arbor, 1961), 108, attributes the work to LT; on Jay's authorship, however, see LT to John Scoble, February 7, 1843, Abel and Klingberg, *Side-Light,* 112. On efforts to find an editor and secretary, see American & Foreign Anti-Slavery Society, Minutes of the Executive Committee, May 17, 1841, and after, AMA MSS, Fisk, formerly at AMA headquarters in New York; G. Smith to LT, January 11, 1841, ltrbk., Gerrit Smith Miller MSS, Syracuse University Library.

33. *British and Foreign Anti-Slavery Reporter* (London), June 17, 136–38; *American and Foreign Anti-Slavery Reporter* (hereinafter *A&FASR*), September, 1840; LT to G. Smith, July 22, 1840, Gerrit Smith Miller MSS, Syracuse University Library; Birney to LT, July 23, 1840, Dumond, *Birney Letters,* II, 584; Frederick

B. Tolles, ed., *Slavery and the 'Woman Question': Lucretia Mott's Diary of Her Visit to Great Britain to Attend the World's Anti-Slavery Convention of 1840* (London, 1952), 22, *passim;* Garrison and Garrison, *Garrison,* II, 367–75.

34. LT to G. Smith, August 2, 1840, March 14, 1841, February 7, 1842, Gerrit Smith Miller MSS, Syracuse University Library; LT to Jay, June 11, 1841; Birney to LT, December 1, 1840; Joseph Sturge and Whittier to LT, June 12, 1841; LT to Seth Gates, July 9, 1840, ltrbk.

35. Goodell, *Slavery and Anti-Slavery,* 464, suggests the number of one to two hundred thousand.

CHAPTER ELEVEN

The Mendi Africans

In late April, 1839, the "Tecora," a Portuguese slaver, took aboard five or six hundred slaves at Lomboko on the west coast of Africa. The "barracoon" or depot there belonged to Pedro Blanco, a former Spanish sailor who had become a millionaire in a few years by selling such cargoes as this to the Pedro Martinez Company of Havana. Escaping British patrol ships, the "Tecora" headed for the open seas and a few weeks later left its consignment at a covert point on the coast of Cuba.[1]

Rubbed with palm oil to make them shine, the Negroes—men, women, and children—were marched in coffles to the Misericordia stockade just outside the walls of Havana. On June 26, some forty-nine of these prisoners were sold to a slave speculator from Porto Principe named José Ruiz. Together with three girls belonging to an old man, Pedro Montez, the group was herded aboard the "Amistad," which would carry them around the island to Granaja. The ship was a fast, eighty-ton, two-masted coastal schooner, built some six years before in a Baltimore shipyard expressly for the slave trade. On the fourth day at sea, the Africans, under the leadership of two of their number called Cinqué and Grabeau, successfully mutinied, killing the captain and cook and taking Montez and Ruiz prisoner. Intending to make for Africa, they spared the masters' lives so that they could serve as navigators.[2]

During the day, Montez and Ruiz did Cinqué's bidding, sailing eastward, but at night they changed course, heading north in hope of reaching a southern slave state and safety. After weeks of boxing about the Bahamas, with provisions exhausted, the ship finally dropped anchor at Culloden Point, near the tip of Long Island. While Cinqué and a small group took the long boat to find fresh supplies, a navy cutter commanded by Lieutenant J. R. Gedney spotted the vessel and captured it from Grabeau and the rest. Rounding up the shore party, Gedney placed them all under arrest for piracy and murder and released the nearly hysterical Cubans from their shackles.[3] Transported across the Sound to New Haven, the Africans were placed in jail to await trial. There they huddled, ignorant of the language and the ways of their captors, undernourished, and cold in the unfamiliar climate. Meanwhile, the news of their strange adventure traveled across the nation.

Most Americans had as little knowledge of Africa and the slave trade as they did of cannibalism or suttee, and there were those who took advantage of that general ignorance and indifference by participating in the slave trade with almost complete impunity. Nicholas P. Trist, United States consul in Havana, for instance, made a fortune from supplying false ships' papers, with which slavers could claim immunity from British inspection. The Van Buren administration was aware of his dealings but did nothing about them, for southern politicians wanted as little to do with British suppressive measures as possible. Only abolitionists like Tappan cared, but their protests were wholly ignored.[4] The "Amistad" prisoners provided a dramatic and even romantic way to bring the fate of hundreds of thousands of captive Africans to the attention of the American public.

Immediately upon hearing the news of the arrest, Lewis Tappan formed a committee consisting of himself, Joshua Leavitt, and Simeon Jocelyn. Although Leavitt was sometimes estranged from Tappan because of their differences over political abolitionism, he had to admit that Tappan's "untiring vigilance, his immovable decision of character, and his facility in the despatch of business" were chiefly responsible for the eventual release of those who were known as the Amistads.[5]

On September 6, Tappan met the Africans for the first time at the jail. He gave an impromptu sermon—his subject was the Providence of God—which they had no way of understanding. More interesting to them, though, was a sample of ice, which some handled "as if their hands had been burned," while the rest,

Tappan observed, "laughed immoderately." The first task, he thought, was to arrange for their spiritual instruction, and he soon hired a group of divinity students at Yale to take on the job, even before he found an interpreter. Equally important was the publication of favorable articles to win friends and raise money for the Africans' defense. Colonel Pendleton, the jailer, was exhibiting his charges to the curious at a New York shilling apiece, while giving a lurid and mostly fictional account of their origins and mutiny. Meanwhile, newspaper men spread all sorts of stories about their "cannibalism." The handsome, twenty-six-year-old Cinqué, of course, and Grabeau got the most attention for having led the mutiny, but Konoma, a Congolese with monstrously disfigured teeth, served as example of the Africans' presumed man-eating propensities. (It was later reported in an evangelical pamphlet that his defacement had been performed *"to make the ladies love him."*)[6]

Later in the month, Tappan again visited the jail to watch one of the "God palavers," as his Yale seminarians called them. "It was interesting, and painful too," he said, "to see these pagans, from a far distant land, gazing at the speaker, and listening to this discourse . . . in a language wholly unknown to them. O, thought I, for the gift of tongues to communicate to them the unsearchable riches of Christ!" The Rev. Thomas Gallaudet, who had developed a sign language for the deaf and mute, tried to reach the prisoners, but to no effect. When, however, two or three wandered off in the course of the service for a smoke, Cinqué "rose from his seat, went to them, and struck the pipes out of their mouths. . . . What an instinctive lesson is this to careless and ill bred attendants in Christian assemblies!" Tappan exclaimed in admiration.[7] Later on, he found out that the Africans believed in a spirit called the Ga-wa-wa, which the missionaries interpreted as a primitive revelation of the true God. In any case, his stress upon their religious training made excellent copy for the church-going public that was called upon to support the effort to free them.[8]

Tappan searched the wharves and ships of New York for an interpreter and found at last James Covey, a cabin-boy on a British African patrol vessel who could speak the prisoners' dialect. Luckily, most of them were from the same tribe, the Mendi, of present-day Nigeria. Covey was their only link with the strange world around them.[9] Finding able counsel was a less difficult task.

Theodore Sedgwick of New York and Roger Sherman Baldwin of New Haven, both able lawyers, responded to the committee's request and began to prepare for the opening trial, scheduled for September 17.[10]

The presiding judge was the same Andrew T. Judson who had prosecuted Prudence Crandall in 1833. There was no reason to think he had altered his views of abolitionism in the intervening years. Van Buren and his cabinet reluctantly had agreed to allow the federal court to handle the matter, in spite of Spanish demands for the captives' immediate surrender, because of the danger of unfavorable northern reaction to any arbitrary action from Washington. The President, Secretary of State John Forsyth, a Georgian, and W. S. Holabird, the local district attorney, all expected Judson to do his Democratic duty.[11]

National interest focused on the trial. As Joshua Leavitt said, "The South is watching with the deepest solicitude to see what disposal a Federal Court holding its session in a free State, will make of self-liberated black men who have asserted their rights Bunker-Hill fashion."[12] Transported by canal boat, the prisoners arrived in Hartford shivering in the autumn air. Before Judson's bench sat Lewis Tappan, next to Montez' little girls, who were wrapped in white blankets and sobbing with fright. Tappan took one by the hand, and Pendleton gave them apples to cheer them up.[13] Surprisingly, the judge, accepting Baldwin's able arguments, threw out the charges of piracy and murder, on the ground of lacking jurisdiction over crimes against foreigners committed at sea. Yet the worst was not over, because the Cubans still could claim their property in his Court of Claims. For the time being, though, the prisoners went back to jail in New Haven.[14]

Unwilling to let interest die before the next trial, Tappan thought of a brilliant counter-stroke. He authorized Baldwin and Sedgwick to set in motion the arrest of the masters on twin charges of false imprisonment and cruelty. Accompanying the New York sheriff to the Spaniards' hotel, he had the pleasure of seeing them locked up in that notorious city jail called the "Egyptian catacombs."[15] Reaction from proslavery elements was immediate. Threatening letters arrived in volume at Tappan's postbox, and James Watson Webb, Major Noah, and James Gordon Bennett scourged him in their papers as they had in years past. "Really, it is time that the community should come to an understanding with Mr. Tappan," cried the New York *Express*. Unless his meddling was stopped, the editor warned, southern citizens on northern visits would soon find themselves in the same predicament as Ruiz and Montez. The *Evening Tatler* urged Ruiz to obtain a writ of habeas corpus and then to have Tappan placed behind bars on the charge of false arrest. But public opinion was not aroused to any action by these appeals. Even Benjamin F. Butler, district attorney for New York and a close friend of the President, refused Van Buren's request to free the Cubans at once.

By some peculiar alchemy, Tappan had made the Amistads' case a "safe" cause. Gentlemen who were silent about more pressing questions of slavery, gentlemen who for years had muttered about the Tappans' subversive activities, congratulated themselves on their liberality in supporting the Amistads. Robert Rantoul, a prominent lawyer, Chauncey A. Goodrich, president of Yale, professors, doctors, and ministers either wrote letters of appeal to the President or found some other means to express their benevolent feelings about the affair. The Garrisonians also momentarily laid aside their hostility toward Tappan and added their financial and polemical support. But of greater significance was the lesson the Amistad case taught complacent citizens about the prejudices of federal officials. As one Ohioan told Lewis, "Such base fraudulence—such *blood-hound* persecutions of poor defenceless strangers cast upon the shores, should call down the manly and scorching rebukes of *universal civilized* man—Yes, of *barbarism* itself." Such virulent criticism of the proslavery policies of the national government would become more common in the 1850's, but the Amistad case helped to stir the beginnings of that mistrust among many Yankees. Tappan was able to enlist the sympathy of the northern public by straightforward reporting of the facts without too much editorial embellishment, a means rather uncommon in antislavery agitation. "Some people marveled that an abolitionist could be so impartial," Lewis boasted to Benjamin after his articles on the first hearings before Judge Judson appeared in the commercial New York newspapers. The "Amistad" committee also kept its operations distinct from those of the American Anti-Slavery Society in order to encourage general northern support. In spite of these wise measures, it was ironic but hardly strange that the fate of a handful of bewildered Africans could arouse the pity of the American people, the intelligentsia especially, in a way that native-born slaves caught in equally cruel circumstances could not.[16]

Not long after his imprisonment, the court released Montez on grounds of insufficient evidence, and Ruiz, who remained in prison until February, 1840, finally got his freedom on bail. (Presumably he failed to take the advice of the *Evening Tatler* by seeking release on a writ of habeas corpus because he had expected that an indignant public would press the courts to give him back his freedom and his property at the same time.) Both men returned to Cuba forthwith, leaving the adjudication of the matter in the hands of the Spanish and American authorities.[17]

By the time the case came to trial, in January, 1840, Lewis Tappan and the lawyers had uncovered evidence that, if justly weighed, would free their clients. Dr. Richard R. Madden, British Commissioner of the Anglo-Spanish board in Havana charged with the suppression of the slave trade, volunteered his services in helping the Amistads. Tappan took Madden to Judson in November to present a deposition which asserted that, under Spanish law, by treaty with Great Britain, these prisoners had to be considered illegal immigrants and must therefore be returned to their homeland. Though their passports for transportation showed native Spanish names, Madden proved the documents had been forged by the Martinez Company.[18] In January, Judson overruled the objections of W. S. Holabird and accepted the deposition and the eloquent appeals of Baldwin and Sedgwick.[19] In rendering his decision in favor of the Amistads, Judson rhetorically asked why the owners had not attempted to ascertain where their property had come from. "This has been the source of all their complicated sufferings, the tale of which will make the stoutest heart to bleed!" In summary, Judson exclaimed "Cinque [*sic*] and Grabeau shall not sigh for Africa in vain. Bloody as may be their hands, they shall yet embrace their kindred."[20] He ordered the United States government to transport the captives home at once. Nowhere, however, did he actually say they were free; Tappan, therefore, in spite of his pleasure at the outcome, was disappointed that Judson's order smacked of the spirit of colonization.[21]

Leading a delegation of abolitionist friends, Tappan went immediately to the jail to give the prisoners the happy news. The young Negroes fell to their knees before their white deliverers, then leaped and shouted in ecstasy. When the tumult subsided, the Rev. H. G. Ludlow offered up prayers of thanks, while James Covey translated his words. The Africans "followed him audibly, and with apparent devoutness," Tappan wrote in the *Emancipator*.[22]

Van Buren, up for re-election and uncertain of his standing in the South, was infuriated by Judson's decision. Seth Staples, one of the "Amistad" committee's lawyers, learned from a reliable source that John Van Buren had declared that his father had been offended because "the decision had a great and important political bearing of which Judson had taken no notice." The U.S.S. "Grampus," which President Van Buren had ordered to stand by at New Haven to take the prisoners to Havana, raised anchor and departed without them. Then the President ordered Holabird to appeal the case to the Supreme Court.[23] When Tappan gave the prisoners the discouraging news, they were not excessively despondent; they were enjoying the attention they received from their pious instructors. Besides, Pendleton allowed them to perform acrobatic acts for money, which they spent in his grog shop next door. (The abolitionists had not yet tried to impose strict temperance upon the Africans. Later, however, Cinqué, under the evangelicals' tutelage, decided that "Mr. P." was a "bad man" who would "go down, down, Devil.")[24]

Two hearings before Smith Thompson, justice of the United States Circuit Court for Connecticut, kept Tappan and the lawyers busy before the January term of the Supreme Court in 1841. Throughout these months, Tappan proved himself as versatile in mastering the intricacies of the case as the lawyers he hired. It was expensive, tiring, and frustrating to carry out the long examinations, attend the proceedings, draw up the reports, and do the other chores connected with the case. Nevertheless, Tappan performed whatever was required unselfishly and efficiently. If he, rather than Benjamin, had become the lawyer in the family, it may be speculated that he would have been a remarkable success.[25]

Leaving no avenue unexplored, Tappan encouraged British intervention through his friends in the British and Foreign Anti-Slavery Society. The effort had some effect on Lord Palmerston, the foreign minister, who directed the British minister in Washington to "interpose his good offices" and to express her Majesty's Government's concern in the outcome of the case.[26] Tappan's success on this score, however, proved something of a liability, for in the Senate John C. Calhoun denounced English meddling in the interest of "a band of barbarous slaves, with hands imbrued in blood," at the same time that the British were enslaving millions of Chinese to the opium habit. Official British sympathy made no impression on the American government, but it lifted abolitionist morale immensely.[27]

As the time for the hearing of the case before the Supreme Court drew closer, Tappan and Baldwin agreed that another lawyer had to be added to the staff. Consulting with Ellis Gray Loring, they decided to approach John Quincy Adams, who after some hesitation finally agreed to the request.[28] Pleased though he was, Tappan considered Baldwin a better trial lawyer than Adams. But he had to admit to Baldwin that, "however erroneous Mr. Adams' legal views may be. . . , his station, age, character, &c &c will give an importance to his services in this cause not to be overlooked."[29] Adams had already taken notice of the case, for as a Congressman he had helped the "Amistad" committee obtain and publish the official State Department correspondence concerning it. These letters, handed over on demand to the House of Representatives, showed how the administration had attempted to comply with the Spanish government's demands, even to the point of contemplating seizure of the prisoners.[30]

While Baldwin's argument before the Supreme Court was the more legally impessive, Adams' eloquent appeal for justice had the greater impact on the Court. Judson's decision was sustained. A letter to Tappan from Adams announced, "The Captives are free!" The old man concluded, "But thanks, thanks in the name of humanity and justice to *you*."[31] Tappan treasured this letter of March 9, 1841, above all those he ever received. Some days later, Tappan left for New Haven to make arrangements for the now liberated Amistads. On his arrival, he discovered that Pendleton still held the girls, wanting them for domestic servants. Armed with a court order, Tappan and two or three friends hustled them into a waiting carriage, while Pendleton and a crowd of Yale students hissed, booed, and threatened violence.[32] All the former captives were soon united at a farm rented to accommodate them near Farmington, Connecticut. They were free at last, yet the problem of getting them back to Africa, trained as missionaries of the Gospel to their people, the Mendi, remained a formidable undertaking.

Tappan's work with the captives was outstanding from every point of view. He had made full use of his abilities as an administrator, legal adviser, publicist, and religious instructor. What made his efforts still more impressive was that they coincided with his fight with Garrison and the political-minded abolitionists, the dismantling of the old American Anti-Slavery Society and the erection of the "new organization," his controversy with the Broadway Tabernacle, the forming of his Negro Sunday school enterprises, and his regular job of sustaining the rapidly sinking Arthur Tappan Company.

Such strenuous activities could not, however, be performed without enormous sacrifices, not only in time taken away from the ordinary things of life, but also to some degree in emotional commitments too, particularly toward his own family. On the whole Tappan was a good father to his children, but he was often absent from home on business. Perhaps unconsciously imitating the rather distant manner of his own father, he seldom set aside a few hours to play with them or to organize spontaneous family outings. He often excused himself from the family circle, even on holidays, to perform a charitable service in the neighborhood. Only when some serious event arose did he devote himself to the needs of the children. When Lewis Henry was dying of rheumatic fever in 1836, for instance, his father was indeed in constant attendance at the bedside. Nevertheless, Tappan could not for a moment forget the religious implications involved. He tried to encourage the boy to announce his conversion, but Lewis Henry was too sick and too stubborn to relent. Tappan's disappointment was keen when all his efforts of persuasion, warnings of the dire consequences, and prayers failed to lead Lewis Henry to the desired deathbed scene of contrition. Yet, Lewis Tappan was too tenderhearted, and perhaps too ashamed of his absences and neglect, ever to spank any of the children. Reviewing his own childhood, he did not feel that his mother's use of physical punishment had done him much good. Instead, he relied on Sarah Tappan's other methods—pious conversations and readings aloud from appropriate devotional sources.

In the midst of his worries over the "Amistad" case, Eliza, eighteen years old, fell dangerously ill with tuberculosis in November, 1840. Like all the Tappan children, she had inherited Susan's gentle disposition, and she was endowed with her father's intelligence and courage. Tappan did his best to comfort her by pointing out the seriousness of her condition. He told Eliza that the doctors considered "her case critical and that *her lungs were affected*." When she began to cry, he asked, as he recorded in his diary, "Eliza, is this unexpected to you—does it distress you to hear it?

She replied that she had not thought she was so ill, and 'when we first hear of things we are apt to be affected.'" Tappan pursued the matter further by stressing that the truth was always preferable to false hope. After praying with her, he left; the child fought back the tears when her mother went into her room a few minutes later.

Just after New Year's Day, 1841, Tappan decided to give Eliza the whole truth of her condition, painful though he realized the revelation would be. He pointed out that, according to the physicians, she had only five or six weeks more to live. Bravely, the girl replied, " 'I hope I am submissive.'" Under her father's supervision, Eliza put aside the essays of Madame de Staël and began reading "The Merchant's Daughter," a popular children's tract, and Richard Baxter's *The Saints' Everlasting Rest*. Tappan was deeply moved throughout her illness by her calm resignation, religious faith, and her remarkable thoughtfulness. Even the family doctors, whose mustard poultices and other painful "cures" did more harm than good, were personally saddened, one of them weeping openly while Lewis told him of "her submission—hope—and faith." Evangelical religion was defective in many respects perhaps, but it provided a family like Lewis Tappan's with an explanation and an appreciation of the beauty of simple things in life and death. Perhaps Tappan was not wrong to tell her of her fate, because he had also prepared her with the means to face it. Eliza was made to feel that through her example she could be useful even in dying, by knitting the family together, by showing that life is not meaningless, and by looking forward to a glory denied the living.

At times it seemed, however, that Lewis' endeavors in various reform causes were a means to escape the very acts of love that he urged Eliza to perform. If he ever wept, as old Dr. A. G. Smith did, he did not record it in his journal. Restless and somewhat disconcerted by the mournful atmosphere of the household, he left home on Sunday, February 7, 1841, to seek solace in a charitable deed. "This forenoon," he noted, "I took a bunch of tracts and went to the Debtors' Jail in Centre st. . . . I conversed with [the inmates] affectionately & faithfully on the subject of . . . Christ & gave each [person] one or more tracts. . . . May the Savior add his blessing to this visit."

Tappan, more emotional than he realized, may have found this kind of work a means of avoiding the helplessness, grief, and uselessness he felt at home. What appeared as an abdication of his duty to show fatherly affection and solicitude could have been somewhat more complicated. It is possible that Susan, his wife, encouraged his absence from the household on occasions such as this. He was not needed; he might only be in the way. Also, one must be wary of accusing him of a lack of feeling. His diary, written in the formal style so common to the times, did not convey sentiments that were probably present throughout this trying period. Lewis Tappan's language was incapable of re-creating the whole circumstance. Beneath the seemingly harsh, almost offensive phrases of piety, more genuine thoughts, recognized by all those present, lay buried. His quaint recital of Eliza's choices of reading materials, his pompous description of the jailhouse visitation, and his interviews with Eliza can be easily misinterpreted, while the silences of loving communion between father and daughter, the hushed conversations between husband and wife, and his gentle explanations to the younger members of the family about what was happening were totally lost in the diary account. A failure to understand himself, to confront the meaning of his attempted flight from intimacy with Eliza, was all too clearly shown, but, in spite of Tappan's unwillingness to shed his reserve, Eliza indicated in the last days of her life that she understood him and loved him deeply. She even thanked him for giving her strength to meet death by telling her the true state of her illness when the doctors had first revealed it months before. After reading some hymns to her, Tappan was very touched when Eliza urged him to stay at her side quietly, for, she said, "I want to talk with you before my voice fails me." She died the following day, May 7, 1841.

Tappan was a strengthening influence in this time of bereavement. He made all the necessary arrangements for the funeral, helped his wife with the greeting of friends, and lightened the household burdens for her. Two days later, however, business took precedence over family duty once more. Tappan had intended to accompany the body to its resting place in Brookline, but, as he reported in his accustomed style in the journal, "as the Amistad Africans were to be on exhibition on Wednesday afternoon and the duty of superintending it divolved [*sic*] on me—and as there was to be a meeting of the Amer. & For. Anti-Slavery Society on Tuesday evening & I was chairman of the committee of arrangements, my friends thought it was my duty to remain." It was characteristic of Lewis to claim to have been compelled by friendly advisers to do exactly what he wanted to do. He hired a Mr. Hulsard to go with the coffin in his place. Tappan reminded himself that, after all, Eliza's chief "desire" was "to be *useful*."[33]

Not long after Eliza's burial, Tappan discovered that the Amistads' freedom had brought new problems. Eager to get home, they grew restless under the management of the abolitionists on the farm. Cinqué was particularly so, as John W. Norton, one of the instructors, told Tappan. For a "shilling he will [take] off his coat to exhibit his feats of ability," he explained. "I met him yesterday running through the streets with a wild boy of sixteen and soon after I saw him in a store with a parcel of dissipated young men." Exercise from chopping wood and pulling stumps was the sort which the evangelicals approved, and as another teacher complained, "to have these men jump in the street" encouraged their association with "the vile and unprincipled."

Unlike the rather self-effacing Negroes who worked in menial jobs in the stores and warehouses of New York, these blacks were much more outspoken, being happily oblivious to the mores of the white society in which they found themselves. Conflicts with their white sponsors were inevitable. Kinna, one of the brightest of the adolescents in the group, proved exceptionally strong-minded. A. F. Williams, an instructor from the Yale divinity school, exclaimed to Tappan that "Kinna is getting as proud as Lucifer & Cinque has just left me . . . urging me to pay for making a coat." Both Mendians were setting a poor example, Williams continued. When the white teacher declined to pay for the new coat, Cinqué, upon whom the abolitionists relied to control his colleagues, refused to order a group of them to return to work; presumably Williams had to relent by purchasing the garment to end the dispute, though he did not confess doing so to his superior in New York. Kinna, who served as chief translator for the teachers after James Covey's departure, was finally disciplined for his impudent behavior by the managers of the farm, who refused to speak to him for a time.[34] In fact, clothing the Mendians was something of an irritation for all concerned throughout the last months of their stay in America. "They seem . . . quite inclined to dress & appear like *Gent*[lemen] *of the Town*," Williams complained to Tappan. Most of the young men disliked the "Hard Times" work clothes given them, perhaps because their "dissipated" young white friends made fun of their wearing outfits worn by southern slaves. In any case, the Africans wanted fancier attire, especially for going to church in the town. On the other hand, the abolitionists rigidly insisted that they should be humble and decorous both in conduct and appearance in order to comply with the white man's notion of their station in life. It was a very small matter, but a rather significant indication of the abolitionists' attitude.

At the same time, the white leaders welcomed a spirit of inquiry and free expression among their charges in other directions. Academically the Africans progressed in a manner gratifying to their teachers. Williams, for instance, concluded "that the Ethiopians are indeed a people not far below if not equal or even superior in intellect to most nations of the earth." The Mendians studied their books and lessons with a will, and they accepted, for a time at least, the simply explained doctrines of Christianity. As they grew accustomed to the routines, the pupils settled down. Then, in midsummer, 1841, a Mendian named Foone drowned in a nearby river. Since Foone was an excellent swimmer, all his friends agreed that his death must have been suicide because of homesickness. They told the instructors that Foone believed that his spirit would return to his native land. The teachers began to report that they could no longer hold the Africans' attention.[35] Although he still felt they were not ready to undertake the Christianizing of their portion of the continent, Tappan realized that another suicide or some other eruption might jeopardize the whole project. Better to plant the seed early than wait for perfect conditions, which might never come in any case. Furthermore, the exciting novelty of dealing with the Africans was wearing thin for all the white participants.

Already Tappan and J. W. C. Pennington, a Connecticut Negro pastor, had formed a special society to sponsor the Mendians' return.[36] To raise money for it, Tappan took the Africans on several tours, exhibited wax works of them, dunned his friends, wrote numerous letters and pamphlets, and formed ladies' auxiliaries.[37] Largest of his fund-raising enterprises was a rally at Broadway Tabernacle, a few days after Eliza's death. Before a capacity crowd, the Africans sang abolitionist hymns, and the younger ones showed their skills at arithmetic and spelling. Most exciting of all was Cinqué's speech in Mendian, which recounted the heroic mutiny with gestures and tones so vivid that the crowd understood him. Tappan then appealed, as he did on all these occasions, for the money to " 'send them back—not slaves but missionaries.' "[38]

By the fall of 1841, Tappan was racing against time to provide for the Mendians' voyage. One major stumbling block was the difficulty of finding out where Mendi country was and what it was like, another the necessity of preventing the re-enslavement of the Africans once they had arrived there. The Mendians themselves were not reliable informants, minimizing the obstacles in hope of speeding their departure. A. F. Williams thought after hearing their reports that their land must be one of the "most productive regions of the world—& the people are of a superior caste."[39] Tappan, however, was not so gullible. He asked his British correspondents for as much information as possible. But even the residents of Sierra Leone had barely heard of Mendi country. When British patrol ships cannonaded the Lomboko compound in 1841, drove Pedro Blanco into early retirement to enjoy his harem, and remained to keep an eye on the Gallinas River mouth, the danger of the re-capture of the Amistads was reduced. Other than this heartening news, Tappan and his friends had little to go on.[40]

Obviously, white missionaries had to accompany the Mendians, but here too there were problems. Tappan tried to interest the American Board of Commissioners for Foreign Missions in supplying the leaders, but the Board was wary of abolitionist associations and politely refused. Two graduates of Oberlin finally volunteered, the Rev. William Raymond and the Rev. James Steel. Both men were thought less than ideal, having little or no missionary experience and doubtful reputations for leadership, but Tappan and his associates decided they would have to do. The Mendians were in too rebellious a mood to wait out another winter in the United States while more suitable companions were found for them.[41]

An unexpected burden of expense loomed when President John Tyler, like his predecessor, refused to transport the Mendians on an American warship.[42] Nor would Great Britain undertake their transportation, probably out of fear of jeopardizing Anglo-American negotiations on Canadian boundary disputes and other issues, though Lord Aberdeen promised the group assistance on its arrival in African waters and at Sierra Leone. With only a few more weeks of good sailing weather, Tappan had to organize a final tour and exhibition of his charges to raise money for the outfitting of a private vessel.[43] Visiting churches in Northampton, Nashua, Lynn, Lowell, Boston, and other towns, the little band collected thirteen hundred dollars, a large sum for a depression year.[44] Joshua Leavitt, who kept the *Emancipator* subscribers informed of every incident regarding the Mendians, described Tappan's efforts of those last days. Leaving for New England with only "an hour's warning," he reported, Tappan discovered on his return two weeks later "nearly a hundred letters of business on his desk to read and answer. . . . " In addition, he had "all the preparation for the embarkation of the Mendians, and their teachers, to be finished in ten days, while as it so happened neither of his associates on the Committee were in town to render even the aid of their counsel to lighten the load of care. That the work was done, and done thoroughly, every thing cared for and every thing provided, could only have been achieved by Lewis Tappan."[45]

At the end of November, the entire group gathered in New York City—the Africans, William Raymond and his wife, two Negro American lay readers, the teachers, and the "Amistad" committee. Exhausted from overwork, Tappan did not attend the final service at the Tabernacle. Simeon Jocelyn took his place, introduced Cinqué and the others, recounted the often-told tale of their troubles, and pointed out its significance. Their suffering, he concluded, had taught the nation the tragedy of human bondage, a lesson not yet learned well but one that in time would also free the American members of the African race.[46]

Margru, one of the little girls, read Psalm One Hundred and Thirty: "Out of the deep have I called unto thee, O Lord; Lord, hear my voice." Then, as Leavitt observed, the Mendians sang a native song "with an energy of manner, a wildness of music, and at times a sweetness of melody, which were altogether peculiar." More to their listeners' taste was the singing of the antislavery hymn:

> When I can read my title clear
> To Mansions in the skies,
> I'll bid farewell to every fear,
> And wipe my weeping eyes. . . .[47]

Many in the audience did weep openly in bidding farewell to

these strange people, whom they expected to carry New England's religion and culture into the dark interior of another continent. Yet the mission could not live up to the quality of that moment in Broadway Tabernacle. Cinqué, proud, alert, and rebellious as ever, returned to Africa to become a chief among his people and to enter the slave trade himself. When he was near death, however, he returned in 1878 to the little mission clearing to renounce his harem and die a Christian.[48] Only Margru, of all the Mendians, served faithfully with the succession of missionaries who lived (and mostly died quickly) at Kaw-Mendi.

On December 4, Tappan, well again, boarded the steamboat that carried the voyagers to their ship, the "Gentleman," waiting at quarantine near Staten Island. On board the ferry were Amos Townsend, A. F. Williams, Jocelyn, and Leavitt, all of whom had worked with the young Africans for two years. As the boat puffed its way toward the "Gentleman," Tappan gathered his friends and the Mendians in the captain's cabin. There he presented each of the Negroes with a little speech and a farewell memento of his stay in the United States. Then he read a valedictory poem to Cinqué, which an abolitionist had composed: "One prayer I breathe, ere yet you leave our land,/ God bless thee, and thy native land." Tappan closed the session with the Lord's Prayer.

When the steamboat reached quarantine, the Africans picked up their meager belongings and followed Raymond up the gangway of the "Gentleman." Pensive and moved, Tappan and his friends watched the ship sail into the distance. But one can picture Lewis, striding off the ferry onto the Manhattan pier with other matters on his mind. Business letters awaited him on his desk; he had just started a new business requiring more attention and energy than he had ever expended at Arthur Tappan's store. There were antislavery chores and Mendi work still unattended—gifts to acknowledge, bills to pay, letters and articles to write, and ministers to consult. The departed Mendians carried his hopes for a continent freed from slavery and Christianized, but Lewis was already thinking of new and better ways to achieve that goal —perhaps a wide religious association for supporting Negro mission work at home and abroad. He had no time for much reflection. There were too many things to do on that brisk December morning. The most pressing were those concerned with his Mercantile Agency.

NOTES

1. Richard Drake, *Revelations of a Slave-Smuggler: Being the Autobiography of Capt. Rich'd Drake, An African Trader for Fifty Years—From 1807–1857* . . . (New York, 1860), 72, 98, copy located in Rare Book Room, LC; New Haven *Record*, quoted by *Emancipator*, October 10, 1839; Dr. Richard Robert Madden, *The Island of Cuba: Its Resources, Progress and Prospects* . . . (London, 1849), 240–41; John W. Barber, *A History of the Amistad Captives: Being a Circumstantial Account of the Capture of the Spanish Schooner Amistad* . . . (New Haven, 1840), 21.

2. Testimony of Cinqué at January 7, 1840, U. S. District Court trial, New Haven, as reported by LT in *Emancipator*, quoted by *Liberator*, January 17, 1840; LT, *Journal of Commerce*, October 12, 1839; Barber, *History of the Amistad Captives*, 1–8; Madden, *Island of Cuba*, 235; *Africans Taken in the Amistad, Congressional Document, Containing the Correspondence &c. in Relation to the Captured Africans, 26th Congress, 1st Session, Document No. 185* (New York, 1840), 30–32; Dwight James to LT, September 6, 1839, Kale to LT, October 30, 1840, AMA MSS, Fisk; *Emancipator*, September 19, 1839; *National Intelligencer* (Washington), September 2, 1839.

3. New York *Sun*, quoted by *Liberator*, September 6, 1839; *Bahama Royal Gazette*, August 21, 1839, quoted by *Emancipator*, September 14, 1839; *Emancipator*, September 26, 1839; *Colored American* (New York), September 28, 1839; *National Intelligencer*, September 2, 1838.

4. Henry Clay to LT, March 29, 1836, Acc. 6643-b, Library, University of Virginia; LT to BT, October 8, November 14, 1839, ltrbk.; John H. B. Latrobe to Martin Van Buren, October 29, 1839, Martin Van Buren MSS, LC; on Trist's complicity, see Alexander H. Everett, Havana, to John Forsyth, secretary of state, "Confidential Report," July 21, 1840, "Havana, July 9, 1840 to August 4, 1840," v. 14, Despatches to Consuls, Department of State, National Archives, Washington, esp. 46–47; indifference of the administration is seen in Forsyth to Trist, October 18, December 18, 1839, February 10, 1841, *ibid.*, v. 10; on Trist's removal see Daniel Webster, secretary of state, to John Tyler (copy), June 22, 1841, and Webster to Trist, July 15, 1841, *ibid.*, a result at least in part of the "Amistad" committee's exposure of his practices arising from the case, though partisan Whiggery also played a part. See LT to "Amistad" committee, September 10, 1839, in *Emancipator*, September 12, 1839.

5. Leavitt in *Emancipator*, December 10, 1841; see Leavitt also in Wilson, *Rise and Fall of Slave Power*, I, 466.

6. Barber, *History of the Amistad Captives*, 26; LT in *Emancipator*, September 12 and 19, 1839; LT's "Index to a Narrative of My Life."

7. LT in *Emancipator*, September 26, 1839; see also his articles in *Commercial Advertiser*, quoted by *Niles' Weekly Register*, September 21, 1839, and *Journal of Commerce*, September 12, 1839.

8. LT in *Emancipator*, September 12, 1839; Barber, *History of the Amistad Captives*, 29.

9. LT to Captain Fitzgerald of H. B. M. "Buzzard," November 1, 1839, ltrbk.; *Emancipator*, September 12, 1839; Samuel Flagg Bemis, *John Quincy Adams and the Union* (New York, 1956), 397; the "Buzzard" was in port to try an American

slaver captured at sea—see Forsyth to B. F. Butler, June 20, 1839, Domestic Letters, v. 30, Department of State, National Archives, Washington.

10. LT to Loring, October 19, 1829, ltrbk.; Amos Townsend to Roger Sherman Baldwin, August 30, 1839, and LT to Baldwin, September 12, 1839, Roger Sherman Baldwin MSS, Yale University Library; another lawyer, Seth Staples, was hired but proved ineffective and was released—see LT to Baldwin, October 10, 1840, *ibid.* On Baldwin's role, see Bemis, *Adams and the Union,* 399; William A. Owens, *Slave Mutiny: The Revolt on the Schooner Amistad* (New York, 1953), 247; Simeon Eben Baldwin, "The Captives of the *Amistad*: A Paper Read before the New Haven Colony Historical Society, May 17, 1886" (n.l., n.d.), offprint in Johns Hopkins University Library's William Birney Slavery Collection, v. 71; Frederick H. Jackson, *Simeon Eben Baldwin: Lawyer, Social Scientist, Statesman* (New York, 1955), 53; William Draper Lewis, *Great American Lawyers . . .* (Philadelphia, 1907–9), III, 527.

11. Forsyth to Van Buren, September 18, 1839, Martin Van Buren MSS, LC, which indicates a cabinet consensus for arbitrarily seizing the prisoners from federal jurisdiction; see also Levi Woodbury to Van Buren, September 22, 1839, *ibid.,* Forsyth to Van Buren, September 23, 1839, *ibid.,* and Forsyth to Felix Grundy, September 24, 1839 (copy), Domestic Letters, v. 30, Department of State, National Archives, Washington. On Spanish demands, see A. Calderón de la Barca to Forsyth, September 6, 1839, and subsequent letters in *Africans Taken in the Amistad,* 4–7 ff.

12. *Emancipator,* September 19, 1839; the Rev. Alonzo N. Lewis, "Recollections of the Amistad Slave Case: First Revelation of a Plot to Force the Slave Question to an Issue More than Twenty Years Before its Final Outbreak in the Civil War. . . ," *Connecticut Magazine,* II (1907), 125.

13. Owens, *Slave Mutiny,* 176; LT in *Emancipator,* September 26, 1839, and *Journal of Commerce,* September 28, 1839.

14. *Journal of Commerce,* September 28, 1839; Baldwin to Adams, November 2, 1840, John Quincy Adams MSS, microfilm #514, Johns Hopkins University Library; *Emancipator,* October 24, 1839; John Bach McMaster, *A History of the People of the United States . . .* (New York, 1906), VI, 605 ff.

15. Warrant for Ruiz's arrest, miscellaneous letters, LT MSS, LC; LT to Sturge, October 19, 1839, LT to Loring, October 19, 1839, ltrbk.; *Journal of Commerce,* October 15, 1839; LT to Baldwin, October 12, 1839, Baldwin MSS, Yale University Library.

16. LT to Sturge, October 19, 1839, ltrbk.; "Reverdy Johnson" to John Quincy Adams [n.d.], Adams MSS, microfilm #514, Johns Hopkins University Library; "Reverdy Johnsting" to LT, April 3, 1841, AMA MSS, Fisk; Forsyth to Argaiz, October 24, December 12, 1839, A. Vail to B. F. Butler, November 9, 1839, A. Vail to Argaiz, November 29, 1839, Domestic Letters, v. 30, Department of State, National Archives, Washington; Bemis, *Adams and the Union,* 294–95 n; *Africans Taken in the Amistad,* 16–45. On positions of respected citizens, see Staples and Sedgwick to Van Buren, September 13, 1839, Miscellaneous Letters of the Department of State, National Archives, Washington; Robert Rantoul Jr., to Van Buren (copy), September 12, 1839, Chauncey A. Goodrich to Van Buren, January 20, 1840, Van Buren MSS, LC; New York *Express* (quotation) and *Evening Tatler* in *Emancipator,* February 20, 1840; J. B. Johnston, Bellefontaine, Ohio, to LT, December 31, 1840, AMA MSS, Fisk (quotation); WLG to LT and others,

November 1, 1839, AMA MSS, Fisk; LT to BT, October 8, 1839, ltrbk. (quotation). It could be argued that the Latimer fugitive-slave case in Boston aroused as much public interest in 1843 as the Amistad case had previously done, but its importance was probably confined to Massachusetts: see Alma Lutz, *Crusaders for Freedom: Women in the Antislavery Movement* (Boston, 1968), 196–97.

17. *Emancipator,* February 20, 1840.

18. Madden, *Island of Cuba,* 233, 237–41; LT to Baldwin, November 11 and 12, 1839, Baldwin MSS, Yale University Library; WLG to LT, AT, Joshua Leavitt, and Birney, November 1, 1839, AMA MSS, Fisk; *Liberator,* December 8, 1839, January 17, 1840; Thomas More Madden, ed., *Memoirs . . . of Richard Robert Madden* (London, 1891), 82; *Emancipator,* November 7, 1839.

19. LT in *Emancipator,* January 9, 1840; *Liberator,* January 17, 1840.

20. LT's transcription of Judson's speech, *Emancipator,* January 23, 1840.

21. LT to BT, January 15, 1840, ltrbk.

22. LT in *Emancipator,* January 23, 1840; *Liberator,* January 24, 1840.

23. Holabird to Forsyth, December 20, 1839, miscellaneous letters, and Forsyth to Holabird, January 6 and 12, 1840, Domestic Letters, v. 30, Department of State, National Archives, Washington; "Memorandum from the Department of State to Secretary of the Navy, January 7, 1840," *Africans Taken in the Amistad,* 47–48; Seth Staples to Baldwin, January 21, 1840, Baldwin MSS, Yale University Library (quotation); LT to Baldwin, January 27, 1840, Baldwin MSS, Yale University Library.

24. LT in *Emancipator,* February 6, 1840; Amos Townsend to LT, March 21, May 17, 1840, Williams to LT (quotation), March 25, 1841, AMA MSS, Fisk.

25. *Emancipator,* May 1, 1840; LT to Baldwin, February 27, 1840, Baldwin MSS, Yale University Library.

26. W. Fox Strangeways to William Paton, &c., of the Glasgow Anti-Slavery Society, December 23, 1839, in *Niles' Weekly Register,* May 21, 1840; see also *ibid.,* February 19, March 7, 1840; H. S. Fox to Forsyth, January 20, 1841, in McMaster, *History of the United States,* VI, 605, 609; Abel and Klingberg, *Side-Light,* 53n, 84; Fox to Adams, January 17, 1841, Adams MSS, microfilm #516, Johns Hopkins University Library.

27. Calhoun's speech in *Niles' Weekly Register,* May 21, 1840; see also *ibid.,* February 29, 1840; LT to Sturge, December 14, 1839, ltrbk.; *Herald of Freedom,* quoted by *Colored American,* September 28, 1839.

28. LT to Baldwin, October 28, 1840, Baldwin to Adams, copy, November 2, 1840, Adams to Baldwin, November 11, 1840, Baldwin MSS, Yale University Library; Bemis, *Adams and the Union,* 299–300. Baldwin drew up the brief and deferentially allowed Adams to be the senior counsel: see his exhaustive brief, January 1841, Adams MSS, microfilm #516, Johns Hopkins University Library.

29. LT to Baldwin, October 28, 1840, and LT to Mrs. R. S. Baldwin, February 27, 1862, Baldwin MSS, Yale University Library; diary, November 20, 1840.

30. Charles Francis Adams, ed., *Memoirs of John Quincy Adams* (Philadelphia, 1874–77), X, *passim; Africans Taken in the Amistad;* LT to Baldwin, September 12, 1839, Baldwin MSS, Yale University Library.

31. Adams to LT, March 9, 1841, copy, Adams MSS, microfilm #514, Johns Hopkins University Library; see also LT to WLG, January 29, 1870, Garrison and Garrison, *Garrison,* IV, 255.

32. *Emancipator,* March 25, 1841; Jocelyn to LT, March 1, 1841, and Kinna

(an Amistad prisoner) to LT, March 20, 1841, AMA MSS, Fisk; *A&FASR*, April, 1841.

33. Diary, November 8, 1840 to May 11, 1841, on Eliza's death and burial; on Lewis Henry's death, see *ibid.*, July and August, 1836.

34. A. F. Williams to LT, March 25, June 3 and 4, 1841, AMA MSS, Fisk; Lewis, "Recollections of the *Amistad*," 127; Norton to LT, March 25, 1841; [?], Westville, Conn., to LT, February 9, 1841; Beriah Green to LT, etc., March 31, 1841, and LT to Baldwin, March 17, 1841, AMA MSS, Fisk.

35. Williams to LT, April 14 and 29, June 3 and 4, August 18, 1841, AMA MSS, Fisk.

36. See Augustus Field Beard, *A Crusade for Brotherhood* . . . (Boston, 1909); Clifton Herman Johnson, "The American Missionary Association," Ph.D. dissertation, University of North Carolina, 1958, University of Michigan microfilm series, No. 59 5561; LT, *History of the American Missionary Association: Its Constitution & Principles* (New York, 1855), 10, all of which ascribe the founding of the American Missionary Association to the Pennington group and the "Amistad" Committee.

37. *Colored American*, September 28, 1839; LT, circular, November 17, 1841, Moses Chamberlain autographs, BPL; the following letters to LT indicate the financial support he received: Charles Torrey, December 13, 1840, Austin Willey, December 14, 1840, J. Holcomb, December 21, 1840, Isaac Parish, December 9 and 12, 1840, Gerrit Smith, March 16, 1841, Phelps, January 20, 1841, AMA MSS, Fisk; *A&FASR*, October, 1841.

38. Grinnell, *Forty Years*, 28–29; *Emancipator*, March 25, November 18, 1841; LT to Adams, April 21, 1841, Adams MSS, microfilm #157, Johns Hopkins University Library; LT to Phelps, May 18, 1841, Phelps MSS, BPL; Williams to LT, August 18, September 7, 1841, S. M. Booth to LT, August 27, 1841, Norton to LT, October 13, 1841, AMA MSS, Fisk; *Emancipator*, September 23, 1841.

39. A. F. Williams to LT, March 25, 1841, AMA MSS, Fisk.

40. LT to John Beaumont, September 25, 1841, in Abel and Klingberg, *Side-Light*, 83–84; unsigned letter to George W. Alexander (copy), March 25, 1841, Alexander to LT, June 18, 1841, J. J. Roberts to LT, September 30, 1841, and Lt. Gov. Ferguson, Freetown, Sierra Leone, to LT and "Amistad" Committee, October 31, 1841, AMA MSS, Fisk; see also Abel and Klingberg, *Side-Light*, 87–88n.

41. Phelps to LT, October 24 and 27, 1841, and Norton to LT, October 13, 1841, AMA MSS, Fisk; *The First Annual Report of the American Missionary Association* . . . (New York, 1847), 5–6.

42. John Tyler to LT, October 21, 1841; LT to Daniel Webster, September 23, 1841, Department of State, National Archives, Washington; Webster to LT, in *Emancipator*, October 21, 1841.

43. See correspondence in references of Abel and Klingberg, *Side-Light*, 83–88; LT to Sir Thomas Fowell Buxton (copy), March 29, 1841, AMA MSS, Fisk; Buxton to LT, October 21, 1841, *ibid.*; William Wemyss Anderson to "Commanders of H. B. M.'s Ships . . . ," November 19, 1841, *ibid.*; Scoble to Earl of Aberdeen, December 20, 1841, and Canning to Scoble, December 23, 1841, in *Liberator*, February 4, 1842.

44. LT to *Congregational Observer*, in *Liberator*, November 5, 1841; *ibid.*, November 12, 19, and 26, 1841; *Emancipator*, November 18, 1841.

45. *Emancipator,* December 10, 1841.

46. *Ibid.,* and *Journal of Commerce,* quoted by *Liberator,* December 3, 1841.

47. *Liberator,* December 3, 1841.

48. *Emancipator,* December 10, 1841; Lewis, "Recollections of the *Amistad,*" 128.

CHAPTER TWELVE

The Mercantile Agency

*I*t *was hardly* surprising that Lewis Tappan should think of quitting the silk firm. Ever since the crash, the company had barely been able to meet its day-to-day commitments. Between October, 1839, and April, 1840, the brothers had to make one hundred thousand dollars above expenses just to stay afloat. Furthermore, Arthur, desperately gambling on a change of fortune, had not given up the expedients which had resulted in his bankruptcy in 1837. "We are, I perceive," Lewis complained, "getting insensibly into the credit system again, and of course, filling up a new Deferred Book with Suspend[ed], and bad debts. This is contrary to my understanding of the principles upon which we were to re-commence and continue business, and it is contrary to my views of the true interest of the concern & of my present principles." Only a "rigid adherence to the cash system," he concluded, could save the partnership.[1] Even so, he insisted on his loyalty to his brother, to whom he still felt an immense obligation for bailing him out in 1827. "I sympathize with you in all the distresses that have come upon you," he wrote him on another occasion.[2]

The depression, the weakness of the firm, and a rising competition led Lewis to conclude that his brother would either fail outright or else muddle along without ever regaining a measure of his old prosperity. Henry C. Bowen and Thomas McNamee, both former apprentices at 122 Pearl, had started a rival business, which already surpassed all the silk wholesalers in volume of trade. Personal loyalty was not the sure cement of the Tappans' partnership that it had once been, for the brothers were no longer as intimate with one another. Arthur's headaches were growing worse, and even Lewis, who seldom took much notice of temperamental changes in other people, remarked that Arthur's "anxieties are great & no doubt affect his physical system."[3] By 1840, matters had almost reached a climax. Discovering to his consternation and embarrassment that the bank was not honoring their drafts, Lewis left a furious note on Arthur's desk advising him that, unless all partners (there were two junior ones as well) were kept fully advised of the firm's situation daily, their connection would have to be dissolved. "I begin to feel that you care very little about my remaining in the concern," Lewis said.[4]

It may not have been altogether fair of him to leave Arthur when his problems were so crushing. Yet, quite apart from the state of the business itself and of his relationship with Arthur, Lewis, already fifty-three years old, had only a limited time left to provide for his own family in old age. Besides, selling umbrellas and handkerchiefs for fourteen years had become drudgery, while a new enterprise would be a challenge. Confident of his talents, Tappan had thoroughly mastered business routines. His smooth efficiency, whether in the management of the store or in organizing an antislavery activity, was actually the chief source of his boredom. Once he had laid down the patterns, their repetition grew irksome.

In order to leave the silk business and all its troubles, Lewis had to find a sound alternative; otherwise, people might accuse him of deserting his hapless brother lightly. He thought of opening a cotton goods store but was influenced by Theodore Weld, who could not bring himself, he said, to deal in the products of slave labor. When Lewis' partner in this venture failed to raise the necessary capital, he gave it up.[5]

Tappan never mentioned how he came upon the credit-rating scheme. Anyone who had tried to collect bad debts during the Panic of 1837, however, might have thought of it. Certainly the brothers had become experts on all the methods of evasion and fraud that country traders used to escape their liabilities. Some took the debtor's oath. Others skipped town: Ellis Gray Loring, the Tappans' lawyer in Boston, reported, for instance, that Saunders, a debtor whom he finally traced to Detroit, "has *some* character," though most likely "it is a very bad one."[6] From the moment the Panic of 1837 began, the Tappans tried to screen each client even more thoroughly than before, and they probably kept records of their credit evaluations. So valuable did their judgment become that other jobbers sometimes stopped by to ask them about particular buyers.[7]

The Tappans' difficulties with country clients differed very little from those of other New York wholesalers. When unfamiliar customers appeared during the spring or fall rush, New York storeowners demanded proof of solvency and reliability in the form of letters from clergymen, bankers, and lawyers and affidavits of assets and liabilities, before honoring orders for cottons or corset stays. A high interest charge on all sales for long-term credit (over six months) gave them some protection, but all too frequently they were deceived. The traders, of course, passed these charges along to their own customers, who also needed and received credit at high rates. Each middleman, from the source to the consumer, acted as a banker, and the whole structure might topple if payments were not made on time at any point in this network of credit. If a community was suddenly depressed, the storekeeper defaulted, leaving men like Arthur Tappan to force collections as best they could.[8]

To avoid bad risks, large firms employed traveling agents to check up on clients, but the system was expensive and inefficient. Its one advantage was that there was less chance of collusion between the credit applicant and the reporter than between the former and those who wrote letters of recommendation for him. Travel was relatively slow, however, and the little country stores were sprinkled thinly over wide areas. Moreover, agents could not return frequently enough to keep accurate running accounts on any district, and in bad times a few weeks or months might change the entire complexion of business. [9]

The opportunity to improve the conduct of credit business was there for anybody to seize. A central office in New York could establish a network of local informants throughout the country. They would forward information on all merchants in their area doing business in New York. The more subscribers to the system, the better the service could become. For a man of Tappan's religious beliefs and temperament, the idea had special appeal; he would be the warden of Wall Street and Merchants' Exchange, making sure that clients told the truth on their semiannual visits to the New York jobbers. Proud of his own integrity, he had little use for the renegade, the marginal operator, and the self-deluded optimist, who sometimes got credit they did not deserve. Borrowing money, thought Tappan, was bad enough in any case, and, like the hard-money Jacksonians of the day, he had no use for banks and paper credit.[10] Perhaps business could not do without them; nonetheless, the nation should, he thought, free itself from addiction to speculation and greed.

Many years later, Tappan wrote that "eagerness to amass property . . . robs a man and his family of rational enjoyment" and "tempts him to doubtful and disreputable acts. . . ."[11] He spoke from his own experience of 1827, and he had long been convinced that material ambitions were unworthy of a Christian merchant. In 1843, he wrote Benjamin, "How much wisdom there is in the advice of the apostle Paul—'Owe no man anything—but to love one another.'"[12]

If he ever noticed the paradox of his founding a company totally dependent upon other people's need or greed for credit, he did not mention it in any surviving paper. He did see that borrowing could be made a more honest and reliable transaction than it was. Tappan himself would at least be free of the toils of paper finance. The agency would also insure him against the ups and downs of the national economy. As he later wrote a nephew, this was a kind of business that did not depend substantially on the profits of his subscribers. "In prosperous times they will feel able to pay for the information and in bad times they feel they must have it."[13] Such protection against disaster suited the nature of his faith as well, for God, in his opinion, was more responsible for the blessing of prosperity or the punishment of depression than were the workings of economic laws. Typical was his comment about the depression of 1857: "Business men have been insane. They are reaping the fruits of their folly. . . . God is chastising us. Let us amend our ways."[14] Immune from the worst fluctuations of the business cycle from 1841 to the end of his life, Tappan only regretted that he had not thought of the Mercantile Agency— as he called his new firm—much sooner and spared himself un-Christian speculations in textile factories and the poor credit policies of Arthur Tappan & Co.

Temperamentally, Lewis Tappan was ideally suited to the new enterprise, because so untried a venture would require imagination, a willingness to take calculated risks, and persistence. No one in New York drove himself harder than he, and few demanded the same level of performance from their staffs. Clerks marveled at his pace. In a despairing letter, one of them wrote, "Mr. T. is a *hard task* master. He has wonderful endurance himself & drives others as if made of the same stuff."[15] Moreover, Lewis' demands for high ethical standards gave him a reputation for personal honesty. While Tappan was not always as disinterested about money as he claimed, few doubted he was well equipped to make his experiment into a profitable business. Only Arthur, somewhat piqued by his brother's departure, predicted that the effort would fail.[16]

Establishing a new company, however, taxed even Tappan's ingenuity. First, he needed correspondents to report from all points in the northern states. Since his acquaintances were mostly abolitionists and churchmen (often one and the same), he relied on their co-operation when he could not obtain the services of lawyers in their localities. Lawyers were preferable because of their experience in handling collection cases and their association with businessmen generally, but, as he later wrote in a note to himself, *"Want some one every where we can write for inf*[orma-tion]*—ministers, abo*[litionists]*, or some one."*[17] Ellis Gray Loring of Boston, Roger Sherman Baldwin of Connecticut, James G. Birney of Michigan, and Salmon P. Chase of Ohio were ideal correspondents, since they were all lawyers and Christian abolitionists as well.[18] While northern correspondents of good character were hard enough to find and to enlist, recruiting southern reporters was almost impossible. Tappan tried to reach them by correspondence and by employing independent credit agents to interview them, but few southerners would join a company run by so notorious an abolitionist. Later in the company's history, Tappan's failure to provide complete national coverage proved a serious handicap.

In addition, he had to face important local problems. He had chosen a poor time to begin. Business, chronically slow between 1837 and 1843, stagnated in the summer months of 1841. After moving into an office opposite the Merchants' Exchange, issuing advertisements to the papers, and consulting friends about the rates he should charge, he set out on July 7 to sign up subscribers. "Committed the plan to Him in whose hands are the hearts of men," he wrote before leaving his desk. It was discouraging work, even though the plan was cheap and clearly valuable. Subscribers risked only fifty dollars a year, if they did less than fifty thousand dollars in annual trade, and only three hundred, the maximum rate, if their sales exceeded half a million.[19] The few merchants still braving the summer heat bowed him out the door with a thin smile or stifled yawn. "Some wanted to see their partners—some declined & most showed considerable apathy," he reported after the first grueling day without a subscriber.[20]

Tappan despised the weak and timid businessman, but even he succumbed to depression. His thoughts often turned to God as he left a suffocating warehouse or store, and he sometimes blamed Him for his discomfort. As if God were his unseen companion on all his rounds, he gave Him a healthy share of the praise or blame for his own efforts:

Today I called on several merchants. . . . Some I found absent . . . & others did not seem to think it would repay them. . . . I felt disheartened [*sic*], but, while I wondered that the Lord should have directed my mind to this new employment, and then disappointed me in my expectations I was brought into sweet submission to His will. I think it was the desire of my heart to make a fair trial & thus perform any duty, & then quietly submit to what w[oul]d appear to be the act of Him who can not err. I called at another place . . . and [the owner] readily subscribed with very kind & flattering words. This elated me much. I was surprised at my former unbelief & at the present revulsion in my feelings. I almost felt guilty. I applied to another, and he, after some persuasion, subscribed. My gratitude now was raised high, & I expressed it in ejaculatory prayer. The Lord, this day, has been better to me than my fears. Blessed be His holy name.[21]

One wonders how Lewis could have carried on if every sale or failure prompted a reappraisal of his relation to God, but Tappan was not the kind of man to meditate for long on metaphysical problems.

Whatever he thought about divine favor or disfavor toward the Mercantile Agency, the difficulties he encountered came mostly from the unpopularity of his reformist views in the business community. New York merchants would have hesitated in any case to put their money into some untried scheme, but to deal with an abolitionist was out of the question for many. When Tappan first issued his prospectus in the papers, he enjoyed a good press in Boston and Philadelphia; but in New York, James Watson

Webb carried a report from a Norfolk paper in which a local attorney named Williams publicly declined Tappan's offer "to act as a spy" on his neighbors—a role, he said, which even a slave would scorn. Webb denounced the Mercantile Agency as a "new clap-trap for notoriety. . . , carrying on the business of a secret inquiry into the private affairs and personal standing of every body buying goods in New York."[22] Tappan was rather amused, remarking that "he thinks I am a better man than I am."[23] Even if New York merchants had not read the article, Tappan's reputation for irascibility and abolitionism traveled ahead of him through the dingy offices of lower Manhattan. Levi Cook, a Pearl Street jobber, frankly advised him to find someone else to solicit customers, since he repelled so many businessmen with his anti-slavery ideas.[24]

The wonder is that Tappan succeeded as well as he did. He piously refused to sell his service to a distillery, and undoubtedly he put off some merchants with his bristling reaction to a dirty joke. Yet by mid-August, 1841, he had accumulated one hundred and thirty-three subscribers, mostly in the dry goods, crockery, and grocery trades. It was a healthy start, athough short of his expectations. Of course, some companies, such as Bowen & McNamee and Tappan & Edwards (the new name of Arthur Tappan's store after Lewis left it), subscribed because abolitionism was their creed, too. Other subscribers soon found the service indispensable, no matter what they thought of the proprietor.[25]

Despite all his problems, Tappan enjoyed the new work immensely. "There is great variety of business connected with the office—complaints of subscribers, complaints of correspondents &c.—and it requires much address to attend to all these matters & adjust them satisfactorily," he wrote a relative.[26] By early 1843, he could say, "The M[ercantile] Agency is now quite popular here. . . . It checks knavery, & purifies the mercantile air."[27]

Any new scheme like the Mercantile Agency was bound to show many crudities and imperfections. Tappan was an expert at ironing out problems in administration. The failure of his subscribers to live up to their contracts vexed him constantly. Although sworn to secrecy, they would not keep the information about their purchasers to themselves. Appealing to their self-interest, Tappan pointed out that if non-subscribers received Agency reports "it will lessen their inducement to subscribe, and

this . . . is equally injurious to you and to me." The more subscribers who signed up, he said, the more funds there would be
for improving and extending the system.[28]

Some merchants even told their customers what Tappan's
reports said of them, much to the embarrassment of all concerned.
He also discovered that some non-subscribers deliberately hired
clerks away from his clients to gain access to the Agency's service
without payment. Lewis tried various schemes to limit the number
of those authorized to obtain Agency information, but none
worked very well. As one means of control, he had the office fitted out with a high counter separating the clients and his staff.
A subscriber or a company representative wrote out the name
of the businessman for whom an evaluation was desired and his
address and handed it over to one of the clerks, who brought out
the appropriate, oversized ledger and read the information while
the customer took notes. The subscribers were on their honor to
hold these notes "CONFIDENTIAL—for their use only," as Tappan
pleaded. Nor were they even to mention to anyone that they
subscribed to his services. In his first year of operation, Tappan
guaranteed his clients a one-third discount on a year's subscription for each new subscriber they obtained. The offer was designed
not merely to attract new subscribers but also to promote a pride
in and a loyalty to the firm among the clients. Yet the inducement
was probably too generous to repeat thereafter, and no doubt it
helped very little in counteracting the demoralizing effects of loose
tongues.[29]

While Tappan had trouble with his subscribers, he also received
complaints from his correspondents at the other end of the business. Some were sure that subscribers misinterpreted their reports, or that clerks had miscopied them, or that their identities
were known to the local traders, who might be led to retaliate.
Most frequently, they insisted that they were paid too little for
their hard work.

Indeed, the arranging of equitable settlements with the correspondents was one of Tappan's most difficult problems. Each
correspondent was to send in his reports twice a year, August 1
and February 1, in time for the fall and spring sales, when inland
storekeepers descended on New York, like a swarm of migrating
fowl. Tappan preferred that correspondents should be compensated by commissions obtained from successful collection suits
initiated by his New York subscribers. But it was not always

possible to find reliable lawyers, particularly in new areas of the West, so that he presumably had to pay bank tellers, ministers, sheriffs, postmasters, and other knowledgeable community leaders a flat fee for their reports. Young lawyers, such as Abraham Lincoln of Springfield, Illinois, whose reports were full of wry humor, made the most satisfactory correspondents. They found the experience of learning about their neighbors and their prospects especially valuable. Whenever a delinquency occurred, the subscriber notified Tappan, who then referred him to the appropriate lawyer-correspondent. The latter would then undertake prosecution, obtaining a percentage fee out of whatever amount he could extract from the defaulting storekeeper. Correspondents operating under this arrangement, therefore, earned no immediate return, only the prospect of business from New York subscribers, who sometimes selected their own attorneys, contrary to the rules of their contracts. If Tappan had paid a set sum to all his local agents, lawyers and non-lawyers alike, he complained, the costs of the Agency would have trebled.

Correspondents who were attorneys aired their grievances to Tappan rather frequently, particularly those living in prosperous, honest neighborhoods. As one lawyer from western New York declared, "I think the tendency of y[ou]r agency is greatly to diminish bus[iness] in the county. If y[ou]r cor[responden]ts make correct reports y[ou]r sub[scriber]s will have but little trouble in collecting their debts and seldom need an attorney."[30]

Tappan could only reply that, as business in New York grew in volume and his list of subscribers increased, the number of collection cases would also climb, in good times as well as bad. To mollify the resident correspondents, he took the unusual step of sending them all a year's subscription to the *Columbian Lady's and Gentleman's Magazine*. Some, however, objected. The magazine was flighty, and even Tappan had to admit that it did not live up to his expectations as a "grave and philosophical" journal. The next year he bought them *The Christian Parlor Magazine*. To supplement the sometimes amateurish reports from the resident agents, Tappan also started hiring experienced traveling reporters. This combination has continued to the present (in Dun & Bradstreet), although the resident amateurs later gave way to professional agents.[31]

Although Tappan often had trouble in prodding the reporters to get their information to him on time, he was generally satisfied with the results. There was a quaintness about these early reports, for they sometimes reflected the religious and social preoccupations of their compilers. It must have occurred to Tappan that his business was rather useful as a means of social control in the hinterlands. The drinker or the philanderer who traded in New York goods might find that his credit had disappeared because of an unfavorable report made out by a pious bank cashier or teetotaling attorney. Yet Tappan insisted that correspondents be scrupulously fair and that they not rely on unsubstantiated rumor. The following example of the kind of report, with its attention to detail, that the Agency wanted, arrived at the office in 1850:

James Samson is a peddler, aged 30; he comes to Albany to buy his goods, and then peddles them out along the canal from Albany to Buffalo. He is worth $2,000; owns a wooden house at Lockport . . . has a wife and three children . . . drinks two glasses cider brandy, plain, morning and evening—never more; drinks water after each; chews fine cut; never smokes; good teeth generally; has lost a large double tooth on lower jaw, back, second from throat on left side . . . purchases principally jewelry and fancy articles.[32]

While such a report as this one might have satisfied the curiosity of the most demanding subscriber, Tappan found that he had as much trouble meeting the criticisms of his New York customers as he encountered in dealing with his correspondents in the field. Attorneys, the jobbers complained, were too slow in collecting bad debts; there was not sufficient coverage across the country and especially in the South; reports were sometimes incomplete and too long delayed; the clerks were surly. (Tappan paid some copy clerks three dollars a week, and even his head clerk made only six hundred dollars a year, a meager sum in view of his responsibilities. Such wages did not encourage courtesy.) As middleman between the correspondents and the subscribers, Tappan could see the weaknesses of both groups. On the one hand, "more than half of the merchants," he wrote a Connecticut lawyer, "are either ignorant of what is equitable & legal, in the charges employed by [lawyers,] or evince great illiberality in their view of them." On the other, he noted that attorneys might be tempted to raise their charges too high, "& both professions would suffer."[33]

The general public also mistrusted the operations of the new

235

company, and inland merchants were convinced it was a conspiracy against them. "Country traders," Tappan warned his associates, "and persons not subscribers here, occasionally tell 'great stories' about what is on my books. . . ."[34] Some called the Agency "jesuitical," and James Gordon Bennett's New York *Herald* played on popular feeling by announcing that Tappan was running "an office for looking after everybody's business but his own."[35] These suspicions were unjustified, since every storekeeper with good credit benefited by having his status known to all the subscribers instead of just to a small circle of his own acquaintances. If credit information became more reliable, eventually the consumer would gain, as lower interest rates brought down the charges on the goods he bought. Nonetheless, several years passed before the public accepted the innovation in credit reporting.

The importance of Tappan's establishing this means of reducing the uncertainties of business transactions cannot be exaggerated. Economic historians have paid too little attention to the subject of credit reporting in the nineteenth century. His contribution was based upon rather simple notions of the puritan ethic; his methods were perhaps as crude and unsophisticated as the first model of a telegraph key, but his Agency was not much less vital to American business communications than Samuel F. B. Morse's famous invention.

Although Tappan did not fully realize it, his Agency was answering a specific need that those institutions which he so much appreciated himself—the church, the family, and the small-town community—were no longer capable of supplying. At one time, the local minister, a relative, or a neighbor could furnish the appraisal of an applicant that a creditor needed. By the 1840's the country had grown too large and too populated and its people were too mobile for the old sources of information to function efficiently. The ties that once had intimately bound family to family, neighbor to neighbor, and creditor to debtor were not strong enough to provide the basis for financial arrangements of an increasingly complex character. Tappan himself was lucky to have belonged to a family with loyalties and resources sufficient to meet the credit needs of its members. While this circumstance was still applicable to many Americans, there were millions more in the country who could not rely on that kind of co-operation but had to seek money from unfamiliar, distant sources. A new, specialized institution was required, and Tappan supplied it. Like the rail-road, the telegraph, and the press, his enterprise was a means of collecting and distributing information efficiently and quickly. He was shrewd enough to see that his service could be no cheaper or more prompt than the postal system enabled it to be; he therefore championed the Cheap Postage movement that developed in the late forties, an effort that further indicated a growing awareness of the necessity for modernizing American communications to keep pace with technological and economic advances.[36]

Although his service provided the nation with its first large-scale network of credit reporting, Tappan discovered that it was not good enough to meet the inexorable demands of the New York community. The crisis came not during the Agency's first stage of development but in 1844, when Tappan had convinced himself that its future, after his three years of hard work, was assured. The problem arose from his antislavery convictions. He had over three hundred correspondents, but nearly all of them were in the free states, parts of Missouri, and the territories of Wisconsin and Iowa. After his difficulties with Mr. Williams of Norfolk and the *Courier and Enquirer,* Tappan had abandoned the southern states almost entirely. Competitors imitating his system and offering southern coverage had opened their doors in 1842, but not until the fall season of 1844 were they a serious threat.[37]

Tappan hated to admit that the company's uncertain state upset him, particularly since his health did not allow him to work much harder. In addition to running his Agency, he had all his mission-ary and antislavery chores, the editing of evangelical journals, and a steady round of addresses before church meetings to keep him busy. He tried to interest Amos Phelps and Elizur Wright in joining his enterprises, but they refused, partly because he offered them insultingly low salaries.[38]

Realizing that his health and inclinations prevented him from a full engagement in reinvigorating the company, Lewis turned to Edward E. Dunbar, a "wide awake" young New Englander, who had opened a Boston branch office the year before.[39] Tappan soon regretted the move, but he simply could not hold the pace of the last three years without relief. "Were I ten years younger," he wrote a nephew, "I would see my way clear to make a fortune out of this business with branches that might be formed."[40] Even in the present state of his energies, there were more important, more Christian things to do, and Tappan preferred to do them rather than to pursue an aggressive policy of expansion.

On his arrival in New York, Dunbar discovered an alarming situation. Subscribers were leaving the company to take advantage of other credit services, and Tappan's unpopularity was affecting the growth of the concern. With some difficulty Dunbar was able to convince his senior partner that a network of southern correspondents had become imperative. "Rival agencies have sprung up," Tappan told his friend Amos Phelps, "& unless we went ahead we should go astern."[41]

Early in 1845, Dunbar, William Goodrich, and three other members of the firm toured the South in search of agents. At the outset, Tappan advised them to instruct the correspondents to address their reports to Edward E. Dunbar & Co., a subterfuge to spare the southern lawyers embarrassment. As originally planned, however, they were privately to mention to these attorneys that Lewis Tappan, an abolitionist, was head of the company. From the discouraging reports he received from the five, Tappan feared that the whole scheme would collapse unless they made no mention of his being in the firm at all. "In the first place," he told Dunbar, "if all the facts are frankly stated you will not be able to establish correspondencies, and if your name alone is mentioned a deception is practised that appears to me improper." Improper or not, Tappan concluded that deception was preferable to a "public explosion that would injuriously affect the M[ercantile] A[gency]."[42] He thought that perhaps the company could be divided, his own agency dealing with northern states and Dunbar handling the southern trade, with an exchange of information between them. Such co-operation would presumably not antagonize southern local correspondents writing to Dunbar & Co.[43]

Tappan's proposal was probably the most ethical arrangement that could have been managed under the circumstances, but indignantly Dunbar turned it down, responding that he would seek out agents in South Carolina as previously arranged, "even against the dagger and pistol chivalry of this chivalrous State" if necessary.[44] In writing the other agents, Tappan did not wait for Dunbar's reply but strongly hinted that their success and safety rested on their silence.[45] The others complied, but perhaps to his own surprise, Dunbar found co-operative lawyers in spite of his frankness. Upon hearing the good news, Tappan changed his mind and reasserted his scruples to justify a return to the original policy.

In a letter to Goodrich, then at Little Rock, Arkansas, he declared:

Mr. D. and myself are now decided that in every instance, the other fact should be stated—not at first, but before you leave the individual. . . . He does this, and meets no difficulty—that is, no insuperable difficulty. . . . We will not have any one deceived about the parties with whom they correspond, and we regret that you have not in all cases, pursued this course. . . . We may not have been so definite as we should have been, but such were our intentions. Dunbar & Co.[46]

When the agents returned to New York, he ordered them to burn those letters of his hinting at a policy of deception.[47]

For the rest of the year, Dunbar continued his work in the New York office, mainly developing the southern end of the business. Goodrich went to Philadelphia to open another branch. Fearing that Tappan's abolitionism would sink the new effort, Dunbar and Goodrich persuaded Tappan to agree not to be a partner in the Philadelphia office, in exchange for a cash settlement. There was to be a transfer of information between the parent and subsidiary offices, however, with the charges determined by the amount of information each office requisitioned from the other. It was a complicated arrangement and a source of endless dispute between Tappan and Goodrich. Dunbar tried to form a third subsidiary in Baltimore upon the same basis as that of the Philadelphia firm. He told Tappan quite frankly, even tactlessly, that he would be a "dead weight" on the branch there. Stung by the remark, Tappan raised the ante so high on his exclusion that Dunbar had to give up the Baltimore project.[48]

From that point to the end of 1845, the partners' relations grew increasingly icy. Dunbar concluded that under Tappan's "profuse professions of high mercantile honor, philanthropy and piety was an avaricious, vindictive and hypocritical spirit."[49] Dunbar convinced himself (with some justice) that it was he who did most of the work, while the senior partner devoted his time to "his anti-slavery affairs, to the injury of the business."[50] Dunbar also believed that he was responsible for the renewed success of the company, especially in its southern department.

When Dunbar decided to force Tappan out of the company altogether, however, he badly misplayed his chances. First, he did not have the necessary capital to buy Tappan out, and the senior partner's reasonable estimate of the company's value—twenty-five thousand dollars—was far beyond Dunbar's means. Second, Dunbar announced his intention to dissolve without first consulting the other partners in the Boston and Philadelphia offices to ascertain their positions. Finally, he grossly underestimated his rival by trying to shame him into acquiescence. He accused Tappan of stirring up the New York merchants with his antislavery work. Immediately Tappan replied, "My reputation is a thing upon which I place no value, and I shall never do anything to bolster it up or compensate for its loss."[51] To use a phrase later circulated by another antislavery firm, Tappan's principles were not for sale, but only his services. When Dunbar first joined the staff, he knew, as Tappan rightly pointed out, the sort of man he was dealing with.[52]

A disagreeable and tedious controversy resulted, with Dunbar insisting that he had rights to the southern reports and Tappan denying him any rights at all beyond an evaluated share of his contribution to the company. Finally, the parties submitted their differences to referees under the auspices of the Chancery Court in Albany. After several weeks of testimony, the referees gave the company and all rights of ownership to Tappan.[53] Barred from engaging in the credit-rating business, Dunbar issued a full, repetitious statement of his side of the dispute and set out for California to start life over again.[54]

Although Tappan experienced some difficulty in patching up the partnerships in Boston and Philadelphia, the Agency weathered the controversy without much loss, and its profits grew steadily for the next three years.[55] He soon added the Jabez Pratt Company of Baltimore. By the end of 1846, the combined agencies had nearly seven hundred correspondents. To take Dunbar's place in the head office, he promoted Benjamin Douglass, his chief clerk, giving him a third of the partnership.[56] Thoroughly acquainted with all branches of the business, Douglass, who had once been a merchant in Charleston, was especially valuable because of his knowledge of the southern country trade. According to one observer, the thirty-year-old clerk was "as smart as a steel-trap."[57] Tappan did not inquire deeply into his religious and political beliefs but instead heartily endorsed his work in expanding the company. "It is owing to his exertions, and popularity," Lewis wrote Arthur, "that my business had increased so much since Dunbar quit. . . . I have never had the slightest discordance with him." By 1848, the Mercantile Agency was earning fifteen thousand dollars a year for the senior partner, five thousand more than two years before. Tappan was at last able to set aside funds for his retirement, to which he looked forward with increasing anticipation.[58]

Meanwhile, Arthur had fallen on evil days again. Not long after Lewis left the silk company, Arthur had to declare himself a bankrupt. Lewis' sympathy went beyond the ordinary, for he had not forgotten his debt of gratitude to his brother. In 1848, Arthur became a junior partner in a silk firm organized by his nephew, Alfred Edwards, but the other members of the firm treated him shabbily. The old tradition of pious deference to elderly relatives and acquaintances apparently did not apply in the turbulent climate of the New York business world. Lewis knew that if Arthur should replace him in the Mercantile Agency his dour personality, crotchety business habits, poor health, and growing introspection would be clear liabilities. But Lewis was still proud of his brother's stern rectitude. "Think of a man owing upwards of a million dollars divided among a hundred creditors," he told a friend, "and paying off every cent while money was worth from 9 to 15 per cent a year."[59]

Putting his misgivings aside, Lewis informed Douglass of his intention to retire from the business upon condition that Arthur should take his place. Douglass strenuously objected to Arthur's participation, but it was finally agreed that Douglass would become an equal partner with Arthur. The young businessman was not altogether pleased, but his promotion mollified him to a degree. Though desperate for a chance to regain something of his fortunes and self-respect, Arthur accepted Lewis' benefaction with only grumpy acquiescence. While generally gratified by the outcome, Lewis had to admit later that Arthur was "chiefly occupied in keeping the cash account and examining the Reports as they are received at the office. The weight of the business falls upon Mr. Douglass, who has an iron constitution, and who loves to labor very hard."[60] Moreover, Arthur's new anxieties brought on a severe headache attack that even the water cure at South Orange, New Jersey, failed to alleviate. Lewis offered to return to the Agency for a period of time while Arthur made his recovery, but his brother had too much pride to accept the suggestion.[61]

Lewis' formal association with the Mercantile Agency was over, but he continued to keep a careful eye on his brother and took a personal interest in the firm's progress. In 1851, he was once more drawn into its problems, when John B. and Horace Beardsley, who were Norwalk, Ohio, merchants, sued him for libel, claiming that in 1848 a local reporter had sent in false information about their company. Tappan was not directly involved, as the new partnership assumed all liabilities in 1849. At the trial, Douglass refused to reveal the name of the confidential correspondent in question, and Judge Betts of the United States District Court in New York City sent him to jail for twenty days for contempt of court. The New York business community applauded Douglass' refusal to testify, thus indicating the esteem in which the Mercantile Agency was held. Tappan ably defended his former colleague in an article in the New York *Evening Post*. Privately, however, he remarked, "The Correspondent, whose name we would not disclose, has behaved either corruptly or foolishly." Luckily for the future of credit-rating agencies, jurists later came to appreciate the value of confidential reporting and protected the acquisition of privileged information by mercantile agencies.[62]

In 1859, Douglass, having bought Arthur's interest five years before, sold his proprietorship to Robert Graham Dun, a young man of Scottish-Presbyterian descent. Dun, who had come to New York from Chillicothe, Ohio, had joined the firm before Arthur's departure. Under Dun's direction, the company expanded into a vast international service with hundreds of branch offices. Thirty-three years after his death in 1900, R. G. Dun & Co., as the Mercantile Agency was usually styled, acquired the Bradstreet Company. It had been founded in 1849 by John M. Bradstreet, another figure in the firm's history with deep roots in the puritan tradition. This company had concentrated on the city trade, whereas the Mercantile Agency had developed a somewhat broader coverage. Subsequently the merged organizations adopted the now famous name—Dun & Bradstreet, Inc.—having long since abandoned the cumbersome partnership system that the Tappans and Douglass had fashioned. Although its later managers, especially John M. Bradstreet's descendants and R. G. Dun, were responsible for the refinement and expansion of the credit reporting service, Lewis Tappan's initial contribution ought to be well remembered. It was the most original of all his institutional creations.

Nonetheless, the Mercantile Agency's purpose, as Lewis conceived it, was hardly different from that of the other institutions that he and Arthur had helped to found—the *Journal of Commerce,* Lane Seminary, Oberlin College, the Sabbatarian and revival enterprises, and even, to a degree, the American Anti-Slavery Society. All these agencies were efforts to conserve the values of an older, more stable New England society in a sea of alien changes. Like them, the Mercantile Agency was designed as a citadel to sustain the ethics and the cultural heritage of an eighteenth-century puritanism, modified to fit the conditions of an expanding society. Abolitionism itself was also an assertion of what was valuable in the Yankee yeoman's way of life, an attempt to extend the freedom to practice that life-style to all Americans, black and white. So too was the Mercantile Agency an attempt to universalize the doctrine of each man's accountability to himself, to those trusting him, and to God. The colleges, newspapers, and societies which the Tappans established were formed to preserve, not disrupt, the religious and social standards of their youth.

Purpose and the method of accomplishing it were not conjoined in the Agency without paradox. Lewis Tappan's commercial venture was a reaction against the hedonism and business anarchy of his time, but its very success helped to promote a specialization of institutions that weakened or at least altered the traditional receptacles of community values, particularly the church and the family. In reacting against the trends of his time, Tappan had founded a company that played a vital role in building the twentieth-century American economic system.

In performing this paradoxical service for his evangelical faith and his country, Tappan showed surprisingly wide vision in financial matters that contrasted rather sharply with the narrow limits of his religious preoccupations. He also evinced an acute sensitiveness to business opportunities that he never matched in his relationship with people. He wrote his brother John that during the Agency's history he had never felt "any desire to accumulate property . . . knowing that my sphere of usefulness lies in another direction."[63] "Desire" perhaps he did not feel; he did "accumulate property" nevertheless, and sometimes, thoroughly abolitionized as he was, with all the will of a Yankee sharper. His inclination to deception in drumming up a southern trade is evidence of that.

When his ambition did outrun his stern code of business conduct, he did not always engage in a show of repentance. He could be perfectly unreflective, and perhaps that selective lack of retrospection had something to do with his decisiveness and dynamic earnestness. It may be noted that these were qualities important to the success of the Yankee entrepreneur *and* the Yankee evangelical in the nineteenth century.

NOTES

1. LT to AT, October 5, 1838, copy; see also Lewis E Atherton, *The Southern Country Store, 1800–1860* (Baton Rouge, 1949), 113–14, 140.

2. LT to AT, February 5, 1840, ltrbk; diary, October 21, 1839; LT to Charles Tappan, November 23, 1839, ltrbk.

3. Diary, June 22, 1841; Scoville, *Old Merchants*, I, 324.

4. LT to AT, February 5, 1840, ltrbk.

5. Diary, August 10, 1841.

6. E. G. Loring to Arthur Tappan & Company, December 10, 1838, Ellis Gray Loring letterbook, Houghton Library, Harvard.

7. Edward Neville Vose, *Seventy-Five Years of the Mercantile Agency: R. G. Dun & Co., 1841–1911* (New York, 1916), 12–13; see also Atherton, *Southern Country Store*, 113–14, on the Tappans' willingness to introduce respectable customers to other New York houses.

8. See Henry E. Resseguie, "Alexander Turney Stewart and the Development of the Department Store, 1823–1876," *Business History Review*, XXIX (Autumn, 1965), for example of one merchant who escaped this problem in the depressions of his career. See also Foulke, *Sinews of Commerce*, 289–90; Lewis E. Atherton, *The Pioneer Merchant in Mid-America*, "University of Missouri Studies," XIV (Columbia, Mo., 1939), 108–9, 112–13; and Atherton, *Southern Country Store*, 117–21.

9. Foulke, *Sinews of Commerce*, 283.

10. LT in New York *Evening Post*, July 8, 1837.

11. LT, *Is It Right to Be Rich?* (New York, 1869), 14.

12. LT to BT, December 12, 1843, ltrbk.

13. LT to Henry Edwards, September 10, 1844, *ibid.*

14. LT to Gamaliel Bailey, October 1, 1857, *ibid.*

15. Henry De Puy to Salmon P. Chase, June 17, 1848, Salmon Portland Chase MSS, LC.

16. *America's Advancement*, 1875, quoted in Vose, *The Mercantile Agency*, 32; P. M. Ross, *The Accountant's Own Book and Business Man's Manual*, quoted in Foulke, *Sinews of Commerce*, 289–90; diary, July 9, 1841, AMA MSS, Fisk. This diary is not to be confused with Tappan's other diary, which, of course, is in the LC (my practice continues to be not to cite location of the LT MSS, LC, each time). Lewis Tappan did promise to give up the experiment, but Arthur naturally demurred in spite of his ill-health; see diary, June 22, 1841.

17. Diary, February [?], 1844, AMA MSS, Fisk.

18. E. G. Loring to Tappan, June 2 and 22, August 7, 1841, Ellis Gray Loring letterbook, Houghton Library, Harvard; diary, September 14, 1841, AMA MSS, Fisk; LT to R. S. Baldwin, June 7, 1841, Baldwin MSS, Yale University Library; LT to J. G. Birney, March 10, 1846, ltrbk.

19. Diary, June 3, 21, 22, 25 and 26, July 7, August 6, 1841, AMA MSS, Fisk.

20. *Ibid.,* July 7, 1841.

21. Diary, August 10, 1841.

22. *Courier and Enquirer,* June 22, 1841, with quotations from Norfolk *Beacon;* diary, June 22, 1841.

23. Diary, June 22, 1841, AMA MSS, Fisk.

24. *Ibid.,* August 16, 1841.

25. *Ibid.,* August 16 and 24, 1841, February 24, July 13, November 8, 1842.

26. LT to Charles Stoddard, February 6, 1843, ltrbk.

27. LT to Lewis Tappan Stoddard, February 6, 1843, *ibid.*

28. LT, printed circular, September 15, 1842, in diary, AMA MSS, Fisk; see also another circular, August 8, 1843, in *ibid.,* and another, January 2, 1844, in *ibid.*

29. See *ibid.,* August 8, 1843 (quotation), and also September 1, 1842, February 10, 1843, and February [?], 1845 (printed card); Foulke, *Sinews of Commerce,* 290.

30. Diary, September 1 and 15, 1842, and also the following printed circulars: October 26, 1842, August 8, 1843, January [?], 1844, and another dated January 2, 1844, February [?], 1844 (quotation), and December 1, 1844, AMA MSS, Fisk; Foulke, *Sinews of Commerce,* 350–51.

31. Diary, June 29, September 15, 1842, AMA MSS, Fisk; traveling agents in LT's day were confined to Connecticut, New Jersey, and New York; see Foulke, *Sinews of Commerce,* 307–8, 334.

32. Foulke, *Sinews of Commerce,* 353–54 (quotation).

33. LT to Lafayette S. Foster, December 26, 1844, miscellaneous papers, Special Collections, New York Public Library; diary, July 22, 1842, February 23, 1843, AMA MSS, Fisk; LT to Dennis Jones, March 13, 1843, ltrbk.

34. Diary, June 4, 1844 (printed circular), AMA MSS, Fisk.

35. Printed circular of January 20, 1847, diary, AMA MSS, Fisk; *Herald,* quoted by Albion, *Rise of New York Port,* 256.

36. These remarks were inspired by Seymour J. Mandelbaum, *Boss Tweed's New York* (New York, 1965), 1–6. LT served as treasurer of the New York Cheap Postage Association for a number of years: see LT to John Scoble, April 3, 1851, in Abel and Klingberg, *Side-Light,* 259–60.

37. Edward E. Dunbar, *A Statement of the Controversy between Lewis Tappan and Edward E. Dunbar* (New York, 1846), 12, 72; see also *Journal of Commerce,* August 30, 1842; diary, January [?], 1844, AMA MSS, Fisk.

38. LT to Elizur Wright, October 15, November 11, 1844, ltrbk; LT to Phelps, October 14, November 19, 1844, ltrbk; Phelps to Tappan, November [?], 1844. I am in debt to Mrs. Virginia Roberts, of Cotey College, for checking the Agency ledgers at Baker Library, Harvard University, to substantiate this claim.

39. Dunbar, *Statement of Controversy,* 11; diary, July 1, 1844 (printed circular),

AMA MSS, Fisk; Vose, *The Mercantile Agency*, 20; LT to Lewis Tappan Stoddard, February 6, 1843, ltrbk.

40. LT to Henry Edwards, September 10, 1844, ltrbk.

41. LT to Phelps, January 13, 1845, Phelps MSS, BPL.

42. LT to Dunbar, January 29, 1845, ltrbk. Dunbar was then in Fayetteville, N. C., on his way to South Carolina.

43. *Ibid.;* diary, January 6, 1845, printed card announcing the extension of business without mention of this rearrangement; nor was there any such mention in the circular of February 10, 1845.

44. Dunbar to LT, February 13 or 23 (illegible), 1845, in Dunbar, *Statement of Controversy*, 17.

45. LT to William Goodrich, January 29, 1845, and LT to Dunbar, February 10, 1845, in Dunbar, *Statement of Controversy*, 19.

46. LT to Goodrich, March 4, 1845, in *ibid.*, 21.

47. *Ibid.*, 21. Dunbar might be considered an unreliable source in view of his later actions, but undoubtedly in unfriendly hands the letters would have been very damaging. In reprinting LT's letters, he was scrupulously accurate, insofar as they can be checked against LT's ltrbk.

48. *Ibid.*, 23; see also 22.

49. *Ibid.*, 24; see also LT to Dunbar, August 12, 1844, ltrbk.

50. Dunbar, *Statement of Controversy*, 55.

51. Dunbar to LT, December 31, 1845, LT to Dunbar, January 5, 1846, in *ibid.*, 25. See also LT to Dunbar, January 7, 14, and 25, 1846, ltrbk.

52. *Ibid.*, 26.

53. *Ibid.*, 3–6, 45–86; LT to A. Crist (a referee), June 16, 1846, ltrbk.; apparently the matter was not fully settled until the end of August, 1846, although the decision was handed down in June, 1846; see Susanna A. Tappan to Julia Tappan, August 24, 1846, transcript by the author of letters in private LT collection.

54. Vose, *The Mercantile Agency*, 27.

55. See LT to Woodward & Dusenberry, November 4, 1846; LT to Joseph W. Clary, Boston, October 3, 7, 10, and 20, November 3 and 14, 1846; LT to Joseph L. Chester, Philadelphia, October 9 and 10, 1846; LT to Stephen Pearl Andrews, June 5, 1846; LT to Edward Russell, Boston, October 28, 1846—all in ltrbk.

56. LT to Benjamin Douglass, November 12, 1846, LT to William Gordon, Boston, February 3, 1846, *ibid.;* diary, August 3 and 27, 1846, AMA MSS, Fisk; LT to AT, October 28, 1848, ltrbk.

57. Foulke, *Sinews of Commerce*, 290; Scoville, *Old Merchants*, I, 236.

58. LT to AT, October 28, 1848, ltrbk.

59. LT to David Hale, August 18, 1847; LT to Joseph Sturge, February 20, 1849 (quotation), ltrbk.

60. LT to John Tappan, October 15, 1849, ltrbk.

61. *Ibid.*, October 6, 1849.

62. Diary, December 18 and 23, 1851; New York *Herald*, December 12, 1851; Vose, *The Mercantile Agency*, 48–50; Foulke, *Sinews of Commerce*, 292–94; New York *Evening Post*, December 24, 1851.

63. LT to John Tappan, October 15, 1849, ltrbk.; Foulke, *Sinews of Commerce*, 294–97. An interesting general discussion of the interrelationship of religious

precepts and economic growth, reviewing in part the familiar works in this area, especially those of Max Weber and Ernst Troeltsch, is found in Karl F. Helleiner, "Moral Conditions of Economic Growth," *Journal of Economic History*, XI (Spring, 1951), 97–116. See also in this connection, as a good example of comparative analysis of puritan and southern ethics, C. Vann Woodward, "The Southern Ethic in a Puritan World," *William and Mary Quarterly*, XXV (July, 1968), 343–70.

CHAPTER THIRTEEN

England and Texas

The early 1840's were a period of readjustment for the antislavery movement, as well as for Lewis Tappan. After the collapse of the American Anti-Slavery Society, abolitionism seemed to have been reduced to petty factionalism. Garrison and his band of Quakers, "infidels, Universalists, Unitarians, worldly men of all sorts," as Tappan called them, rather inaccurately, were not only preaching heresies but also accusing him of fraud and thievery. "You see how low they have sunk in the moral thermometer," Tappan wrote his friend Joseph Sturge in England.[1] In their desire for public office, the political activists, Tappan thought, also were skittering close to the edge of immorality.

Some reformers left the movement altogether. Elizur Wright worked for a while in the Liberty party ranks, editing the *Free American* and then the *Emancipator,* which was transferred from New York to Boston. He resigned to publish an illustrated translation of La Fontaine's *Fables.* James G. Birney went off to the wilderness of Michigan, and even brother Arthur, busy with financial troubles and wracked by ill health, withdrew from antislavery activity.[2] Most sorely missed was Theodore Weld, who retired to a farm near Belleville, New Jersey, with his wife Angelina and sister-in-law.[3] Weld's excuse was an injury to his vocal chords, but his inactivity stemmed also from a growing skepticism of evangelical theory and perhaps a fear that controversy, even in a good cause, could lead to an uncontrollable trend toward violence, bitterness, and disillusion. As a young visitor to the Belleville farm later recalled, Weld "had been laboring to destroy evil in the same spirit as his antagonists. He suddenly felt that fighting was not the best way to annihilate error. . . ." His inaction was not spiritually satisfying for him, but it was not until the Civil War that he returned to the fight for emancipation. Though sanguine at first that he could induce Weld "to wage war with sin & Satan," Tappan finally realized that Weld was a hopeless defector. When Whittier requested news, in 1847, Tappan replied, " 'Where is Weld?' He is in a ditch opposite his house, doing the work any Irishman could do for 75 cents a day. His wife is 'suckling fools and chronicling small beer.' *The quakers did it,* they say."[4] Weld's absence was a heavy blow to the "new organization," the American and Foreign Anti-Slavery Society, desperately in need of a fund-raiser. John Rankin, David Leavitt (another quarter-millionaire and former abolitionist), and William Green were no longer active. Tappan did not miss them much, but in their places there were no other wealthy backers of his efforts. "Our rich men," he mourned, "have all failed—in purse or principle."[5]

The truth was that Christian antislavery had aged, with younger men either turning to political action or joining the Garrisonians. The religious enthusiasm that had fostered interdenominational co-operation had given way to a revived sectarianism. Denominations, faced with schisms, depression debts, bitter personal quarrels, and antislavery disruption, drew back from the evangelical movement. By the mid-forties both the Baptist and Methodist churches had split along sectional lines, while the Presbyterians had divided doctrinally between the New and Old Schools, a separation with some sectional overtones.[6] When Tappan hired Niblo's Saloon for another Finney revival, competition from "lectures and debates on every sort of subject," as Lewis explained, showed that religious observances were facing strong challenges from other forms of public ceremonies. Besides, Finney's doctrine that full sanctification was open to man on earth was too radical a departure from traditional Calvinism for many churchgoers even though it was attuned to the notions of human progress of the day.[7]

Finney traveled on to Washington for another revival, which Lewis urged Benjamin Tappan, Senator from Ohio, to attend. According to Lewis, the preacher believed "Pres[ident Jonathan]

Edwards' great error consisted in teaching physical depravity."
Benjamin, of course, refused "to waste his time" on a canting
evangelist, but he and Lewis enjoyed their game of religious
parrying immensely. "You have never examined this subject, with
a mind strong and acute," Benjamin wrote on one occasion. "You
are a man of impulses & I suppose will ever be. I do not dislike
you for this but I marvel you do not tire in trying to proselyte
me." Lewis never did; on the other hand, Benjamin never quit
his efforts to win Lewis to deism (both brothers were equally
evangelistic).[8]

Not only was Finney unable to arouse the populace, but Christian ministers themselves, Tappan discovered, were bringing disgrace upon the evangelical movement. The editor of the New
York *Evangelist,* which Tappan had helped to found, was drinking
himself insensible, attending the theater, and, Tappan gossiped,
roistering with "dissolute women!!" An Episcopal bishop and a
Presbyterian cleric of the city were exposed as incurable drunkards.[9] The case of J. R. Judd, a minister to one of the few surviving
free churches, was most shocking. Under the pseudonym "A
Friend of Virtue," Tappan himself publicized the clergyman's
offense. Judd had been "taking the most indecent familiarities
with several of the little girls belonging to the Sabbath School."
Tappan hoped "that this loathsome display of wickedness will
make parents be watchful and faithful—lead all to cease from
man—and direct the views of many to the Lamb of God who
taketh away the sins of the world."[10] Judd's transgressions were
a grim commentary on the present state of the free-mission system.
Lewis' only solace was that Judd had never accepted Finney's
"sanctification" ideas; otherwise Tappan and Finney might have
been touched by the unpleasant publicity.[11]

Since evangelicalism was in a state of decline and antislavery
reformers were pursuing independent paths, Tappan had to seek
new sources of inspiration. His solution, for the time being, was
involvement in an international dispute—Anglo-American rivalry
over the fate of Texas.

Ever since its successful revolution against Mexico, the Republic of Texas had been close to financial bankruptcy. Its credit
was low, its government weak, and its army and navy almost
nonexistent. While most Texans looked to the United States to
bail them out of trouble by means of annexation, Stephen Pearl

Andrews, a New-England-born lawyer who had moved from Louisiana to Texas to speculate in real estate, looked to Great Britain. During this period of his career, Andrews was a devout Presbyterian, but in the 1850's he became a perfectionist and ardent advocate of John Humphrey Noyes's free-love doctrines. Among his many communitarian projects was "The Grand Order of Recreation," a high-minded lonely hearts club on Broadway which degenerated into a place of assignation that the Manhattan police raided in 1855. Prior to his rebellion against Calvinist orthodoxy, however, Andrews was so true to his Yankee convictions, including an outspoken hostility to slavery, that he was forced to flee the South, arriving in New York in the spring of 1843. Andrews brought with him an exciting proposal for emancipating the slaves of Texas. Its success depended upon the co-operation of the British government and the bankers of London, as well as on the willingness of the Texas slaveholders to give up their property with compensation, a set of improbabilities as unlikely of fulfillment as his later dreams for a millennial society. "My plan is for the British nation to buy up Texas . . . and . . . make it most obviously in the interest of Texas to abolish slavery," he exclaimed. He believed that the Texas Republic's vast holdings in land could be sold to British investors, with the gold thus obtained being used for state purchase of all slave property. The thirty-one-year-old lawyer pressed his views on Lewis Tappan, already concerned over the growing agitation for the admission of another slave state and eager to find some way for Great Britain to prevent it.[12]

After investigating Andrews' credentials, Tappan introduced him to Gulian Verplanck, a Whig politician; William Cullen Bryant of the *Evening Post;* Theodore Sedgwick; and John Jay, son of the old judge. At a conference that Tappan arranged, Andrews outlined his proposition. With Great Britain underwriting the whole experiment, either by a government loan or by assistance in obtaining private English loans, the Republic would abolish slavery, enjoy British military and economic protection, and serve as a bastion against American encroachments in the Southwest. The cost, he reasoned, was minimal—about ten million pounds. England would gain, first, enhanced prestige as the friend of reform and of underdeveloped nations and, second, political advantages arising from the creation of a buffer state on the American border, completely tied to the English imperial economy. Texas would serve as an example to the South of the superiority of free labor in raising cotton and sugar, and special British tariff concessions would assure economic success, bring about the decline of slavery in neighboring states, and encourage a vast immigration of free laborers from Germany and Ireland. Moreover, Negroes in the United States could take advantage of having the refuge of a southern Canada nearby, and the institution would thus be rendered more precarious and expensive than ever. Would Texas accept the plan? Of course, Andrews replied, citing President Sam Houston's own antislavery statements and current dissatisfactions with American diplomacy. Perhaps the conferees expressed doubts about American reaction to British interference, but Tappan, at least, was enthusiastic.[13]

Shortly afterward, Lewis and Susan Tappan accompanied Andrews to Boston. The two men went off for an interview with John Quincy Adams, who offered them little hope for success. The Peel government, he complained, was not sound on antislavery, since the Tories had not yet made it clear whether the recent Webster-Ashburton treaty's extradition clause included the return of fugitive slaves in Canada. Lord Palmerston and the Whigs were much more outspoken in their antislavery, but they were out of power. Nonetheless, Adams gave the mission his blessing and endorsed Tappan's proposal to go to England with Andrews.[14]

Tappan's sudden decision to go abroad was also prompted by the duty he felt to attend Joseph Sturge's second World Anti-Slavery Convention. Garrison would not be there to cause trouble, and the American and Foreign Anti-Slavery Society might finally come to life if its representatives at the meeting made a good showing. However necessary the trip seemed to Lewis, it did not seem so to Susan, who was furious about it. It was all very well for Lewis to claim "to love my family more & more," but even he had to admit that he "had lost much happiness by not cultivating domestic affection more." Usually she could count on him to take a short vacation at a cool resort with his family or else to spend the holidays with her relatives in Brookline. Despite his wife's objections, Tappan boarded the "Caledonia" with Andrews for England on June 1, 1843. Susan he left with the Augustus Aspinwalls in Brookline. During his absence of over two months, she refused to write him a single line.[15]

Tappan set out for England at a curious moment in the history

252

of Anglo-American relations. The Webster-Ashburton treaty, resolving difficult questions of boundaries and extradition, had helped to clear the diplomatic air, but other problems remained. Businessmen in Britain were angry about the American states' repudiation of debts during the depression and the high tariffs on English textiles. In literature, Charles Dickens' *American Notes,* describing his discomforts as a celebrity and tourist, fed the steady current of criticism of America, particularly of the Yankee assumption of national superiority. Aristocrats found comfort in Alexis de Tocqueville's forebodings about the democratic "tyranny of the majority," and British intellectuals had by this time learned that the United States was not the Eden that Jeremy Bentham had once assumed it was.[16]

Tappan could feel at home in England in the circumscribed society in which he moved. The Anglo-American world of reform, tied together by the constant traveling back and forth of ministers and philanthropists, had few of the problems of misunderstanding, conflicting national interests, and provincial chauvinism that affected other transatlantic relations. The two groups of evangelicals admired one another with a warmth that is surely rare in the history of international sentiments. That bond of friendship, while productive of accord between the Union and the Empire during the Civil War, in this peculiar adventure in reform diplomacy blinded evangelical leaders on both sides to the adverse effects their alliance might produce in the sensitive United States, eager to prove in war and conquest, if necessary, its claims of power.

After conferences with Joseph Sturge, George Stacey, and John Scoble, secretary of the British and Foreign Anti-Slavery Society— all no less keen about the Texas mission than themselves—Tappan and Andrews accompanied a delegation of pious Englishmen to see Lord Aberdeen, the foreign secretary. An evangelical himself, whose clothes were "suggestive . . . of a nonconformist minister," Aberdeen was interested but wisely noncommittal. Privately, he hoped Texas would abolish slavery and remain independent, but he certainly had no intention of carrying his convictions to the point of a fracas with the United States.[17]

Texas did not absorb all of Lewis' time. As he had planned, he attended the World Anti-Slavery Convention at Freemasons' Hall. He reacted to the first session of the Convention just as he had to meeting brother Arthur's evangelical set in New York for the first time in 1827. Republican though he was, Tappan was dazzled by the agglomeration of nobility, wealthy men, and "the many valuable persons," as he called them, who attended: not just Quaker Radicals and Dissenting clergy but men like Lord Morpeth, later the Earl of Carlisle, whose sister the Duchess of Sutherland had expended a portion of her enormous wealth on antislavery and other charitable causes. Representing the last surviving link with the age of Wilberforce was Thomas Clarkson, the honorary president of the Convention, though he was too feeble to attend its sessions. Later in the summer, Tappan visited Playford Hall, Clarkson's ancestral home, and was shown the original manuscript of his host's Cambridge Prize Essay of 1784 on the slave trade and other mementos of the British cause of long ago. The two men struck up a friendship that lasted until Clarkson's death in 1846.[18]

He also visited the aged William Allen, a Quaker peace advocate and chemical manufacturer, but found him practically senile. Leadership of the British antislavery movement had fallen to Joseph Sturge. Sturge resembled a great lumbering bear as he moved his huge frame around the convention hall. He was always in the midst of things with his hearty laugh and vigorous handshake. "There was about him," said his friend John Bright, "a ripeness of goodness which is rarely seen among men."[19] Despised by the Tories for his ceaseless and often forceful agitation, Sturge received few honors in his own time. He has gained little recognition since. Yet his work in renewing the British fight against slavery after 1838, his promotion of adult education in Birmingham, and his opposition to the Corn Laws, limited suffrage, the Opium War, and later the Crimean War, placed him at the center of British reform. He was too radical to suit Richard Cobden, leader of the Anti-Corn Law League. Sturge tried to unite the working-class Chartists with the middle-class Leaguers, but Cobden, among others, disapproved.[20] Sturge's inspiration came from the promise he had observed in the Liberty party when touring America in 1841 with John Greenleaf Whittier. (Both the American and the English Quakers, with their quietistic dislike of politics, frowned upon the political activities of Sturge and Whittier.) Although Sturge's scheme later collapsed because of distrust between the two social classes, Tappan was at this time well impressed by the so-called Complete Suffrage effort. He in turn was encouraged to rethink his own attitudes toward the struggling Liberty party at home.[21]

254

No two reformers ever suited each other better than Tappan and Sturge; they shared an almost identical philosophy of reform and a similar faith in evangelism. Richard Cobden once said of Sturge, "I have sometimes wondered what such men would do, if the world's crimes and follies did not find them plenty of employment in the work of well-doing." The same remark may be applied to Lewis Tappan. Not only did the two reformers exchange antislavery views but also sentiments about the abolition of war. Together they attended "The First General Peace Convention," another international venture in reform which Sturge had helped to organize. Sturge saw to it that Lewis Tappan had an opportunity to address this body. The American reformer proposed a resolution condemning the current British effort to force sales of opium, "a most deleterious drug," upon the Chinese people. In support of his motion of censure, Lewis observed that the British opium trade "lessens the confidence" of Americans "in the disinterestedness and in the real philanthropy" of England, for such commercial policies were at variance with her benevolence toward the West Indian Negroes.[22] At the next session of the World Anti-Slavery Convention, Tappan displayed his own and Andrews' romantic conjectures about the Texas question. If a loan from London bankers at the rate of three-and-a-half per cent were forthcoming, he told the delegates, slavery in Texas would disappear in three months. What an easy, inexpensive victory for the cause, he pointed out, when compared with the twenty millions spent on compensating West Indian planters.[23] At a second interview, however, Lord Aberdeen punctured the romance by informing the delegation "that with regard to the general views expressed he concurred most heartily & sh[oul]d look upon the annexation of Texas to the U. S. with great concern, but if she chose voluntary to unite he could not see how G. B. could interfere." A government loan, furthermore, was totally out of the question. The only gratifying result of the interview was the statement, which Tappan demanded in order to satisfy John Quincy Adams, that the extradition agreement did not, in Aberdeen's view, extend to fugitive slaves in Canada, even if they stole property to make good their escape from their masters.[24]

Although Aberdeen had practically closed the door, Tappan and Andrews were not utterly discouraged. Each tried to convert the eccentric Lord Brougham on different occasions. Brougham proved too "intellectually insane" to suit Tappan, whose interview

255

with him was marked by rather rude manners on both sides. Andrews was apparently a better diplomat than his partner, for he later persuaded Brougham to raise the Texas question in the House of Lords.[25]

In pursuing the Texas question, however, the abolitionists were playing into the hands of President Tyler and the other annexationists in Washington. The resolutions and speeches at the World Anti-Slavery Convention, the political maneuverings of Tappan and Andrews, and the rumors these incidents stimulated permitted the annexationists to take the initiative by claiming that, unless Texas were soon annexed, Great Britain would snatch Texas for herself and free the slaves in the Republic. On July 20, Ashbel Smith, Texan chargé, demanded an explanation from the foreign secretary. Naturally enough, Aberdeen was forced to back down from the faintly antislavery statements he had been making for consumption at home.[26] When Tyler gave the Senate his annexation treaty in April, 1844, he stressed that unless it was ratified the United States would be encircled and isolated by Great Britain, with Texas the last link in the surrounding chain. The treaty failed of passage on that occasion, but the anti-British propaganda was effective in mustering public support until the expansionists did triumph.[27]

There were obvious limits to international co-operation for humanitarian purposes. Nationalism was a strong counter-force. If Tappan's participation had proved anything, it was that emancipation would have to come without the assistance of foreign powers. Yet, there were positive results too. Opportunities for British antislavery men to assist the American cause were infrequent; the Texas venture at least exercised their interest and presumably helped to maintain that concern, expressed in specific issues, even though the British reformers were incapable of affecting the broad course of American history.

Tappan's visit was not all spent in fruitless negotiations, antislavery meetings, and other reform business. He did some sightseeing—Windsor Castle, Eton College, the Royal Academy, and the House of Lords, where he saw the ancient Duke of Wellington peering bleakly from beneath his hat.[28] Unfortunately, not all his outings were so pleasant, for London was in the throes of a severe depression. Returning one evening from one of Sturge's Free Suffrage and Chartist gatherings, Tappan was accosted by "great numbers" of strolling prostitutes along two miles of thoroughfare. He found their overtures most "impudent" and "indecent." Yet, even ugly experiences must be put to use; he wrote up the incident in the *Advocate of Moral Reform* under the title, "Righteousness Exalteth a Nation, But Sin Is a Reproach to Any People." Although prostitutes were a common sight at any time in Victorian London, Tappan was right when he said, "Lasciviousness has doubtless increased in London." He failed to note that the cause might be partly economic.[29]

His reaction was hardly unique for his day, for few members of the middle class in either Great Britain or the United States tried to penetrate to the root causes of social ills. It never occurred to Lewis that wages paid by the middle class and the restrictive welfare system endorsed by it might to some degree be responsible for the conditions of working-class life. Reformers, when they did attempt to relate themselves to the suffering poor, were apt to deliver statements no more profound than that of Sturge's Chartist friend, Richard Oastler: "the very streets which receive the droppings of an 'Anti-Slavery Society' are every morning wet by the tears of innocent victims at the accursed shrine of avarice."[30] Though a city-dweller, Tappan feared, like most people, the slums, poverty, and the mysterious, impersonal throb of city life. New York was still small enough for him to cover most of it in his daily stride. London, on the other hand, was vast. To venture out of the West End and the City could be dangerous, but he was curious enough to wander one afternoon through the worst area near the Smithfield Market:

I walked . . . many narrow streets, courts & lanes, & saw thousands & tens of thousands of poor people sitting by their doors, standing on the side walks, or strolling about. I felt that there was a great need of religious instruction—that but few went to church—and that the largest part of the population were wholly destitute of the means of grace.

He came out at the marketplace, in the midst of abattoirs, carcasses, butchers, draymen—and a temperance gathering, led by a seedily dressed teetotaler on a small platform. With a sense of relief at finding a familiar, comprehensible sight, Tappan rushed to the front row and soon invited himself to address the crowd.[31]

Some critics of that day complained that men like Tappan really sought to press their views and their Bibles upon the poor because they looked "to their heavenly Father as they would do to the bank for interest. . . ." Charity thus was only a matter of the exchange of earthly merchandise for celestial profit.[32] Tappan made no such cynical calculations. He was, simply, devoted to all the *right* attitudes an evangelical was supposed to have; he was no less conformist in his evangelical convictions than he had been as a young merchant and Unitarian in Boston many years before. Such conformity, while preserving him from a shallow "economic" motive, prevented him from achieving any deep and sympathetic understanding of the problems of poverty, vice, and deprivation he saw with his own eyes, even though the same evangelicalism gave him some inkling of the cruelty of a slavery he had never studied firsthand.

Depressed from his tour of Smithfield, Tappan concluded in his diary, "Alas, how little does a stranger know of the real condition of the inhabitants of such a city as this by a residence of a few weeks."[33] That was his way of washing his hands of responsibility, an all too common reaction in his time or any other. Later, however, he turned to Joseph Sturge for answers to the problem of supplying the basic wants of the poor. A man with similarly restricted views, which were blended, however, with an earnest sympathy, Sturge did the best he could for the needy, though his charity may seem niggardly now. "1½ lbs Rice," Tappan recorded in his diary, "with ½ lb flour for thickening will make a dinner for 7 persons, adults and 2 children; or a Porridge can be made with ½ lb flour & 3 lbs bread in; or 15 lbs Potatoes."[34] Meager though Sturge's recipe was, his charity far outdistanced that of most members of the English middle class, just as Tappan's exceeded that of his fellow countrymen.

It is easy enough to criticize these men, self-righteous, snobbish, addicted to such doubtful formulae as the Magdalen asylums or the abolition of grain tariffs, and insistent on their own religious pre-eminence as they were. It is true that they neglected or underestimated the misery under their noses to meddle in problems elsewhere. For example, the pompous radical Dr. John Bowring, an Anti-Corn Law advocate with whom Tappan spent hours in happy discussion on his visit, was as far from famine as Tappan was from slavery. The romantic "interest in unhappy far-off things" that they shared was so keen that it seemed, in contrast to the mythical Antaeus, that they gained strength from their flights above the earth, not from their contact with it.[35]

Even if Victorian romanticism prevented the English and the Yankee reformers from coming to grips with the evils in their own societies, the evangelicals were at least responsive to evils somewhere. In addition, their methods of agitation, so consciously similar in the two nations, may reasonably be represented as an advance in the history of social and political reforms. Richard Cobden, like Tappan during the postal effort of the early years, had recognized *"that a moral and even religious spirit may be infused into that topic* [Corn Law repeal], *and if agitated in the same manner that the question of slavery has been, it will be irresistible."*[36] A latent quality of revolutionary fervor flavored both the British Anti-Corn Law and the American antislavery crusades. In both movements there was enough hot rhetoric to permit the forceful expression of dissatisfaction and yet enough institutional dependency to win over respectable numbers of the middle class. Reform became, for the first time in modern history, a secular institution with a wide, popular basis of support.

The evangelicals of both nations no longer believed in the static society of Wilberforce, Hannah More, or John Pintard and John Jay. As transportation and industry developed, the eighteenth-century notion of teaching the poor to be satisfied with their lot in a Christian spirit of submission gave way to a more dynamic philosophy. In evangelical theory, anyone who was Christian and hardworking was capable, whatever his color, of improving his condition and ought to have the chance to do so. The antislavery cause in America and the agitation for Corn Law repeal in England, although still infused with the language and some of the forms associated with the Christian church, represented a striking evolutionary advance over the authoritarian view of philanthropy of the previous era, even though the Victorian stress upon each individual's right to free opportunity was itself conceived in too restrictive, paternalistic terms and was hardly sufficient to meet the conditions of an industrialized, impersonal, and increasingly secular society. By preaching to the poor the lessons of work and thrift as the elements of advance, bleak though the message was, Tappan, Sturge, and their kind helped to prepare the way for the development of the social activism divorced from theology that was evident in the yearning of a Jane Addams for a better world. The abolitionist crusade in America had a deeper impact upon the social thinking of the nineteenth-century American than has been recognized, in spite of its limitations in the antebellum period and in spite of its apparent demise in the throes of post-Civil War problems.[37]

If Tappan was disturbed by the despair of London's poor, he was hardly more comfortable in the presence of English wealth. Throughout his visit, he was entertained lavishly by antislavery Quakers—Isaac Braithwaite and members of the Gurney, Forster, Fry, and Buxton families. He had dinner with the family of London banker Samuel Gurney and several guests who belonged to the French nobility. They dined on soup, veal, lamb, duck, salmon, fresh peas, cauliflower, potatoes, strawberries, jellies, and custards. Wryly, Tappan remarked in his diary that the five liveried servants "were offering things to the guests &c continually & thus saved much trouble to Mr & Mrs G."[38] Tappan was disturbed that these wealthy and apparently pious Quakers drank the best of French vintage—"five kinds of wine!" at Gurney's table, for instance.[39] Tappan was unaware that in earlier days Wilberforce had taken large doses of opium; that William Cowper, a poet whom his mother Sarah had always admired, drank quantities of gin; and that John Newton, who had converted Wilberforce to antislavery, enjoyed nothing better than a good pipe.[40] Perhaps the Victorian code had grown more rigid since those days, but the evangelicals were few who did not at least take their food seriously, including the dapper, portly Lewis Tappan himself.[41]

To his astonishment, he found that even England, that lighthouse of religion, had progressed no further along the way of Sabbatarianism than his own country. "People here, professors & all, do not scruple to use the omnibuses on the Sabbath. They fly in all directions."[42] He was shocked to find that, even at Buckingham Palace, Sunday drives were taken in the carriages, and he turned away, refusing to gaze "at such folly & profanation. . . ."[43] It was ironic, but not surprising, that the puritan New Englander was more "Victorian" than the queen who lent her name to the era.

Tappan found it agreeable to be able to censure people outside his own land for a change. True to his republican principles, he ridiculed with obvious relish the signs of aristocracy and privilege he saw. "What a 'House of Lords' will be in the pit!" he exlaimed to Amelia Opie, an English friend, when he heard that Lord Brougham's conversation was "shockingly profane." On the way to his ship at Liverpool, Tappan watched the Bishop of Norwich on a train platform in a drizzling rain, searching for his luggage. Lewis was amused and noted, "the more equalization between the bishops & other clergy the better." The steam engine, he realized, was helping to bring about the change.[44] The only sign that English sophistication had influenced him to any degree was the reading matter he chose for the homeward voyage: Dickens' novel about America, *Martin Chuzzlewit,* Tappan's first fiction in a long time. His taste in literature had apparently improved since his trip to England, when he was occupied with Mrs. Lydia Howard Huntley Sigourney's *Pleasant Memories in Pleasant Lands.*[45]

Tappan's stay in England of almost nine weeks could hardly result in any substantial change in his habits of thought. After all, he was fifty-five, long past a malleable age. Yet, he did form a new relationship with two ladies whom he met in England. It was a novel experience for him. In this romantic era, the cultivation of sentimental friendships, no matter what the age, sex, or marital status of the parties, was very much in fashion, especially among religious people. The exchange of spiritual intimacies had led the unsuspecting Theodore Weld to the altar with Angelina Grimké, and Charles Stuart had shared similar confessions by letter with Weld many years before.[46] Until 1843, however, Tappan had not had close ties of this sort with anyone, much less with women, outside his family. Seldom did his letters intentionally reveal anything of the inner man. He seemed to wear his religion inside out, presenting its most confident aspect to the world and reserving to himself his fears and despondency.

Sophia Sturge, Joseph's maiden sister who ran the widower's household in Birmingham, was one of those who was smitten with his charm. According to James G. Birney, "Why, our friend, Sophia Sturge is quite enraptured with you. I have not known her to deal in such high praises of any one else."[47] Since her letters have disappeared, the basis of their cordiality is hard to guess. Furthermore, they did not have much chance to talk, since Tappan spent only a few days in Sturge's Birmingham house before departing for Liverpool and home. Nonetheless, Sophia Sturge was the only person ever to learn of Tappan's reservation about his conversion to evangelical religion in 1827. In a long letter to her, he described his spiritual history—his hostility as a child to the dreary discipline of his mother, the influence of William Ellery Channing upon him, and his return to orthodoxy in reaction to Sarah Tappan's death. He failed to mention, of course, the financial problems that accompanied the crisis, but otherwise the exposure was frank. Tappan concluded the letter:

Since abandoning the U[nitarian] Church I have not had that spirituality of mind, and benevolence of heart, that the Gospel of Christ requires. I have been zealous for the truth, anxious for the conversion of men, liberal in supporting the institutions of religion, but have not to the extent I should have done, had that love for fellow-Christians, and that compassion for sinners, that Jesus inculcated.[48]

Perhaps the expression of these sentiments was a routine fulfillment of the requirements befitting this kind of relationship, but it is very likely that Tappan had recognized a flaw in his character that indeed existed. In addition, he confessed to Sophia his deep attachment to Channing, a love he held for no other spiritual leader. In a letter to his widow in 1842, after Channing had died, Tappan expressed his gratitude that, when he told Channing of his change of heart about Unitarianism, her husband never made "an unkind, trifling, jocose remark" or "reproached" him or "impeached" his motives. Tappan had also published anonymously an obituary in the New York *Evangelist,* a sensitive and quite unsentimental analysis of Channing's Christian character. Aside from Mrs. Channing and Sophia Sturge, few of Tappan's friends were aware of his lasting affection for his Unitarian pastor.[49] Too little of Channing's gentleness worked its way into Lewis' behavior, but at least he was able to express the deficiency to his English friend.

Tappan's friendship for Amelia Opie, his other soulmate across the waters, was not so intimate, although he had apparently made the same impression on her as on Sophia Sturge. Mrs. Opie, a sprightly old lady, was the most colorful member of that interesting group, the Norwich Friends. In spite of her intimacy with the Fry, Forster, and Gurney clans, she had once been a confidante of Mary Wollstonecraft (later Godwin's mistress and Mary Shelley's mother) and also a highly popular novelist who dealt with such unevangelical themes as adultery, seduction, and prostitution. After her conversion to Quakerism, Mrs. Opie composed only pious tracts when she wrote at all. Her exchange with Tappan, whom she playfully called a "comical man," mainly concerned the value of fiction, which she still read and admired. Eventually, she convinced him of the merits of the literature of imagination too.

"Every young lady," he had to admit, "will not read 'Practical Piety' nor every young man Locke's 'Reasonableness of Christianity.' Interesting tales therefore, conveying moral truths, may find access to such minds, and leave a lasting good behind."[50]

Tappan returned to the United States with a feeling of accomplishment, even if he had not fulfilled his dream of procuring a free Texas. He wrote a friend, "My visit was supposed to be useful." Yet, when he stopped at Quincy, he found Adams hardly more cheerful than at their last meeting. "The policy of the British Government is to cherish, sustain, and protect the institution of slavery in the United States and Texas, and their task is to do it by humbugging the abolitionists in England into the belief that they intend directly the reverse," Adams wrote in his diary.[51] He was probably closer to the truth than Tappan realized. Certainly, later events would bear out the old diplomat's acid appraisal. Tappan yearned to regale Adams with stories about the English philanthropists, but Susan was waiting impatiently in the carriage. Once more, he felt the tug of the domestic harness, and there was business waiting on his desk in New York.[52]

In fact, Tappan had accomplished very little by his English adventure. He had not learned a great deal about himself or his country, and his mission had been a failure. He thought, though, that England, undergoing a period of ferment over Chartism, Irish unrest, and middle-class indignation about the Corn Laws, resembled the United States with its crises over slavery and expansion. The objective difference between the two nations was that England would shortly achieve a stability and social balance during the "High Noon of Victorianism," while America was headed toward the shattering of its national institutions and the republic itself. Tappan, of course, was not aware of this; he was too hopeful to entertain gloomy predictions that slavery would fall only by blood and iron. In a letter to an Englishman, however, he later drew a valid distinction: "The abolition of your Corn Laws made no change in the social relations of your people, & therefore was not dreaded as large portions of . . . [our] people . . . dread emancipation." Of abolitionist efforts, Tappan would have liked to have used the words of Richard Cobden about the victory of 1846: "The sharpest weapon we wielded was the pen, and the loudest artillery was the voice of the orator. We never sought to slay an opponent, but only to *convert* him."[53] Meetings of Dissenting ministers, Anti-Corn Law tea parties, and rallies at Freemasons' Hall were sufficiently forceful to impress Sir Robert Peel, who finally brought about the repeal of the bread tax, as it was called, but the same kind of effort in America was inadequate to fulfill Tappan's dream of Negro emancipation. If so pacific means as Cobden described failed in their application to the slavery issue in this country, it was not Tappan's fault nor that of any other abolitionist. Some problems in universal history cannot be resolved in any other way than by violence, tragic and corrupting though it may be. Southern slavery was one of them, while repeal of the Corn Laws was not.

In spite of his ill success, Tappan did make one decision as a result of his English experience. His association with Sturge and the Free Suffrage cause and his talks with Sturge's Chartist friends inspired him to join the Liberty party. Envying the engagement in affairs of the moment of his political-minded friends at home, aware that his "new organization" languished in spite of all his efforts to revive it, Tappan had already begun a reassessment of his views of third-party action. On his return from England, he vowed to do all he could to promote it.

NOTES

1. LT to Sturge, October 11, 1844, ltrbk., to G. Smith, March 24, 1840, ltrbk.; LT to John Beaumont, January 30, 1844, Abel and Klingberg, *Side-Light*, 174; LT to G. Smith, January 18, 1841, Gerrit Smith Miller MSS, Syracuse University Library.

2. Fladeland, *Birney*, 212–14; LT to Wright, October 15, November 8 and 11, 1844; LT to Gamaliel Bailey, August 9, 1844, ltrbk.

3. Thomas, *Weld*, 176–77, 212, *et passim;* Weld to LT, April [?], 1842, Barnes and Dumond, *Weld Letters*, II, 938.

4. LT to Whittier, April, 1847, Whittier-Pickard MSS, Houghton Library, Harvard; LT to Weld, October 12, 1844, ltrbk.; see also Thomas, *Weld*, 216–17; Charles Stuart to Weld, January 31, 1843, Barnes and Dumond, *Weld Letters*, II, 968; Weld to LT, May 2, 1844, *ibid.*, 1004–5 and n; LT to Weld, April 1, 1844, *ibid.*, 1003: inviting him to give a speech at Brooklyn, LT wrote, "If you will only take a little brandy and water . . . —swear a little—get into a spree etc., . . . I could have the Lyceum filled . . . . But TRUTH's HINDRANCES!! . . . it smells of radicalism—mad dog!" Henry Blackwell, the young visitor, is quoted by Gerda Lerner, *The Grimké Sisters from South Carolina: Rebels Against Slavery* (Boston, 1967), 313–14.

5. LT to Whittier, November 8, 1844, ltrbk.; Brooklyn *Evening Star*, February 10, 1844, back of clipping, LT scrapbook.

6. Donald G. Mathews, "Orange Scott: The Methodist Evangelist as Revolutionary," in Duberman, *The Antislavery Vanguard*, 91–97; Mathews, *Slavery and Methodism*, 230–82; David Benedict, *A General History of the Baptist Denomination in America* . . . (New York, 1848), I, 906–9; LT's comment on the Methodist split is found in LT to Jay, June 14, 1844, ltrbk.

7. LT to Deacon H. C. Taylor, Oberlin, December 23, 1842, LT to Finney, December 2, 1842, and LT to Taylor, February 18, 1843 (quotation), ltrbk.

8. LT to BT, January 11, 1843, ltrbk.; BT to LT, December 28, 1842, January 13, 1843, BT MSS, Ohio Historical Society (hereinafter, OHS).

9. LT to George Whipple, June 12, 1844 and to Augustus Aspinwall, June 13, 1844, ltrbk.

10. Brooklyn *Evening Star*, February 10, 1844, clipping scrapbook.

11. LT to Weld, February 1, 1844, ltrbk.; LT to Finney, February 1, 1844, *ibid.*

12. Quotation from Madeleine B. Stern, *The Pantarch: A Biography of Stephen Pearl Andrews* (Austin, 1968), 39; see also *ibid.*, 36, 89–91, *passim;* Charles Shively, "An Option for Freedom in Texas, 1840–1844," *JNH*, L (April, 1965), 77–90; LT to Scoble, March 1, 1843, Abel and Klingberg, *Side-Light*, 115–17; William Ellery Channing to LT, December 28, 1840, Channing MSS, Houghton Library, Harvard.

13. Madeleine B. Stern, "Stephen Pearl Andrews, Abolitionist, and the Annexation of Texas," *Southwestern Historical Quarterly*, LXVI (April, 1964), 499, 506; David Urquhart, *Annexation of Texas: A Case for War between England and the United States* (London, 1843), 50; cf. more realistic opinion of Ashbel Smith to Anson Jones, July 2, 1843, in George P. Garrison, ed., *Diplomatic Correspondence of the Republic of Texas, Annual Report of the American Historical Association for the Year 1908* (Washington, 1911), II (2), Part III, 1101 (hereinafter, Garrison, *Texas Correspondence*); LT to William Jay, May 18, 1843, ltrbk., gives a report of this conference in New York City.

14. Adams, *Memoirs*, XI, May 31, 1843, 380; LT to Scoble, March 20, 1843, in *Anti-Slavery Reporter* (London), IV (May 17, 1843), 75–76; and LT to Scoble, April 24, 1850, Abel and Klingberg, *Side-Light*, 239–40; diary, May 26, 1843; Wilbur D. Jones, *Lord Aberdeen and the Americas* (Athens, Ga., 1958) (showing that Peel had already turned down a request from Texas for loans), 8, 9, 17–18; on LT's decision, see letters to Scoble above and diary, May 31, 1843.

15. Diary, August 6, 1841 (quotation), June 1 and 29, 1843; LT to Sturge, February 22, 1843, to Leavitt, May 3, 1843, to Phelps, March 2, 1843, ltrbk.

16. "How They Manage things in the 'Model Republic,'" *Blackwood's Magazine*, LIX (April, 1846), 439–40, is a good example of the conservatives' criticism of the United States; Jones, *Aberdeen and Americas*, 25; Leland H. Jenks, *The Migration of British Capital to 1875* (London, 1963 ed.), 99, 103; David Paul Crook, *American Democracy in English Politics, 1815–1850* (London, 1965), 11–22, 166–98.

17. Algernon Cecil, *British Foreign Secretaries, 1807–1916: Studies in Personality and Policy* (London, 1927), 91, 92, 115; Garrison, *Texas Correspondence*, II (2), Part III, 911 and n; Sir Reginald Coupland, *The British Anti-Slavery Movement* (New York, 1964 ed.), 179; E. D. Adams, *British Interests and Activities in Texas, 1838–1846* (Baltimore, 1910), 55–60.

18. *Proceedings of the General Anti-Slavery Convention* . . . (London, 1843) (hereinafter, *Proceedings, G. A.-S. C.*); LT to Sturge, August 14, 1843, in *A&FASR*, September 6, 1843, 166 (quotation); diary, July 11, 1843.

19. William Allen to Arthur [*sic*] (Lewis) Tappan, June 2 [*sic*] (July 2), 1843; quotation from Conrad Gill and Asa Briggs, *History of Birmingham* (London, 1952), I, 381n; Frank Thistlethwaite, *America and the Atlantic Community, Anglo-American Aspects, 1790–1850* (New York, 1959), 80, 88, 97, 152; diary, June 30, 1843; LT to Allen, MS copy, 1843.

20. Asa Briggs, *The Making of Victorian England, 1784–1867: The Age of Improvement* (New York, 1965 ed.), 320–21; Norman McCord, *The Anti-Corn Law League* (London, 1958), 113–15; "Anti-Corn Law Agitation," *Quarterly Review,* LXXXI (December, 1842), 269; Asa Briggs, "Chartism Reconsidered," *Historical Studies: Papers Read before the Third Conference of Irish Historians,* II (London, 1959–   ), 53, 55; Gill and Briggs, *Birmingham,* I, 393, 404, 405; Asa Briggs, *Victorian People: A Reassessment of Persons and Themes, 1851–1867* (New York, 1963 ed.), 214–15.

21. Joseph Sturge, *A Visit to the United States in 1841* (London, 1841), 48; LT to G. Smith, April 6, 1841, Gerrit Smith Miller MSS, Syracuse University Library; John L. and Barbara Hammond, *The Bleak Age* (New York, 1947), 183, and *The Age of the Chartists, 1832–1854: A Study of Discontent* (London, 1930), 271; Llewellyn Woodward, *The Age of Reform, 1815–1870* (Oxford, 1962), 140–42.

22. C. D. H. Cole, *Chartist Portraits* (London, 1941), 164, 165; Thistlethwaite, *America and Atlantic Community,* 156–57; Harold U. Faulkner, *Chartism and the Churches: A Study in Democracy,* "Columbia University Studies," LXXIII (New York, 1916), 22–23. LT quoted from *Herald of Peace* (London), August, 1843. John Tappan was a delegate to the Peace Convention but did not attend the antislavery meetings.

23. *Proceedings, G. A.-S. C.*, 306.

24. Diary, June 30, 1843; LT to Birney, August 9, 1843, ltrbk.; Thomas Clarkson to LT, June 30, 1843; Adams, *Memoirs, XII,* July 1, 1844, 66; see Wilbur Devereaux Jones, "The Influence of Slavery on the Webster-Ashburton Negotiations," *JSH,* XXII (February, 1956), 45–58, which surprisingly ignores this aspect of the problem.

25. Diary, June 29, 1843; LT to Brougham, draft, June 29, 1843; but cf. Brougham's speech *Parl. Debates,* 3, LXXI (1843), August 18, 1843, 913–17, 918, and Stern, "Andrews and Annexation," 510.

26. See *Parl. Debates, loc. cit.*, 918; Smith to Jones, July 31, 1843, Garrison, *Texas Correspondence,* II (2), Part III, 1116–19; Thomas Hart Benton, *Thirty Years' View* . . . (New York, 1856), II, 606–8; Harriet Smither, "English Abolitionism and the Annexation of Texas," *Southwestern Historical Quarterly,* XXXII (January, 1929), 199–200 (Smith to Calhoun, June 19, 1843); Jesse S. Reeves, *American Diplomacy under Tyler and Polk* (Baltimore, 1907), 126–27; Adams, *British Interests,* 139–43; LT to Beaumont, January 30, 1844, Abel and Klingberg, *Side-Light,* 169–72.

27. "Message of the President . . . April 22, 1844," *British and Foreign State Papers, 1844–1845,* XXXIII (London, 1859), 254–57; Reeves, *Diplomacy under Tyler and Polk,* 127–30; Bemis, *Adams and the Union,* 469–73.

28. Diary, June 29, July 1, 1843.

29. LT in *Advocate of Moral Reform,* November 1, 1843; New York *Express,* August 17, 1843.

30. Quoted by Asa Briggs, *Victorian Cities* (New York, 1965), 60.

31. Diary, July 9, 1843.

32. Quoted by Brown, *Fathers of the Victorians,* 322, from *Figaro in London.*

33. Diary, July 9, 1843.

34. *Ibid.,* July 16, 1843.

35. G. R. S. Kitson Clark, "The Romantic Element, 1830–1850," in John H. Plumb, ed., *Studies in Social History: A Tribute to G. M. Trevelyan* (London, 1955), 232; see also Kitson Clark's "Hunger and Politics in 1842," *Journal of Modern History,* XXV (December, 1953), 358–59, 360; see, for an example of Bowring's romanticism, his poem in the *Anti-Bread Tax Circular,* quoted by *Quarterly Review,* LXXXI (1842–43), 264. See also Douglass Hurd, "Sir John Bowring: Radical Governor," *History Today,* XVIII (October, 1967), 651–59.

36. Cobden to Frederick W. Cobden, October 5, 1838, in John Morley, *The Life of Richard Cobden* (London, 1903), I, 126.

37. Asa Briggs, *Victorian People,* 118; Asa Briggs, "The Language of Class in Early Nineteenth Century England," in Briggs and John Saville, eds., *Essays in Labour History* (New York, 1960), 43–52; E. M. Forster, *Marianne Thornton: A Domestic Biography* (New York, 1956), 54; see David Brion Davis, *The Problem of Slavery in Western Culture* (Ithaca, 1966), 333–37, which explains the British phenomenon of blindness at home but vision abroad as a symbolic transfer of guilt—a general human tendency, as Christ made clear in his parable of the mote and beam.

38. Diary, July 3, 1843; see also June 14 and 16, 1843.

39. Diary, July 3, 1843; David E. Swift, *Joseph John Gurney, Banker, Reformer, and Quaker* (Middletown, 1962), 85–86, on his brother's fears of Samuel's worldliness.

40. Brown, *Fathers of the Victorians,* 325–26; G. M. Young, *Victorian England: Portrait of an Age* (New York, 1954), 33, noted the change in formal Victorianism; Leonard Elliott-Binns, *The Evangelical Movement in the English Church* (London, 1928), 43–64.

41. LT's diary of his trip is a fascinating and detailed account of an American evangelical's reaction to British life in the Victorian era.

42. Diary, June 24, 1843.

43. *Ibid.,* June 25, 1843; G. R. S. Kitson Clark, *The Making of Victorian England* . . . (Cambridge, 1962), 29–31.

44. Diary, July 18, 1843; LT to Opie, September 20, 1845, ltrbk.

45. Diary, June 5, July 21, 1843.

46. Thomas, *Weld,* 17, 150–61; Barnes, *Antislavery Impulse,* 168.

47. Birney to LT, August 22, 1843; Cole, *Chartist Portraits,* 168.

48. LT to Sophia Sturge, January 24, 1844, ltrbk. (almost illegible).

49. LT to Mrs. William Ellery Channing, November 15, 1842, ltrbk.; "Sketch of Dr. Channing," LT scrapbook clipping from an October, 1842, issue of New York *Evangelist.* BT misunderstood the article: see BT to LT, January 13, 1843, BT MSS, OHS.

50. LT to Opie, December 30, 1844, ltrbk.; see Opie to LT, May 14, 1844, March 25 and October 20, 1844; Swift, *J. J. Gurney,* 9, 168–69.

51. Adams, *Memoirs*, XI, August 7, 1843, 406; LT to William T. Hubbard, August 11, 1843, ltrbk.; Bemis, *Adams and the Union*, 471.

52. Adams, *Memoirs*, XI, 405.

53. "Mr. Cobden's Speech at the Free Trade Banquet at Madrid, 14th October, 1846," in Mrs. Salis Schwabe, compiler, *Reminiscences of Richard Cobden* (London, 1895), 13 (quotation); LT to James Hurnard, Colchester, England, March 17, 1855, ltrbk.

CHAPTER FOURTEEN

The Frustrations of Christian Politics

Within a few days of Tappan's return from England, he wrote his friends that he was going to support the Liberty party. The old societies, he said, were "well-nigh defunct," and maintaining them only prolonged the war with Garrison without materially aiding the cause. The best antislavery men had already gone into political work, and "Rallying [*sic*] under this banner will be bearing a testimony against the two great political parties, & encourage people to regard moral principle in their political act &c &c." Yet, he doubted that even Liberty men would stay "true to their principles."[1] He was right.

In 1856 Theodore Parker summarized the difference between the political and the non-political reformer, a distinction that Tappan, for all his doubts, did not wholly grasp. The former owes allegiance to his constituency, the law, and the Constitution, but the latter "is not to deal with institutions; he is to make the institutions better." While the political reformer has to convince a majority, "the non-political reformer has done something if he has the very smallest minority, even if it is a minority of one." The purpose of moral agitation, as Garrison and Parker understood it, was to revolutionize the civil and social climate of the North in such a way that all political questions would be seen in their bearing upon the overriding issue of slavery. This could be accomplished by a determined handful of reformers who concentrated upon the politician's basis of support—his constituency, or at least its most vocal elements. Essentially this approach was the original plan of the American Anti-Slavery Society, a point the Garrisonians constantly reiterated. The essence of the policy was that moral reformers should act not as a political body themselves but as a pressure group affecting the regular party organizations by forcing them to comply with the antislavery demands of the people, particularly the middle class, whom the agitators pledged themselves to arouse to passionate conviction. The Garrisonians' almost obsessive preoccupation with political events and maneuvers attested to their perception that in America politicians react to the clamorous minority faster than to the vague yearnings of the apathetic majority.[2]

Slaveholders were a minority with political influence far out of proportion to their number. Parker reasoned that a group comparably united in opposition to slavery could also exercise disproportionate power. To some degree, antislavery men adopted the techniques of their southern opponents. Indeed, Garrison's call for northern disunion was intended to be more than a dramatization of the extent of American political corruption. It was also an attempt to create a counterforce of dissent that could break the old constitutional compromises. The Garrisonian approach was both original in its appreciation of the psychology of democracy and old in its stress upon religious rhetoric. "The non-political antislavery party," said Parker, combining these factors, "is the Church of America [acting] to criticize the politics of America. It has been of immense service; it is now a great force" that makes "every political man in the North . . . afraid of it."[3] Like John C. Calhoun, Garrison and his followers were able students of the power of minority action.

Basic to the Garrisonian policy of provoking dissent (without advocating violence and insurrection) was the belief in keeping the roles of politician and reformer as separate as possible. Accordingly, the moral agitator should not enter into any accommodation with the established order, either by voting or running for office. To refuse to do so was to bear testimony to the false promise of majoritarian politics, *as then constituted,* and its inadequacy for handling basic flaws in the constitutional system. The perfectionist, no-human-government doctrine was, of course, a vision of the millennial future (analogous to the nineteenth-century Marxist utopia of a classless, post-revolutionary society), but its pragmatic effect, which the Garrisonians increasingly appreciated, was to hold together the group of traveling lecturers, agents, and journalists who made up the core of the Boston group and to prevent them from succumbing to the desire for holding office and from compromising themselves by making choices at the polling place.

Garrison and his friends quarreled with the Liberty party that Tappan was about to enter because they believed that its program weakened the militant resolve of the moral reformer, exposed him to the temptations of conciliation, bound him in institutional fetters, and misled the public about his ability to bring about genuine change. "I distrust the atmosphere of Washington and of politics," said Wendell Phillips. Even the most sincere antislavery men "move about, Sauls and Goliaths among us," until they arrive there and suddenly shrink in "stature." While Garrison gave space to Liberty party activities in the *Liberator,* he felt its leaders were deserters from true antislavery enthusiasm who tried "to make bricks without straw—to propel a locomotive engine without steam—to navigate a ship without water."[4] It was not surprising that he reserved some of his most forceful language for attacking the defrocked Jeremiahs, now involved in third-party action. His attitude was analogous to the reaction of orthodox Marxists of France, Italy, and Germany in the latter half of the nineteenth century to those socialists who supplanted old faith in the moral awakening of the masses to revolution with participation in the ordinary parliamentary process.

While peculiarly American in its religious vision and in its fascination with political measures, Garrisonianism was an experiment unique in the annals of the country, a venture worthy of a serious analysis it has never received. Its purpose was to influence the average voter toward antislavery by demonstrating the alienation of eloquent, thoughtful antislavery leaders from the sources of power. In short, it was antipolitics with a strong political message. Garrisonian disunionism, conceived in these terms, was a method of translating moral outrage into political force. In that sense it was an advance over the old policies of the Tappans' Executive Committee in New York, which sought to transform moral indignation into action primarily against the ecclesiastical bulwarks of slavery and the religious community generally. In Garrison's mind, the Liberty party, a more conventional experiment in reform action, threatened to misguide the public about the real purpose of abolitionism. His quarrel was not with its principles or the "right" of abolitionists "to band together politically for the attainment of their great object" but with its inevitable loss of moral conviction, its confusions over means and ends, and its underestimation of the power of institutions to stifle thought and action, a fear unhappily justified by later events.[5]

From a theoretical point of view, Tappan's concept of politics was as conventional and unimaginative as Garrison's was new and provocative. Lewis was essentially a businessman, and a very creative one, while Garrison was perhaps the first American to develop agitation into a genuine profession. Each had a considerable self-confidence, sense of purpose, and innovativeness in his chosen field. Tappan would never display that expertise and instinct for discovering the essence of things that Garrison brought to bear upon political problems. The New York leader was as far out of his element when he turned to politics as Garrison was when he had to puzzle over the *Liberator*'s ledgerbooks. Lewis believed that power and principle could be wholly united, that it was possible for men to be thoroughgoing reformers and wise statesmen at the same time, that events could always be controlled by the proper application of moral principle. He could not fully accept, with Garrison's and Theodore Parker's relish in partisan strife, those political concessions that even the most earnest antislavery politician had to make in order to survive. As a result, Lewis was likely by turns to be unhappy about a Congressional friend who voted for a slaveholding speaker of the House, for instance, and then overly elated when a shift in political fortunes afforded him some reason for momentary cheer.

In Tappan's Boston years as a Federalist ward canvasser, when one could frighten a child by "'whispering Thomas Jefferson,'" party loyalty had been a simple matter.[6] The forces of statesmanship and religion, order and peace, were united against the evils of atheism, anarchy, and war. But the rise of popular suffrage had somehow destroyed that harmony. Only if one believed that the people themselves spoke with divine authority could there be any hope of reuniting the political and religious elements. When the Rev. Thomas Spencer, vicar of Bath, friend of Sturge and Universal Manhood Suffrage, gave Tappan his pamphlet on *Religion and Politics* after a London Chartist rally, he supplied the American with that very notion. Spencer (who was the philosopher Herbert Spencer's uncle) had a supreme faith that Christianity and democracy offered solutions to all problems of human suffering. Echoing William Ellery Channing's idea of "Self-Culture," Spencer declared that " 'the creation of a new power in the state, the power of the people,' " was a force for good, in fact the work of God himself. If people followed Him in their political acts, "men who dare to obey God rather than man" would be elected to carry out social reforms—factory inspection to ensure the welfare of the workers, licensing and prohibition to control intemperance, secular and universal education, the abolition of privilege, the extension of the franchise, and so on. Tappan was won over to this proto-Social Gospel. "Politics and religion," he wrote Sophia Sturge, "cannot be long divorced."[7]

Yet religious action was fragile, easily contaminated by the dirty business of politics, Tappan realized. Shortly after his conversion to the Liberty party, he learned that Gerrit Smith was going about the countryside giving political sermons at Sunday services. Tappan worried that not only God would be offended but ministers and "the truly good in their flocks" as well. Smith, however, assured him that the politically oriented sermon was a form of religious education, and Tappan confessed to Arthur, "He is trying to emancipate me from *superstitious* regard to such forms & usages. I doubt not he is doing good."[8] Presumably Gerrit Smith was only practicing what Spencer preached.

However unsure he may have been about the proper nature of Christian politics, Tappan did know that parties had to win elections or go under. As long as James G. Birney headed the ticket, he judged, there was little chance of success. Lacking experience and public exposure and displaying little gift for campaign management, Birney was not Lewis' choice for the White House. He had agreed with William Jay in 1840 that "Birney's canvass will render abolitionists contemptible in the eyes of politicians, & perhaps in their own," and his opinion did not change materially when the party mustered only 6,784 votes in that election.[9]

Perhaps as a consequence of that tally, Birney had become increasingly skeptical of democracy, believing that the people had insufficient moral wisdom to be entrusted with the franchise, and the people to whom he particularly referred were recent immigrants, Masons, and Catholics. Gamaliel Bailey, his successor as editor of the *Philanthropist* in Cincinnati, frankly told Birney, "You have always appeared in the character of a Moralist, a reformer, rather than as a Politician or Statesman. . . . You denounced the people—and . . . gave them over to destruction. . . ."

Prophets make poor politicians, Bailey was saying. With Birney's antidemocratic views Tappan did not agree; he himself had become "more democratic," as he told Benjamin, "than I was when I lived in Boston." The political game had to be played by democratic rules; gloomy manifestos from the Michigan swamp-lands, to which Birney had "exiled himself," were not going to win elections, in Tappan's opinion.[10]

What Tappan really wanted was a reconstruction of the moderate Federalist philosophy of a generation earlier: the election of "Upright—moral—disinterested public men" with experience, education, and social standing.[11] He discarded Hamiltonian economics, the B.U.S., and other Federalist dogmas, merely wishing to have, as he told Governor William H. Seward of New York, "a better state of things prevailing—to see men . . . who value post-humous fame [and] the favor of God more than the applause of office-seekers. . . ."[12]

The Whigs came closer to his ideal than the Democrats, though he had no use for the *bon vivant* slaveholder Henry Clay. Regretting that William Henry Harrison had turned his back on the abolitionists in the 1840 campaign, Tappan wrote Joshua R. Giddings, antislavery Whig Congressman of the Western Reserve, "I fully believe that if the Whigs should honestly and courageously take . . . [antislavery] ground, they would have great accessions; but if they do not, they are ruined."[13] In default of a candidate that wholly satisfied him, Tappan gave his vote to Birney.

But Tappan hoped a different candidate would be selected in 1844, someone who could command the respect of the best classes of society. Writing Giddings in 1841, he suggested that the five antislavery Whigs in Congress announce their support of John Quincy Adams for President. All they had to do was "blow the trumpet—buckle on the sword and adopt the motto—For God and country" and the movement would begin. Soon he was vigorously writing other antislavery leaders along the same lines.[14]

Tappan found supporters for his program of uniting Whiggery with the Liberty party among his Ohio friends Salmon P. Chase, Gamaliel Bailey, Samuel Lewis, and General Leicester King. All these Liberty men, particularly Chase, an ambitious Cincinnati lawyer, were thoroughly dissatisfied with Birney. Elated by this discovery, Tappan wrote Judge Jay, "The Ohio party is truly National in its principles, aiming only to [divide?] the general Gov[ernment] from all participation in Slavery or the Slave Trade."

Bailey and the rest, he pointed out, did not believe, as Birney, Alvan Stewart, and Leavitt did, that the Constitution was an antislavery document and that it was within the powers of Congress to abolish slavery in all the states.[15] Tappan and Jay agreed that too radically antislavery an interpretation of the Constitution would only alienate the people, and an adherence to a more moderate course could enhance the party chances.[16]

Chase was overjoyed to find that Tappan viewed political action the same way he did. "Warm, ardent, uncompromising men began" the party, he wrote Lewis. "They required . . . faith in . . . absolute unconditional and immediate emancipation" and acted primarily "upon our ecclesiastical bodies" rather than upon the voters as a whole. With a man like Adams, William Jay, or William H. Seward to head the party, Chase, as he wrote to Giddings, expected that the united Whigs and abolitionists could "carry on their banner, not just 'Northern Rights' exactly but Constitutional Rights, Liberty, Justice, Free Labor." He urged Tappan to sound out the three possible candidates and bring in all the eastern abolitionist support he could.[17]

Tappan did his best, but Jay refused to run, still believing, Tappan reported, "that what little virtue there is in politicians is with the Whigs."[18] In any case, the Birney faction was skeptical of the old judge, Elizur Wright remarking that "I should eat & sleep only on a hatchet lest he should fall into a fit of prudence and *disclaim* us to death."[19] Adams, Tappan found, was unapproachable on the subject, and Birney disliked Adams intensely, considering him something of a fraud despite his help in presenting petitions from abolitionists to Congress.[20] Tappan also sounded out William Seward, the wily Whig governor of New York and protégé of Thurlow Weed. Lewis did not feel very sure of Seward's antislavery convictions and was relieved when Seward showed little interest.[21]

It proved equally difficult for Tappan to reunify eastern abolitionists for political efforts. Tappan tried to win over the New York Garrisonians, David and Lydia Maria Child, who ran the *National Anti-Slavery Standard,* the American Anti-Slavery Society's replacement for the *Emancipator,* and James Gibbons, to whom he proposed a reunion of the "old" and "new" organizations. Mrs. Child was rather disillusioned with the Boston faction. "I have long felt that the judicious and moderately conservative among us gave up the reins too much to these Jehus," she told

275

Ellis Gray Loring. Although troubled by Garrison's disunionism and his interference in editorial policies of the *Standard,* the Childs refused to act with Tappan. The rest of the Garrisonians, Tappan told Chase, were of course beyond hope.[22]

Shortly after Tappan's return from England, the Liberty party renominated Birney at its Buffalo convention. Chase took his defeat with the aplomb of a genuine politician, predicting to Lewis that 1848 would bring a change of luck.[23] Tappan also tried to show the right spirit by holding a dinner in New York for Birney, seating him "at the head of the table with . . . Weld at his right, Sec. of State! Poor S. S. J[ocelyn] blushed," Tappan wrote to Whittier, "when I called him P[ost] M[aster] General." For a few months more, Lewis continued to work on his plan for substituting Jay or Adams, until finally he gave up and reconciled himself to Birney's candidacy.[24]

Having made up his mind to work in party harness again, Tappan took to the political hustings in the election summer of 1844. Stressing the theme that the Liberty party was the true heir of Washingtonian principles, he toured New England towns where Federalism had once been strong—Northampton, Norwich, and New London. His greatest success was in his home town. At a meeting there, an old patriarch challenged Tappan's antislavery facts. "Quick as sunbeams, and as pleasant," recalled a witness many years later, "Mr. Tappan retorted: 'Art thou a ruler in Israel and knowest not these things?'" According to Deacon Stoddard, Tappan's performance "turned our whole town into Abolitionists."[25] His influence was also strong in his Brooklyn neighborhood, where he formed a political club.[26] Undoubtedly his efforts helped to account for the party's relatively better showing in New York state than in the 1840 campaign. Yet, politics Lewis could only take in small doses still, for his fears of dishonesty and shady deals persisted.

The bickerings within the Liberty party over purity of program and coalition with Whigs were petty matters compared with the rising national storm over the Texas issue. With the dying patriarch Andrew Jackson gasping for Texas annexation before the *"golden moment"* passed and England plucked it away, Democratic expansionists such as Robert Walker of Mississippi were preparing the party and the country for the admission of slaveholding Texas.[27] For once in their lives, Benjamin and Lewis had the same political aspiration—the prevention of Texas annexation —and Benjamin was in a position to do something about it.

Ousting Senator Thomas Morris because of his antislavery views, the Ohio legislature in 1838 had sent Benjamin Tappan to take his place. Naturally Lewis fumed over his brother's success at the expense of abolitionism: "To tell you the honest truth I should have preferred to have heard that you had become a deacon of a church."[28] Although cool toward abolitionism throughout his senatorial years, Benjamin was indignant when he discovered that John C. Calhoun, Tyler's secretary of state, wanted Senate ratification of the treaty of annexation in the spring of 1844, without public debate. "Suppose I send you the Treaty & Correspondence," Benjamin wrote Lewis, "will you have it published in the Evening Post in such a way that it cannot be traced back?" Lewis was pleased that at last his brother was beginning to show some antislavery leanings, but he had no desire to be hauled before a Senate investigating committee and charged with sole responsibility for the leak. After several days of indecision, Tappan approached Albert Gallatin, then an aged New York banker, for advice. He urged immediate publication, and Tappan was relieved. The treaty appeared in the *Evening Post Extra,* and Lewis wrote his brother happily that it was making a sensation. (Cannily enough, the *Post* also hinted that insiders expected to make a killing in Texas bond speculations if the treaty passed.)[29]

Shortly afterward, the Democrats held their convention in Baltimore. Coerced by the pressure of events, Van Buren finally took his stand in opposition to the admission of Texas, and the expansionists nominated James K. Polk instead. If Benjamin Tappan intended his exposure of the secret treaty arrangements to aid his friend Van Buren, he had failed miserably. Yet, Tyler and Calhoun had handled the issue so badly that the Senate refused to ratify the treaty.[30]

Benjamin's antislavery posture did not last long, for the Ohio legislature instructed him to vote for admission at the next opportunity. Much to Lewis' distress, the Senate in February, 1845, carried the joint resolution inviting Texas into the Union by a margin of twenty-seven to twenty-five. A tie would have defeated it.[31] Benjamin was still furious that Van Buren had lost the nomination and Polk had won the election, but he voted, as requested, for annexation anyway. Urging Lewis to forget a Whig alliance, Benjamin wrote, "It is in the power of the Liberty party to place the democratic party in Massachusetts, Ohio & the other free states beyond the influences of the state of things which has so long existed & *in no other way can you succeed in freeing the blacks.*"[32] Still infatuated with antislavery Whiggery, Lewis did not agree with Benjamin's analysis, but coalition with abolitionists and Democrats was the course the Liberty men chose to take in 1848.

In casting his vote for Texas' admission, Benjamin did not solely, as he claimed, bow to the popular will in Ohio. Shortly after Tyler signed the joint resolution admitting Texas, the Senator instructed his brother "to cast all the money you have of mine in Texas stock. . . . I say to you privately that the debt of Texas will be provided for by our government."[33] On receiving these instructions, Lewis exploded that he absolutely declined and admonished Benjamin for pursuing a course "dishonorable to you as a man & as a Senator. By your single vote you could have stopt the nefarious project. What honor you would have gained if you had had the consistency & patriotism to have done it!"[34] Far from taking Lewis' advice "to have nothing to do with that Stock," Benjamin marshalled his resources and made from his Texas transactions an estimated fifty thousand dollars, a somewhat quicker way to wealthy retirement than his brother's mercantile house provided. The abolitionist's grandiose hopes for a free Texas had unexpectedly ended, after all Lewis' labors, on a very dismal note.[35]

Lewis Tappan was not altogether unhappy about the results of the election of 1844. Henry Clay had been defeated—"I prefer an out & out friend & advocate of Slavery [like Polk]," he wrote Benjamin, "to an intriguer [like Clay], or 'northern man [like Van Buren] with southern principles.' "[36] The Liberty party had not done well, except in New York, where, as Tappan admitted, Whigs voted for the Liberty party in sufficient numbers to give Polk the state's electoral votes and the national election, too.[37] It was a consolation to him that Polk was a teetotaler, a Sabbatarian, and a Presbyterian. Hoping to prevent a war with Mexico, Tappan sent the President's wife Jay's pamphlet on peace.[38]

More than pamphlets and good wishes were required to counteract the advance slavery had made in acquiring Texas. In March, 1846, with the United States on the threshold of war with Mexico, Tappan began his most important contribution to political antislavery, the founding of the Washington *National Era*. Under the editorship of Gamaliel Bailey, Tappan's first choice for the position, the paper served effectively as the Liberty party's most popular journal.[39] As usual, Tappan organized the fund-raising for Bailey's salary and the paper's operation until it was self-supporting. He depended largely on old friends of the American and Foreign Anti-Slavery Society on both sides of the Atlantic, who responded well.[40] When the first issue appeared, on January 7, 1847, Tappan was pleased with its neat appearance and moderate tone. "Dr. Bailey," he boasted, "is . . . never ultra or vulgar or coarse. . . ."[41] Some abolitionists, such as Beriah Green, grumbled that Tappan and Bailey put too much faith in discretion, "a virtue, which Sir John Falstaff spoke highly of," while the times actually required "a little *bravery*. . . ."[42] Tappan had altered his antislavery views very little over the years (unlike Garrison in this regard). Lewis was still pretty much the agitator of the mid-thirties, while others, including Beriah Green, were adopting more forceful views about how the federal Constitution could be used to give Congress and the President the legal justification for emancipating the slaves. Yet, modest political demands, confined to ending slavery in Washington and supporting the Wilmot Proviso (exclusion of slavery from the territories acquired from Mexico), paid off handsomely in circulation increases. "Candid men, in slave States, as well as in the free States," Tappan predicted, "will learn to distinguish between furious denunciators and those who aim to promote the true welfare . . . of both master and slave."[43]

The growing conservatism of eastern Liberty party leadership, as evidenced in the Tappan-Bailey editorials, led to a splintering of the party. William Goodell, Gerrit Smith, and a few other New York leaders formed the Liberty League at Macedon Lock, with Smith and the peace-advocate Elihu Burritt as their Presidential team. Tappan tried to prevent the movement but only confirmed the Liberty-Leaguers' opinion that the old party was about to be interred in a conservative grave. The selection of Tappan's choice for the regular Liberty ticket, John P. Hale, a New Hampshire senator whose antislavery credentials were too new to be fully tested, was not calculated to calm the fears of Goodell and Smith.[44]

Through Tappan's aggressive campaign in his behalf, Hale won the nomination over Gerrit Smith at the Buffalo Liberty convention in 1847. Although a man of limited talent for leadership, Hale was enough of a political animal to hesitate before leaving his fortunes in the hands of Tappan or of Joshua Leavitt and Henry Stanton, who by this time also hankered for a popular nomination. After some weeks of indecision, Hale accepted the honor, much to Tappan's relief, and began to act as a candidate should—attending rallies and making the proper antislavery statements.[45]

Behind the scenes, Salmon P. Chase was again busy with intrigues, this time with the purpose of removing Hale and of forming a much wider coalition with dissident elements of the major parties. As early as the Buffalo convention, he had warned against Hale's nomination, foreseeing that events later in the election year might make his selection an embarrassment and restrict maneuvering. By the spring of 1848, Chase's prediction came true, as the agitation over the Wilmot Proviso reached a crescendo and threatened to divide both the Whigs and the Democrats along sectional lines. Furious that Van Buren was once more rejected by their party, Democratic bolters nominated him on their own "Barnburner" ticket. The antislavery Whigs, John G. Palfrey, Charles Francis Adams, Joshua R. Giddings, and Charles Sumner, left their party after the nomination of the slaveholder Zachary Taylor.[46]

Tappan, of course, refused to accept Chase's idea of substituting Van Buren for Hale, though Chase argued that Van Buren had not only proved himself of Presidential stature but also commanded the largest single following, the Democratic insurgents. Even Hale was willing to see the substitution made, but Tappan urged him to halt the trend toward "expediency," and for the time being he held his post. At an exciting meeting of the antislavery factions—Liberty, Barnburner, and Conscience Whig—in August, 1848, at Buffalo, the climax occurred. Having won the support of Leavitt and Stanton, leaders of the old Birney faction, Chase secured the nomination for Van Buren by a vote of 244 (to 181 for Hale). The Free Soil party, based on the exclusion of slavery from the territories, was born. Tappan *"felt stabbed in the vitals"* by this course of events and lashed out at Stanton for his "extraordinary & unjustifiable" desertion of Hale at the convention. His fears of 1840 had turned out to be fully justified. Even reformers like Leavitt and Stanton could not forever resist the temptation of office and power.[47] In fact, Stanton did degenerate thereafter into the most ordinary of political hacks in the Free Soil and later the Republican parties, displaying a loss of conviction that hardly surprised the Garrisonians who had warned the abolitionists of this dereliction for many years. Shocked by the convention's decision, Tappan refused to wheel into line, particularly after receiving an unsatisfactory reply from Van Buren about his role in the "Amistad" case, which Tappan could hardly be expected to forget.[48] Instead, he voted, with about twenty-five hundred other abolitionists (including the all but forgotten James Birney), for Gerrit Smith, wrong though he previously thought the Liberty-Leaguers to be for running their own candidates.[49]

Tappan's decision was understandable, impractical and almost ludicrous though it appears. At least Gerrit Smith stood solidly for racial equality and immediate abolition, while the Free Soil party was, at best, the weakest of the antislavery vehicles. The Barnburners, led by Van Buren, his son John, and David Wilmot, cared nothing for Negro freedom. Their Free Soilism was almost openly racist and opportunistic; by excluding slavery they also meant to exclude Negroes from the former Mexican lands, saving them for white Yankee settlement alone. Generally, abolitionists like Tappan were unaware of this aspect of the Democratic insurgency, but they instinctively mistrusted its advocates, whose records in national and local politics were not very reassuring. In regard to the abolitionists in the Free Soil effort, Whittier warned Tappan after the election, "I am not without fear that they may be drawn into some un[w]orthy compromise." Under the circumstances, he exclaimed, genuine reformers needed all the "vigilance & wisdom" they could muster to hold "the line of principle." Yet even the pioneers in the cause, like Tappan and Whittier, who had suffered years of abuse, were not willing to admit to themselves that northern hatred of slavery could mask a bitter hostility to the enslaved as well. There was nothing incompatible, though, in the Free Soil dream of prosperous free-labor farms dotting the West and a complementary nightmare of Negro competitors poisoning the atmosphere of Western skies.[50]

Busy with the negotiations for the sale of the Mercantile Agency and other affairs, Tappan gave little time to such gloomy meditations. It was impossible for him to despair for long. Writing to Julius LeMoyne, another disaffected Liberty man, he said, "Let us not sink into despondency. There are very many in the country who love the ancient antislavery principles, who prize the moral and religious aspects of the cause, who would be glad to unite in defence & diffusion of such principles." Tappan suggested a reorganization of the old American and Foreign Anti-Slavery Society or else the establishment of "a central Com. & State Com.s" with an active secretary. "Now is the time to press the anti S. subject upon the community. . . . Nil disperandum!"[51] But the day had passed for that kind of work. Instead, Tappan threw most of his energies into church antislavery. His greatest contribution to the movement lay in that area and not in political activity, which he neither enjoyed nor fully understood.

NOTES

1. LT to Seth Gates, October 21, 1843, ltrbk.; LT to E. Wright, October 9, 1843, ltrbk. and to others in same period, ltrbk.

2. Theodore Parker, *The Great Battle between Slavery and Freedom* . . . (Boston, 1856), 15; cf. Thomas, *Liberator*, 324–33, in which the author is most scornful of Garrison's "hokum" about the Liberty party and about non-resistant, disunionist "purity." Actually, Garrison's criticisms were justified; Liberty party men turned out to be poor politicians and good prophets, or else consummate politicians at the expense of original convictions. Garrison, more realistic than might have been expected, approved of the Free Soil and Republican movements, to a degree, because they were indications of the growth of antislavery sentiment and were led by real politicians, not agitators turned politicians. Of course he was critical of the halfway measures of Free Soilism and Republicanism at the same time that he welcomed the formation of legitimate antislavery political organizations. James B. Stewart is studying this interpretation of Garrisonianism, and I am deeply indebted to him for his original approach to the Boston group.

3. Parker, *Great Battle*, 32.

4. "The Philosophy of the Abolitionist Movement," in Louis Filler, ed., *Wendell Phillips on Civil Rights and Freedom* (New York, 1965), 61; Garrison and Garrison, *Garrison*, III, 34.

5. Garrison and Garrison, *Garrison*, III, 34 (quoted from *Liberator*).

6. Wendell Phillips, *Disunion; Two Discourses at Music Hall* . . .(Boston, 1861), 7, a reminiscence about Federalist Boston.

7. LT to Sophia Sturge, October 13, 1843, ltrbk.; Thomas Spencer, *Religion and Politics; Or, Ought the Religious Man to be Political?* (London, 1840), 5, 13–14; LT to G. Smith, September 19, 1843, LT to William Jay, August 9, 1843, ltrbk.; Henry B. Stanton, *Sketches of Reforms and Reformers* . . . (New York, 1849), 320; Cole, *Chartist Portraits*, 174.

8. LT to AT, September 14 or 15, 1843, ltrbk.; see also LT to Phelps, October 6, 1843, Phelps MSS, BPL; Phelps, however, continued to disapprove—see Phelps to LT, December 5, 1843: "G. Smith's explanation was a handsome back-out—

just saying that what he meant by politics, was not politics but religious instruction in regard to it!" Quotation in text is from LT to Smith, September 2, 1843, ltrbk.; see also Harlow, *Gerrit Smith*, 203 ff.; LT to Smith, September 9 and 18, 1843, Gerrit Smith Miller MSS, Syracuse University Library.

9. Jay to LT, September 12, 1840, Jay MSS, Columbia University Library; LT to J. H. Tredgold, August 20, 1840, in Abel and Klingberg, *Side-Light*, 74–75; LT expected one per cent to vote for Birney, but he drew less than a tenth of one per cent—see Theodore Clarke Smith, *The Liberty and Free Soil Parties in the Northwest* (New York, 1897), 46; LT to G. Smith, June 29, 1840, Gerrit Smith Miller MSS, Syracuse University Library; see also Leavitt to Birney, February 10, 1843, in Dumond, *Birney Letters*, II, 716; Gerrit Smith blamed LT and Bailey in advance of the election for Liberty failures in Ohio—see G. Smith to LT, June 19, 1840, ltrbk., Gerrit Smith Miller MSS, Syracuse University Library.

10. Birney to Bailey, March 31, 1843, Dumond, *Birney Letters*, II, 726, and Birney to Bailey, April 12, 1843, *ibid.*, II, 734; Fladeland, *Birney*, 233–34; LT to BT, March 13, 1840, BT MSS, LC; LT to BT, April 23, 1848, ltrbk.; LT to R. D. Webb, October 25, 1842, WLG MSS, BPL.

11. LT to Seth Gates, June 17, 1840, Seth M. Gates MSS, Syracuse University Library; see also *ibid.*, June 9 and 12, July 12, December 8, 1840.

12. LT to Gates, July 9, 1840, *ibid.*; LT to Smith, June 17, 1840, Gerrit Smith Miller MSS, Syracuse University Library; LT to Seward (quotation), March 18, 1842, William H. Seward MSS, Rochester University Library; LT to Giddings, April 24, 1840, ltrbk.

13. LT to Giddings, February 17, 1840, in George W. Julian, *The Life of Joshua R. Giddings* (Chicago, 1892), 90; LT to Seth Gates, March 10, 1840, ltrbk.; LT to Editors, May 27, 1840, *National Intelligencer*, June 1, 1840; LT to Luther Bradish, March 2, 1840, Luther Bradish MSS, New-York Historical Society; LT to G. Smith, June 17, 1840, Gerrit Smith Miller MSS, Syracuse University Library.

14. LT to Giddings, July 24, 1841, Joshua R. Giddings MSS, OHS; Wilson, *Rise and Fall of the Slave Power*, I, 436–37; Birney to Chase, February 2, 1842, Chase MSS, LC; LT to Gates, June 12, 1841, Gates MSS, Syracuse University Library; LT to G. Smith, February 17, 1842, Gerrit Smith Miller MSS, Syracuse University Library.

15. LT to Jay, March 13–16, 1842, ltrbk.; see also *Philanthropist*, January 12, 1842; Wilson, *Rise and Fall of Slave Power*, I, 551; Alvan Stewart to Birney, April 14, 1842, Dumond, *Birney Letters*, II, 689–90.

16. Jay to LT, October 5, 1844.

17. Chase to LT, May 26, September 15 (quotation), 1842, Chase MSS, LC; Chase to Giddings, February 9, 1843 (quotation), Joshua R. Giddings-George W. Julian MSS, LC; Joseph G. Rayback, "The Liberty Party Leaders in Ohio: Exponents of Antislavery Coalition," *Ohio State Archeological and Historical Quarterly,* LVII (1948), 165–78.

18. LT to Bailey, March 6, 1843, ltrbk.; LT to Chase, March 20, 1843, *ibid.;* Bailey to Birney, March 31, 1843, Dumond, *Birney Letters*, II, 727.

19. Wright to Chase, January 20, 1843, Chase MSS, LC.

20. Chase to Giddings, January 21, 1843, Giddings-Julian MSS, LC; Birney to Chase, February 2, 1842, Chase MSS, LC; Chase to LT, February 15, 1843, Chase MSS, LC; Rayback, "Liberty Party Leaders," 172; Adams, *Memoirs*, XII, 79–80; G. Smith to editor, *A&FASR*, November 1, 1842; Fladeland, *Birney*, 217–18;

Birney to L. King, January 1, 1844, Dumond, *Birney Letters,* II, 767; Birney, *Birney,* 343–44; Jay to LT, October 3, 1842.

21. LT to Seward, March 18, 1842, Seward MSS, Rochester University Library; Chase to LT, September 12, 1842, Chase MSS, LC; Harlow, *Gerrit Smith,* 166.

22. Child to Loring, May 16, 1844, personal miscellaneous letters, New York Public Library; see also *ibid.,* February 28, December 6, 1842, March 6, 1843; Mrs. Child to LT, September 20, 1843, Child miscellaneous file, New-York Historical Society; LT to David Lee Child, September 23, 1843, David Lee Child MSS, BPL; see also LT to Mrs. Child, January 11, 1843, Child MSS, BPL; LT to Chase, September 20, 1843, ltrbk.; Garrison and Garrison, *Garrison,* III, 91–92.

23. Chase to LT, September 12, 1843, Chase MSS, LC; Harlow, *Gerrit Smith,* 167–68; Rayback, "Liberty Party Leaders," 172; J. W. Schuckers, *The Life and Public Services of Salmon Portland Chase . . .* (New York, 1874), 69–70.

24. LT to Leavitt, August 29, 1843, ltrbk.; Jay to LT, October 3, 1843, an attempt to stop him from exciting "new distractions"; LT to Adams, January 21, 1844, ltrbk.; *Philanthropist,* January 10, 1844; quotation, LT to Whittier, December 9, 1843, in Filler, *Crusade Against Slavery,* 176.

25. Newspaper clipping, n.d., scrapbook, 1857–95; LT to BT, October 26, 1844; LT to Scoble, July 31, 1844, in Abel and Klingberg, *Side-Light,* 186.

26. LT to BT, August 6, 1844, ltrbk.; LT to Scoble, July 31, 1844, Abel and Klingberg, *Side-Light,* 186.

27. Quoted by James P. Shenton, *Robert John Walker: A Politician from Jackson to Lincoln* (New York, 1961), 34, 38; see also anti-British activity of Secretary of State Upshur, in Claude H. Hall, *Abel P. Upshur, Conservative Virginian, 1790–1844* (Madison, 1964), 199, and Tappan's response, LT to Scoble, October 19, 1843, Abel and Klingberg, *Side-Light,* 148; for LT's response to Walker's expansionism, see LT to Scoble, January 30, 1844, in Abel and Klingberg, *Side-Light,* 169–72, and March 28, 1844, 180; and see also Frederick Merk, "A Safety-Valve Thesis and Texas Annexation," *MVHR,* XLIX (December, 1962), 413–36.

28. LT to BT, December 28, 1838, BT MSS, LC; Smith, *Liberty and Free Soil Parties,* 25.

29. BT to LT, April 22, 1844, BT MSS, OHS; LT to BT, April 27, 1844, BT MSS, LC; LT to BT, May 3, 1844, ltrbk.; James C. N. Paul, *Rift in the Democracy* (New York, 1961), 120.

30. Paul, *Rift in the Democracy,* 123, 144–68, and 65, 76, 78, 90, 127, for BT's associations with Van Buren; BT was censured for revealing the treaty—see *Senate Journal,* 28 Cong., 1 sess., 426–43.

31. Elbert B. Smith, *Magnificent Missourian: The Life of Thomas Hart Benton* (Philadelphia, 1958), 198–200; LT to BT, January 10, 1845, ltrbk.

32. BT to LT, December 9 and 22 (quotation), 1844, January 18, 1845, BT MSS, OHS; LT to BT, December 13, 1844, ltrbk.

33. BT to LT, March 10, 1845, BT MSS, OHS.

34. LT to BT, March 13, 1845, ltrbk.

35. Filler, *Crusade against Slavery,* 179–80; LT refused to do much anti-Texas propaganda work thereafter; he was too busy and the prospects of a reversal too slim; LT to Smith, October 25, 1845, Gerrit Smith Miller MSS, Syracuse University Library.

36. LT to BT, October 14, 1844, ltrbk.

37. Birney, *Birney,* 354–55; Smith, *Liberty and Free Soil Parties,* 78–84; LT to Charles Tappan, November 7, 1844, ltrbk.; LT to Sturge, November 15, 1844, Abel and Klingberg, *Side-Light,* 200; LT to George Thompson, December 2, 1844, ltrbk., explaining Clay's defeat.

38. Tappan also disapproved of Clay's running-mate, Theodore Frelinghuysen, the old promoter of Arthur's Valley projects; LT considered it cynical for Whigs to place "the Christian Statesman" on the same ticket with the reprobate Clay: see LT to BT, May 3, 1844, BT MSS, LC; LT to Sturge, February 28, 1845, and LT to Mrs. Polk, April 4, 1846, ltrbk.

39. LT to Birney, March 10, 1846, ltrbk.; see also Dumond, *Birney Letters,* II, 1006; see minutes of the American and Foreign Anti-Slavery Society (A&FASS), March–September, 1846, AMA MSS, Fisk; LT to Whittier, November 5, 1846, autograph collection, Houghton Library, Harvard; LT to Smith, August 24, 1846, Gerrit Smith Miller MSS, Syracuse University Library.

40. LT to W. W. Patton, November 5, loose letter (copy), LT MSS, LC; LT to J. N. Hobard, Pittsburgh, November 3, 1846, and LT to Sturge, October 31, 1846, January 16, 1847, ltrbk.; LT to Smith, October 26, 1846 (circular), Gerrit Smith Miller MSS, Syracuse University Library.

41. LT to James Whiton, Boston, August 4, 1847, ltrbk.; see also LT to Sturge, January 30, 1847, ltrbk.

42. Green to Birney, August 2, 1847, in Dumond, *Birney Letters,* II, 1078.

43. *National Era,* February 4, 1847; see also LT to Smith, July 5, 1848, Gerrit Smith Miller MSS, Syracuse University Library.

44. Smith, *Liberty and Free Soil Parties,* 100–101, describing also a western split, with Birney off on a tangent; LT to Smith, July 30, September 10, December 15 and 30, 1847, January 7, 1848, Gerrit Smith Miller MSS, Syracuse University Library; see also LT to W. H. Childs, Niagara Falls, June 21, 1847, ltrbk.; *National Era,* August 5, 1847.

45. Richard H. Sewell, *John P. Hale and the Politics of Abolition* (Cambridge, 1965), 90–94; Harlow, *Gerrit Smith,* 177–80; LT to Sturge, January 14, 1848, and LT to Mrs. A. H. Richardson, January 14, 1848, ltrbk.; Smith to LT, February 10, 1848, ltrbk., Gerrit Smith Miller MSS, Syracuse University Library; Birney to LT, July 10, 1848, in Dumond, *Birney Letters,* II, 1108–9; *National Era,* May 18, 1848; LT to Scoble, April 22, 1848, in *Anti-Slavery Reporter,* June 1, 1848 (III), 107.

46. Frank Otto Gatell, "Conscience and Judgment: the Bolt of the Massachusetts Conscience Whigs," *The Historian,* XXVII (November, 1958), 18–45; Martin B. Duberman, *Charles Francis Adams, 1807–1886* (Boston, 1961), 110–47; Schuckers, *Chase,* 82–83.

47. LT to Stanton, September 1 and 28, 1848, ltrbk.; see also LT to Bailey, November 6, 1848, ltrbk.; LT to Julius LeMoyne, November 18, 1848, LeMoyne MSS, LC; LT to Smith, July 14, September 11, December 17 (quotation), 1848, Gerrit Smith Miller MSS, Syracuse University Library.

48. LT to Van Buren, September 30, 1848, ltrbk.; Van Buren to LT, October 2, 1848; LT to Smith, November 28, 1848, Gerrit Smith Miller MSS, Syracuse University Library.

49. LT to Sturge, November 8, 1848, ltrbk.; LT to Smith, December 5 and 6, 1848, ltrbk.; Birney to John J. Crittenden, January 8, 1849, Dumond, *Birney Letters,* II, 1124.

50. James B. Stewart, "Joshua R. Giddings and the Tactics of Radical Politics," Ph.D. dissertation, 1968, Case Western Reserve University, Chapter VIII; Whittier to LT, July 14, 1849.

51. LT to LeMoyne, December 18, 1848, LeMoyne MSS, LC; *ibid.*, November 18, 1848; LT to Smith, November 18 and 28, December 17, 1848, Gerrit Smith Miller MSS, Syracuse University Library.

CHAPTER FIFTEEN

The American Missionary Association

The abolitionist movement was primarily religious in its origins, its leadership, its language, and its methods of reaching the people. While the ideas of a secular Enlightenment played a major role, too, abolitionists tended to interpret the Declaration of Independence as a theological as well as a political document. They stressed the spiritual as much as the civil damage done to the slave and the nation. Antislavery sentiment, of course, found its political expression in the Free Soil, and later the Republican, parties. Yet their limited program of containing slavery within the old states could hardly satisfy those who believed in immediate emancipation, without compensation or transitional procedures. For them what was required was the kind of moral protest from the religious community that would overthrow the entire slavery system.

Whatever the sizes, degrees of influence, or the eccentricities of the various camps within the antislavery movement, there was little doubt that the cause, originating and still strongest in the middle-class, religious segment of the New England settlements in the North, was having a national impact. Tappan recognized that effect when he wrote Joseph Sturge, "Although the number of those who think slavery is, under all circumstances, wrong does not rapidly increase, yet . . . newspapers throughout the country now contain facts, arguments &c against the extension of slavery & very many of them against slavery itself."[1] Until the raid on

Harpers Ferry, the central focus of abolitionism continued to be moral and religious, giving the movement a coherence and unity that transcended the superficial factionalism dividing it after 1840 and that contributed to its national influence. After John Brown's conspiracy, with its profound catalyzing effect on opinion in both sections, the issue could only be resolved by political and military means.

It has been claimed that Garrisonian disunionism, first proclaimed in 1842, represented an aberration from the old religious orientation of the cause. Like "Immediate Abolition," the slogan of the thirties, "No Union with Slaveholders," the motto of the forties, was not a political rallying cry in the usual sense. It was an extension of the the old religious plea that all institutions, habits, and traditions should be governed by strictly moral precepts. It was a disposition of mind that some Americans adopted in order to impress others, at least in some measure, with the profound sickness of society. O. B. Frothingham, a Garrisonian and Transcendentalist, declared in 1857 that disunionism should bring about "no greater convulsion than is experienced in passing from one frame of temper to another." Disunionism was a moral weapon to force politicians and voters, clergy and laity, to consider what the true purpose of union, nation, and established government was supposed to be. Some men, Phillips said, "prate about 'nationality,' and the 'empire,' and 'manifest destiny,' using brave words" to convey the petty concerns of "white States making money out of cotton and corn." Phillips urged that "American nationality" ought to be perceived as "the last best growth of the thoughtful mind of the century, treading underfoot sex and race, caste and condition, and collecting on the broad bosom of what deserves the name of empire, under the shelter of noble, just, and equal laws, all races, all customs, all religions, all languages, all literature, and all ideas."[2] An American Union that rejected these principles as the basis for practical political action deserved rupture and ruin.

When Garrison spoke of disunion, he was speaking not as a political reformer but as a moral agitator. "The separation of North and South," he wrote Elizabeth Pease, "is required by every principle of morality, justice, and religion. . . . Slaveholders, warriors, worshippers of mammon, enemies of holiness, are all embraced in the Christian fold."[3] This was not the language of a politician; it was the platform of a religious perfectionist. Garri-

288

son had not taken leave of his senses, but it can only be concluded that he had if his statement to Miss Pease is read as a *political* comment. On the basis of that rationale, political logic would have required him to forswear all connections with national and local governments—to refuse to pay taxes, to incite those eligible to evade or refuse militia calls, and otherwise to demonstrate dramatically a withdrawal from civil duties. These acts of disobedience were contemplated, but Garrison, for the most part, held aloof from such radical responses. He did not disrupt church services with antislavery speeches, as did S. S. Foster and Parker Pillsbury, and he frequently tempered his anticlericalism with a caution rather inappropriate to his reputation as an infidel.[4] Throughout his career, he refused to countenance violence, even withholding his blessing from Kansas Free Soilers and reproaching them for excluding free Negroes from the territory.[5] Although radical in a religious sense, he and those who followed his non-resistance, disunionist gospel were in many ways conservative in their tactics. His harsh language was a conscious attempt to arouse angry reaction in others (not dissimilar to nonviolent provocations of public anger through mass demonstrations, a technique of agitation of more recent development). Garrisonians could always count upon hostile outbursts from proslavery forces to dramatize their own nonviolence.

Lewis Tappan, like most of the moderate, church-oriented abolitionists, did not understand the Garrisonian method, but even he occasionally found himself defending the Boston editor against proslavery attacks. Tappan had to admit that Garrison's disciples had "talent & industry" and that they "utter a great deal of truth, although they seem to do it in a bad spirit, reminding me of a zealot of whom it was said 'he serves God as if the devil were in him.'" As a subscriber to the *Liberator*, Tappan recognized that the editorials were often right, although he found them too censorious in judgment.[6]

The quarrel between the two did not concern the nature of the malady afflicting the nation but the proper way to cure it. Garrison wanted wholesale purgatives of the American conscience, and even amputation, while Tappan sought restoratives. Garrison indulged the prophetic pleasures of denunciation and sought a polarization of opinion—with dissent on the one extreme and conservatism on the other. Tappan looked for a gradual transformation of national sentiment, both in the North and in the South.

"May the day be hastened," he wrote in the *National Era*, "when *practical godliness* shall be preached from every pulpit. . . , when the majority of preachers and church members will not be as far from the teachings of Christ as a majority of the politicians of the day from the principles of the Declaration of Independence."[7] His mission was not to denounce the old ways of doing things but to reform them in the traditional sense.

To accomplish this purpose, Tappan had to deal with much more complex moral problems than Garrison did, whose approach was to reduce options to their simplest components. To shout up to the ramparts from the outside required a loud voice, a clear message, and persistence, but to make reforms from within the city gates was another matter. Tappan thought of himself not as an outlander but as a man of wide connections and influence. His trip to England in 1843 was based on that assumption, and his disagreement with Garrison stemmed in part from his fear of being identified with one whom he considered a social leper capable of destroying his access to the respectable classes of society.

Lewis believed that, given the proper circumstances, he could deal even with members of the proslavery "establishment" on an equal and gentlemanly basis. Garrison, on the other hand, could never have tried such an experiment, and he thought it a useless waste of time anyhow. To him, the South was beyond recovery and therefore should be quarantined, as though its social diseases were communicable. Lewis Tappan, however, still thought that the New England sense of communal responsibility for evil could be transferred to the South if the molders of southern opinion were reached and converted to the New England way. (The aim of this evangelism was actually similar to Garrison's goal of a universal society devoted to the puritan ethic, in which blacks and whites pursued their ambitions in equality while suppressing age-old tendencies to sloth, inebriation, and purposeless sport.) Visiting his brother Benjamin in 1843 at a Washington boardinghouse, Lewis met several southern Congressmen, who treated him "with entire respect." Introduced to some slaveholding Senators in the capitol building, he talked pleasantly with them about abolition and related matters.[8] As far as Tappan could see, an approach of the kind had led to the passage of the revolutionary West Indian Emancipation Act of 1833: discreet conversations with the leading M. P.'s, backed by formidable agitation.

Tappan also corresponded with ex-Governor James H. Hammond of South Carolina in a friendly way a few years later, urging him to make his state the leader of a general emancipation movement. "I sometimes wish I could go among your people—not to spirit away slaves or to excite revolt—but to reason with the best part of your population," he wrote. "Would they hang me? I trow not if you were in the Executive chair." Tappan may sound grossly naive in announcing to Hammond his desire "to free the slaveholder from disquietude, loss, remorse, retribution" while freeing the slave from "moral darkness, heathenism, disruption of domestic ties, chattelism. . . ." Yet who has not assumed that he could convert a man of opposite opinion at one time or another? In questions that tend to violent opinion, who has not preferred to believe that answers may be acquired by reason? The Garrisonians were perhaps almost cynical in their rejection of this kind of exchange, but Tappan still believed, as he had in the thirties, that missionary work among southern community leaders was the most promising approach. Hammond, for his part, did remain courteous throughout their correspondence. He thanked Tappan for sending antislavery materials and even said of Theodore Weld's *The Bible against Slavery,* "I thought it erudite & able, but *not precisely to the point.*"[9] In testing the sentiments of a Christian gentleman like Hammond, Tappan was attempting a much more difficult task than his Boston rival set himself. To do it well required subtlety, restraint, and diplomatic skill. Tappan was too impulsive to be a good diplomat, though he and Hammond were able to rein in their tempers fairly well. In the end, however, this kind of effort was, as the Garrisonians predicted, hopeless.

More typical of his frustrations as a northern Christian gentleman trying to touch the heart and conscience of a southern squire was his colloquy with John B. O'Neall, a temperance, tract, and missionary enthusiast of South Carolina. In 1844, Judge O'Neall sentenced a free Negro to death for helping his slave mistress to escape from her owner. To probe the judge's motives and bring him to an awareness of his inhumanity, Tappan sent him the protests from Thomas Clarkson and the Congregational ministers of Lancashire, as well as other English and American petitions for leniency. What infuriated O'Neall more than anything else that Tappan wrote him was the implication that he was not a Christian in good standing. Although the governor commuted the sentence to thirty-nine lashes, both Lewis Tappan and Judge O'Neall grew increasingly sarcastic and abusive, the altercation culminating with Tappan's self-righteous comment that God would not allow the southerners "to manage their slaves as they please," any more than Yankee abolitionists would allow them to do so. "In mercy or in judgment He will soon, I doubt not, lead the poor slaves out of the house of bondage—I am afraid it will be in judgment." Tappan soon had to grieve over O'Neall's election as one of the vice-presidents of the American Bible Society, an honor not balanced by the selection of an abolitionist as another.[10] Such evidences of moral cowardice among northern church leaders seemed to confirm Garrison's contempt for organized religion. But Tappan's response was to couple his protests with institutional substitutes for the old ecclesiastical organizations. These alternate organizations he hoped would eventually bring about that transformation of the public conscience necessary to make all men brothers under God.

In August, 1841, a few months before the departure of the Mendi Africans, J. W. C. Pennington, a Negro Congregational minister of Hartford, Connecticut, founded the Union Missionary Society. Its purpose was not only to aid the Mendi effort but also to establish other antislavery missions at home and abroad. Most of its original directors were Negro clergymen, but when LaRoy Sunderland, the antislavery Methodist preacher, Simeon Jocelyn, and Tappan merged their "Amistad" committee with it at a meeting in May, 1842, the whites rapidly assumed control. They replaced some of the Negro officers, though they retained Pennington as president for the time being. Tappan wrote Phelps, "Still it is intended to give the intelligent & excellent men of color their full share in our cause. I have the honor to be Treasurer & Secretary." Lewis considered the arrangement very generous, and, of course, it was unusual for a benevolent society to have a racially mixed directorship. But it was not long before the Negroes occupied only minor and honorary posts.[11] Tappan and his friends could not resist taking charge; that was their nature. It never occurred to them that the decision was itself a commentary upon the character of the antislavery movement and upon the nature of race relations in the North. It should be added, though, that none of the Negroes who had been displaced protested his removal, at least in public.

Soon the Union group absorbed several minor associations

originally founded by Oberlinites. Tappan started the *Union Missionary* to describe the development of the Society and publish its requests for funds. With Amos Phelps as secretary, the organization won new friends and support as the only nonsectarian antislavery missionary body in the country. In 1846, Tappan organized a convention of the "Friends of Bible Missions" in Albany, where William Jackson, a Massachusetts banker and railroad owner, was elected president of the enlarged and reconstituted American Missionary Association.[12]

From then on, the organization grew at a rapid pace, adding new missions, including one in Siam formerly operated by the American Board of Commissioners for Foreign Missions (A.B.C.F.M.). Amos Phelps, Tappan's long time friend, did not live to see its full development; after a rest cure in Jamaica, where he visited the A.M.A.'s stations, he died of consumption. George Whipple, an energetic Oberlin professor, took his place. In time, Simeon Jocelyn also accepted a secretaryship, and the basic leadership was shared by the three—Whipple being in charge of foreign missions, Jocelyn directing the domestic ones, and Tappan functioning as treasurer and policy-maker in the executive committee. Jocelyn, sweet-natured to a fault, was the least efficient of the three and caused Tappan much irritation. Yet, his gentle good humor was sorely needed in the businesslike atmosphere of the Association headquarters. Tappan drew little salary from the A.M.A. over the years, although he worked as hard as the professionals, particularly after his retirement from the Mercantile Agency in 1849.[13]

Despite the A.M.A.'s dependence upon Congregational support, Tappan and his friends hoped to keep the organization nonsectarian. "As the *American Missionary Association* belongs to no sect," he declared, "it has a claim upon all. Its simple object is to send out a pure gospel, free from every compromise." His hope was that eventually it would supplant the "old Boards," which still sheltered proslavery sentiments and members.[14]

Much of Tappan's work in the new enterprise was similar in nature to his other activities in those reform organizations that he had joined previously. He raised money, wrote thousands of letters, edited the *American Missionary* whenever Whipple was out of town, gave advice, organized the annual conventions, paid bills, hosted missionaries when they visited the city, arranged for their return to distant lands, and performed all those labors that gave him so much personal satisfaction and the Association so much efficiency and success.[15]

By 1852, the A.M.A. had five missions, thirteen stations, sixteen ministers, thirty-three assistants, and sixteen physicians in the foreign field. At home, it was aiding thirty-one churches. It even invaded the slave states; it sponsored a mission in Kentucky, as well as a traveling colporteur who went about the state distributing Bibles to both Negroes and whites. A brave soul, the latter reported in the *American Missionary* that, though persecuted "and having my name cast out as evil, yet in these things do I rejoice; for Christ has said, 'Blessed are they that suffer persecution for righteousness' sake; for theirs is the kingdom of Heaven.' "[16] Most of the society's missionaries faced other perils: jungle and swampland climate, disease, and undernourishment, rather than the hostility of the natives. Despite them, the organization throve, thanks to the skill of Lewis Tappan.[17]

One of the most promising and yet disappointing ventures that the A.M.A. undertook was its West Indian mission. Ever since West Indian emancipation, American abolitionists had taken a special interest in the freedmen of the sugar islands. The American reformers were convinced that English experience could point the way toward freeing the slaves in the United States. Tappan asked Amos Phelps to set down his opinions and recommendations after he returned from Jamaica in 1847. Although he had only a few months to live, Phelps complied, presenting readers of the *American Missionary* with some rather astute and well-reasoned proposals.

First, Phelps suggested that the mission force be urged to try a new approach, "dealing with the people in all things as men, and not as serviles, and aiming to make them a New England farming population." Although his suggestion sounded somewhat parochial, what he meant was that the whites should encourage the development of family farm life, with Negroes owning their own land, improving it, and taking pride in their efforts, until economic self-sufficiency prepared them for cultural and political education. "Nothing will give them a feeling of independence, and make them act like men, sooner than this," he predicted. It was also important for their advisers to spend less time in the pulpit and more time in training them how to work the land, even getting down in the muck to show the Negroes that white men knew how to use their hands as well as their tongues. "The missionaries should identify themselves with the people," he stressed, probably because most of them associated with the planter class almost exclusively. They ought not to live near the plantation estates in comfortable style; instead, they should locate their stations where there was land available on which the freedmen could develop their farming skills.[18]

Tappan was much impressed with these comments. "To buy land wherever they can, in little properties of their own, and put up their little houses, and get their other little comforts around them"—what a vision it must have created in his mind, the Jeffersonian (and indeed puritan) dream fulfilled with a black yeomanry. Phelps, however, recognized the formidable obstacles in the way. None of the English Caribbean islands, with the exception of Antigua, had thriven after 1833, though the cause was not so much emancipation as the blundering British colonial policy and the continued intransigence of the planters. As one governor pointed out, "the absence of self-control" of the "ruling classes"; the constant battles among colonial administrators in London, the Parliament, and the island legislative assemblies; and the Parliamentary intoxication with free trade (fostered by the Anti-Corn Law League) had disrupted political and economic life. A mounting depression in the late forties, accompanied by reduced wages, coolie competition, and the bankruptcy of many employers, frustrated hopes for an easy transition from a slave to a free-labor system. Because of these troubles, an abolitionist complained to Tappan, "We have not had anything to prove the good results of immediate, & unconditional Emancipation, etc."; he asked Tappan to do something to demonstrate British success in the Caribbean.[19]

In 1854, the Richmond Estate, located near the A.M.A. missionaries' Brainerd station in Jamaica, came on the market at the bargain price of $2,500. The plantation, consisting of 1,090 acres, including a sugar mill, mansion, and outlying buildings, was worth $50,000 in better times. From the reports of the A.M.A. missionaries, Tappan surmised that it was an ideal spot to try out Phelp's ideas. "Hitherto," Tappan wrote Sturge, "land owners would not sell in small parcels or the price demanded was so great that the purchase of land . . . was beyond the reach of the people."[20] The missionaries would sell the land in small lots, thus laying the groundwork for a demonstration to the white Jamaicans that

Negroes could become independent, industrious, and resolute farmers when given the chance.

Tappan's job was to raise the necessary funds to buy the plantation. That proved difficult, partly because his British friends were apparently sensitive about the failures of colonial policy and took little interest in the project. He made the down payment of $500 from the A.M.A. treasury, however, and over the next few years sold shares in the enterprise to antislavery friends as a way to obtain the remaining sum. Throughout these negotiations, he found the missionaries quarrelsome, petty, and oddly devious.[21]

He soon located the trouble. The missionaries had discovered what they hoped were rich copper veins on Negro-owned properties nearby and were taking more interest in arranging geological studies than in the Richmond Estate. Tappan did not care for this venture: "Nothing divides the mind more from spiritual things than the supposed wealth of mines." In response to his criticism, the Rev. A. D. Olds told Lewis bluntly to mind his own affairs. Although he did not know the details of how the missionaries intended to involve themselves in the copper business, Tappan sent Olds a lesson in morality; he wrote that he had given up trading on the Wall Street market because he had discovered that he always turned to the financial page instead of the religious column when he opened the morning paper. Instead, Tappan said, he invested in Brooklyn real estate, which offered security and fewer anxieties. He closed by warning that the Richmond Estate project would have to be dropped unless the missionaries showed greater zeal.[22] Then another A.M.A. agent bought land on his own and sold it to Negroes at a one hundred per cent profit. "Ought missionaries to do this?" Tappan exclaimed. "I think not. This mixing up of the merchant & missionary does not suit my views of things. Would Paul or Peter have done so?"[23]

In spite of these troubles, Tappan proceeded with the experiment. "If it can be demonstrated at Jamaica beyond cavil that the emancipated are benefitted in their social, moral, religious, & industrial capacities we can strike a very effective blow at American Slavery," he wrote Seth Wolcott, one of the few missionaries who did not engage in private speculations. "What sanguine hopes we had of this 17 years ago. How have these hopes been baffled in various ways." Gradually, the New York headquarters was able to increase its support of the Richmond venture; an industrial school was established in the large mansion, and parts of the estate were sold to Negroes in lots of five to ten acres at low interest charges.[24]

The experiment afforded Tappan the chance to call attention to English mistakes and to suggest better ways for Americans to handle the transition to freedom when the opportunity came. Ruefully, he told the readers of the *American Missionary* that the British had compensated the wrong individuals under their plan of 1833. "Justice required that part of the bounty should have been expended in supplying education, agricultural implements, and small lots on reasonable terms, to the freedmen." In addition, he said, the white planters did nothing to help the Negroes but forced them to rent small farms at four or five dollars per annum, if they were lucky, or else to serve as day laborers, if they were not. "In this way," he continued, more or less repeating Phelps's conclusions a decade earlier, "a spirit of servility and dependence, hostile to a free and healthful development of character[,] is fostered, and the degrading influence of slavery perpetuated."[25]

Tappan was not a social scientist; he had never visited the islands, nor did he ever go south, even after the Civil War. Yet, he was aware, like Phelps, that property and liberty could not be separated. It was an old Anglo-American tradition that neither could be safe in the absence of the other. Abolitionists had their weaknesses, but their study of the Negro led them sometimes to very sensible conclusions, even though they often failed themselves to live up to them. Lewis Tappan was not so completely devoted to religious instruction that he failed to see the need for secular education and economic opportunities for the race. In the *American Missionary*, he observed that sermonizing was insufficient. Negroes, he said, "need to be taught the mechanic arts, to be impressed with the dignity of labor [in contrast to the West Indian planters' latinized views of manual work], and the importance of self-exertion and self-dependence."[26]

The Richmond Estate did not fulfill Tappan's high hopes; it never served as an eloquent model for future American action. It was like most utopian communities of the era: its aims were lofty, but its performance disappointing. If all the land was ever sold to enterprising Negro farmers, the A.M.A. never bothered to acknowledge the achievement. By 1861, the original conception of the mission had largely been forgotten. Writing in the *American Missionary*, the Rev. C. C. Starbuck, one of the missionaries at the Richmond Estate, showed none of the characteristics of sympathy and goodwill recommended by Phelps. Far from regarding the black Jamaicans as equals, Starbuck recorded that they were "simple, unreflective, childlike," with a tendency to lie. He and his fellow agents found it hard to steer a course between "a rigor that finds no response in their own conscience and an indulgence that winks at what they themselves know to be wrong." He decided that "rigor" was the better plan. The industrial school continued to operate. Seth Wolcott declared that it was "designed to meet the wants of the mass—to develop self-dependent, and hence independent, manhood."[27] At the beginning of the Civil War, Tappan wrote a pamphlet that did not hesitate to pronounce West Indian emancipation a remarkable success. He did not use the effort at Richmond as a model for American action. Presumably, he accepted the verdict of Starbuck and the others, though Tappan at least could claim that the British policy proved the safety of immediate abolition.[28]

Tappan had little more success with the missions assigned to the fugitive slaves in Canada. Here, too, there was a concerted effort to plant freehold communities as a means of proving that Negroes were not inferior in talent or industry to whites. Hiram Wilson, one of the earliest of Weld's Oberlin apostles in the 1830's, had started a "model" community called the Dawn Institute near London, Ontario.[29] Wilson lacked administrative skill, and he soon was embroiled with Josiah Henson, a fugitive slave who sought to dominate the experiment himself. Although the A.M.A. and other agencies supported the enterprise, debts piled up quickly, and the internal squabbling dragged on for years. Finally, in 1851, John Scoble, Tappan's associate and secretary of the British and Foreign Anti-Slavery Society, crossed the Atlantic to conduct an investigation in behalf of the English benefactors backing the movement.

As if the Dawn Institute was not already in enough trouble, Garrisonian nostrils on both sides of the Atlantic quivered with the smell of Tappanite conspiracies in Canada. Mary Estlin, an English friend of Garrison and Maria Weston Chapman, warned the Bostonians that "we must do the best we can . . . to bring to light the various subterfuges by which people here are led astray, & keep them on their guard against Scoble [and] his ally Lewis Tappan." Miss Estlin, a Bristol spinster, had convinced herself that the two collaborators were "full of plots and counterplots. . . ." Exactly what she expected them to gain from association with the bankrupt Canadian experiment remained a mystery.[30] In any case, Scoble decided to take over the management of the Institute permanently.

Unfortunately, the Englishman, however good his intentions, was barely more successful than his predecessor. (Perhaps it would have been better to have let the Negroes manage their own affairs; even if they had managed them badly, they could hardly have been much less successful than their white leaders.) In 1857 Tappan gave Scoble advice that, though sound, was difficult to apply: "There needs an *esprit de corps* amongst the colored people—industry—economy—a desire to have their children educated. . . ." Discouraged by the ineffectiveness of his plans and the continuance of internal friction, Scoble wrote that colored people were simply ungrateful and "that a white man can do but little for them." They, on their side, found him aristocratic, impatient, and overbearing. Tappan was sympathetic: "It would be strange indeed if you, brought up in London, amidst intelligent & polished society, could so identify yourself with the colored people in Canada as to bear with them . . . & do them good. It requires almost super human qualities. Our Saviour was equal to it, but who of us is?" Scoble did the best he could, however, and the utopian venture stumbled along until 1868.[31] Once again, as in the Richmond effort, Tappan found that a significant obstacle was not that the black man was unprepared for his own freedom but that the white man was not prepared to co-operate with him in the proper spirit.

He wrote Sarah Grimké that "our progenitors were thought more contemptibly of than are the negroes by the whites of this country; that the millions of Irish &c pouring into this country do not endanger our institutions," and that probably the blacks would "excel the papists in this country in a half century, if emancipated, in intelligence, in capacity as electors, and as moral beings." The problem lay with the whites, whose cruelty had damaged the subjected race, contaminating even those tribes living on that part of the coast of Africa open to European intrusion. If it were ever proved that Negroes were an inferior race, he said, that inferiority would be the consequence of the ordination of God that the children of parents unnaturally brought together in slavery would suffer the defects of that state. Tappan concluded that what the abolitionists could do to right these evils was to prepare both races to live together in equality.[32]

In founding the A.M.A., with all its defects, Lewis Tappan had begun a worthwhile effort to make the American dream of equality come true. By 1860, the Association had expended over one million dollars on antislavery missions—in Africa, Jamaica, Siam, Turkey, and the Marquesas and Sandwich Islands, as well as in over one hundred places in this country. Although its unusual experiments were unsuccessful, the Association laid the groundwork for wartime and Reconstruction efforts to give Negroes both religious and secular education. Few abolitionists could claim to have played a more creative role than his. He sought not just the extermination of the gross injustices of the present but looked forward into the trying times of emancipation itself.

During these years, Susan Tappan's health declined. Managing the Tappan household was hard work. For years she had entertained her husband's clerical friends at a moment's notice, and in 1844 she supervised the move from New York City to a bigger house in Brooklyn Heights. Tappan felt sorry for his "poor wife," as he wrote Weld, but he was seldom on hand to help, and he never relaxed, even on summer vacation.[33] Instead, he spent the sultry days writing articles, reading religious reports, or speaking at a neighboring church or picnic about antislavery and missions.

Susan lost one of her favorite and gentlest daughters when Eliza died in 1841, but the rest of the family was healthy and active. Lucy Maria, a pretty girl, small like her parents, married the silk merchant Henry C. Bowen in 1844. The young couple lived in an outrageously grand style by Tappan's standards, for Bowen had accumulated money as only a sharp Connecticut Yankee could. For the summer holidays, he built a house in the wooden domestic Gothic style in his native town of Woodstock, near the Massachusetts border. A lover of roses, he had the house painted pink with red trimming and laid out elaborate flower beds and boxwood mazes; later, he added a bowling alley and a croquet court, though neither was used on Sundays. Some time in the 1850's he also built a mansion in southern colonial style in Brooklyn Heights, not far from the much more modest Tappan house on Pierrepont Street. Susan was happy about the first marriage in the new generation, and, as Lewis said in admiration, she "worked very hard making preparations for Lucy & has achieved all with her accustomed good taste & judgment."[34]

Susan, named in memory of their eldest child, who died in 1817, also married well. Hiram Barney, a former member of the Young Men's Anti-Slavery Society of New York City, was a lawyer with a clientele drawn mainly from dry-goods houses. He later joined the prosperous firm of Benjamin F. Butler, an associate of Martin Van Buren and a Free Soiler.[35] Julia was still unmarried. She was an intelligent young lady but, like so many women of that era, was unable to find good use for her talents. She was very helpful to her father as a secretary and lessened the burden of housework for her mother. Susan once wrote her on the occasion of one of Julia's infrequent trips from home, "I miss my little *hand-maid very much.*"[36]

William, after completing his law training, worked for a while in the Mercantile Agency. Association with his father was not pleasant to him, however, and they shortly broke their connection. Rebelling against his father's puritanism, he grew interested in Transcendentalism and literary pursuits. A friend of Nathaniel Hawthorne and Ralph Waldo Emerson, William could hardly have expected his father to approve of his inclinations. "I have been apprehensive that William's acquaintance with Mr. E[merson] would be disadvantageous to him. Let us pray," he wrote a relative, "that it may not be so & that God will add to Wms many amiable qualities the riches of His grace."[37] In 1847, William married Caroline Sturgis, daughter of a wealthy Boston merchant and a Transcendentalist herself. They lived for many years on a farm in the Berkshires called "Highwood," though by the time Miss Mary Aspinwall Tappan and Mrs. Gorham Brooks, their daughters, donated the estate to the Boston Symphony Orchestra in 1913 it was known as "Tanglewood."[38]

With three daughters still at home—Georgiana, Ellen, and Julia—the household was still large enough to prevent Susan from fully recovering from the trials of the years since leaving Brookline. Unfortunately, the letters between Lewis and his wife are so few and his diary entries so full of public business that it is impossible to say with any certainty how happy the couple were in each other's company. Susan loved her husband, it may be said, even if his work often carried him from home. In a letter to Julia, she remarked with a certain pride after Tappan had given an antislavery address, "He bears his popularity modestly."[39] Tappan, for his part, seems to have taken his wife somewhat for granted.

In 1853, Susan collapsed from exhaustion and, after an illness of several weeks, died on March 24. Tappan did not record his feelings in much detail in his diary, but he wrote the Welds, "In the midst of the sorrow that I feel under this heavy bereavement I am grateful to that Good Being who spared my dear companion so many years & made her such a blessing."[40] But Arthur Tappan believed that Susan's death called for something more from Lewis. Julia seemed on the verge of a nervous breakdown, and the younger sisters, Georgiana and Ellen, also took the loss very hard. Approaching Lewis about the need for a comforting and steadying influence at home, Arthur urged him to spend more time with them than at his "public duties." "I think so to[o]," Lewis noted in his diary, "but am in a dilemma about what is due from me to each & whether, after devoting proper time to them I can be an efficient Sec. of the Soc. May God direct!"[41]

It did not take Lewis long to reach a decision. A few days later, a Mrs. Rose Porter arrived in New York City with a nine-year-old Negro girl whom she had kidnapped from Charles Trainer, her father, in Cincinnati. A white friend there telegraphed Tappan to bring legal action against the woman, whom Tappan's hired agent located in "a house of ill-fame" on Mercer Street. For several weeks thereafter, Tappan was busy attending the court sessions, consulting with the lawyers he had retained, and publicizing the case in the local and antislavery press. Eventually Trainer and his daughter were reunited, though Mrs. Porter was never indicted for kidnapping.[42]

Meanwhile, Julia's condition grew worse. Tappan sent her off to a water-cure establishment near Rochester, while he took Ellen and Georgiana on a tour of the White Mountains for the summer. It must have been rather dull for the girls, since their father disapproved of "young ladies waltzing with strangers," but they did not know the dance anyway, as he was pleased to learn.[43] After he returned to Brooklyn, Julia sent him a telegram from Rochester, urging him to come at once. He left on a Sunday morning, breaking his Sabbatarian rule. On arrival, he found her near hysteria. When she had calmed herself, she let him know that she had become the dupe of "a clown, an ignoramus, an adulterer, a liar"— namely, the doctor in charge of the health resort. For the first time in his life, he had to deal with a domestic problem without Susan's help. He took Julia to another hotel and stayed with her there for over a month, giving her the understanding and sympathy she desperately needed. With his aid, she finally recovered her usual spirits. Nevertheless, there was little occupation for a daughter of Lewis Tappan, or indeed for any woman, outside the home. She could have become a missionary, but, like William, she was not religiously inclined.[44]

Her father, however, had no intention of being lonely for very long. Although he was sixty-five when Susan died, Tappan felt as fit and virile as ever. After an A.M.A. convention at Worcester, he visited William Jackson, the society's president, at his home in Newton, Massachusetts. There he met Jackson's daughter Sarah, a lady of mature years whose deceased husband had been a mayor of Boston. Although childless, she considered herself an expert on the moral training of youth. "Remember, too, that religion does not consist in joy," she warned young ladies in her *Letters to a Young Christian,* a small book published by the Female Guardian Society. "The question is not 'How have you felt to-day?' . . . but *'For whom are you living? Is all on the altar?'*" Like Lewis Tappan, Sarah believed that it was wrong to be *"unequally yoked together with unbelievers."* After a courtship of six months, the couple were married on April 4, the year after Susan's death. They returned immediately to New York, where Tappan plunged again into his labors, though he managed to take his bride to hear a public lecture by a Dr. Folger on "The Present State of Europe."[45]

Lewis Tappan did not honor Susan with a word in his diary on the first anniversary of her death. Yet he did pay special tribute to the memory of his mother two days later, on March 26. "Sweet spirit," he wrote after gazing at Gilbert Stuart's portrait of her, "I looked this morning at thy benign & peaceful countenance— thought of thy tender love—of thy joyful life that now is—and prayed that we might see each other & dwell with each other thro' the endless ages of eternity." Tappan's diary often reads as if it were suitable for a public gathering. Perhaps his praise for his mother was a substitute for his failure to observe Susan's death day. Sarah probably read all his entries. Unlike Finney, who had remarried a few years before, Tappan did not embarrass her "by talking about his first wife."[46]

According to family tradition, the second marriage was a matter of convenience, not love. Certainly Julia disliked the new occupant of the Tappan house in Brooklyn Heights. One anecdote has it that Sarah took all the Aspinwall heirlooms to the nearest auctioneer and that Julia, Lucy Maria, and the other daughters had to buy them back at fancy prices. The story may be true; Lewis

Tappan can be expected to have agreed with Sarah that there were too many unnecessary pieces about the place. Unlike his daughters, Tappan found Sarah a delightful and useful lady. She shared all his hopes for an evangelized world and devoted her time to sending packages to A.M.A. missionaries and performing other charitable tasks. She replaced Julia as his secretary, scanning articles and reports for him, and she accompanied him on many of his excursions. Unencumbered by family duties, she was ideal for Tappan in his declining years, and he loved her as much as, perhaps more than, Susan, though for different reasons.[47] Indeed, so successful was this second marriage that it seemed to restore Lewis' energies and equip him for new antislavery assignments.

If Tappan displayed no special loyalty to Susan, he was as faithful as ever to his luckless brother. In 1854, Arthur Tappan sold his shares in the Mercantile Agency and put his holdings into a machine-making plant in New Jersey; once again, he was seeking compulsively to turn a quick fortune and thereby to assume his former role of benefactor. Shortly afterward, he discovered that his business associate had enticed him into the arrangement only as a means of sharing his misfortunes with a gullible partner. The factory was heavily in debt, and Arthur as partner was liable. Soon, Arthur's funds had entirely disappeared into the pockets of creditors, and the factory was put up for bankruptcy sale. Once more Arthur was faced with humiliation and penury.

Lewis took great pains to lead Arthur out of the morass into which he had plunged almost suicidally. He inspected the factory ledgers, conferred with lawyers, and assisted in the final disposal of the company's property. The problem about Arthur's future still remained. Lewis' solution was to bring suit against Benjamin Douglass, their former colleague in the Mercantile Agency. After all, Douglass was in a sense fair game: as Lewis later said, "an Old School Presbyterian—a pro Slavery man—and a Buchananite" (though these characteristics had not kept Lewis from allowing Douglass to resuscitate the Agency years before). The idea of the suit was to extract another large payment for the dissolution of Arthur Tappan's partnership in the Agency on the grounds that the original settlement was grossly inadequate because all of the company's assets had not been included in that settlement. Months of complicated court action were required, but the new litigation ultimately resulted in an additional twelve-thousand-dollar settlement in Arthur's favor. Although it was some eight thousand dollars less than Lewis anticipated, the sum provided the merchant, still sick with worry and as querulous as ever, with a modest income for his remaining years.

Arthur husbanded his reserve with reasonable success until the Civil War. By then, many charities were clamoring urgently for funds for worthy measures that Arthur could not resist. In spite of his advanced age and years of obscurity, he invested much of his capital in real estate speculations in war-torn West Virginia. Coal, it had been whispered, was likely to make the area a second California. The boom was only a dream. Perhaps fortunately, Arthur died before the coal speculations collapsed; there was enough cash, however, to fulfill most of the benevolent donations he had stipulated in his will.

Lewis' uncomplaining and persistent support of his brother reveals the affection in his nature more clearly than any other aspect of his personal relations.[48] As he wrote John Tappan of Arthur, "Though he has made some great mistakes in money matters, yet his many valuable qualities should induce us to show him all the substantial marks of affection we can. . . ."[49] In a country that honored monetary success so highly and considered the bankrupt as morally unfit for decent society, Lewis bravely insisted that Arthur was a great and good man, a better man than John, for instance. While Arthur lived, Lewis always made certain that his brother was kept abreast of antislavery news and that he was appointed to honorary offices in the religious abolitionist organizations. After his brother's death, Lewis wrote a biography of Arthur to prove to posterity that business failings did not dull the luster of Arthur's benevolent deeds.

NOTES

1. LT to Sturge, February 20, 1849, ltrbk.; Barnes, *Antislavery Impulse,* 197, recognizes this continuance of the moral spirit, though he considers Garrison a deviant from it and ends his account in 1844, thus neglecting the persistent efforts against conservative church bodies after that period.

2. *Liberator,* June 12, 1857.

3. WLG to Elizabeth Pease, July 2, 1842, WLG MSS, BPL (quotation).

4. Parker Pillsbury, *The Acts of the Anti-Slavery Apostles* (Boston, 1884), 49–

51, 131; Louis Filler, "Parker Pillsbury: An Antislavery Apostle," *New England Quarterly* XIX (September, 1946), 323 ff.; Garrison and Garrison, *Garrison,* III, 27–28; see also Mrs. Chapman's remark, as quoted by Oscar Sherwin, *Prophet of Liberty: The Life and Times of Wendell Phillips* (New York, 1958), 96.

5. See Wyatt-Brown, "Garrison and Antislavery Unity," 5–24.

6. LT to Sturge, October 7, 1846, ltrbk.; LT to Julius LeMoyne, December 26, 1849, LeMoyne MSS, LC; scrapbook, clipping of LT in *Watchman and Crusader* (New York), March 8, 1856; LT in *National Intelligencer,* March 5, 1850.

7. LT in *National Era,* August 9, 1851.

8. *National Anti-Slavery Standard,* October 19, 1843.

9. LT to James H. Hammond, March 25, June 6, 1845, James H. Hammond MSS, LC; see also *ibid.,* June 22, 1850; James Hammond to LT, June 17, 1845, Claude W. Unger MSS, Pennsylvania Historical Society; see also diary, June 30, 1850.

10. LT to O'Neall, September 28, 1844, ltrbk.; see also *ibid.,* April 29, July 19, 1844; LT to Clarkson, May 6, September 14, 1844, LT to William Jay, June 14, 1844, LT to Giddings, April 30, 1844, LT to Sturge, April 30, 1844, ltrbk.; Abel and Klingberg, *Side-Light,* 184–85; LT, "From an Unpublished History of Slavery," *Independent,* February 26, 1857; diary, February 15, 1857; E. Wright to editor, March 23, 1844, *Anti-Slavery Reporter,* V (April 3, 1844), 59.

11. LT to Phelps, September 26, 1842, Phelps MSS, BPL; the best source for a history of the A.M.A. is Clifton Herman Johnson, "The American Missionary Association," Ph.D. dissertation, University of North Carolina, Chapel Hill, 1958; LT, *History of the American Missionary Association* (New York, 1855), 1–11; *First Annual Report of the American Missionary Association, Read at New York, September 29, 1847* (New York, 1847); A&FASR, June, 1842.

12. LT to Phelps, January 4, 12, and 16, April 25, May 17, 1844, Phelps MSS, BPL; *Union Missionary,* May, 1844, April and October, 1845; LT, *AMA History,* 17–20; *American Missionary,* I (October, 1846), *passim.* The Union Missionary Society supported missions to the Obijue Indians west of Lake Superior in Minnesota, a Jamaica mission, and the Sandwich Island (Hawaii) station of Jonathan S. Green, brother of Beriah Green, with whom Tappan corresponded for many years; see LT MSS, LC. Pennington had an unfortunate career after this period; Tappan learned in 1854 that he had become "a confirmed drunkard, has used his friends wrongfully, is greatly in debt, is neglecting his parishioners, and contriving . . . to obtain money under false pretenses": diary, February 13, 1854. Samuel Francis Smith, *History of Newton, Massachusetts . . .* (Boston, 1880), 785; Henry K. Rowe, *Tercentenary History of Newton, 1630–1930* (Newton, 1930), 104, 110–11, 118, 119, 121; diary, February 13, 1854, 88 (quotation).

13. LT's obituary for Phelps, *American Missionary,* I (September, 1847); LT to Whipple, interoffice, December 1 and 7, 1847, AMA MSS, Fisk; *American Missionary,* II (September, 1848), 86–87. The MSS of Dr. D. B. Bradley are in the Oberlin College Library and AMA MSS, Fisk. Diary, April 14, 1853. See LT's complaint to Jocelyn, January 20, 1856, ltrbk.; Jocelyn to LT, December 10, 1856; diary, December 11, 1856.

14. [LT,] "A Friend of Free Missions," "The American Missionary Association— Its Claims on Anti-Slavery Christians," *American Missionary,* VII (October, 1853), 101.

15. LT to Whipple, December 1, 7, 1847, March 30, April [?], 1848, and

Whipple to LT, May 1, 1848, AMA MSS, Fisk; "Farewell to Missionaries," *American Missionary*, III (November, 1849); LT to Sturge, December 18, 1849, October 29, 1850, ltrbk., give examples, though a complete citation would be too long to include here.

16. *American Missionary*, VII (September, 1853), 91.

17. Certainly the most pestilent of all the assignments was the Mendi mission, where missionaries died with depressing regularity after a few months or years. Dr. Raymond, for instance, only lasted until 1847. On learning of the deaths of two Mendi missionaries, LT wrote, "Sad news! But the Lord reigns. . . . I will not let the melancholy intelligence . . . engross my mind, but, by God's help, resign it all to Him & press forward in the work in which I am engaged" (diary, December 9, 1855).

18. *American Missionary*, I (September, 1847), 81; LT to G. W. Alexander, February 23, 1847, Abel and Klingberg, *Side-Light*, 218.

19. Sir Alan Burns, *History of the British West Indies* (New York, 1965 ed.), 652–53 (quotation); see also *ibid.*, 651–63; James M. McPherson, *The Struggle for Equality: Abolitionists and the Negro in the Civil War and Reconstruction* (Princeton, 1964), 185–86n, and "Was West Indian Emancipation a Success? The Abolitionist Argument during the American Civil War," *Caribbean Studies*, IV, No. 2, 28–34; James W. West to LT (quotation), October 3, 1854.

20. LT to Sturge, November 27, 1854, January 3, 1855, ltrbk.; LT in *American Missionary*, X (August, 1856), 77.

21. LT to A. M. Richardson, January 4, 1855, ltrbk., in which he said that a friend in England (Sturge) did not think the missionaries capable of running the estate and that, furthermore, most Negroes were already landowners; LT to Seth T. Wolcott, Jamaica, December 2, 1854, LT to A. D. Olds, December 19 and 24, 1854, January 3, 1855, LT to Whipple and Jocelyn, interoffice, January 4, 1855, ltrbk. Later, Sturge gave generously to this effort; see LT to Mrs. L. E. Sturge, August 3, 1857, *ibid.*

22. LT to A. D. Olds, December 19, 1854, January 3, 1855, LT to Bailey, January 10, 1850, LT to A. M. Richardson, January 4, 1855, and LT to Jocelyn and Whipple, January 4, 1855, ltrbk. LT to Julia Tappan, November 4, 1857, *ibid.*, estimates his wealth at $60,000.

23. LT to A. M. Richardson, January 31, 1855, *ibid.*

24. LT to Wolcott, May 24, 1855, LT to S. W. Jones, February 10, 1856, ltrbk.; *American Missionary*, X (August, 1856), 76-77; see also *ibid.*, II, new series (February, 1858), 26.

25. *American Missionary*, X (August, 1856), 77; see also LT to James Hurnard, Colchester, England, March 17, 1855; LT to Sarah Grimké, March 21, 1857, ltrbk.

26. *American Missionary*, X (August, 1856), 77; diary, July 8, 1853.

27. Starbuck in *American Missionary*, V, new series (November, 1861), 253; *ibid.*, II (January, 1858), 4; Wolcott in *ibid.* (February, 1858), 25–26; *ibid.* (April, 1858), 75–78.

28. LT, *Immediate Emancipation: The Only Wise and Safe Mode* (New York, 1861), 1–16; see also LT to William A. Stearns, May 24, 1855, ltrbk. Luckily, Negro dissatisfaction did not erupt in Jamaica until 1865, or southerners would have had additional arguments against the safety of emancipation. See Arvel B. Erickson, "Empire or Anarchy: the Jamaica Rebellion of 1865," *JNH*, XLIV (April, 1959), 99–122.

29. William H. and Jane H. Pease, *Black Utopia: Communal Experiments in America* (Madison, 1963), 63–65, 70–71.

30. M. A. Estlin to Maria Weston Chapman [?], 1851, Mary Estlin to E. Weston, December 29, 1851, J. B. Estlin to C. Weston, March 20, 1852, J. B. Estlin to Maria Weston Chapman, April 3, 1852, Weston MSS, BPL.

31. LT to Scoble, June 19, 1857, ltrbk.; LT to Richard Littleboy, June 18, 1857, ltrbk.; see also Scoble to LT, April 5, 1860, AMA MSS, Fisk. There is also a collection of letters from Josiah Henson and others at Dawn to LT and the Union Missionary Society at Rutgers University, giving some descriptions of the conditions of fugitives in Canada during the early 1840's; see also LT to Thomas Henning, Toronto, April 3, 1853, *Frederick Douglass' Paper*, April 22, 1853; diary, April 13, 1853; Pease and Pease, *Black Utopia*, 81–83; LT to Richard Littleboy, June 18, 1857, ltrbk.; diary, October 25, 1855, clipping.

32. LT to Sarah Grimké, March 21, May 23, 1857, ltrbk.

33. LT to Weld, July 17, 1844, LT to Julia Tappan, July 30, August 8, 1844, LT to Birney, July 29, 1844, ltrbk.

34. LT to John Tappan, June 9, 1844, LT to Charles Tappan, May 3, 1844, LT to Weld, June 26, 1844, *ibid.*

35. See "Hiram Barney," *Dictionary of American Biography;* obituary by W. A. Butler, New York *Tribune,* May 20, 1895, scrapbook clipping.

36. Susan Tappan to Julia Tappan, June 5, 1848, private collection.

37. LT to Mrs. John Bigelow, March 31, 1846, ltrbk.

38. Louise Hall Tharp, *The Peabody Sisters of Salem* (Boston, 1950), 350–51; see also Susan Tappan to Julia Tappan, July 10, 1849, Julia to Susan Tappan, January 26, 1850, private collection; Leon Howard, *Herman Melville: A Biography* (Berkeley, 1958 ed.), 160; Randall Stewart, ed., *The American Notebooks by Nathaniel Hawthorne* . . . (New Haven, 1932), September 17, 1849, 129, September 4, 1850, 132, July 29, 1851, 217, August 5, 1851, 226, 305n, 329n.

39. Susan Tappan to Julia Tappan, July 5, 1848, private collection.

40. Copy, diary, March 30, 1853; see also *ibid.*, March 25–30, 1853; obituary, *Independent,* March 31, 1853; LT to BT, March 9, 1853, Charles Tappan to BT, March 22, 1853, BT MSS, LC. The children inherited Susan's property in Brookline; LT's description of the land and other documents, deeds, and wills in the Caroline Sturgis MSS, Houghton Library, Harvard.

41. Diary, April 21, 1853.

42. Diary entries for May 9 to June 13, 1853; *Anti-Slavery Reporter,* I (August 1, 1853), 169–72, and I (September 1, 1853), 193–99. Trainer later sued Mrs. Porter and received $775; see diary, February 27, 1854.

43. Diary, July 30, 1853; LT to BT, August 11, 1853, BT MSS, LC.

44. Diary, August 17, 1853 (quotation); see also *ibid.*, April 22, 1853; August 14, 15, and 18 and August 29–September 14, 1853; LT to Julia Tappan, June 12, 1857, ltrbk., warning her against the bogus spiritualism of Andrew Jackson Davis.

45. Sarah (Jackson) Davis, *Letters to a Young Christian* (New York, 1852), 25, 59; diary, October 4, April 4 and 7, 1853.

46. LT to T. B. Hudson, December 22, 1858, ltrbk.

47. The family anecdotes and impressions of Sarah were undoubtedly handed down by "Aunt Julia"; see diary, October 17, 1854.

48. LT to John W. Sullivan, May 3, 1857, ltrbk. (quotation); AT to Henry C. Bowen and S. B. Hart, October 13, 1854, Clarence W. Bowen Scrapbook, Ameri-

can Antiquarian Society, Worcester; LT to BT, November 17, 1854, ltrbk., and December 10, 1855, BT MSS, LC; LT to Frances (Antill) Tappan, December 10, 1854, LT to Naylor & Co., December 19, 1854, LT to AT, December 19, 1854, January 4 and 18, October 31, November 12, 1855, LT to Josiah S. Leverett, December 19, 1854, LT to John Tappan, January 18, 1855, LT to Benjamin Douglass, March 9, 1855, ltrbk.; diary, May 18, December 9 and 24, 1855; LT to J. H. Mott, July 25, October 11, 1855; LT to John F. Seymour, October 9, 1855, and other ltrbk. entries for October and November, 1855; LT to Hiram Barney, December 20, 1855, ltrbk.; AT to LT, December 12, 1863; diary, August 30, 1865; LT to William H. Edwards, November 19, 1870 (copy ?), LT MSS, LC.

49. LT to John Tappan, May 20, 1857, ltrbk.

CHAPTER SIXTEEN

Antislavery and the Evangelical Movement

*T*hroughout *the 1840's,* Lewis Tappan and William Lloyd Garrison shared the leadership of the antislavery crusade. Garrison retained his control of the radical elements, exercising an influence that was perhaps disproportionate to his effective power and the size of his following, but Tappan served as the co-ordinator of the activities of a great number of abolitionists. His influence cannot be measured by popular vote, since he made no serious attempt to gain political or church office, nor can it be assessed by his management of the "new organization" or the A.M.A., important though that was. Instead, his correspondence and other association with hundreds of clergymen, reformers, and pious laymen both here and abroad gave him a wide network of channels of advice and persuasion, actively maintained from 1840 to 1860.[1] He owed his pre-eminence in religious antislavery circles not primarily to his speaking abilities (though he was a good orator) but to his persistence. With the exception of Garrison, J. Miller McKim, John Greenleaf Whittier, and perhaps a few other delegates to the Philadelphia Convention of 1833, no other abolitionist could boast a longer or more dedicated life of reform. None had a more consistent policy spanning the antebellum and war years. No layman in the evangelical movement used his influence on clerical policies to better purpose.

Attrition among the ecclesiastical reformers also helped to single him out. Some died or retired, but many renounced their orthodox faith. Elizur Wright, for instance, published an attack in 1846 on the doctrine of future punishment in a weekly paper he had started in Boston. In spite of Lewis Tappan's rejoinder, Wright also denied the Hopkinsian principles of a "hell-spurred religion."[2] Gerrit Smith, the eccentric Stephen Pearl Andrews, the Welds, Joshua R. Giddings, James Birney, George W. Julian, and Julia Ward Howe were among those outside the Garrisonian camp who also adopted some form of a religion of humanity. According to Julian, an antislavery Congressman from Indiana, "They were theologically reconstructed through their unselfish devotion to humanity and the recreancy of the churches to which they had been attached. They were less orthodox, but more Christian." Giddings, who was raised in the same faith as the Tappans, could shiver nostalgically when he recalled his childhood faith, for he considered himself as having been emancipated from a fear-ridden cult. By 1856, he was predicting that slavery and other kinds of oppression and barbarism would be wrecked upon "the sterile coast of political and religious conservatism" and that a new world, free from corruption and outmoded superstitions, would emerge.[3] For him, humanitarianism and Calvinism were irreconcilable, as they had been for the Garrisonians since 1837. In general, the ideas of what was sometimes called Free Religion were not formally institutionalized, partly in reaction to the formalism of the orthodox churches, but their popularity among intellectuals, in New England especially, was bound to affect the abolitionist leaders. Ironically, Lewis Tappan, leader of the traditional wing of the antislavery movement, had helped to engender the new spirit, for his own agitation for immediate and unconditional emancipation had been one of the causes of the weakening of the church system to which he was so faithful.

William Jay was particularly alarmed by the development of religious deviancy, writing his old friend Lewis Tappan, "Very many abolitionists are running headlong into infidelity & jacobinism; & thus absolutely exclude from all co-operation with them the sober-minded men. . . ."[4] He was not complaining only about the Garrisonians. Though few abolitionists went so far as to deny the validity of institutional Christianity itself, the rebellion against Calvinism was reaching its climax.

Tappan's loyalty to church antislavery in a sense increased his own power with the rank-and-file abolitionists in the forties, although it cut him off from some former associates. A new generation of clerical abolitionists appeared in the 1850's—Henry Ward Beecher, George B. Cheever, and others—whose fame outdistanced his own as the spokesmen of ecclesiastical antislavery. The new group was rather distinct from the old abolitionists who had attended the Philadelphia Convention of 1833. Perhaps the character of a second generation of reformers or revolutionaries is always somewhat different from that of the first. In the antislavery movement, this later set did not have to face the degree of scorn and rough handling that had been the lot of Tappan and his associates. Perhaps because violence had impinged less directly upon them, they were generally less hesitant to advocate it—for righteous purposes to be sure. But to Beecher antislavery was less a commitment burned into the soul than a badge memorializing that conviction. Tappan and his friends had convinced the true-hearted Yankee evangelical that antislavery was his birthright and the proper means of expressing his sectional identity. The new generation of church-minded reformers to carry forward the banner of antislavery acted mostly from force of habit and therefore felt the need of reassurance and recommitment, sometimes in calls to arms. Just as evangelicalism for Lewis Tappan was an emotional allegiance to but not an intellectual acceptance of the faith of his mother, so antislavery was becoming by the 1850's an expression of something imperfectly remembered but nostalgically moving. Antislavery was gradually being modified to fit the growing complacency of the reformers themselves. Antislavery success, though still modest, was breeding its own failure; abolitionists of the Cheever and Beecher stripe (and also the former Liberty men like Leavitt and Stanton) could be reasonably well satisfied with the Free Soil and Republican movements as the embodiments of the antislavery tradition. At the same time they were beginning to look upon Garrisonian disunion with a disapproval that time had somewhat tempered. The radical rhetoric had lost some of its novelty and thus some of its impact; they could even listen to the speeches and conversations of Garrison, dean of antislavery, with that respect and indulgence that is usually accorded chieftains past their prime and retired statesmen.

Lewis Tappan prepared the way for these new leaders; he tried to keep them true to the old doctrines of racial equality and immediate emancipation. But the lines of argument that he took in the 1840's to bring the evangelical movement to what seemed to him the right ground were developed by others in the following decade. Beecher, Cheever, and their kind did not urge a renewed effort to bring Negroes into white churches in fellowship; they did not add new ideas to those that Lewis Tappan helped to promulgate; principally, they repeated the antisouthern abolitionist arguments, with increasing effect, following along the paths that Lewis had laid out.

As early as 1834, the American Anti-Slavery Society had tried to convert the other benevolent societies to its position. Initial rebuffs, however, kept the Society from pursuing that aim with much vigor thereafter, and it concentrated upon building a hard core of antislavery followers. Once the evangelicals separated from Garrison, however, the attack against the so-called "benevolent empire" was renewed in earnest. Most conservative and powerful among these agencies was the American Board of Commissioners for Foreign Missions (the A.B.C.F.M.). In 1842, Lewis Tappan was writing colleagues that the Board ought to be investigated and exposed.[5] What aroused his attention was the fact that its missionaries to the Cherokee and Choctaw tribes condoned slaveholding as well as polygamy. The Board defended the policy on the grounds that it was hard enough to win converts to Christianity without interfering in established customs. Antislavery sentiment grew, however, and the Board took a strongly antislavery position at its meeting in Brooklyn in 1845, though it left the missionaries in the field with discretionary powers. Tappan was pleased with this change, even if it was not up to the abolitionist mark. "We think," he wrote Sturge optimistically, "that when the 'American Board' gets right we shall have but little difficulty in persuading the people that Slavery is altogether disgraceful to church & state."[6]

Three years passed without further developments in the Board's policies, and Tappan grew impatient. "Nothing will bring the A.B.C.F.M. to right action so soon as outspoken remonstrance, withholding of funds, and commendation of the A.M. Assoc.," he wrote a clerical supporter. Abolitionist agitation, which included the jabs of the Garrisonians, was constant against the Board throughout the 1850's. No less concerned than Tappan, William Jay published articles announcing that the proslavery agency winked at "atrocities unknown to the despotisms of Europe." It was wrong, the abolitionists declared, to misrepresent Christianity in this way by not preaching the sinfulness of enslaving fellow creatures. A clergyman at an antislavery gathering in Chicago in 1851 urged his audience thereafter to give its money to the American Missionary Association.[7] The propaganda began to have its effect, as evangelicals transferred their allegiance in growing numbers to the A.M.A. Under these pressures, the Board endorsed some modestly liberal suggestions of its secretary Selah Treat in 1854 and denounced the Cherokee nation for not allowing Negro children the chance for education. Such a display was not enough to satisfy Tappan, but what irked him especially was that so slight a thaw encouraged the northern religious press, including the *Independent,* which represented Beecherite antislavery, to hail the Board for its courage and humanity. He protested vigorously and with telling effect.[8]

The following year the A.B.C.F.M. elected General John Hartwell Cocke as one of its vice-presidents. Tappan was outraged. The general held over a thousand slaves, he reported, in gross exaggeration. Undoubtedly, Lewis was really trying to embarrass his brother John, who he knew had engineered the appointment for his friend. Appearing as a card in the New York *Tribune,* Tappan's attack on the Christian slaveholder aroused considerable agitation. Conservatives maintained that Lewis had gone too far. The publicity may have been a factor in the more liberal line adopted at the next A.B.C.F.M. convention, when a resolution inimical to slavery passed, much to Tappan's satisfaction.[9]

The Board's responses to pressure from proslavery and antislavery forces were characteristically nerveless, and its ultimate decision was to abandon the Indian missions altogether. By 1861 all missionary stations in the Indian territories were closed, and the Board contented itself with maintaining a sulky neutrality on these moral issues. Tappan had won no commanding victory by the time war began, but he had awakened the conscience of many northern clergymen and laymen and gained their support for his own A.M.A.[10]

The other benevolent societies were hardly less conservative than the A.B.C.F.M. The American Bible Society, for instance, had long been the target of the Tappan brothers, ever since the Tappans' 1834 campaign to supply Bibles for distribution to slaves. In 1851, William Jay examined the Society's records and discovered that the fund allocated for southern Negro efforts varied from $1,222.69 in 1848, when Joshua Leavitt had conducted a drive for that purpose, to an absurd $5.50 in 1851.[11] Tappan and Jay wrote resolutions for the American and Foreign Anti-Slavery Society conventions, published articles, and made other kinds of entreaties of the usual pattern, but the Bible Society, though embarrassed, refused to be coerced, insisting that its auxiliaries had full autonomy to treat the slave issue as they chose.[12]

Other organizations also received the attention of the two antislavery partners. While Jay, for his part, protested the absence of antislavery materials in the American Tract Society catalogue, Tappan, for his, exposed the expurgations of unfriendly comments on slavery from the Sunday School Union publications. The publicity worried Francis Packard, secretary of the latter group, but no substantial change of policy resulted. Taking over from Judge Jay, who was seriously ill, Tappan spoke for over an hour before the Life Directors of the Tract Society in 1858, but his proposal that the Society publish a mild admonition to slaveholders on the treatment of slaves was soundly defeated.[13]

Although primarily concerned with the conversion of the Congregational-Presbyterian denominations and the benevolent associations they led, Tappan did not spare any evangelicals who deviated from abolitionist principles. Generally, he could count on the support of British Dissenting churchmen. Though they sometimes failed to speak out against slavery when traveling in America, they usually aligned themselves with his branch of the cause when they were on safer soil. "We are strengthened by the sympathy and example of the abolitionists of Great Britain," he once wrote.[14]

American Protestants rejoiced at the founding of the Scottish Free Kirk, led by Dr. Thomas Chalmers, in 1843. Not only was the Free Kirk a blow to the prestige of the Established Church of Scotland, but it constituted a powerful addition to the Calvinistic forces in both countries. Chalmers, however, solicited "bloodstained" money from Southern Presbyterians on a tour in 1844. In vain Tappan urged the Free Kirk representatives to avoid that sort of compromise. When Chalmers vigorously assailed his abolitionist critics, Tappan wrote Sturge that he was afraid that the churchman's defense "is to put down what we have been attempting for 10 years to build up. . . . It is administering an opiate to Northern proslavery ministers who have been placed in an awkward position by Anti-Slavery arguments & entreaties." Since Scotland was perhaps more thoroughly attuned to antislavery

315

principles than other parts of the Kingdom, Chalmers' policy was a serious defeat for American abolitionists.[15] Tappan urged his British friends "to bring public sentiment to bear" on the Free Kirk through the regular means of agitation. Meanwhile, the American and Foreign Anti-Slavery Society issued a strong "Remonstrance," which circulated widely as a pamphlet and in the religious press of both countries. Not surprisingly, Garrison also turned his guns on the Scottish sect and sent Frederick Douglass and James Buffum to join George Thompson on the rostrum against it in Great Britain. Later, he went over himself. The Garrisonians were as convinced as Tappan "that there is no power out of the Church that could maintain Slavery, if the Church attacked it in earnest."[16] For all their contempt for each other's "bigotry" and "infidelity," both antislavery groups attached more importance to the reformation of the churches than to any other aspect of the cause.

So virulent was the abolitionists' reaction to the Chalmers' American tour that the Evangelical Alliance, formed to unite all evangelical elements in the United States and England against the threat of popery and other "heresies," was seriously weakened, though it continued to exist. Chalmers, the American Old School Presbyterian Robert Baird, who had once helped Arthur with his Mississippi Valley missionary campaign, and its other leaders could blame the rise of antislavery for their failure. Writing to John Scoble, then secretary of the British and Foreign Anti-Slavery Society, Tappan boasted that the Alliance stood "but little better here than the Colonization Society," which by this time had fallen on very evil days.[17]

Tappan was always vigilant in insuring that his English friends did not accept every American clerical visitor at face value. Some years later, a member of the Alliance, Dr. Chickering of Maine, took a clear antislavery position while in England. When Tappan learned of it, he publicized the incident thoroughly, pointing out that moderate clergymen like Chickering seldom spoke out at home. "It is no libel on our great body of Northern clergy to say that, in regard to the wrongs of the colored people . . . their highest merit consists in [not] afflicting new injuries on their wounded brother." While a few Yankee pastors—"Cotton Parsons," they were called—such as Nehemiah ("Southside") Adams of Boston, defended slavery on humanitarian and Biblical grounds as if they had been southerners themselves, most Protestant ministers were sluggishly indifferent and timid.[18] Tappan's unremitting efforts had the limited effect of pressing some of the national benevolent institutions into a defensive position, creating a new moral spirit in regard to slavery, particularly among the churchmen of the North, and frightening southerners into an awareness of their growing isolation.

In the early 1850's, the evangelical movement, which had lain in the doldrums in the 1840's, regained impetus. After the split between the New and Old School Presbyterians in 1837, new leaders appeared to take the place of Lyman Beecher, Nathaniel Taylor, Finney, and the other figures of the first crusade. Though these men were still active, a new breed arose to preach much the same message, though adapting it to the task of evangelizing the cities. Included in this new group were such men as Albert Barnes, Edward N. Kirk, and Horace Bushnell.

In New York City, the younger generation was more powerful than it had been in the heyday of Arthur Tappan and Finney. George Barrell Cheever, Joseph P. Thompson, Richard S. Storrs, and Henry Ward Beecher held churches fully independent of the discipline of Old School Presbyterians like Gardiner Spring. They were liberal in theology, alive to reform issues, and less sectarian in approach than the Old School Presbyterians. While these four were all preachers of rare ability, Beecher outshone the rest. Like his father, Lyman, he was more politician than theologian, dressing his religion in the accepted styles of the middle-class churchgoer of the day. His power came not from doctrinal orthodoxy but from an easy manner and flamboyant flights of oratory. "Popularity," a contemporary remarked, "has clothed him with pomposity and egotism," leading him to a strenuous overuse "of the mighty 'I'! and 'Myself'!" Yet, even Lewis and Sarah Tappan were impressed enough to join his Brooklyn parish in 1856, "after long hesitation."[19]

Brooklyn had grown from a little town across the river to a city of over two hundred thousand by 1855, third largest in the nation. It was known as a hotel and bedroom city, where "all the world comes to stay over night, to rise up early in the morning, to quarry its breakfast from a mountain of hash, and go on its way grumbling." Beacher's Plymouth Church, located strategically in the center of city life, became the spiritual capital of middle-class America. Henry C. Bowen, Tappan's son-in-law, not only had personally hired Beecher from Indianapolis but also had loaned the money (at some profit to himself) for the huge auditorium structure on prime Brooklyn Heights property.[20] Arthur and Lewis Tappan had sent the senior Beecher west and been disappointed by his performance there; Bowen had brought his son East and also regretted the decision, though many years later. Tappan never fully trusted Beecher, but he welcomed his rising fame, admired his ability to raise thirteen thousand dollars for the pew rentals (Tappan had abandoned the free-church idea), enjoyed his company when they met in Lucy Maria's parlor, and served with him on several antislavery rostrums.[21] Beecher strengthened the cause of antislavery Christianity, whenever popular Yankee opinion indicated that it was safe to do so.

Tappan liked George Barrell Cheever better, but his church was in New York and Tappan refused to cross the river by ferry on Sunday. More than once, Cheever had stirred up his congregation by preaching on the sinfulness of slaveholding without the equivocations that marked Beecher's statements (though Cheever's outbursts were not sustained long enough to have much permanent effect). Tappan urged Cheever to greater efforts for the cause. "I pray you," he wrote him in 1856, "to sound the gospel trumpet, on the walls of Zion [?], in thunder tones," since the voluntary associations "are doing more to undermine & bring into contempt the religion of Christ than the efforts of all the Infidels, sceptics & non-professors in the land." Although he sometimes backslid, Cheever complied this time by denouncing the American Tract Society, the A.B.C.F.M., and the others for their policy of silence. "In reference to this iniquity [of slavery]," he declared, "they hate him that speaketh at the gate, and they abhor him that speaketh uprightly."[22]

The new evangelists were free of some of the quixoticism of their predecessors, but their methods of reaching the people by press and pulpit were identical. Cheever re-established and edited the New York *Evangelist*, and in 1848 Henry Bowen started the *Independent*, which dominated the religious press of the North with a circulation of thirty thousand by the end of 1856. According to Theodore Tilton, one of its youngest and ablest editors, its original purpose was twofold: to promote "the Congregational as against the Presbyterian Church polity" and "the freedom of the slave against the tyranny of his master." Though forceful in pursuing the former goal, it did not show the spirit Tappan would have liked to see on the latter.[23] The trouble, he said, was that the journal, "though called an anti-slavery, is not an abolition paper."[24]

Tappan did not blame the proprietors, for Henry Bowen, Seth Hunt, and Thomas McNamee were all loyal alumni of Arthur Tappan's school at 122 Pearl, and the publisher was Seth W. Benedict, who had long been one of the brothers' printers. Besides, the *Independent* was not always neutral about slavery. In 1850, an editorial on the Fugitive Slave Act went so far as to urge Christians to disobey it. When Samuel Chittenden, another merchant-member of this latter-day Association of Gentlemen, resigned in protest and proslavery merchants denounced the paper and its managers, Bowen and McNamee inserted a card in the New York *Herald* declaring that "our goods, not our principles, are on the market." Tappan was proud of their stand and their paper, on that occasion at least.[25] For its neutrality at other times he blamed the editors—Richard S. Storrs, Leonard Bacon, and especially Joseph P. Thompson, pastor of the Broadway Tabernacle. Antislavery though these men were, they were closer to the Free Soil position than to abolitionism.

In 1854, Thompson denounced the A.M.A., claiming that it duplicated the work of the A.B.C.F.M. and was schismatic and radical. Calling the accusation "wholly unjustifiable," Tappan launched a vigorous barrage of explanations and exhortations. Soon the controversy spilled into all the major Congregational newspapers on both sides of the Atlantic.[26] The *Independent* also criticized the Reform Book and Tract Society, which Tappan and the Rev. James Vincent of Cincinnati founded in 1852 to fill the gap left by the Tract Society. On that subject, however, Tappan was silent, perhaps because he had to admit privately that Vincent was indeed rather hotheaded.[27]

On only one occasion did Tappan chastise Bowen himself, noting that the *Independent* too often boasted about its influence among the leading men of the age. "Refuting the charge of being abolitionist! Placing stress on the fact that distinguished men, instead of God and Truth, are on the side of the paper! . . . I feel ashamed. . . ." He was uneasy about the materialism and irreligious behavior of these evangelicals as well as their circumspect, casual attitude toward reform. "My heart has ached at the supineness, man-worship, and expediency-policy of the ministry," he wrote Richard Storrs, another editor and clergyman.[28]

319

In spite of these failures to win over the *Independent* and the leading clergy of New York City and Brooklyn to his abolitionist position, Tappan hoped that many Christians were at last awakened to the issue. Time and unceasing agitation would eventually bring them to right ground. The most optimistic sign was the development of an antislavery Congregational church. In 1852, Lewis attended the Maine Religious Convention, where speakers called for the organization of abolitionist Christians. There had been many such conferences before, but this conclave, coupled with similar gatherings in Ohio, led to another and larger affair at Albany the following October. Joshua Leavitt, Seth Gates (the old antislavery Congressman from western New York), Henry Bowen, George Cheever, Richard Storrs, Joel Hawes, Henry Ward and Lyman Beecher, Absolom Peters of the American Home Missionary Society, and Lewis Tappan were among the leading delegates. The chief business at hand, aside from dealing with slavery in the churches, was to strengthen Congregationalism outside New England. Bitter complaints were heard about the treatment of Congregational and New School Presbyterian missionaries in the West. Old School Presbyterians, still distrustful of Finney, Lyman Beecher, and Taylor, quizzed their missionaries unmercifully, threatened them with heresy trials, and sometimes actually brought them before ecclesiastical tribunals. Denouncing the Plan of Union, which forbade Congregational expansion, one delegate declared that Presbyterians "have often come from the West to our New England, and ranged over our fat pastures, and borne away the fleece from our flocks; they have milked our Congregational cows, but they have made nothing but Presbyterian butter and cheese."[29]

Shortly after this debate, Henry Bowen rose to announce that his silk house would offer ten thousand dollars toward a drive for forty thousand in matching funds to support western missions. The proposal had as electrifying an effect as Arthur Tappan's offer to support the Mississippi Valley campaign of 1830. No longer was the barbarism of the frontier the issue, but the aim was basically the same—the extension of New England religion into the West. "Silks, feathers and piety" had combined once more to leave Presbyterian conservatism behind in a great effort to evangelize the New England way. By the terminal date of the drive, the fund was oversubscribed.[30]

Unlike Arthur Tappan's original crusade, this one included antislavery as a chief goal. The convention endorsed the proposition that slavery was an individual as well as a social sin. Unless this line was adopted, Jonathan Blanchard of Illinois predicted that the western churches "would wheel off." The proslavery Home Missionary Society, which operated fifty missions in the South, was in danger of losing its Congregational support unless it adopted the same position on individual responsibility. When Peters, the Society's secretary, sought to prevent that loss, Leonard Bacon, formerly a colonizationist and a critic of the Tappans' measures, made it clear that he would not be disturbed if the A.M.A. replaced the older group entirely. When such men as Leonard Bacon could speak favorably of antislavery measures and organizations, there had indeed been a rather serious shift in Yankee opinion about the antislavery cause. Tappan had every reason to suspect that many of the delegates to the convention were adopting liberal positions simply to be abreast of the times or for reasons of political convenience. If he entertained such doubts, he kept them to himself and did not apparently take much part in these proceedings on the floor. He was pleased, however, with the debate about the Home Missionary Society. Later, he said, "It was no part of the design of the Convention to *dictate* to the Home Missionary Society [but] to inform . . . the public respecting the views" of Congregationalists on the slave issue. But the A.H.M.S. did not surrender to the demands.[31]

Even though the *Independent* continued to be indifferent to the issues raised by the A.M.A., Congregationalists gradually left the A.H.M.S. Its treasury became depleted, and the rival group gained ground. Throughout the 1850's, the warfare between the Presbyterians and the Congregational missionaries continued. One A.M.A. agent reported, "Sectarian Presbyterians are very much afraid of Anti-Slavery preaching, & unite with . . . the lager beer, & whiskey drinkers [to drive] *political* preachers from their schoolhouse."[32] Gradually, the A.M.A. lost its ecumenicism and took on something of the character of an institutional element of the Congregational church.

Tappan considered Congregational expansion a fulfillment of a quarter-century dream—the creation of a denomination dedicated to Christian reform. The old benevolent societies had not lived up to his expectations, but he was gratified that the church of his fathers was proving to be an effective alternative for the encouragement of antislavery beliefs among Yankee Christians. Yet he realized that even the Congregational church was too often timid and its spokesmen too preoccupied with pew sales and too little concerned with principles. In some ways, Lewis was not very far from Garrison's "come-outer" position. Even before the Albany meeting, he had written a Cincinnati convention of antislavery Christians, "We ought not to continue in Church relations where we cannot have freedom of speech and action in regard to . . . Slavery." Tappan continued to work alone with his Bible and mission classes for Negro children; he seldom had much support from his antislavery pastors. Despite the shortcomings that Tappan recognized in the churches, he wished not to disband "the divinely appointed institutions and instrumentalities of Christianity" but to save them from "disgrace" and to put them into a right relationship with God and man.[33] Those who, like Giddings and Garrison, followed the path toward a secular humanitarianism despaired that the American church would ever accept the racial challenge. Lewis Tappan, on the other hand, believed that his son-in-law Henry Bowen, Beecher, Cheever, and other members of the new generation of reform-minded, practical men of affairs might succeed in making the Congregational church the vehicle of millennial reform that Lewis and Arthur had for so long tried to create.

NOTES

1. See Emerson Davis, *The Half Century* . . . (Boston, 1851), 160–61. Taking the sample dates, April 19, 1855, to April 18, 1856, LT received during that period of time 1,082 articles, letters, etc., and wrote 913 letters (see his diary and ltrbks.). This prodigious outpouring did not include letters and memoranda of which he made no copies on his letterpress, or much of his correspondence on behalf of the A.M.A. and other organizations having their own files.

2. Boston *Weekly Chronotype*, December, 1846; see *ibid.*, LT, "Future Punishment"; LT to Wright, November 25, 1846, ltrbk.

3. George W. Julian, *The Life of Joshua R. Giddings* (Chicago, 1892), 401; see also letter to his wife, March 14, 1856, 403, and Julian's comments, 402. Julia Ward Howe, *Reminiscences, 1819–1899* (Boston, 1900), 48–50, 62, 206–8; Thomas, *Weld*, 228; Fladeland, *Birney*, 289–90; LT to Gerrit Smith, July 24, 1851, ltrbk.

4. Jay to LT, June 11, 1849; see also *ibid.*, November 20, 1845, February 8, 1847.

5. LT to Henry Cowles, July 25, 1842, Cowles MSS, Oberlin; LT to Phelps, July 26, September 26, 1842, Phelps MSS, BPL; Phelps to Cowles, November 4, 1842, Cowles MSS, Oberlin; see also Thomas Lafon, *The Great Obstruction to the Conversion of Souls at Home and Abroad* (New York, 1843), which LT had published and distributed; LT to Scoble, July 31, 1844, Abel and Klingberg, *Side-Light*, 187–88.

6. LT to Sturge, September 12, 1845, ltrbk.; Phelps to LT, February 27, 1845; see also Robert T. Lewit, "Indian Missions and Antislavery Sentiment: A Conflict of Evangelical and Humanitarian Ideals," *MVHR*, L (June, 1963), 39–55; J. B. Walker, "Report of the Existence and Influence of Slavery in the Mission Churches of the American Board of Commissioners of Foreign Missions," *Anti-Slavery Reporter*, VI (December 1, 1854), 191–92, a history of the question, and *A&FASR*, August, 1845.

7. LT to Thomas Boutelle, North Woodstock, Conn., January 11, 1848, ltrbk.; Jay to LT, March 8, 1853, *American Missionary*, VII (May, 1853), 51; *ibid.* (September, 1853), 89; *ibid.*, VIII (April, 1854), 45; see also LT to Charles D. Cleveland, October 26, 1849, ltrbk.; *Anti-Slavery Reporter*, VI (December 1, 1851), summary of Chicago convention of Evangelical Abolitionists, 191–94 (quotation) 193; on Garrisonian anti-Board propaganda, see American Anti-Slavery Society, *Annual Report* (1855), 83–93, 99.

8. William E. Strong, *The Story of the American Board* (Boston, 1910), 53; Lewit, "Indian Missions and Antislavery Sentiment," 51–52; LT, letter, November 23, 1854, *Anti-Slavery Reporter*, III, 3rd series (January 1, 1855), 15–18; LT, "The Mission Boards, Caste, Polygamy and Slavery," *American Missionary*, VIII (April, 1854), 45; LT to C. Cushing, November 8, 1854; LT to S. D. Hastings, November 27, 1854; LT to Editor, *Non-Conformist*, November 23, 1954; LT to Editors, *Congregational Herald*, November 23, December 11 and 27, 1854, January 12, 1855; LT to James B. Walker, to C. B. Boynton, to William Patton, December 15, 1854; LT to "Bro." Baldwin, December 31, 1854, LT to Jonathan Blanchard, December 6, 1854, January 17, April 5, September 18, 1855, LT to James Vincent, March 17, 1855, LT to L. A. Chamerovzow, March 20, 1855; LT to S. B. Treat, January 26, March 21, 1855, ltrbk.; diary, January 12, 1855, clipping from *Congregational Herald*.

9. LT to Gerrit Smith, September 12, 1855, Gerrit Smith Miller MSS, Syracuse University Library, with clipping from *Evening Post*, September 12, containing reprint of card from *Tribune*, September 8, and reply of *Commercial Advertiser;* LT to Cocke, n.d., ltrbk., with note that letter was published in *Tribune* and New York *Times*, September 8; see also diary, September 8, 1855; LT to E. C. Delavan, September 14, 1855, LT to David Banks, March 1, 1856, ltrbk.; on A.B.C.F.M. action, see diary, October 30, 1856.

10. LT to Chamerovzow, June 16, 1855. For LT's continued agitation from 1856, see the following: LT to William Lillie, Edinburgh, February 12, 1856, LT to AT, October 23, 1857, ltrbk.; LT in *American Missionary*, X (October, 1856), 92–93; AT to LT, February 2, 1858; Theodore Tilton, *The American Board and American Slavery: The Speech of Theodore Tilton in Plymouth Church, Brooklyn, January 28, 1860*, a defense of LT's policy, the A.M.A., and Christian opposition to the A.B.C.F.M.; see also *American Missionary*, IV, new series (January, 1860), 15, and IV (March, 1860), 59.

11. Jay to LT, September 11, 1851; see also *ibid.*, February 2, 1848, May 3,

1851, February 28, 1857; LT, letter, April 22, 1848, *Anti-Slavery Reporter*, III (June 1, 1848), 107; LT, "Supplying Slaves with the Bible," *American Missionary*, II (April, 1848); Griffin, *Brothers' Keepers*, 180–81; LT in A&FASS *Annual Report* (1850), 64; LT, *Arthur Tappan*, 322–23; on Leavitt's campaign, cf. Lysander Spooner to George Bradburn, March 5, 1847, Lysander Spooner MSS, New-York Historical Society; on earlier LT efforts, see American Anti-Slavery Society, *Annual Report*, I (1834), 32–33, and LT to C. B. Campbell, February 29, 1856, ltrbk.

12. LT to Chamerovzow, October 29, 1854, in Abel and Klingberg, *Side-Light*, 343–44; Griffin, *Brothers' Keepers*, 181–82; Jay to LT, March 14, 1849; LT, letter, April 13, 1850, *The Minutes of the Christian Anti-Slavery Convention Assembled, April 17th–20th, 1850* ... (Cincinnati, 1850), 81; A&FASS, *Annual Report* (1850), 11; A&FASS *Annual Report* (1851), 10, 68; Jay to LT, May 3, 1851; A&FASS *Annual Report* (1853), 120.

13. LT, *Letters Respecting a Book 'Dropped from the Catalogue' of the American Sunday School Union in Compliance with the Dictation of the Slave Power* (New York, 1848), see especially Francis Packard to LT, February 11, 1848, 22–26; see also the large file of letters in LT MSS concerning other expurgations in religious and national journals and books. LT apparently intended to publish the collected data but never found the time. See Charles K. Whipple to LT, May 15, 1855, and LT to Whipple, May 17, 1855, ltrbk. On Jay's antitractarian drive, see Griffin, *Brothers' Keepers*, 192–93; Jay in *Frederick Douglass' Paper*, April 22, 1853; Jay to R. Hayter, June 1, 1857, LT MSS, LC; Jay to LT, June 12, 1855, and October 6, 1857. On LT's antitractarian effort, see diary, May 16, 1858; *National Era*, clipping, diary, 275; and *Independent*, June 10 and 24, 1858.

14. LT, letter, April 26, 1848, *Anti-Slavery Reporter*, III (June 1, 1848), 107; *ibid.*, VI (September 1, 1857), 149. On English reticence in this country, see LT to Sturge, November 26, 1845, March 31, 1846, and LT to Augustus Aspinwall, November 24, 1845, ltrbk.; Jay to LT, November 20, 1845, concerning the Rev. Thomas Spencer. On a similar problem with George Stacey and William and Josiah Forster, Quaker stalwarts of the British and Foreign Anti-Slavery Society, see LT to Sturge, March 31, September 12, 1845, ltrbk. On his work opposing the New School Presbyterians, see *Proceedings of the American and Foreign Anti-Slavery Society at its Anniversary, May 6, 1851* ... (New York, 1851), 9–10. Diary, July 31, 1851, and LT to William Lillie, February 12, 1856, ltrbk.

15. LT to Sturge, November 15, 1844, Abel and Klingberg, *Side-Light*, 197; see George Shepperson, ed., "Notes and Documents, Thomas Chalmers, the Free Church of Scotland, and the South," *Journal of Southern History*, XXVII (November, 1951), 520 (quotation); Thomas Chalmers' defense is reprinted in Abel and Klingberg, *Side-Light*, 196, in his published letter to Thomas Smyth, D.D., of Charleston, September 25, 1844; LT to Birney, June 4, 1845, ltrbk.

16. American Anti-Slavery Society, *Annual Report* (1855), 92, a rendering of the words of the Presbyterian Albert Barnes; LT quotation from LT to Sturge, November 17, 1844, ltrbk.; LT to Phelps, July 6, 1844, Phelps MSS, BPL; *Union Missionary*, I (May, 1844), contains the "Remonstrance"; Garrison and Garrison, *Garrison*, III, 150–55, has the Garrisonian story.

17. LT to Scoble, June 30, 1847, Abel and Klingberg, *Side-Light*, 224–25; Thistlethwaite, *America and Atlantic Community*, 83; LT to Sturge, October 7, 1846, ltrbk.; Garrison and Garrison, *Garrison*, III, 150–75; Griffin, *Brothers'*

Keepers, 197. LT was rather indifferent to the Alliance's anti-Catholicism; see LT to Joseph Soul, London, March 15, 1851, ltrbk., but cf. diary, July 30, 1851.

18. The Chickering affair was particularly bitter: see, for quotation, LT to Editor, London *Patriot,* April 5–10 [?], 1852; LT to *ibid.,* April 13, 1852; LT to *Puritan Record,* "The [London] *Banner* on Abolition," February 23, 1852; LT to William Jackson, March 5, 1852, LT to Sturge, April 10, 1852, ltrbk.; LT in *Anti-Slavery Reporter,* VI (October 1, 1851), 160–61; LT and editorials in *Christian Mirror* (Bangor, Maine), December 30, 1851, February 24, March 2, April 27, May 4, June 15, 1852; diary, February 11, April 21, 1852; see also Jay to Goodell, copy, January 24, 1853, LT MSS, LC; diary, August 14, 1857, clipping, "Letter to Rev. Seth Bliss," *Congregationalist,* and August 28, 1857.

19. Diary, November 2, 1856; Rev. Galbraith Hall, "A Contemporary Glimpse at Henry Ward Beecher," *Journal of Presbyterian History,* XL (September, 1962), 187–88. Discussing the new generation of evangelical clergymen in an authoritative and scholarly way is Timothy L. Smith, *Revivalism and Social Reform: American Protestantism on the Eve of Civil War* (New York, 1965 ed.), 45–62, 185, 203. See also, on the importance of antislavery and Presbyterian developments, C. Bruce Staiger, "Abolitionism and the Presbyterian Schism of 1837–1838," *MVHR,* XXVI (1949–50), 395–409.

20. Harold Coffin Syrett, *The City of Brooklyn, 1865–1898* (New York, 1944), 12; Paxton Hibben, *Henry Ward Beecher: An American Portrait* (New York, 1942 ed.), 101–7.

21. Diary, January 12, 1855, clipping from *Congregational Herald;* LT to Chamerovzow, May 20, 1855, ltrbk.; diary, January 15, 1854, July 12, 1855; see also LT to William J. Bowditch, March 20, 1850, ltrbk.; LT to Charles Sumner, April 25, 1851, Charles Sumner MSS, Houghton Library, Harvard; LT to John G. Fee, July 10, 1855, ltrbk. The *Independent,* February 19, 1857, in "The Cost of Worship in New York" attacked the free church idea as "contrary to the whole genius of the American people," but LT did not dispute the point publicly.

22. LT to George B. Cheever, February 24, 1856, October 21 and 26, 1858, George Barrell Cheever MSS, in Cheever Family MSS, American Antiquarian Society, Worcester; Cheever's quotation in "Conservative Associations in Defense of Popular Sins," *Independent,* February 19, 1857; see also diary, May 27, 1858; LT in *American Missionary,* X (October, 1856), 92–93; George I. Rockwood, *Cheever, Lincoln, and the Causes of the Civil War* (Worcester, 1936), 40–55. LT helped Cheever to publish and distribute his sermons: *God Against Slavery* . . . (New York, 1857) and *The Fire and Hammer of God's Word Against the Sin of Slavery* (New York, 1858). Although mildly antislavery, Horace Bushnell, in contrast, refused to support the A.M.A.; see Bushnell to A.M.A., September 29, 1857, AMA MSS, Fisk.

23. "An Historical Sketch of the *Independent* on the Occasion of Its Twenty-First Birthday," reprinted in *Independent,* LXV (December 10, 1908), 1373; Louis Filler, "Liberalism, Anti-Slavery, and the Founders of the *Independent,*" *New England Quarterly,* XXVII (September, 1954), 291–306; *Independent,* January 1, 1857.

24. LT to Editor, *The Nonconformist,* November 23, 1854, ltrbk.; see also the first editorial of December 7, 1848, reprinted in *Independent,* LXV (December 10, 1908), 1370.

25. LT to Charles Stuart, January 13, 1854, ltrbk.; Filler, "Liberalism," 296–97; Foner, *Business and Slavery*, 44; see also *Independent*, October 23, 1851. In 1863, however, Chittenden helped Bowen to capitalize the Brooklyn *Union*, a Republican paper to rival the anti-Lincoln *Eagle*; see Syrett, *City of Brooklyn*, 21. Joshua Leavitt was managing editor of the *Independent*, but he was less radical than he had been in the mid-forties. Timothy Smith's *Revivalism and Social Reform* does not treat the influence of the Tappans, Henry Bowen, and other laymen in clerical circles during this period.

26. LT to Thompson, March 26, 1854, ltrbk.; diary, March 26, 1854, May 25, 1854, July 28, 1854; LT to Hastings, November 24, 1854, LT to Editor, *Non-Conformist*, November 23, 1854, LT to Editor, *Congregational Herald*, December 9 and 11, 1854, January 12, 1855, LT to J. B. Walker, December 15, 1854, LT to C. B. Boynton, December 15, 1854, LT to William W. Patton, ed., *Christian Herald*, October 19, December 16, 1854, LT to Jonathan Blanchard, September 18, 1854, ltrbk.; *American Missionary*, VIII (April, 1854), 37–38; LT to R. S. Storrs, July 28, 1854, diary; *Congregational Herald*, November 3, 1854; LT in *Anti-Slavery Reporter*, III (April 1, 1855), 15–18; *Non-Conformist*, October 25, 1854. J. P. Thompson later became more outspoken; see his *Teachings of the New Testament on Slavery* (New York, 1856).

27. *Independent*, March 12, 1857; LT to J. B. Mason, February 1, April 14, June 18, August 19, 1855, LT to James Vincent, March 17, 1855, LT to Blanchard, September 18, 1855, ltrbk.; *Anti-Slavery Reporter*, II (April 1, 1854), 78–79.

28. LT to Storrs, July 28, 1854, diary; LT to Henry C. Bowen, June 10, 1858, in William Hayes Ward, "Sixty Years of the *Independent*," *Independent*, LXV (December 10, 1908), 1352; see also LT to William Marsh, February 10, 1856, ltrbk.

29. *Proceedings of the General Convention of Congregational Ministers and Delegates in the United States, Held at Albany, N.Y., on the 5th, 6th, 7th and 8th of October, 1852* . . . (New York, 1852), 71; *Independent*, July 8, 1852; on Maine meeting, see LT, *National Era*, April 29, 1852; see also Frederick Kuhns, "End of Joint Missionary Work by Presbyterians and Congregationalists in 1861," *Journal of Presbyterian History*, XXVIII (December, 1960), 255, the first indication of trouble regarding the Plan of Union in 1846, though it culminated in 1852; see *An Address to the Anti-Slavery Christians of the United States* (New York, 1852), published by the A&FASS, and Jay to LT, February 2, 1852, for complementary action of "new organization."

30. *Proceedings of the General Convention*, 65–69; *Independent*, April 14, 1853.

31. *Proceedings of the General Convention*, 82, 83; LT, in *American Missionary*, VII (February, 1853), 31 (quotation), and VII (April 1, 1853), 45–47; LT to Editor, *Anti-Slavery Reporter*, October 26, 1852, reprinted in Abel and Klingberg, *Side-Light*, 299, with copy of the antislavery resolution; see also Leonard Bacon, *Slavery Discussed in Occasional Essays from 1833 to 1846* (New York, 1846), 132–36, in which he denounced LT and A.M.A. efforts, prior to his change of mind.

32. L. Bridgman to Jocelyn, Westfield, Wisconsin, July 30, 1857, and J. H. Parsons to Whipple, December 3, 1859, AMA MSS, Fisk; LT to AT, October 23, 1857, ltrbk.; *American Missionary*, VII (March, 1853), 38–39, and VII (April, 1853), 45–47; LT to Bro. Baldwin, December 31, 1854, ltrbk.

33. *The Minutes of the Christian Anti-Slavery Convention, Assembled April 17th–20th, 1850* (Cincinnati, 1850), 81. William Goodell, LT's friend, also showed the influence of Garrison's ideas when he wrote *Come-Outerism, the Duty of Secession from a Corrupt Church* (New York, 1855). See also LT in *Anti-Slavery Reporter*, VI (December 1, 1851), 189–91; William Jay to LT, April 12, 1851; *American Missionary*, VII (April, 1853), 38–39.

CHAPTER SEVENTEEN

The Violent Decades

*F*or the *"mob-tried church-centered confessors"* of the 1830's, the decade of the 1850's was bewildering. Antislavery sentiment was growing in the North, but southern hostility matched its progress. In Congress the session which did not reflect these tensions was exceptional, and in the nation violent reactions met every sectional incident. Veterans like Tappan welcomed the signs of Yankee aggressiveness, but they were suspicious of its authenticity. As Whittier remarked in 1849, it was almost as hard to locate a proslavery man in the North as it used to be to uncover an abolitionist; "yet, I have scarcely charity enough to suppose that this marvelous conversion is altogether genuine & heartfelt."[1] Tappan thought that any glimmering of a sense of national guilt about slavery was an advance, and he accepted the credentials of antislavery newcomers with less suspicion than Whittier.

In politics, there was no abolitionist party at all. Liberty men had sold out to the Free Soilers in 1848, and even that party was fast expiring. Salmon P. Chase and Henry Stanton, who had helped to found it, paid no visit to the deathbed. "In my sober judgment the day for '*third* parties' on the slavery question is gone," Stanton said. Chase rejoined the Democratic party to which he had once belonged and obtained a Senate seat by promising "two worthless fellows" seats on the Ohio State Supreme Court. "Alas! that such a man should, for the sake of an office, commit such an act," Tappan sighed.[2]

National events dictated the need for a new political vehicle for abolitionist principles. Political antislavery had been shattered by the defeat of 1848. Fearing that Congress might capitulate to southern demands in 1850, Tappan traveled to Washington to reorganize the politics of the movement. He found the excitement in the capital intense and contagious. Controversies raged over the territorial rights of North and South in the areas taken from Mexico, the admission of California as a free state, and settlement of the Texas boundary. Giddings' bill for the abolition of slavery and the slave trade in the District of Columbia and James M. Mason's bill to commit the national government to the protection of slave property were fiery issues. On March 7 Tappan heard Daniel Webster give his impassioned plea for acceptance of Clay's compromise to settle these disputes. He helped John P. Hale write his reply to Webster's late-blooming southernism, and he witnessed Seward's eloquent attack on the slavocracy. At a party given by Dr. Bailey, he congratulated the antislavery group—Hale, Giddings, Seward, and Chase—on their performances. "What a fall for D. Webster!" he gloated to a Whiggish relative afterward. "He seems to have lost his moral sense. Seward's speech is magnificent." For the moment at least, Free Soilers and abolitionists were more united than ever before, lending hope for future collaboration.[3]

Tappan's Free Soil colleagues were unable to prevent the passage of the Compromise of 1850, but the Fugitive Slave Act, which the Yankee politicians had to swallow, gave the antislavery forces a chance to regroup, and they soon capitalized on the bill's unpopularity. Contradicting the personal liberty laws of various free states, the law aroused fierce northern resentment. Even Tappan, while still an opponent of bloodshed, felt the stirrings of the new spirit of violence that was arising in the North. In a tract he displayed a stridency from which he would have recoiled a decade earlier. Not only was the measure unconstitutional, he said, but it made everyone "a *slave-catcher*." The Yankee, with his heritage of "Hampden and Sydney," had no choice but to open the doors of his house to the "panting fugitive. . . . HE MUST DISOBEY THE LAW" or disgrace his Revolutionary forebears.[4]

Tappan had always stood ready to aid the fleeing Negro. He had helped David Ruggles and the other managers of the New York Vigilance Committee, a free Negro organization, ever since its founding in 1836 and had passed whatever useful information

he overheard to his many friends in the Negro community whenever masters were hunting their lost property. By and large, Negroes hid their own people, but occasionally Lewis and Arthur
helped.[5]

How extensive the so-called Underground Railroad was in New
York City is a matter of speculation. In 1844, Lewis told Thomas
Clarkson that "these railroads mean horses and wagons and men
to guide them," but in all probability the effort was not well organized. In any case, Tappan's interest did not lie in the direction of
assistance to escapees, for prior to 1850 he recorded only two cases
of his having assisted slaves in flight himself. One of the fugitives
belonged to Amos Kendall, Jackson's former postmaster-general,
and the other to R. M. Johnson, Van Buren's Vice-President.[6]

After the passage of the Fugitive Slave Act, a few celebrated
escapes made up in emotional impact for all the obscurity of previous crossings into freedom. Tappan had nothing to do with the
spectacular affairs of Shadrach, Anthony Burns, and Ellen and
William Craft, which excited so much attention and even mob
action in Boston. He did participate in a quieter case in New York.
Failing to save James Hamlet, a Negro porter of the city, through
court action, Tappan raised eight hundred dollars for his purchase
from his Baltimore mistress and saw him returned to his wife and
children. Reports of rescues and happy reunions of this kind
inflamed antisouthern feeling more than a host of antislavery
resolutions. "The Fug. Slave Bill," Tappan said, "is awakening the
country to the horrors of slavery & creating widespread sympathy
for the slaves."[7] In 1855, he and Sarah hid a young girl, dressed
as a boy, in their Brooklyn house and then sent her in the custody
of a Negro minister to the Dawn Institute in Canada to join her
parents. In this instance, the full paraphernalia of passwords,
disguises, aliases, and a relay of escorts was used in the romantic
manner that made the saga of Negro escapes so popular. The
evidence seems, however, to indicate that, even after 1850, the
efforts of groups like the Vigilance Committee, directed almost
wholly by Negroes themselves, were much more important than
the occasional exertions of white abolitionists that received so
much contemporary and historical attention.[8]

One of the consequences of the uproar over fugitives was the
publication of Harriet Beecher Stowe's *Uncle Tom's Cabin*. Tappan was impressed enough by the reception of the book to put
aside his fears of the immorality of fiction and read it himself. He

had some doubts about it. Mrs. Stowe sends George Harris to Liberia at the end of the story. While some Negroes may have gone to Liberia with the feeling that white America could never offer them the true freedom and real opportunity for self-development that they could find in Africa, many other Negroes rightly believed that Liberia was a symbol of white escapism from racial realities and that the "return" to Liberia should therefore not be countenanced by the black community. Lewis Tappan agreed with the latter position, and he conducted a private campaign to convert Mrs. Stowe from further endorsement of that experiment. Apparently he was successful, for she did abandon her inclination to colonization and supported Tappan's Reform Book and Tract Society that denounced it.[9]

With the addition of Charles Sumner to the Senate antislavery forces and the rise of popular feeling against the South, Tappan expected great results from a conference that he attended in Cleveland in 1851. Joshua Giddings had called the meeting so that the "friends of freedom" could form a new political organization. Returning for the moment into the abolitionist camp, Chase assured Tappan that this time he was really "opposed to all coalitions & compromises &c." Reviewing Chase's odyssey from party to party throughout his long political career, a fellow Ohioan reminisced that Chase "had membership in more political parties, with less enjoyment in any of them and with less mutual obligation arising therefrom than any other public man America has produced." Somehow Chase always conveyed a spirit of the utmost sincerity, and Tappan, eagerly seeking signs of co-operation in antislavery work, believed him. The platform adopted at the convention was a radical one, and Tappan approved. He asked the delegates to hold another meeting the following year to make nominations for the President and Vice-President of the United States. All indications seemed to point to a revival of the old Liberty party.[10]

Yet the usual pattern prevailed. Samuel Lewis of Ohio issued an invitation to a convention, to be held at Pittsburgh, limited to those who supported Van Buren and the Buffalo platform of 1848. Protesting in behalf of veteran Liberty men, Tappan denounced the resurrection of a milk-toast Free Soilism. "I think I did wrong in voting for Hale," he sulked. "He is too much of a joker. Chase is not reliable enough. Giddings I have no confidence in. Lewis is not the man." He attended the meeting anyway, but he did very little to help Hale and George W. Julian, the candidates selected, in the campaign.[11] Hale could be said to have done well at the polls only if his vote of about 150,000 was compared with Birney's in 1844, for he was far short of Van Buren's showing in 1848. Moreover, the Democrat Franklin Pierce won handily, without third party assistance to divide the Whig vote, as had happened in Polk's election.[12]

Tappan was indifferent about the election results, but he could not escape the fact that southerners and "doughfaces" dominated the Pierce regime, and that domination led to the abrogation of the Missouri Compromise by the Kansas-Nebraska Act of 1854. No longer was slavery bound by the 36° 30′ parallel. In response to this open invitation for slavery expansion, Tappan altered his tactics. In 1845, Lysander Spooner, a Boston lawyer of eccentric beliefs, had published a pamphlet, *The Unconstitutionality of Slavery,* which claimed that human laws to be valid had to coincide with natural rights. His argument imposed on Congress the duty to abolish slavery even where it had always existed. Tappan now embraced the doctrine, although for years William Jay had influenced him against it. In early 1855, he joined William Goodell, Gerrit Smith, and Simeon Jocelyn in founding the American Abolition Society, which was based on the advocacy of "the illegality and unconstitutionality of Amer. Slavery." It superseded the old American and Foreign Anti-Slavery Society, whose affairs Tappan quickly wound up.[13]

The new group held a meeting in Syracuse in June, 1855, boldly claiming a loyalty to the Constitution's *"righteous language"* as opposed to the southerners' *"unrighteous intentions."* The program was new, but the membership was all too familiar, consisting mostly of "new organization" friends and A.M.A. missionaries. Only the presence of Frederick Douglass, who was earlier a Garrisonian, was novel. Though glad of Douglass' break with Garrison, Tappan had no great hopes for the Society. "It will receive the sneers of many professed abolitionists, the contempt of political men, and the neglect of very many," he concluded.[14] Gerrit Smith made extravagant promises of support, and Goodell started a paper called the *Radical Abolitionist,* but Tappan told them not to expect much aid from him.[15]

The Society, which was also intended as a revival of the Liberty party, got off to a bad start, suffering from financial anemia and already bickering over a new schism in the antislavery movement.

Some abolitionists opposed not only the clerical, the political, and the Garrisonian wings of the cause but also the chief unifying principle of the movement itself, namely, its nonviolence. At the Syracuse convention, a tall, fiery-eyed shepherd named John Brown called for arms to fight slaveholders in Kansas. When an A.M.A. missionary from Canada supported Brown, Tappan objected: "Would not one Uncle Tom do more good by his pious submission to God . . . than a score or a hundred men who should act exactly opposite?"[16] Frederick Douglass, Charles Stuart, and Gerrit Smith took Brown's side, and the issue exposed a new rift in antislavery ranks potentially more serious than previous disputes.

Tappan grew increasingly alarmed by the trend toward violence. When he learned that John G. Fee, head of the A.M.A. mission in Kentucky, allowed his escorts to bear arms in case of sudden mob attack, he admonished him to rely on God to keep him safe. Yet, the chorus for armed defense of Kansas settlers grew more insistent as atrocity stories reached the eastern journals. Horace Greeley, Henry Ward Beecher, and Theodore Parker spoke for the collection of Sharp's rifles to protect the embattled freemen. Both Garrison and Tappan denounced these hotheads, but to little effect. Tappan's solution was to send peace-minded missionaries, not bullets and guns, to the territory. They had their own troubles, however, falling into the vices which seemed to beset A.M.A. missionaries wherever they went—squabbling with each other and lending money at usurious rates to settlers.[17]

Discouraged, Tappan wrote Sturge, "In this community I am almost alone in inculcating the duty & sound policy of maintaining peace. Rifles, it is said, are peace weapons. It is hard to withstand the multitudes, but I have aimed to be firm & thorough. . . ." Goodell took the same position, but Gerrit Smith, leader of the "Radical Abolitionists," was eager to bring war to the southern doorstep.[18] At least Tappan was able to prevent Douglass from waging a full-scale campaign to encourage slave uprisings in the South. In the 1840's, while still a Garrisonian, Douglass had influenced Negro abolitionists against Henry Highland Garnet's proposals for unremitting warfare against slavemasters, but his association with Brown and Gerrit Smith had converted him. When Douglass' paper reflected his new belligerence, Tappan threatened to withdraw his financial support, and Douglass ceased for a while to be quite so militant. Nevertheless, the American

Abolition Society, weak enough to begin with, could not be effective when its leadership was so divided on a major question.[19]

Repelled by the radicalism of his associates, Tappan voted in 1856 for John C. Fremont, nominee of the Republican party, which had arisen out of the ashes of the Free Soil movement. Tappan cared little for the new party and soon regretted his decision. Republicans smelled too much of old-line Whiggery to suit him; "it was a white man's party united for selfish purposes." Moreover, Tappan himself had nominated Gerrit Smith at a convention of the Radical Abolitionists, and he felt a little guilty about deserting his friend.[20]

If northerners were prone to a violence that Tappan could not approve, southerners were still more blameworthy. Preston Brook's attack on Sumner, the Lecompton Constitution in Kansas, the Supreme Court's decision in the Dred Scott case, and other signs of the "slave power's" success inflamed Lewis' desire for Yankee revenge as much as any other abolitionist's. Brutality and wrongdoing, though, had to be met with a superior force of love. Then, in 1859, came John Brown's raid on Harpers Ferry. Tappan had not approved of Brown's activities in the Kansas troubles. He had written Gerrit Smith, "Respecting what you intimate about money for Kansas I am in the dark, and have had nothing to do with 'dark designs' since I bought Calicoes of that name in Manchester, Eng. in 1811."[21]

Because he could not condone physical violence, Tappan regretted the raid on the arsenal, as Garrison did. But like Garrison he regarded Brown as a martyr, feeling compelled to admire the grizzled rebel for his "courage, self-denial and truthfulness."[22] While others glorified the filibuster as a holy crusade, however, Tappan was busy publicizing the hysterical persecution of A.M.A. missionaries in the South that it had prompted.

John G. Fee, a Kentuckian and product of Lane Seminary, had begun a "college" for Negroes and whites at Berea, Kentucky. Tappan believed that the missionaries were ill equipped for so ambitious a project, but he appreciated Fee's aims and his courage. After Brown's Raid, Fee and his associates were forced to leave Kentucky, and Berea College was not to be established again until after the war. Another victim of southern retaliation was Daniel Worth, an aged Methodist missionary in North Carolina. Worth, who received A.M.A. support, was arrested for distributing copies of Hinton Helper's *Impending Crisis*. Tappan and other philanthropists raised the money to secure his release on bail from Ashboro prison, and the grateful minister promptly paid them back after a successful lecture tour of the North. Tappan was more concerned with these signs of southern hostility to peaceful religious work than he was with the rights and wrongs of Brown's actions.[23]

The truth was, Tappan was getting very old. Although his correspondence was as prodigious as ever, he showed signs of weariness after 1857. That was the first year he suffered from rheumatism and also the first of many to come in which he had to bury old friends and relatives. While some of them departed with pious phrases on their lips, Benjamin took his leave without the deathbed repentance scene Lewis hoped for. Nevertheless, he remarked in his diary that Benjamin "had always been affectionate to me & was endeared to me on many accounts."[24]

The old veterans were passing on, too. William Jay suffered a severe stroke in the summer of 1857, rallied for a few months, and then died the following year. James Birney succumbed in 1857, Ellis Gray Loring in 1858, and Joseph Sturge and Gamaliel Bailey in 1859.[25] By and large, however, Yankee reformers—Tappan included—were a tough, long-lived breed, and most of them survived to see the day of triumph, perhaps by sheer determination to defy the laws of biology. Lewis Tappan's active career was unofficially over by the time war broke out in 1861, but he was listening for the sound of the trumpets blowing for freedom.

Throughout the war years, Tappan alternated between two fears: that the Union would win so quickly that slavery would survive; and that the war would be so bloody and lengthy that the North would finally give up. Indeed, he had good reason to worry. In spite of the years of abolitionist agitation, most northerners were prepared to fight only for the Union, not for emancipation. John Tappan, for instance, wrote his old friend General John Hartwell Cocke a most revealing letter as the fighting commenced. In it he expressed the feelings of old-line Whigs and conservatives generally:

We had looked to the States bordering the secessionists to curb their violence and bring them to reason, but alas when old and glorious Virginia proved faithless to the union and upheld the outrage upon Fort Sumter, it was impossible to repress the uprising of our whole population to put down the insurrection. Be assured my dear friend, there is and will be but one sentiment— the Constitution must and will be supported—altho' it may cost us the blood of our sons. Would that we had been spared such awful calamity as is now impending over us, but it is not our seeking and should we both live I trust we shall agree that this calamity was brought about not by the true friends but by the enemies of that liberty acquired under Virginia's noblest son, the immortal Washington.

Even that earnest apologist for the South, Dr. Nehemiah Adams, John Tappan's pastor, patriotically called for a one-hundred-thousand-dollar fund to support the veterans' widows and dependents. Lewis Tappan, of course, welcomed these signs of clerical unity in suppressing secession; he sometimes mistook them for genuine fervor for abolition. Old Dr. Gardiner Spring, whose ecclesiastical conservatism he had once fought, apologized to him for past snubs, and Tappan rejoiced in his conversion in 1864 to antislavery as a means to promote the war. Yet the hostilities stirred the blood of conservatives and abolitionists for different reasons. Most northerners were not unequivocal on the question of Negro slavery, much less on the reformers' cry for racial equality. Wartime propaganda smothered doubts for a while, but John Tappan's view was more indicative of the country's prevailing mood than that of his New York brother. Lewis Tappan, however, was rightly convinced that if the war was lengthy and costly enough, slavery would be the most dispensable casualty.[26]

Every day, he went by the offices of the New York *Evening Post* to see the military bulletins outside printed in large letters. Then he proceeded to the A.M.A. headquarters to take his customary place behind the ledgers. His hearing was not as keen as it used to be; he even asked a friend whether an ear trumpet would help. Nevertheless, he followed events, wrote up articles for the *American Missionary,* the *Evening Post,* and other journals, distributed tracts on the safety of immediate emancipation, and corresponded with war leaders, particularly Charles Sumner, whom he admired more than any other Washington politician.[27] Like most root and branch men, he eyed Abraham Lincoln with some suspicion.

In 1860, Tappan could not bring himself to repeat his mistake of 1856. He voted for Gerrit Smith, though his sons-in-law, Barney and Bowen, were enthusiastic about the Illinois lawyer. Abolitionists were skeptical of the Republican party during the 1860 campaign. Elizur Wright declared to Beriah Green, who was more favorably inclined to it, "When you pitch into the anti-republican Republican party and blow up its sneaking, lily livered, pharisaical, humbug platform, I feel like holding the bott[le] and sponge. Oh the conglomeration of sapheads, paltroons and Pecksniffs!" Republican indifference to the fate of slaves in the existing states and a scarcely disguised hostility to Negro demands for equal citizenship accounted for Tappan's preference, futile though it was, for Gerrit Smith. As Elizur Wright frankly told Beriah Green, "the poor black man" would hardly owe any gratitude to "Abe. Lincoln who is only 'honest' enough to see that enslaving him damages the white man, while he isn't wise enough to see that giving him all the rights of a man must benefit all parties." As the war progressed and as Tappan grew older and mellower, he gradually changed his mind, particularly when the President issued the Emancipation Proclamation in 1862.[28]

Tappan considered the measure a revolutionary act fulfilling an old hunch of John Quincy Adams about how slavery would be abolished—through emergency executive action in wartime. Lewis was pleased that Lincoln did not mention any scheme of removing Negroes to Africa, compensating masters, or lengthening the process by transitional apprenticeships. Nonetheless, the administration was much too slow in accepting Negro recruits and too conservative during the war period to endorse racial equality in national suffrage, in Tappan's opinion. Lewis wrote Charles Sumner, "When will the poor negro have his rights? Never, I believe, until he has a musket in one hand and a ballot in the other." Moreover, Tappan urged an ending of the "absurdity of excluding people from [railroad] cars on account of their complexion," a practice which "must excite, as the poet says, 'the loudest laugh in hell.' "[29]

An "Emancipation Jubilee" was held in January, 1863, at Cooper Union. After the Negro minister Henry Highland Garnet read the Proclamation and the crowd gave three cheers for Lincoln, Lewis Tappan made a few remarks. It must have been an affecting sight, for the seventy-five-year-old "patriarch" symbolized the history of the movement in New York City better than anyone else present. Holding in his hand the letter of March 9, 1841, from John Quincy Adams, informing him that the Supreme Court had freed the "Amistad" captives, Tappan gave a picture of the cause in those unhappy days. Then he observed that the Proclamation, while not as sweeping as he would have liked, promised the general overthrow of slavery in the near future. Some, he continued, questioned the capacity of Negroes to conduct themselves properly in freedom. Sir John Bowring had once told him that the Negroes were actually superior in intelligence and physique to the white man, but Tappan said he wasn't so sure. He believed "that a white man was as good as a black man, if he behaved himself. (Cheers and laughter.)" He closed with a poem:[30]

> Judge not of virtue by the name,
> Or think to read it on the skin;
> Honor in white and black the same—
> The stamp of glory is within.

Except for his attendance at A.M.A. conventions, this was his last appearance in public. Impressed with Lincoln's slow but sure arrival at abolitionist ground, Tappan had nothing to do with the schemes of some radicals to replace him with Chase or Fremont; instead, he voted for "Old Abe" in November, 1864, the first time in his life he had voted for a winning candidate.[31]

The war years were a period of unity reminiscent of the early thirties. Garrison, like Tappan, had thrown over his extreme peace principles with a show of Yankee practicality few ever expected. The bitter memories of ancient offenses prevented a quick accord between Lewis and Garrison, but Arthur received a friendly note from the Bostonian inviting him to attend the thirtieth anniversary of the American Anti-Slavery Society. Garrison assured him "that my gratitude to you is as fresh and overflowing as it was when I was delivered from my incarceration." From his quiet retirement at New Haven, the seventy-eight-year-old Arthur replied in kind, though illness prevented his attendance.[32]

Lewis' contributions to the war effort were two, both undramatic but both useful. In 1861 he had saved the *Independent* from being sold to pay Bowen's debts when the latter went temporarily bankrupt owing to the loss of his southern trade in silks in the months following the firing on Fort Sumter. Lewis ran the paper's business affairs (though he had no control over the editorial policy) for several months, until Bowen was back on his feet and resumed its direction. Under Henry Ward Beecher's editorship, the paper became one of the more influential sheets to support the war, Lincoln, and emancipation.[33]

As well, Tappan helped to set A.M.A. policy in regard to the freedmen. During the summer of 1861, General Benjamin Butler at Hampton Roads defined Negro refugees who reached Union lines as "contrabands," property seized from traitors that should not be returned to them. The term appealed to conservatives and abolitionists alike, and Tappan congratulated the general on his "wisdom and intrepidity in defense of the right." Tappan had always believed that the Negroes should be emancipated on southern soil, where they should be urged to remain, but he asked Butler for permission to remove the contrabands near Norfolk from the battle area and to bring them North, where his organization would see to their needs. Apparently he had no idea how great the number of fugitives around Fortress Monroe was. In any case, Butler replied that the contrabands were better off where they were, though he welcomed any assistance Tappan wished to offer in caring for these people there.[34] The A.M.A. acted promptly on this suggestion, commissioning several missionaries to work in the Norfolk area and, as Union armies widened their occupation, sending in their agents as soon as permission could be secured. Tappan took an active part in the growing responsibilites of the missionary society, which was by far the largest of the religious organizations to undertake this important work. Lewis' duties were mostly routine but were no less important for all that. By the end of 1865, the Association was operating on a budget of $139,000, with 350 agents and missionaries in the field.[35] Though an assistant treasurer, William E. Whiting, did most of the accounting, Tappan continued to influence policy. Working with Jocelyn and Whipple, he told a young member of the staff, "has been very agreeable," though Jocelyn was not as prompt and thorough as Lewis wished. Yet they in turn, he concluded, had had to put up with his "impetuosity" and had borne it well.[36]

Tappan's conviction that the time was fast approaching for his complete retirement from the Association was perhaps confirmed by the news that Arthur Tappan lay dying at his home in New Haven. On July 21, 1865, Lewis reached his brother's bedside. "I took his hand & spoke to him," he recorded in one of the last entries in his diary. "I said, 'Do you know me?' He replied, 'I think I ought to.'" Arthur died the following day without speaking again. Among the pallbearers at the small funeral were Simeon

Jocelyn of the A.M.A. and Amos Townsend, who had labored many years before with the "Amistad" captives. Although several Negro families attended the ceremony, none of the major abolitionists, black or white, were present. In writing Arthur's obituaries for the *Commonwealth* and the *American Missionary*, Lewis recalled his brother's remarkable career, his many charitable donations, amounting to a perhaps overestimated fifty thousand dollars a year in the early 1830's, and his unswerving loyalty to emancipation. Lewis did not altogether overlook his brother's austerity of manner and his other failings: "No one knew better than himself, his sinfulness by nature, and the many imperfections of his maturer life; and no one could lament them more, or strive more earnestly to overcome them."[37] Apparently, both Lewis and Arthur had forgotten Finney's Arminianism and sanctification ideas as they grew older and had turned to the faith of their mother Sarah, at least to some degree. Already Lewis had told Whipple and Jocelyn privately that this was his last year as treasurer. The words set down at Arthur's passing were appropriate also to himself: " 'I feel that I can say, Lord, now lettest thou thy servant depart in peace, for mine eyes have seen the emancipation of the poor colored people.' "[38]

Although Arthur Tappan had died, Lewis could rejoice that Charles, whose arrival upon antislavery ground came late in life, had decided to spend his last years as a missionary to the Negro freedmen, a belated but, in Lewis' eyes, a welcome gesture. Lewis pointed out "the hardships & exposures of such work," but Charles was insistent; in mid-winter, 1865, he joined the A.M.A. missionaries at Port Royal, South Carolina, there participating in one of the earliest wartime efforts of the Association. For his part, Lewis thought himself "too old to enter upon such perils," but retirement did not come easily to him. He kept up with the news, observing with growing amazement and chagrin that Andrew Johnson was subverting the cause of Reconstruction and northern victory. After the death of Lincoln, Tappan had hoped for the best, predicting that Johnson would be "an able & faithful magistrate," but a year later he wrote in the margin of his diary, "This prophecy falsified by his treachery."[39]

Yet, Lewis' spirit of optimism could not be long extinguished. Rebel atrocities, evil Presidential policies, and national greed would all eventually pass away, and "Our grandchildren will live in a more healthy political & moral atmosphere than we have done." God would prove the abolitionists right and bring about the "supremacy of the colored race & the humiliation of the proud and domineering . . . Anglo-Saxons." Like most abolitionists, Tappan underrated the problems facing the nation, the depth of national racial prejudice, and the complexity of adjustment. Yet he was too old to take an active part in formulating new solutions; that task belonged to the Henry Ward Beechers and the Henry Bowens. Tappan realized that this generation of evangelicals was not up to the standards of his own. He wrote Finney, who wanted to launch an eastern revival crusade, that his style and his sentiments were both unhappily old-fashioned; Henry Ward Beecher, "whose gold is not in ingots but in gold leaf," was the ecclesiastical rage.[40]

Tappan realized that he and Finney were living by precepts that did not command much observance in the get-rich-quick war and postwar period. In his retirement, Lewis published *Is It Right to Be Rich?*, a heavy indictment of the materialism of the age, though one couched in such old-fashioned terms of piety and distrust of credit and paper money that this forlorn echo from the puritan past sounded only weakly in the harsh atmosphere of Grant, Daniel Drew, and Mark Hopkins. Although he had almost rebuked Finney for proposing another mission effort in New York, Lewis was not prevented from suggesting a revival measure of his own. In an article published in a religious journal, Tappan urged that the old free mission experiment of the 1830's be tried again as a way of rekindling that spirit of evangelism that had done so much to propel social reform and religious enthusiasm. Did not the Christians of the 1860's know that Christianity was supposed to be "an *aggressive movement*"? he asked. Instead of paying outrageous sums for pews as a demonstration of their wealth, they ought to work with "the sick, the imprisoned, the ignorant, the vicious, and the unconcerned." Six hours a day of office work, Tappan declared, were sufficient to give a man a competency; the remaining time should be spent, as he had spent it, in tending to the needs of the less fortunate.

Another effort to recapture an outworn time was his biography of Arthur Tappan, completed and published in 1870. It was a tribute to his brother but also to the kind of Christianity and antislavery for which he had fought. Tappan's style here too was as archaic as his sentiments, but somehow the book quaintly breathes the spirit of the Yankee cause. The book was a labor of love, a

341

final sign of gratitude for Arthur's generosity in 1827, the discharge again of a debt that had been repaid many times over since that wretched year. While many old-timers read the work with sympathy, Lewis was surprised to hear from William Lloyd Garrison. Though they had continued their warfare through the 1860's, the Boston editor now sent him a generous note, remembering "your early friendship, your generous hospitality, your courageous and whole-souled espousal of the Anti-Slavery cause. . . ." Lewis responded cordially.[41]

Shortly after completing the biography, Tappan had a stroke, from which, however, he recovered. Sarah and Julia found him well enough for the usual summer trips to vacation spots, and he still had his keen eyesight for reading. In fact, the two ladies thought him rather hard to handle. Julia complained to Sarah Grimké, "Mrs. T. certainly has enough [cares] with Father, and I share these, being chief-driver in all his drives, croquet player &c. &c. His still active mind is too much occupied in reading for the health of his body at his age, and it is our constant care to walk with him, while he leans upon us. . . ."[42]

Presumably the family did its best to withhold from him the news of the Beecher-Tilton scandal. Theodore Tilton's wife had confessed to being a paramour of Henry Ward Beecher, her husband's associate on the staff of the *Independent*. Tilton, whose word on this score is still the only evidence, learned from Bowen that his wife Lucy Maria, Tappan's daughter, had also confessed to the same offense when she lay dying in 1863. While the affair did not reach the newspapers until 1873, knowledge of it traveled months before that time in the family circles involved. If Tappan ever learned of this unfortunate business, he did not record his feelings.[43]

On June 21, 1873, when he was eighty-five years old, Tappan suffered a second and fatal heart attack at his home in Brooklyn Heights. At the funeral, Henry Ward Beecher gave the chief address, but, appropriately, the service was conducted, by A. N. Freeman, the minister of a Negro Presbyterian church. Except for the faithful Simeon Jocelyn, there were no old abolitionists present, nor was there a later memorial service. Already Tappan was an obscure figure as the Reconstruction sun was setting. The new era, which Tappan himself had done so much to bring into being, took little notice of his great contributions to American reform.

NOTES

1. Whittier to LT, July 14, 1849.

2. LT to Julius LeMoyne, December 26, 1849, LeMoyne MSS, LC; Stanton to Chase, September 23, 1850, Chase MSS, LC.

3. LT to Augustus Aspinwall, March 14, 1850, LT to G. Smith, March 13, 1850, LT to Mrs. Stoddard, March 12, 1850, LT to Birney, March 15, 1850, LT to William J. Bowditch, March 20, 1850, LT to BT, July 25, 1850, ltrbk.; Sewell, *Hale*, 129.

4. LT, *The Fugitive Slave Bill: Its History and Constitutionality; with an Account of the Seizure and Enslavement of James Hamlet, and His Subsequent Restoration to Liberty* (New York, 1850), 1, 28; *Proceedings of the American and Foreign Anti-Slavery Society at its Anniversary . . .* (New York, 1851), 7.

5. LT at Vigilance Committee Meeting, November 21, 1836, in *Emancipator*, December 15, 1836; LT in William Still, *The Underground Railroad . . .* (Philadelphia, 1872), 681–88; LT, *Arthur Tappan*, 313. AT, according to LT, was said to have kept a horse near the Susquehanna River for the use of fugitives, but LT was probably the real owner. The only white abolitionist in New York City to make this sort of work his chief antislavery contribution was Isaac Hopper, a Quaker merchant; see Lydia Maria Child, *Isaac Hopper: A True Life* (Boston, 1853).

6. Amos Kendall to LT, March 4, 1843; see also *ibid.*, January 18 and 31, 1843; LT to Thomas Clarkson, September 14, 1844, Thomas Clarkson MSS, Moorland Room, Howard University Library; see also LT, "Jesse Harod," *Emancipator*, June 18, 1837, and LT to R. M. Johnson, Martin Van Buren's Vice-President, November 18, 1837, copy, LT MSS, LC; Larry Gara, *The Liberty Line: The Legend of the Underground Railroad* (Lexington, 1961), challenging the myths of the "North Star"—see especially 93–105.

7. LT to [?], September 4, 1851, ltrbk.; LT, *Fugitive Slave Bill*, 1–5; Filler, *Crusade Against Slavery*, 202; LT to Joseph Soul, March 15, 1851, ltrbk.; LT to Chamerovzow, October 29, 1854, Abel and Klingberg, *Side-Light*, 347; LT and the Henry Long case in *National Era*, December 26, 1850, January 9, 1851; LT to Sumner, December 26, 1850, Charles Sumner MSS, Houghton Library, Harvard; *Liberator*, January 17 and 24, 1851.

8. The girl was a member of the Weems family, some of whom escaped from Alabama; others were bought by the abolitionists. See diary, July 19, November 30, December 3, 1855; LT to Ellwood Harvey, December 4, 1855, LT to J. Bigelow, December 3 and 5, 1855, Sarah Tappan to Richardson, July 27, December 8, 1855, ltrbk. On the other cases, see LT to Mrs. Eliza Wigham, Edinburgh, February 6, 1857, ltrbk.; diary, July 25, 1857; Alexander Milton Ross, *Recollections and Experiences of an Abolitionist: From 1855 to 1865* (Toronto, 1875), 27–28, apparently a reference to LT's fugitive work; LT to E. L. Stevens, July 4, 1857, ltrbk.; LT to J. Smith, Glasgow, March 3, 1857, ltrbk. "The Vigilance Com. makes a good use of the funds committed to it. Every week almost fugitives arrive here in destitute circumstances."

9. Diary, July 28, December 21 and 23, 1852, January 21, February 2, 15, 18, 1853; LT to J. Miller McKim, February 1, 1853, WLG MSS, BPL; Harriet Beecher

Stowe, "To the Ladies' New Anti-Slavery Society of Glasgow," November 18, 1853, in *Anti-Slavery Reporter*, II (January 2, 1854), 8–9; LT to Mrs. Stowe, December 9, 1855, ltrbk.; LT to Mrs. E. L. Sturge, April 19, 1852, ltrbk.; LT as "Manhattan," *National Era*, May 6, 1852. See also Jay to LT, August 14, 1852.

10. Diary, September 25, 1851; *National Era*, October 2 and 9, 1851; Joseph P. Foraker, "Salmon P. Chase," *Ohio Archeological and Historical Publications*, XV (1906), 315.

11. Diary, July 15, 1852 (quotation); see also *ibid.*, August 12, 1852, and clipping, *Christian Press*, October 1, 1852, 224, clipping, *Pennsylvania Freeman*, October 23, 1852, 225; LT to Charles Allen, June 17, 1852, LT to Giddings, June 17, 1852, LT to Bailey, June 23, 1852, ltrbk.; LT to Chase, June 23, 1852, in *National Era*, July 8, 1852, and *National Era*, August 19, 1852; *Frederick Douglass' Paper*, July 23, 1852.

12. Sewell, *Hale*, 149–50.

13. Diary, March 17, 1855 (quotation); see diary, April 3, 1855, *passim*; A. John Alexander, "The Ideas of Lysander Spooner," *New England Quarterly*, XXIII (June, 1950), 202, *passim*; see LT at Pittsburgh convention, *National Era*, August 19, 1852; on Jay's opposition, see Jay to Joseph C. Hornblower, July 17, 1850, Jay MSS, Columbia University Library; Jay to LT, May 27, 1851, Jay to LT, October 11, 1852, LT MSS, LC; LT to Chamerovzow, May 16, 1855, ltrbk.

14. LT to Sturge, July 10, 1855, ltrbk.; *Proceedings of the Radical Political Abolitionists, Held at Syracuse, N. Y., June 26th, June 27th and 28th, 1855* (New York, 1855), 6–7.

15. LT to Goodell, April 10, 1855, ltrbk.; LT to Smith, July 4 and 12, 1855, ltrbk.

16. Diary, clippings from *The Reformer*, August 30, 1855, and September 2, 1855, 58. See also LT to "The Rev. C. C. Foote, for *The Reformer*," September 1, 1855, ltrbk. On Foote, who supported Brown, see Pease and Pease, *Black Utopia*, 115, 117, 119, 120. Oswald Garrison Villard, *John Brown, 1800–1859: A Biography Fifty Years After* (Boston & New York, 1910), 85.

17. LT to Fee, July 20, August 13, 1855, ltrbk.; LT to John H. Byrd, Leavenworth, Kans., December 9, 1856, ltrbk.; LT to S. L. Pomeroy, Kansas City, Mo., September 11, 1855, ltrbk.; A. Finch to Jocelyn, March 12, 1857, William H. Sears to "Joslin," May 20, 1859, S. L. Adair to Jocelyn, June 30, 1859, AMA MSS, Fisk; diary, "To the Friends of Missions," November 10, 1855.

18. LT to Sturge, February 17, 1856, ltrbk.; see also, LT to Smith, May 22, 1856, Gerit Smith Miller MSS, Syracuse University; Goodell to Smith, April 23 and 29, 1856, American Abolition Society Letterbook, Oberlin College Library.

19. LT to Douglass, December 19, 1856, Frederick Douglass MSS, microfilm, LC; *ibid.*, December 8 and 27, 1856; *Frederick Douglass' Paper*, October 17, December 12, 1856; LT to Edmund Sturge, December 7, 1856, ltrbk.; LT to G. Smith, August 3, 1857, ltrbk; Garnet *v.* Douglass, in W. M. Brewer, "Henry Highland Garnet," *JNH*, XIII (January, 1928), 44–47; Howard H. Bell, "National Negro Conventions of the Middle 1840's: Moral Suasion vs. Political Action," *JNH*, XLII (October, 1957), 250–52.

20. LT to Henry Richardson, Newcastle on Tyne, February 7, 1857, ltrbk.; *American Missionary*, X (October, 1856), 93; *Radical Abolitionist Extra*, June 2, 1856; diary, November 4 and 5, 1856; LT to D. Baldwin, January 11, 1857, ltrbk.

21. LT to Smith, August 3, 1857, ltrbk.

22. LT, "John Brown," *American Missionary*, III (December, 1859), 280; LT to Whipple, December 10, 1859, AMA MSS, Fisk.

23. On the history of Berea and Tappan's relation to it, see Elizabeth Sinclair Peck, *Berea's First Century, 1855–1955* (Lexington, 1955); John A. R. Rogers, *The Birth of Berea College . . .* (Philadelphia, 1903); William Goodell Frost, *For the Mountains: An Autobiography* (New York, 1937); John Gregg Fee, *Autobiography* (Chicago, 1891); *American Missionary*, X (January, 1856), 14; LT to Fee, April 3, 1855, May 26, 1857, Fee to Jocelyn, April 18 and 22, 1859, G. Candee, copy, to Jocelyn, April [?], 1859, and other letters in AMA MSS, Fisk. On Worth, see Worth to LT, from Ashboro prison, April 3, 1860, AMA MSS, Fisk; *American Missionary*, IV (May, 1860), 109, 129; Richard L. Zuber, *Jonathan Worth: A Biography of a Southern Unionist* (Chapel Hill, 1965), 111–12; C. Prinelle to Whipple, July 19, 1860, AMA MSS, Fisk.

24. Diary, April 21, 1857, April 25, 1857; cf. diary, clippings, n. d., 1857, and March 29, 1857, 196, on the pious death of sister Rebecca Edwards, and William Jackson, diary, clipping, February 27, 1855, from *Evening Telegraph*, February 28, 1855, 280.

25. LT to Jay, July 26, 1857, ltrbk.; LT to Smith, July 27, 1857, ltrbk.; Jay to LT, August 5, 1857; John Jay to LT, October 15, 1858; LT, obituary, *Daily Tribune*, October 21, 1858, diary, 358; LT, obituary for Sturge, *Evening Post*, June 9, 1859, clipping, diary, June 9, 1859, 316; Fladeland, *Birney*, 293; Garrison and Garrison, *Garrison*, III, 352.

26. LT to Sumner, December 12, 1860, Charles Sumner MSS, Houghton Library, Harvard; LT, "Courage, Courage!" *Independent*, December 27, 1860, clipping, diary, 351; LT to Wright, August 17, 1861, Wright MSS, LC; John Tappan to Cocke, May 9, 1861, Cocke MSS, Moore Deposit, Library, UVA; diary, January, 1864, 327.

27. LT, *The War: Its Cause and Remedy* (New York, 1861), *Immediate Emancipation: The Only Wise and Safe Mode* (New York, 1861), *Caste: A Letter to a Teacher among the Freedmen* (New York, 1867); diary, September 12, 1861; there are about sixty letters of LT in the Sumner MSS at Harvard, dated from 1850 to 1870.

28. McPherson, *Struggle for Equality*, 19–23, and n. 19; Jonathan S. Green to LT, November 15, 1860, ltrbk.; Fee to Whipple, July 16, 1860, AMA MSS, Fisk; Clifton H. Johnson, *American Missionary Association Archives as a Source for the Study of American History* (New York, 1966), 10–11; Wright to B. Green, November 3, 1860 (quotation), Wright MSS, LC. LT's suspicions of Lincoln: LT to Sumner, February 2, 1861, Charles Sumner MSS, Houghton Library, Harvard; LT to Smith, January 29, 1861, Gerrit Smith Miller MSS, Syracuse University Library. Barney was Lincoln's collector of the port of New York throughout the war, and Bowen was appointed a revenue collector. On LT's vote in 1860, see LT to U. F. Brayton, November 13, 1860, MSS 2421, Western Reserve Historical Society.

29. LT to Sumner, January 9, 1863, Charles Sumner MSS, Houghton Library, Harvard; McPherson, *Struggle for Equality*, 77, and diary, n.d., 294, relating to events of September 12, 1861; LT to G. Smith, September 14, December 3, 1861, Gerrit Smith Miller MSS, Syracuse University Library; LT in *American Missionary*, VI (August, 1862), 178; LT to Sumner, February 13, 1865 (quotation), ltrbk.; LT to Morrow B. Lowry, January 28, 1865 (quotation), ltrbk.

30. New York *World*, January 6, 1863.

31. Diary, November 7, 1864; LT to Amos Townsend, June 10, 1864, and to Gerrit Smith, June 9, 1864, ltrbk.

32. Garrison to AT, November 12, 1863, Leffingwell Autograph Collection, New-Haven Colony Historical Society; *Proceedings of the American Anti-Slavery Society, at Its Third Decade, Held in the City of Philadelphia, Dec. 3d and 4th, 1864* [*sic*; 1863] (New York, 1864), 5–6.

33. See AT's pathetic letter on LT's activities, February 7, 1861; LT to G. L. Ford, September 18, 1861, personal miscellany file, New York Public Library; diary, December 7, 1861, 295–96; William Hays Ward, "Sixty Years of the Independent," *Independent*, LXV (December 10, 1908), 1345–47; a collection of documents relating to Henry Ward Beecher's editorship of the paper, Bowen and Holmes to Beecher, May 11, 1861, Bowen to Beecher, May 16, 1862, Henry Ward Beecher MSS, LC.

34. LT to Major-General Butler, Commanding U. S. Army at Fortress Monroe, Va., August 8, 1861, Butler to LT, August 10, 1861, ltrbk.; LT to Butler, August 14, 1851, Benjamin F. Butler MSS, LC. See also E. Wright to Butler, August 10, 1861, E. L. Pierce to Butler, August 10, 1861, H. Hamlin (A.M.A. missionary, offering his services to the Negroes), August 14, 1861, *ibid.*

35. LT to G. Buckingham Wilcox, November 21, 1864, *American Missionary*, IX (December, 1865), 265.

36. LT to M. E. Streiby, January 14, 1864, ltrbk.

37. *American Missionary*, IX (September, 1865), 203–5; diary, July 21–August 30, 1865.

38. AT obituary, *American Missionary*, IX (September, 1865), 205; *Commonwealth*, July 29, 1865; LT to Whipple, June 7, 1865, ltrbk.

39. Diary, April 30, 1865 (quotation); LT to Charles Tappan, January 31, 1865 (quotation), LT to W. J. Richardson, Port Royal, S. C., February 1, 1865, LT to AT, February 25, 1865, LT to Charles Tappan, March 13, 1865, ltrbk.

40. LT to Charles Greeley Loring, January 18, 1867, Charles Greeley Loring MSS, Houghton Library, Harvard; LT to Fee, May 24, 1865, LT to [?], May 6, 1866, LT to Phillip A. Bolling, December 15, 1869, ltrbk.; LT to Finney, October 15, 1866, photostat, LT MSS, LC.

41. WLG to LT, January 27, March 3, 1870; Whittier to LT, May 2, 1870; LT to Gerrit Smith, October 17, 1870; LT to R. D. Webb, October 27, 1870; LT to Whittier, May 5, 1870—letters of congratulation on his biography—LT MSS, LC. See LT to WLG, January 29, 1870, "Anti-Slavery Figures" file, BPL; LT, "Important Religious Movement," clipping, June or July, 1866, scrapbook, 1857–95 (quotation).

42. Julia Tappan to Sarah Grimké, n.d., Weld MSS, Clements Library.

43. *Beecher-Tilton Investigation. The Scandal of the Age* (Philadelphia, 1874), 21–25, containing Bowen-Tilton correspondence; Tilton to Bowen, January 1, 1871, in *The Great Brooklyn Romance, All the Documents in the Famous Beecher-Tilton Case, Unabridged* (New York, 1874); *Proceedings of the Advisory Council of Congregational Churches and Ministers Called by the Plymouth Church of Brooklyn, N.Y., and Held in Brooklyn from the 15th to the 24th of February, 1876* (New York, 1876), 291–92, with Bowen's equivocal testimony on Beecher's guilt or innocence.

Bibliographical Essay

MANUSCRIPTS

The chief source for a biography of Lewis Tappan is the collection of his papers at the Library of Congress. Tappan lost many of his records in the fire of 1835, but after 1839, when he started his letter-press system, the files of outgoing correspondence are reasonably complete except for the years 1840–42 and 1850–52. There are only 220 incoming letters, however. As noted earlier, these letters as well as other materials from the Tappan collection are cited without designating their location. Much to his brother's dismay, Arthur Tappan did not keep any records at all. The large Benjamin Tappan manuscript collection at the Library of Congress has a few letters from Benjamin, Sr., Sarah, and Arthur Tappan, as well as a large number from Lewis. Other papers the author used at the Library of Congress include the fascinating Elizur Wright MSS, the American Colonization Society MSS, the papers of Salmon Portland Chase, James Gillespie Birney, Joshua Leavitt, Frederick Douglass (microfilm), Benjamin F. Butler, Henry Ward Beecher, Martin Van Buren, James H. Hammond, and Joshua R. Giddings–George W. Julian, and the Julius LeMoyne letters in the Carter G. Woodson Collection. A transcript of eighteen letters of Susan and Julia Tappan, in the possession of Miss Anna Hulett at the time of her death, is held by the author.

Oberlin College provided a number of important collections. The treasurer's office still holds the records of Arthur and Lewis Tappan's financial arrangements with the school. The autograph file, the miscellaneous file, the Robert S. Fletcher transcripts, the very rich Charles Grandison Finney and Henry Cowles MSS, and the American Abolition Society's letterbooks are located in the college library.

The antislavery collections of the Boston Public Library form the core of any study of the reform movement: the William Lloyd Garrison MSS; the Weston, Chapman, and Elizur Wright family papers; and the Amos A. Phelps holdings were used. Lesser collections at the BPL include the George Bond and Moses Grant MSS, autograph files, and American Anti-Slavery Society official records. The Gerrit Smith Miller papers, which also include the Seth M. Gates MSS, at

347

the Syracuse University Library, are among the best organized sources of anti-slavery history. The William H. Seward MSS in the Rush Rhees Library of the University of Rochester contain a number of Tappan letters. The John Quincy Adams MSS, now available at some libraries on microfilm, were used at the Johns Hopkins University Library.

The New-York Historical Society holds the papers of the Manumission Society of New York City, the Luther Bradish and the Lysander Spooner letters, and in Slavery Box II some important letters of Theodore Weld and Lewis Tappan. The Lydia Maria Child and Ellis Gray Loring correspondence at the New York Public Library gave some details. Columbia University has the William Jay papers, but an additional number of significant letters from Arthur Tappan, Lewis Tappan, and William Jay are located at the John Jay House, Mt. Kisco, New York. The American Bible Society at Bible House, New York City, has some records of Arthur's participation.

The archives in Philadelphia provided useful materials. The Simon B. Gratz and the Claude W. Unger collections in the Pennsylvania Historical Society contain some valuable items. Also used at the Pennsylvania Historical Society were the Mathew Carey MSS and the records of the Pennsylvania Abolition Society. The American Sunday School Union headquarters in Philadelphia has one of the largest missionary collections in the country, since nearly all incoming correspondence to the organization has been preserved in bound volumes.

The Ohio Historical Society in Columbus holds some newly acquired Benjamin and Lewis Tappan correspondence, as well as the Joshua R. Giddings Collection. The William L. Clements Library at Ann Arbor has the Theodore Dwight Weld and James G. Birney Collections. Fisk University's Amistad Room in the main library building is the depository for the American Missionary Association's three-hundred-thousand item collection. The Mercantile Agency diary, 1841–45, and the American and Foreign Anti-Slavery Society *Minutes,* formerly at the Board of Home Missions headquarters in New York, have been added, I believe, to the A.M.A. holdings since I microfilmed them.

At Yale University I surveyed the Lyman Beecher MSS, miscellaneous MSS, the Roger Sherman Baldwin MSS, and the Samuel Farrar MSS. The records of the State Department in the National Archives, Washington, D.C., were consulted for the Amistad chapter. For supplementary purposes, other collections were also consulted: the John Pierce journals at the Massachusetts Historical Society; the Charles Sumner, Ellis Gray Loring, William Ellery Channing, Whittier-Pickard, Charles Greeley Loring, Jared Sparks, and Caroline Sturgis Tappan Collections at the Houghton Library, Harvard; the Thomas Clarkson MSS at Howard University's Moorland Room; the John Greenleaf Whittier MSS at the Essex Institute, Salem, Massachusetts; the General O. O. Howard MSS, Bowdoin College Library; the variously titled John Hartwell Cocke MSS at the Alderman Library, University of Virginia; the Lane Seminary archives at the McCormick Theological Seminary, Chicago; the American Home Missionary Society MSS, Chicago Theological Seminary Library; #2421 MS and the Hitchcock Family Papers, Western Reserve Historical Society; the Clarence W. Bowen scrapbook and the Cheever Family MSS, American Antiquarian Society, Worcester; the Union Missionary Society MSS, Rutgers University; and the Leffingwell autograph collection, New-Haven Colonial Historical Society.

NEWSPAPERS

Standard equipment on any expedition into abolitionism is Garrison's lively *Liberator* (Boston). Other antislavery journals used include the *Emancipator* (New York and later Boston); *Human Rights* (New York), 1835–38, available in the Moorland Room, Howard University Library; the *Slave's Friend* (New York), 1835–37, also in the Moorland Room and at the Western Reserve Historical Society; the *American and Foreign Anti-Slavery Reporter* (LC and Oberlin College Library), which Tappan published intermittently; the *Union Missionary*, 1844–46, and the *American Missionary*, its successor, both of New York, located in complete files at the Oberlin College Library. Also consulted were Lundy's *Genius of Universal Emancipation*; the Colonizationists' *African Repository and Colonial Journal*; the *Philanthropist* (Cincinnati); the *Abolitionist* (Boston, 1833); the *National Inquirer* and *Pennsylvania Freeman*, both of Philadelphia; the Liberty party's *Massachusetts Abolitionist* (Boston, 1840–42) and *National Era* (Washington); the *Anti-Slavery Reporter* and the *Anti-Slavery Record*, both of New York; *Friend of Man* (Utica); *Anti-Slavery Reporter* (London), organ of the British and Foreign Anti-Slavery Society; and four Negro papers: *Colored American* (New York), from the complete file in the Western Reserve Historical Society, *Rights of All* (New York), *Freedom's Journal* (New York), and *Frederick Douglass' Paper* (Rochester). The *National Anti-Slavery Standard* (New York) was the American Anti-Slavery Society's official journal after the Garrisonians' victory in 1840. William Goodell published the *Radical Abolitionist* (New York) for the American Abolition Society in the 1850's (complete file in Oberlin College Library). The New York *Independent* was founded by Lewis' son-in-law Henry C. Bowen.

Religious journals were frequently consulted. The New York *Evangelist; McDowall's Journal* (New York); Beecher's *Spirit of the Pilgrims* (Boston); the New York *Observer*; the Boston *Recorder*; the *Christian Examiner* (Boston); the Rochester *Observer*; the *Western Recorder* (Utica); the New York *Israel's Advocate*; the *Christian Register* (Boston); E. S. Ely's *Philadelphian*; and Elizur Wright's *Weekly Chronotype* (Boston) were used for particular points. Extremely hostile to the Tappanite reforms were Theophilus Fisk's *Priestcraft Unmasked* (New York); the New York *Sentinel*; the *Gospel Herald and Universalist Review* (New York); Frances Wright's *Free Enquirer* (New York); the *Evangelical Magazine and Gospel Advocate* (Utica); and the *Ohio Watchman* (Ravenna, Ohio); while the orthodox *Christian Mirror* (Bangor) engaged in a lengthy dispute with Lewis Tappan later in his antislavery career.

The story of antiabolitionism and antievangelicalism is found also in the secular press. Among the New York papers useful in this way were James Watson Webb's *Morning Courier and New York Enquirer*; Mordecai M. Noah's *Evening Star*; George Henry Evans' *Working Man's Advocate*; and James Gordon Bennett's New York *Herald*. Other New York papers consulted include: William Cullen Bryant's and William Leggett's *Evening Post*; the *American*; the *Commercial Advertiser* (and its country edition, the *Spectator*); the *Tribune*; and the Tappans' paper, the *Journal of Commerce*, purchased by David Hale. Boston papers used were the *New England Palladium and Commercial Advertiser, Daily Advertiser*, and *Repertory and General Advertiser*. Southern papers were helpful for the postal campaign chapter, especially: the *Southern Patriot* (Charleston), the Richmond *Whig,* the Nashville *Banner and Whig, Niles' Weekly Register* (Baltimore), the Washington *Globe,* and the *National Intelligencer* (Washington). The Ravenna *Star* was the only Anti-Mason paper used. Other newspapers consulted were the London *Times* and several papers of Harrisburg, Pa.

PAMPHLETS AND PUBLISHED REPORTS

Tracts and annual reports were one of the chief methods by which the evangelicals and abolitionists got across their message—cheaply, efficiently, and pungently. So many exist that only those that Tappan wrote himself or helped to publish will be given complete attention here. The American Anti-Slavery Society, the American Missionary Association, and the American and Foreign Anti-Slavery Society *Annual Reports* are not difficult to find in scattered numbers. One of the few complete sets of the American Missionary Association reports is found in the Oberlin College Library. Tappan wrote many of these reports from 1846 to 1861. His tracts include *Prisons and Prison Discipline* (Boston, 1826); *Letter from a Gentleman in Boston to a Unitarian Clergyman of That City* (Boston, 1828); *Letter to Eleazar Lord, Esq. in Defense of Measures for Promoting the Observance of the Christian Sabbath* (New York, 1831); *Broadway Tabernacle Anti-Slavery: Proceedings of a Meeting* (New York, 1838); *Address to the Churches of Jesus Christ, by the Evangelical Union Anti-Slavery Society . . . of New York* (New York, 1839); *Proceedings of the Sessions of the Broadway Tabernacle against Lewis Tappan, with the Action of the Presbytery and General Assembly* (New York, 1839); *Letters Respecting a Book 'Dropped from the Catalogue' of the American Sunday School Union in Compliance with the Dictation of the Slave Power* (New York, 1848); *Fugitive Slave Bill: Its History and Unconstitutionality; with an Account of the Seizure and Enslavement of James Hamlet, and his Subsequent Restoration to Liberty* (New York, 1850); *American Slavery: Letter to the Editor of the British Banner* (London, 1851); *Reply to Charges against the American and Foreign Anti-Slavery Society* (London, 1852); *History of the American Missionary Association: Its Constitution and Principles* (New York, 1855); *Immediate Emancipation: The Only Wise and Safe Mode* (New York, 1861); *Is It Right to Be Rich?* (New York, 1865); and *Caste: A Letter to a Teacher among the Freedmen* (New York, 1867). As the titles indicate, Lewis Tappan did not venture into political or religious theory about abolitionism or evangelicalism. Mostly, the tracts are anecdotal and factual in content. He also helped William Jay publish his tract, *Address to the Non-Slaveholders of the South on the Social and Political Evils of Slavery* (New York, 1843), though its authorship has sometimes been attributed to Tappan.

Casting an unfavorable light on Lewis Tappan's business methods is Edward E. Dunbar, *A Statement of the Controversy between Lewis Tappan and Edward E. Dunbar* (New York, 1846). David Hale, editor of the *Journal of Commerce,* published in Tappan's defense *Facts and Reasonings on Church Government: Report of a Discussion Held at a Meeting of the Broadway Tabernacle* (New York, 1839). A pamphlet of considerable value is the American Tract Society's *Arthur Tappan, Tract No. 677* (New York, n.d.).

PUBLISHED LETTERS, DIARIES, MEMOIRS, AUTOBIOGRAPHIES, AND COLLECTIONS

Historians of abolitionism are fortunate that New England reformers were indefatigable publishers. Later scholars and memorialists have supplemented this literature. Most appropriate to this study are the heavily annotated Annie H. Abel and Frank Klingberg, eds., *A Side-Light on Anglo-American Relations, 1839–1858, Furnished by the Correspondence of Lewis Tappan and Others with the British and Foreign Anti-Slavery Society* (Lancaster, Pa., 1927); Gilbert H. Barnes and Dwight L. Dumond, eds., *Letters of Theodore Dwight Weld, Angelina Grimké Weld, and Sarah Grimké, 1822–1844*, 2 v. (New York, 1934); and Dwight L. Dumond, ed., *Letters of James Gillespie Birney, 1831–1857*, 2 v. (New York, 1938). Lewis Tappan compiled letters of his mother in a *Memoir of Mrs. Sarah Tappan* . . . (New York, 1834). Also, a descendant published *Lewis Tappan's Wedding Journey, September 7, 1813* (n.l., n.d.), and I believe I have the only copy available for the use of scholars.

Other important collections of letters include Samuel T. Pickard, ed., *Whittier as a Politician, Illustrated by His Letters to Professor Elizur Wright, Jr.* (Boston, 1900); *Letters of Lydia Maria Child* (Boston, 1883); Dorothy C. Barck, ed., *Letters of John Pintard to His Daughter Eliza Noel Pintard Davidson, 1816–1833*, 4 v. (New York, 1940–41), still in print and very interesting. Charles Francis Adams, ed., *Memoirs of John Quincy Adams*, 12 v. (Philadelphia, 1874–77), was useful in conjunction with Tappan's dealings with the ex-President. For a portrayal of New York life, Bayard Tuckerman, ed., *Diary of Philip Hone*, 2 v. (New York, 1889); Allan Nevins, ed., *The Diary of Philip Hone, 1828–1851* (New York, 1927); and Allan Nevins and Milton Halsey Thomas, eds., *Diary of George Templeton Strong, Young Man in New York, 1835–1849* (New York, 1952), I, were all valuable.

Directly appertaining to the Tappan brothers are the following: Charles G. Finney, *Autobiography* (London, 1903); Barbara M. Cross, ed., *The Autobiography of Lyman Beecher*, 2 v. (Cambridge, 1961), with a perceptive introduction; Asa Mahan, *Autobiography, Intellectual, Moral and Spiritual* (London, 1882); and Joseph Sturge, *A Visit to the United States in 1841* (London, 1841). Richard R. Madden, *Memoirs Chiefly Autobiographical* . . . (London, 1891), tells of Madden's role in the "Amistad" case. Samuel J. May, *Some Recollections of Our Anti-Slavery Conflict* (Boston, 1869), relates Arthur Tappan's work in the Prudence Crandall case. John Neal's *Wandering Recollections of a Somewhat Busy Life* (Boston, 1869) recalls the Clinton Hall mob. Joseph A. Scoville [Walter Barrett, pseud.], *The Old Merchants of New York City*, 3 v. (New York, 1863–72), was a mine of information in spite of the author's inaccuracy. Joseph P. Thompson, *Memoir of David Hale* (New York, 1850), and Henry B. Stanton, *Random Recollections* (New York, 1887), added various details about the Tappans' editorial and journalistic work.

Louis Filler has edited *Wendell Phillips on Civil Rights and Freedom* (New York, 1965); William H. Pease and Jane H. Pease have published *The Antislavery Argument* (Indianapolis, 1965); and Staughton Lynd has collected opinions on *Nonviolence in America: A Documentary History* (Indianapolis, 1966). Louis

Ruchames, ed., *The Abolitionists: A Collection of Their Writings* (New York, 1964), is also a convenient source.

BIOGRAPHIES

When he was eighty-two, Lewis Tappan composed the only biography of Arthur Tappan (New York, 1870). With becoming modesty, Lewis relegated himself to a position of distinctly secondary importance. He hardly appears in the book, and one suspects that many accomplishments that Lewis attributes to Arthur are really attributable to himself. Lewis is preoccupied with Arthur's merits, both real and imagined.

William Birney, *James G. Birney and His Times* (New York, 1890), contains many valuable letters and interesting but biased accounts of Garrison's place in the movement. It has been superseded, however, by the able work of Betty Fladeland, *James Gillespie Birney, Slaveholder to Abolitionist* (Ithaca, 1955). Although highly partisan, Wendell Phillips Garrison and Francis Jackson Garrison, *William Lloyd Garrison, 1805–1879 . . .* , 4 v. (Boston, 1885–89), reprints many useful items of correspondence and editorials. Oliver Johnson, *William Lloyd Garrison and His Times* (Boston, 1880), is apologetic but worthy of restudy. Two recent biographies of the Boston reformer are Walter M. Merrill, *Against Wind and Tide: A Biography of Wm. Lloyd Garrison* (Cambridge, 1963), and John L. Thomas, *The Liberator, William Lloyd Garrison: A Biography* (Boston, 1963). Both are thoughtful and well written. Merrill, however, is perhaps insufficiently critical, while Thomas is too unsympathetic, though some challenging ideas about the nature of American romanticism and reform emerge from the book. The best short life of Garrison is Russel B. Nye, *William Lloyd Garrison and the Humanitarian Reformers* (Boston, 1950).

Benjamin Thomas, *Theodore Weld, Crusader for Freedom* (New Brunswick, 1950), is a short, lively life of the great antislavery orator, though it accepts uncritically the anti-Garrisonian interpretations popular at the time of its composition. Merton L. Dillon is to be highly congratulated for his *Benjamin Lundy and the Struggle for Negro Freedom* (Urbana, 1966). He has largely compensated for the unfortunate lack of a set of Lundy materials (burned in the Pennsylvania Hall fire, 1838) with a new and rewarding study of the movement's history before and after Garrison. Also useful is Dillon's *Elijah P. Lovejoy, Abolitionist Editor* (Urbana, 1961). Though largely unsympathetic, Ralph V. Harlow, *Gerrit Smith: Philanthropist and Reformer* (New York, 1939), deserves reissue. A new biography to replace Henry Steel Commager's idealistic *Theodore Parker: Yankee Crusader* is much needed. Irving Bartlett, *Wendell Phillips, Brahmin Radical* (Boston, 1961), merits greater attention than Oscar Sherwin's *Prophet of Liberty: The Life and Times of Wendell Phillips* (New York, 1958).

The Boston agitators have been rewarded with scholarly treatment more than have the evangelicals of Tappan's immediate circle, but Bayard Tuckerman's uncritical *William Jay and the Constitutional Movement for Abolition of Slavery* (New York, 1893) will suffice until a better work appears. There is no good biography of Joseph Sturge, Amos A. Phelps, Joshua Leavitt, or Elizur Wright.

The latter has been treated with insufficient depth by Philip Green Wright and Elizabeth Q. Wright, *Elizur Wright: The Father of Life Insurance* (Chicago, 1937). David French of Case Western Reserve University is working on a study of Wright's antislavery career, and James B. Stewart, also of Case Western Reserve, has completed a dissertational biography of Joshua R. Giddings, which will be published by the Press of Case Western Reserve University. George W. Julian, *The Life of Joshua R. Giddings* (Chicago, 1892), is dated but informative. A first-rate study of a second-rate politician is Richard Sewell's *John P. Hale and the Politics of Abolition* (Cambridge, 1965). Madeleine Stern has published her able life of Stephen Pearl Andrews, *The Pantarch* (1968), with the University of Texas Press. Elizur Wright memorialized another political abolitionist in his *Myron Holley and What He Did for Liberty and True Religion* (Boston, 1882). A new biography of the antislavery poet-politician, Whittier, Edward Wagenknecht's *John Greenleaf Whittier: A Portrait in Paradox* (Oxford, 1967), is superior to John A. Pollard, *John Greenleaf Whittier, Friend of Man* (Boston, 1949) but is insufficient on Whittier's reform career.

More attention is now being given to women in the antislavery cause. Gerda Lerner, *The Grimké Sisters from South Carolina: Rebels Against Slavery* (Boston, 1967), is the most recent biography of these interesting ladies. Otelia Cromwell, *Lucretia Mott* (Cambridge, 1958), treats another feminist, while Alma Lutz, *Crusade for Freedom, Women in the Antislavery Movement* (Boston, 1968), describes the careers of a number of white ladies in the movement, including Prudence Crandall.

Biographies of leading clergymen are mostly of uneven quality. Outstanding, however, are Arthur W. Brown, *Always Young for Liberty: A Biography of William Ellery Channing* (Syracuse, 1956), and David E. Swift, *Joseph John Gurney, Banker, Reformer and Quaker* (Middletown, 1962). Henry Ward Beecher deserves a more sophisticated study than the muckraking Paxton Hibben's *Henry Ward Beecher: An American Portrait* (New York, 1942 ed.). Two works concern George B. Cheever: George I. Rockwood, *Cheever, Lincoln, and the Causes of the Civil War* (Worcester, 1936), and Robert York, *George B. Cheever, Religious and Social Reformer, 1807–1890* (Orono, Me., 1955). While dissertations abound on the work of Charles Grandison Finney, there is no good, modern life in print. New biographies or at least sketches of the antislavery Negro ministers who contributed more to the movement than historians have so far recognized should be written to add a dimension to the subject that is desperately needed.

SECONDARY WORKS: BOOKS, ARTICLES, AND ESSAYS

Although this is the first biography of Lewis Tappan to appear in print, the influence of the Tappan brothers' antislavery work has been well known at least since Gilbert Hobbes Barnes published *The Antislavery Impulse, 1830–1844* (New York, 1933). Although mistaken on a considerable number of facts and interpretations, Barnes's absorbing study is still a landmark in abolitionist historiography.

Another eminent scholar, Dwight L. Dumond, follows Barnes's emphasis on western abolitionism and anti-Garrisonian interpretations in his *Antislavery Origins of the Civil War of the United States* (Ann Arbor, 1939) and *Antislavery: The Crusade for Freedom in America* (Ann Arbor, 1961), both of which are marked by scholarly depth in spite of their partisanship. Louis Filler's *The Crusade Against Slavery, 1830–1860* (New York, 1960) contains the mine of bibliographical information and the very useful synthesis of current studies that Dumond's *Antislavery* lacks. Also worthy of mention as a general introduction is Merle Curti's *The Growth of American Thought* (New York, 1964), Chapter XV, a balanced view of the abolitionist effort.

Two historians have observed the international nature of antislavery: Allan Nevins, "The Pulse of Reform," in *Ordeal of the Union*, 6 v. (New York, 1947–60), I, 113–51, and Frank Thistlethwaite, *The Anglo-American Connection in the Early Nineteenth Century* (Philadelphia, 1959). Both skillfully interweave British and American reform ideas. David Paul Crook, *American Democracy in English Politics, 1815–1850* (London, 1965), offers a challenge, however, to the Anglophiles with its brilliant intellectual history of British-American relations. Ford K. Brown's discursive *Fathers of the Victorians: The Age of Wilberforce* (Cambridge, England, 1961) is much too critical, but the author knows his subject enviably well. Other works used in dealing with Anglo-American reform connections were: Conrad Gill and Asa Briggs, *History of Birmingham* (London, 1952), I; Asa Briggs, *The Making of Victorian England, 1784–1867: The Age of Improvement* (New York, 1965 ed.); Asa Briggs, "Chartism Reconsidered," *Historical Studies: Papers Read Before the Third Conference of Irish Historians* (London, 1959–); Asa Briggs, *Victorian People: A Reassessment of Persons and Themes, 1851–1867* (New York, 1963 ed.); Asa Briggs, "The Language of Class in Early Nineteenth Century England," in Briggs and John Saville, eds., *Essays in Labour History* (New York, 1960), 43–52; G. R. S. Kitson Clark, "The Romantic Element, 1830–1850," in John H. Plumb, ed., *Studies in Social History . . .* (London, 1955); C. D. H. Cole, *Chartist Portraits* (London, 1941); Harold U. Faulkner, *Chartism and the Churches: A Study in Democracy,* "Columbia University Studies," LXXIII (New York, 1916); and E. M. Forster, *Marianne Thornton: A Domestic Biography* (New York, 1956).

Martin Duberman, ed., *The Antislavery Vanguard: New Essays on the Abolitionists* (Princeton, 1965), is a most impressive anthology of the opinions of the so-called New Left historians. There is no doubt that Howard Zinn, Martin Duberman, Staughton Lynd, and others whose work is represented in this volume have enriched the study of American reform. Also, I am indebted to James McPherson, *The Struggle for Equality: Abolitionists and the Negro in the Civil War and Reconstruction* (Princeton, 1964), and Willie Lee Rose, *Rehearsal for Reconstruction: The Port Royal Experiment* (Indianapolis, 1964), for inspiration as well as information. Both works carry the antislavery story beyond the usual terminal date of 1861. David Brion Davis, *The Problem of Slavery in Western Culture* (Ithaca, 1966), deserves the highest praise, but one hopes that the second volume will relate the movement to changes in the theology of Jonathan Edwards' disciples. Larry Gara, *The Liberty Line: The Legend of the Underground Railroad* (Lexington, 1961), and Leon F. Litwack, *North of Slavery: The Negro in the Free States, 1790–1860* (Chicago, 1961), are both able re-evaluations of the Negroes' life in antebellum America. Litwack demonstrates the high incidence of racial prejudice that pervaded Yankee society, taking a position that is in contrast to the more self-congratulatory style of Dumond and others. P. J. Staudenraus, *The African Colonization Movement, 1816–1865* (New York, 1961), replaces Earle Lee Fox, *The American Colonization Society, 1817–1840,* "Johns Hopkins University Series" (Baltimore, 1919), as the most comprehensive study to date of the southern deportation effort. William A. Owens, *Slave Mutiny: The Revolt on the Schooner Amistad* (New York, 1953), has no footnotes but describes in vivid detail the odyssey of the Mendi Africans.

Contrasted with the neoabolitionist "vanguard" is Stanley Elkins, *Slavery: A Problem in American Institutional and Intellectual Life* (Chicago, 1959). As mentioned before, the final chapter of this work criticizes the abolitionists for their anti-institutional behavior but fails to account for church and political abolitionists like Lewis Tappan. In the same category is David Donald's *Lincoln Reconsidered: Essays on the Civil War Era* (New York, 1961 ed.), wherein Donald, too, disputes the wisdom and sanity of the radical abolitionists. It must be obvious that I am critical of these volumes. Yet, both works have left a mark on our reform historiography, and their conclusions must be taken into account by any serious antislavery student. Furthermore, Professor Donald's incisive, though unsubstantiated, assumptions warn the serious scholar of the danger of too sympathetic and unthoughtful evaluations. George M. Frederickson, *The Inner Civil War: Northern Intellectuals and the Crisis of the Union* (New York, 1965), has portrayed the conservatism of some northern intellectual supporters of the war, thus (inadvertently) illuminating what the abolitionists had to face both during and before the war. It is marred, however, by insufficient research and easy judgments. Two other works may also be classified as hostile to evangelical reform: Charles I. Foster, *An Errand of Mercy: The Evangelical United Front, 1790–1837* (Chapel Hill, 1960), and Clifford S. Griffin, *Their Brothers' Keepers: Moral Stewardship in the United States, 1800–1865* (New Brunswick, 1960), but they were most useful to this study from a factual point of view.

Concerning religious history, H. Richard Niebuhr's *The Kingdom of God in America* (New York, 1959) retains its pre-eminence as the best short study of its kind, while Alan Heimert, *Religion and the American Mind from the Great Awakening to the Revolution* (Cambridge, 1966), is a fascinating reappraisal of the Edwardsean contribution to American social, civil, and reform traditions. William G. McLoughlin, Jr., *Modern Revivalism: Charles Grandison Finney to Billy Graham* (New York, 1959), is the best analysis of the evangelical reform and missionary effort, in spite of the more recent publication by Perry Miller of *The Life of the Mind in America from the Revolution to the Civil War* (New York, 1965), the chapter on evangelicalism in which is somewhat disappointing. Timothy L. Smith, *Revivalism and Social Reform: American Protestantism on the Eve of the Civil War* (New York, 1965 ed.), makes use of few primary and manuscript sources and neglects the role of the laymen, but it offers most suggestive points about the evangelical background to the social gospel. Donald G. Mathews, *Slavery and Methodism: A Chapter in American Morality, 1780–1845* (Princeton, 1965), suffers from a pedantic style, but it set a high standard for scholarship in religious history. Whitney R. Cross, *The Burned-Over District: The Social and Intellectual History of Enthusiastic Religion in Western New York, 1800–1850* (Ithaca, 1950), is a classic. Also meriting that term is Robert S. Fletcher, *A History of Oberlin College from Its Foundation through the Civil War,* 2 v. (Oberlin,

1943). L. Nelson Nichols, *History of the Broadway Tabernacle of New York City* (New Haven, 1940), is, surprisingly, much less parochial than the subject indicates. There is no modern published history of the American Missionary Association, but Clifton Herman Johnson, "The American Missionary Association," Ph.D. dissertation, University of North Carolina, 1958, ought to be issued to fill the need.

Commercial and demographic studies include the following: Roy A. Foulke's able *The Sinews of American Commerce: The Dun & Bradstreet Company, 1841–1941* (New York, 1941); Edward Neville Vose, *Seventy-Five Years of the Mercantile Agency: R. G. Dun & Co., 1841–1916* (New York, 1916); Dixon Ryan Fox's neglected *Yankees and Yorkers* (Port Washington, 1940); Robert G. Albion, *The Rise of New York Port (1815–1860)* (New York, 1939); Lewis E. Atherton, *The Southern Country Store, 1800–1860* (Baton Rouge, 1949), and *The Pioneer Merchant in Mid-America,* "University of Missouri Studies," XIV (Columbia, Mo., 1939).

Most of the articles with particularly interesting points of view have been given editorial comment in the footnotes. The best collections of them are: Charles Crowe, ed., *The Age of Civil War and Reconstruction, 1830–1900: A Book of Interpretive Essays* (Homewood, 1966); Richard O. Curry's more balanced *The Abolitionists: Reformers or Fanatics?* (New York, 1965); and Hugh Hawkins, ed., *The Abolitionists, Immediatism and the Question of Means* (Boston, 1964). Only a few others will be cited here. Donald G. Mathews, "The Abolitionists on Slavery: The Critique behind the Social Movement," *Journal of Southern History,* XXXIII (May, 1967), 163–82; Anne C. Loveland, "Evangelicalism and 'Immediate Emancipation' in American Antislavery Thought," *ibid.,* XXXII (May, 1966), 172–88; and David Brion Davis, "The Emergence of Immediatism in British and American Antislavery Thought," *Mississippi Valley Historical Review,* XLIX (September, 1962), 209–30, indicate a growing awareness of how little we appreciate the arguments the abolitionists employed (see Mathews on this point). I have published "William Lloyd Garrison and Antislavery Unity: A Reappraisal," *Civil War History,* XIII (March, 1967), 5–24, and "Abolitionism: Its Meaning for Contemporary American Reform," *The Midwest Quarterly,* VIII (Autumn, 1966), 41–55. Frank Tracy Carlton, "Humanitarianism, Past and Present," *International Journal of Ethics,* XVII (October, 1906), 48–55, is a cruder and earlier version of the points raised by David Donald in his "Toward a Reconsideration of the Abolitionists."

Articles dealing with the Texas issue include: Charles A. Shively, "An Option for Freedom in Texas, 1840–1844," *Journal of Negro History,* L (April, 1965), 77–96; Madeleine B. Stern's thorough "Stephen Pearl Andrews, Abolitionist, and the Annexation of Texas," *Southwestern Historical Quarterly,* LXVII (April, 1964), 491–523; and Harriet Smither, "English Abolitionism and the Annexation of Texas," *ibid.,* XXXII (January, 1929), 193–205. I am indebted to Linda K. Kerber, "Abolitionists and Amalgamators: The New York Race Riots of 1834," *New York History,* XLVIII (January, 1967), 28–39. Dixon Ryan Fox, "The Protestant Counter-Reformation in America," *ibid.,* XVI (January, 1935), 19–35, is an interesting piece.

There are not many articles as yet on the psychology of the abolitionists, except those essays already cited. Yet, Martin Duberman, "The Abolitionists and Psychology," *Journal of Negro History,* XLVII (July, 1962), 183–91, provides an alternative to Freudian analyses. Gerald W. McFarland, "Historians of American Reform: Working Toward a Doorless Corner," an unpublished paper, is a still more elaborate challenge to the Freudian view.

Finally, these articles should not be overlooked: William G. McLoughlin, "Pietism and the American Character," *American Quarterly*, XVII (Summer, 1965), 163–86; John L. Thomas, "Romantic Reform in America, 1815–1865," *ibid.* (Winter, 1965), 656–81; Sidney E. Mead, "The Rise of the Evangelical Conception of the Ministry in America (1607–1850)," in H. Richard Niebuhr and Daniel D. Williams, eds., *The Ministry in Historical Perspectives* (New York, 1956), 207–49; and Ralph Gabriel, "Evangelical Religion and Popular Romanticism in Early Nineteenth-Century America," in Grady McWhiney and Robert Weibe, eds., *Historical Vistas, Readings in United States History*, 2 v. (Boston, 1963), I, 407–19.

Index

359